THE TRIPLE INCARNATIONS OF
SAI BABA

THE TRIPLE INCARNATIONS OF
SAI BABA

*Sri Shirdi Sai Baba, Sri Sathya Sai Baba
& Future Prema Sai Baba*

SATYA PAL RUHELA

PARTRIDGE
A Penguin Random House Company

To order additional copies of this book, contact
Partridge India
000 800 10062 62
orders.india@partridgepublishing.com

www.partridgepublishing.com/india

CONTENTS

SECTION I

The First Sai Baba
Sri Shird Sai Baba
(1838-1918)

SECTION II

The Second Sai Baba
SRI SATHYA SAI BABA
(1926-2011)

SECTION III

The Future Sai Baba
The Third Sai Baba
SRI PREMA SAI BABA
Future Incarnation in the 21st Century

Select Bibliography

PRAYER TO GURU

Salutations to the real Guru who is the embodiment of the Bliss of *Brahman* (Divinity) who bestows supreme bliss of *Brahman* (Divinty) who bestows supreme happiness and is detached, knowledge personified, beyond duality, who is like the sky and is indicated by such Vedic dicts as 'Thou art That', and who is the One, eternal, pure, immovable, the witness of all the workings of the intellect, beyond all states and devoid of the three *Gunas*.

PREFACE

I am now 80 years of age. Forty years ago, I got the first opportunity of having the *darshan* (Divine glimpse) of the world famous God man Sri Sathya Sai Baba when he visited Delhi in early April, 1973. Then I witnessed a dazzling halo or aura of silver color around his face. Within three days a very serious problem of my life then was solved. I felt that was due to his miraculous grace on me when I had his *darshan* only for a few minutes. Thereafter, soon one night I had a dream in which he (Sri Sathya Sai Baba) poured *vibhuti* (holy ash) on both my palms and told me to come to his *ashram* via 'that station' (later on I found out that he was referring to Penukonda railway station). I soon felt that happy time was returning in my life due to his *darshan* and divine grace.

After nine months, I visited his Prasanthi Nilayam ashram and his native village Puttaparthi, which is adjacent to it, for the first time on the occasion of holy *MahaShiva Ratri* (Lord Shiva's night) festival in early February 1974. I was overjoyed, thrilled and uplifted in my spirits by the peaceful, soothing and fragrant divine environment of his ashram which was full of about 30,000 devotees, first time visitors and local residents on that festive occasion. I was fascinated by so many things which I observed and heard in the ashram and discovered in course of my modest social survey of his village, meeting his family members, close relatives and several others in order to collect information on Sai Baba's life, mission, activities and grandeur during my 4 day stay in the *ashram*. I still vividly remember these three most wonderful miraculous events witnessed by me there which have been vividly imprinted in my memory since then:

(1) In the forenoon of that festive day Sri Sathya Sai Baba miraculously materialized a lot of (may be about 10 kilograms) of fragrant *vibhuti* (holy ash) by vigorously rotating his right palm in an empty small metal pitcher held by his close devotee, secretary and biographer Prof. N. Kasturi, which torrentially rained on the silver statue of Sri Shirdi Sai Baba for about 25 minutes from the pitcher before all the thousands of people in the big Poorna Chandra Hall of the ashram.

(2) In the afternoon he materialized a beautiful dazzling rectangular gold locket with gold chain for a school girl who had just concluded her moving speech describing the poignant scriptural story of the ancient old tribal female devotee Shabari who had been very impatiently

waiting for a number of days for the arrival of Lord Rama in her hut, and when he actually arrived there she welcomed him by offering *ber* (berries) to eat, each one of which she had pre—tested by half eating it to ensure that only ripe and sweet berries be offered by her and eaten by her divine guest Rama.

(3) In the *ShivaRatri* (whole night devoted to the singing of *bhajans* (devotional songs on Shiva) at about 9 P.M. in the Poorna Chandra Hall Sai Baba miraculously created and emitted from his mouth the wonderful a '*Atma Lingam*' which was flashing out multi-colored light of the divine flame within it in all directions

In the following dawn Sai Baba appeared on the stage of Poorna Chandra Hall and gave a short and very thrilling discourse on the significance of '*Atma Lingam*' materialized by him last night and blessed all those who had witnessed it then in these words;

"You have had the good fortune of looking at the Divine Vision. You have also seen the Divine significance of the *Lingam* and that will grant you complete salvation. So far as you are concerned you have attained complete salvation and there are no more rebirths for you. Why is it that of all the *crores* (tens of million) of people in the world only you have seen this manifestation of Divinity? It is a piece of great fortune for you . . ."

His full discourse and the photo of the miraculously materialized *Atma Lingam* were later published in the thrilling and beautiful publication "*Vision of Divine*'(1975) by Dr.Fanibunda.

On this first visit to Prasanthi Nilayam in February 1974, there I came to know a lot about Sri Sathya Sai Baba, something about his previous incarnation Sri Sai Baba of Shirdi village in Maharastra state and also some thing about the future Prema Sai Baba. In course of my return journey I eagerly visited Shirdi and learnt a lot about Sri Shirdi Sai Baba there.

Since then I have been greatly attracted towards all the three Sai Baba *Avatars* (incarnations). I visited Prasanthi Nilayam—Puttaparthi complex about 20 times and Shirdi about 15 times between 1974 and 2002. I was privileged to get the opportunity of having four rare and very eagerly desired personal interviews with Sri Sathya Sai Baba and receive his blessings. As I had eagerly wished and prayed in my heart, I was invited to deliver two lectures on 'Education in the Sai Age India' in the second 'Summer Course on Indian Culture and Spirituality' in the first fortnight of June 1974 which had been organized by Shri Sathya Sai Trust in the presence of Sai Baba at his second ashram Brindavan in Kadugodi, Whitefield, Bangalore. I read all available books and articles on Sai Baba with great interest and in all seriousness and was deeply influenced by them and greatly attracted to the Sai Trinity phenomenon.

Being a trained sociologist and social anthropologist and then enriched by my extensive study, field observations and varied experiences, I decided to write some books on Sri Sathya Sai Baba and Sri Shirdi Sai Baba and their unique spiritual and social movements in sociological perspective.

Like a beggar who goes on collecting whatever small coins from whomsoever he can get, I greedily collected innumerable pieces of information about the Sri Shirdi Sai Baba, Sri Sathya Sai Baba and the future Prema Sai Baba from all available sources—collecting and reading all printed materials and meeting many devotees—Indian as well as foreign devotees and others who had any information on Sai incarnations to share.

My earliest source of information on the future Prema Sai Baba incarnation was an earnest Sai devotee Mrs. Veena Varma of Janakpuri colony in New Delhi in 1974 (who is now residing in Flat No. C-6/7567, Vasant Kunj, New Delhi). She used to do meditation daily and converse with the spirit of Sri Sathya Sai Baba in meditation and then record all revelations to her and her thrilling spiritual experiences and poignant feelings soaked in her love for Sai Baba in her daily diary. On my fervent request she kindly lent me all her three personal diaries as such to read in 1974 and thereby I was all the more drawn towards the enchanting Sai Trinity phenomenon of the present *Kali Yug* (Age of Kali)

She only had revealed to me in 1994 the startling prophetic revelation about the third Sai Baba—the future Prema Sai Baba *Avatar* that whereas the first two Sai Baba did not marry, the future Prema Sai *Avatar* would certainly marry and he would have a very illustrious son who would be very wise like Lord Ganesh— the widely venerated son of Lord Shiva.

Till that year no Sai devotee or other person had this rare information, I found none in Prasanthi Nilayam or anywhere else who knew it. My intuition then was that what she had told me about the future Prema Sai *Avatar* must be reliable and I should not hesitate to share it with others.

I kept on gathering bits of information on the trinity of Sai Baba incarnations from all possible sources for 20 years. In 1994 a very strong idea suddenly arose in my mind that I should compile and bring out a small book on all the three Sai Baba incarnations based on my two decades long collection and study of materials on them and to reveal this rare information about Sri Prema Sai Baba in my book. I enthusiastically compiled a small book 'The Sai Trinity' in a few months and self-published it as a pocket book of just 130 pages with my very limited resources under the banner of Sai Age Publications, Faridabad in 1994. That book was very much appreciated by Sai devotees. I was inspired to translate it into Hindi also and for that my friend (Late) Prof. Adhya Prashad Tripathi, Head of the Hindi Department, Sri Sathya Sai Institute of Higher Learning, Prasanthi Nilayam readily helped me in translating it and updating certain information with his vast personal knowledge about Sri Shirdi Sai Baba and Sri Shirdi Sai Baba being an ardent long time devotee of both these *Sai Avatars.*

'The Sai Trinity' became very popular among Sai devotees within a few months and its two reprints had to be brought out within six months. It sold as hot cakes and it become rather impossible for me to meet the market demands for its copies, So I soon decided to approach Vikas Publishing House, India's prominent publisher to publish it. They immediately published its edition towards the end of 1994 and then brought out its several reprints during the period 1995-1999. Then the book was thoroughly revised, updated and enlarged by me in 1999-2000 and Vikas Publishing House sold it all over the world. Many Sai devotees of Sai Baba in India and foreign countries very much appreciated it.

Unfortunately, '*The Sai Trinity*' suddenly became out of circulation soon after the untimely death of my friend publisher Mr. C.M.Chawla since his son as his successor Managing Director of the firm abruptly changed the publishing policy of the company and decided to stop publishing all general books and concentrate only on publishing books on Management and Information Technology. I could not contact any other reliable publisher in India for it as I remained ill for many years and was surrounded by many personal problems and even then desperately trying to complete other writing commitment. In 2007 I had suddenly an attack of coronary thrombosis and paralysis and was virtually bed-ridden and under treatment. Then my life was saved and I recovered in three years and this could be possible solely by the divine grace and blessings of both Sri Shirdi Sai Baba and Sri Sathya Sai Baba. In three years I recovered and regained the energy, moral and spiritual strength and motivation to resume my spiritual study and writing work.

In 1999 I received from an unknown Sai devotee from a foreign country (perhaps it was Malaysia) hurriedly written brief letter along with a book '*Liberation! Here Itself! Right Now!*' *(1997)* authored by a Sai devotee Vasantha Sai from Vadkampatti village in Madurai District of Tamil Nadu state whom he had just visited and was greatly impressed by her divine personality and devotion to Sri Sathya Sai Baba. He was returning to his country and while doing so he had thought of sending the book by post hoping that I might be interested in reading the book. Who he was, how he knew my address and what motivated him to send the book of his favorite spiritual personality to me was a mystery to me. Any way, I read the book very seriously and found it very interesting and soon sent my comments on it about to the author Vasantha Sai and expressed my desire to meet her. She replied that I was welcome to meet her any time. I wanted to travel to her very distant place but my health was not good enough to venture to do so. In June 1999 my wife and were planning to go to Prasanthi Nilayam, and so I suggested Vasantha Sai that we could meet if she too would kindly come there. She replied that she won't come to Prasanthi Nilaym but reach Anantapur town near that and we could meet at her devotee's house on 11th June. She came there with her husband and principal devotee S.V.Venkarraman and one more person and they brought copies of certain ancient *naadi* (palm leaf records) written by great sages revealing her past birth connection with Lord Krishna over 5000 years back and thrilling predictions about her present and future divine life.

With the help of a long structured schedule I interviewed her in depth for 10 hours on 20th June, 1999 in order to know her background, mystery, claims of being Lord Krishna's beloved Radha and her devotion to Sri Sathya Sai Baba. She gave me very convincing and enlightening replies, the whole interview was tape recorded and also written in fast hand by me. I later on brought out a booklet entitled 'Radha's reicarnation as Vasantha Sai which was later published by her and also put on the website www.geocities.com/research/triangle/facility/4014.index,htm by a devotee Krishnan of Delhi and also published by a devotee from Madurai in 1999 and later on also by me in my book *Radha's Reincarnation as Vasantha Sai—Pictorial Biography of a Unique God Woman of Our Times'* (2002).

Since then I have been in touch with her and have come to know from her and believe:

- That she is indeed a very great spiritualist;
- That she is the present reincarnation of Lord Krishna's beloved Radha of over 5000 years ago;
- That she has been worshipping Sri Sathya Sai Baba for decades firmly believing him to be Lord Krishna's re-incarnation
- That she has been in constant contact with Sri Sathya Sai Baba as he is always near her and converses with her in his *sookshma Sharir* (Spirit form) in all her regular thrice-a-day meditation sessions and it is even now when he in not physically alive;
- That Sri Sathya Sai Baba had foretold and assured her many times— and even now after his *samadhi* (passing away) he been reiterating—that

she would be his wife/divine consort when he incarnates as Prema Sai Sai Baba in the 21st century itself;

- That he (Sri Sathya Sai Baba) has been blessing her by pouring many kinds of miraculously created gifts like *vibhuti* (holy ash), *kum kum* or *Sindoor* (vermilion) *akshat* (consecrated rice), *haldi* (turmeric), honey, dry fruits etc. on her manuscripts being written by her daily. He has been giving her many spirituals hints and thrilling messages and his miraculously putting his initials on her manuscripts of books being written by her most of the time daily.

I have myself seen and reliably heard about a number of such miraculous things occurring to her and I have full faith in her truth, integrity, and superb spirituality and her words.I am fully convinced in my conscience about her genuine revelations as under. That is why, I have mentioned her as the crucial point of reference while writing about the future Prema Sai Baba In this book.

- That she firmly believes that she is '*Shakthi*' (the female counterpart of *Sai Avatar*). In her recent e book '*Shanti Sutra*' (2013) she has declared:

"...*Purusha* (the male aspect of God) and *Prakriti* (Nature, the female aspect of God) have never descended as Avatars. This is the first time they are comings here. This is a principle no one can understanding. In the previous ages, the *Avatars* came to destroy the demonic and wicked people and establish *dharma* (righteousness). Swami (Sri Sathya Sai Baba) and I have now come to remove the bad qualities. The demonic qualities that are present in all must be removed and good qualities established."
—Vasantha Sai, *Shanthi Sutra* (e book), August, 2013, p.13.

She has boldly revealed all these wonderful predictions in her books and she is even now doing so relentlessly through her *e books* on her site Mukthinilayam on the internet. Her countless devotees in India, U.K., Canada, Greece, South Africa, Malaysia, Australia, Sri Lanka and other countries very well know them well as they read her books and *e-books*, latest being *New Shanti Sutra* (2013. She has written over 50 books and e books published by Vasantha Sai Books and Publications Trust, MukthiNilayam—Pin Code 625 706 (Madurai District), Tamil Nadu State. They can be procured by any one in the world by contacting: *mukthinilayam @gmail.com* and read.

It may, however, be mentioned that just as Sri Sathya Sai Baba Incarnation is '*the least known and vastly unknown*', in the words of Mr. Krishnamani, President, Bar Association of the Supreme Court of India, had very aptly written in his book 'Divine Incarnation—a Mystery'(2001), the same holds true for Vasantha Sai. It is really a matter of pity and surprise that her spiritual status and unique divine role as the complementary *Avatar* to spread the glory and message of Sri Sathya Sai Baba are not yet recognized by many high ups in the Sai organizations and millions of Sai devotees and many who know her have been looking at her with wrong notions, misunderstanding or just sheer ignorance or prejudice.

Vasantha Sai had very kindly come thrice and stayed with my small family in Faridabadad for a number of days—once with her husband for 16 days and then twice with her group of close devotee ashramites—foreigner and Indian companion ashramits. Thus we had the rare opportunity of serving as host to her and her party for a number of days on each visit during 2000-2003. With her and her party of some very close devotees I visted the holy places like Haridwar, Mathura, Vrindavan, Barsana, Palani, Madurai, Patna, etc. Later on I visited her native Vadkampatti village with my friend Martin Evind, a young Sai devotee and spiritual healer from Santa Rosa, California, U.S.A. My wife and I traveled to her newly founded Mukhti Nilayam *ashram* in Madurai District to participate in the inaugural ceremony of the erection of *Mukhti Stupi* (Liberation Pillar) in her ashram in 2006.

Thus I had many rare opportunities of knowing many new things about her, Sri Sathya Sai Baba and his revelations about the future Prema Sai Baba on those rare memorable occasions. From these contacts, I have learnt a lot about her, her past incarnation as Radha—Lord Krishna's closest beloved devotee about 5200 years ago and then as Sri Sathya Baba's unique and most fortunate devotee who has been assured and foretold by him innumerable times that she would be his wife/divine consort when he reincarnates as Prema Sai Baba in the 21st Century therby her very long cherished ardent wish to get married to God would ultimately be fulfilled in her next birth in the 21st century itself. She has been revealing all such assurances and predictions in her talks and writings.

I have updated my information on Sri Prema Sai Baba believing in her prophetic predictions and revelations made to this most authentic spiritual source Vasantha Sai, Spiritual Head of the unique Mukthi Nilayam *ashram* about whom most of the Sai devotees and spiritual seekers are just ignorant and many skeptics and non-believers and pseudo-spiritualists may perhaps never accept her out of their false sense of ego or whatever else may be the cause.

As a sociologist I have been seriously and objectively studying the phenomena of Sai Baba incarnations and their unique spiritual and social movement since 1975. Therefore, it is my academic commitment and duty as independent social researcher to honestly report my findings on these existing social reality in this area:

- While on the one hand billions of devotees of Sri Sathya Sai Baba have been for decades invariably and equally believing in Sri Shirdi Sai Baba also and reverentially worshipping him along with Sri Sathya Sai Baba throughout the world, on the other most of the Shirdi Sai Baba's devotees and those die-hard ones who have been establishing and running Shirdi Sai temples and publishing journals and books on him do not accept Sri Sathya Sai Baba's claim that he was Sri Shirdi Sai Baba's reincarnation.

- This is so despite the existence of a number reliable testimonies or concrete proofs given by Sri Shirdi Sai Baba's devotees like Dixit, Boddu Pottu etc who had met him before his *Maha Samadhi* (death) in 1918 in Shirdi and then come under the divine protection of Sri Sathya Sai Baba, and the testimonies of many objective, research-minded writers like R.T. Kakde, G.R. Sholapurkar, G.R.Veer Bhadra Rao, V.K.Gokak, T.S.A.Murthy, Chakor Ajgaonkar, B.S.Goel (Siddheswar Baba), A.P.Tripathi, Sarla Joshi etc. and many other impartial, well informed, and open-minded devotees of both the first two Sai Baba *Avatars* had actually experienced and found thrilling experiential proofs to show that Shirdi Sai Baba and Sri Sathya Sai Baba are really one and the Same. Actually there exists a website 'Shirdi *Sai* and Sathya Sai are One and the Same' created by Arjan Das Bharwani. Obviously, most of the devotees of Sri Shirdi Sai Baba do not know about them or do not care to discover the truth. They just refuse to believe that Sri Shirdi Sai Baba reincarnated as Sri Sathya Sai Baba.

To expect of them that that they will even like to hear about the idea of the third Sai Baba—the Future Prema Sai Baba—will be futile. They may perhaps believe only after Prema Sai Baba will actually emerge in the later half of this very century and his name, fame and contributions will resound in all corners of the world, and even then many may not do so.

Any way, in the modern age of democracy every one has the fundamental right to have his or her own religious and spiritual belief. Now most people

18

throughout the world believe in God. Both Sri Shirdi Sai Baba and Sri Sathya Sai Baba also reiterated this spiritual truth:

- *"Sab Ka Malik Ek."* The Master (God) of all is One.

—Sri Shirdi Sai Baba

- There is only one Caste   — the Caste of Humanity
  There is only one religion   — the Religion of Love;
  There in one only Language   — the Language of the Heart;
  There is only God   — He is omnipresent."

—Sri Sathya Sai Baba

Therefore, it is meaningless for any one to argue against any spiritual personality. Spiritual seekers should be really concerned with the foremost phenomenon of Divinity that is GOD and have respect for all spiritual masters.

This book has been compiled by me on the basis of my firm conviction and is meant for the Believers and those who may be eager to know and understand the significance of the Trinity of Sai Baba incarnations in correct and comprehensive perspective.

I have brought out many books on Sri Sathya Sai Baba, Sri Shirdi Sai Baba and spirituality. I consider this book to be my most cherished publication as it presents my precious experiences of 40 years as an open-mined and impartial Sai devotee and modest seeker who has tried to be keep my identity and objectivity as a sociologist all through these long years.

March 30, 2015

Satya Pal Ruhela
'Sai Kripa',
126, Sector 37,
Faridabad-121003
E-mail: spruhela@gmail.com

ACKNOWLEDGEMENTS

Grateful acknowledgements are made to the authors/publishers/ web sites of their following materials which have been reproduced in this book by their courtesy:

* **Background story of the origin of Sai Trinity**:
  Boons to Rishi Bhardwaja by Lord Shiva
  File:http://www.Prema Sai Avatar-a very interesting htm
  Sri Sathya Sai Baba's full discourse revealing this important ancient story to the world for the first time on Guru Purnima day on 6 July, 1963 at Bombay is available in the following Internet file:
  File:htttp://www,sathyasaiorg/discource/1963/d630706.htm

* Prostrations to Sri Shirdi Sai Baba—Taken from '*Sainath Manan*' by B.V.Narsimha Swamy ji, Madras: All India Sai Samaj in 1930s.

* **Who is Sai Baba?**
  The Section I of this chapter has been taken from Gunaji, an English translator's note in the Preface of '*Shri Sai Sat Charitra*'—the famous authorized biography of Shirdi Sai Baba published by Sai Baba Trust, Shirdi.

* **Sai Baba's *Darbar*** (Court)
  This chapter has been taken from the excellent book '*Life and Teachings of Shirdi Sai Baba*' authored and self published in 1974 by the Sai devotee T. Anantha Murthy, then retired Judge, Bangalore by his kind permission given personally in June 1974 when he had come to Sri Sathya Sai Baba's second ashram Brindavan at Kadugodi, Whitefield, Bangalore during Sai Baba's Second Summer Course on "Indian Culture and Spirituality", to present the first copy of the book to Sri Sathya Sai Baba. He then gave its copies also to the dignitaries and guest speakers including me there.

  His book was the first one in which thereto unknown facts of the parents of Shirdi Sai Baba and the thrilling circumstances of his birth in the forest near Pathri village due to the divine boon granted to his mother Devagiriamma by Lord Shiva on his unexpected visit to her house in a rainy night, was revealed to Sai devotees from the detailed Introduction by Prof.V.K.Gokak, Vice Chancellor of Sri Sathya Sai Institurte of Higher Learning, which information he had got from Sai Baba himself. The author Anantha Murthy had kindly permitted me to reproduce any of the chapters of his most informative book in any of my books for the information of Sai devotees and general public.

- **Full Significance of Sri Shirdi Sai Baba**

Rare pieces of very significant information on Sri Shirdi Sai Baba, which are still unknown to most of the Sai devotees throughout the world have been culled from the following important books and reproduced by the courtesy of their authors and publishers:

o *Sai Baba; The Holy Man And The Psychiatrist* (1975) by Samuel Sandwiss, San Diago: Birthday Publishing Co, 1975.

o *Shri Sai Satcharitra,* Shirdi: Sai Baba Trust, 1992 (10th ed.).

o *Sai Baba: The Perfect Master.* Poona: Avatar Meher Baba Poona Centre, 1991.

o *The Dawn of New Era: Vision of Master Rishi Ram* by A. Somasundaram, Markapur: Divine Centre, 1969.

o *The Dawn of New Era and the Need for Universal Religion by* Somasundaram, Markapur: Divine Centre, 1991.(2ND ed.)

o *Romance of A Soul* by *M.K. Spencer,* Coimbatore: Spiritual Healing Centre, 1954.

o *How I Found God* by *M.K. Spencer* Coimbatore: Spiritual Healing Centre, 1957.

o *How I Found God by M.K. Spencer (Edited by S.P.Ruhela), New Delhi: New Age Books, 2011.*

o *Sai Baba: The Master* by Acharya E. Bhardwaj, Ongole:Guru Paduka Publications, 1991 (3rd ed.)

o *Sai Baba of Shirdi,* Wikipedia.

o *Twenty-six Years in Contact With the Spirit World* by V.S.Krishnaswami.

o *Devotees' Experiences of Shri Shirdi Sai Baba* by B.V. Narsimha Swamiji Madras: All India Sai Samaj, 1985.

o *Sai Baba's Charter and Sayings* by Narsimha Swamy ji. Madras: All Sai Samaj, 1986.

o Sai Literature
   File:///c. my document: Sai Literature

- **Sri Shirdi Sai Baba's Miracles**

  The two miracles of Shirdi Sai Baba in this chapter were sent to me by an old Zoroastrian Mr. Baxey from Bombay who claimed that he was close to the Zoroastrian mystic M.K.Spencer and the family of his cousin H.S.Spencer in Bombay.

- Pilgrimage to Holy Shirdi

  The Daily programme of the Sai Baba Samadhi Mandir, Shirdi is taken from:

  File: http://www.shrisaibaba.org/new_eng_%20templte shirdi/daily program . . .

- Shirdi Sai Temples and Centers in the World

  This has ben taken the internet.

- Important Sri Shirdi Sai Baba organizations

  This has been taken from the Internet.

- Sri Shirdi Sai Web sites

  This has been taken from the Internet.

- Sainath Give me Assurance (Prayer)

  Courtesy the authoress Ms.N.B.Sanglikar

- Who is Sri Sathya Sai Baba? Testimony of the Modern Day Masters

  Courtesy: The author R.D. Awle

  File 1:// Who is Sathya Sai Baba—Testimony of the Modern Day Masters.htm

- Sri Sathya Sai Baba: The Cosmic Ruler
  o *Rig Veda*
  o *Sanathana Sarthi,* the official month of Sathya Sai Trust, Prasanthi Nilayam ashram, December, 1999,
  o *Bhagwat Gita*
  o *Godman: Finding Spiritual Master* by Sant Kripal Singh. Virginia (USA): Bowling Green, 1970.
  o *Sanathana Sarthi,* Prasanthi Nilayam ashram, April 1995, pp.83-89.
  o *Sanathana Sarthi,* Prasanthi Nilayam ashram, February 1995, p.333.
  o *Students with Sai: Conversations* 1991-2000, Prasanthi Nilayam.
  o Wayne Peterson, *Extraordinary Times, Extraordinary Beings.* Internet File :*http://Wayne Peterson, Sai Baba and Maitriya.htm*

- Comic Power and the Universe
  Courtesy: The author M.L.Chibber and Editor. *Sanathana Sarathi.*

- Uniqueness of Sai Avatar
  Courtesy: The author A.V.Gokak and the Editor, *Sanathana Sarathi.*

- Sri Sathya Sai Baba: The Divine Alchemist
  Courtesy: The authoress Tina Sadhwani and the Editor, *The CHAKRAS News,* 18 April.2012.
  File: Sri Sathya Sai Baba: The Divine Alchemist The Chakra News. Htm

- 85 Years of Divine: A Saga of Love and Service to Mankind
  Courtesy: Editor, *Sanathana Sarthi,* 2011.

- Universal Sai
  Courtesy: The Editor, *Times of India.*

- A Love Supreme
  Courtesy: The Editor, *Times of India,*

- Sai's Baba's Precious Teachings
  Courtesy: The author Samuel Sandweiss and Editor, *Sanathana Sarthi*

- Sathya Sai Education Overseas Countries
  Courtesy: The Author Pal Dhall

- Some Thrilling Miracles of Sri Sathya Sai Baba: R.D.Awle *et al*
  o Howard Murphet: The Mirculous Vibhuti in Australia *Sai Baba: Invitation to Glory* by Howard Murphet, Macmillan, 1962,.33-41.
  · Mind boggling Miracles of Sathya Sai by Ghandikota V.Subba Rao, from *Sri Sathy Sai Avatar of Love,* Prasanthi Society, 23 November, 1993.
  File://Mind-boggling Miracles of Sathya SaI.htm
  Courtesy: The author R.D.Awle

- Apparitions
  File: //SATHYA SAI BABA AVATAR.htm
  o Miracles at Sri Ranga Patna (Ranga Patttanam) Orphanage

File://1Sathya Sai Baba Miracles: Miracles at Sri RangaPatna orphanage in Myore, 1 . . .

o   Sri Sathya Sai Baba—*Namaskar* Miracle in UK 2011
    File:// Sri SathyaSaiBaba—Namaskar Photograph Miracle in UK 2011.HTM

- The Guru Who Became a Living God
  Courtesy: The Editor, *The Times of India*, 25 April, 2011.

- 80 Ways to Serve Mankind
  Courtesy: The Editor, *Sanathana Sarathi*. November 2005.

- Sai Empire
  Courtesy:The Editor, *The Times of India* (New Delhi) 24 April, 2011.

- Sri Sathya Sa Baba Organizations & Centres Worldwide
  File://I:Intl I:\Sai Baba of India-Sri Sathya Sai Baba of India—Sai Baba-Centers—Sai Baba organisation worldwid 2 . . .

- Sathya Sai Organization sites
  File://I:Intl Sai Org sites.htm

- The Future Sai Baba—Sri Prema Sai Baba
  o   *Prema Sai Avatar I Saiprema:Blog*
  o   *http;//sathyasaibaba.wordpress.com/tag/prema-Sai-Baba*
  o   *tttp:// www.sathyasai.org/intro/premaasai.htm*
  o   *http://www.sathyasai.org/premasai.htm*
  o   *http://www.satyasaibooks.com/*
  o   *http://www.saiprema,wordpress.com/2011/05/0/prema-sai-avatar*
  o   *http;//www.sathyasaibooks.com*
  o   *Prema Sai Baba Avatar. Information*
  o   <u>*http://www,saisathyasai.com/India_hinduism_gods_goddesses/sai-baba*</u> *trinity-shirdi-s . . .*
  o   *Vedic Books.com*
  o   *http://groups.yahoo.com/group/saidevotesworldnet*
  o   *Prema Sai Avatar* by Vasantha Sai, Mukthi Nilayam, 2006.
  o   *Prema Sai Digest* by Vasantha Sai, Mukthi Nilayam: Vasantha Sai Publications, 2007.
  o   *Avatar's Secrets* by Vasantha Sai.Mukthi Nilayam: Vasantha Sai *Publications*

E Mail: _mukthinilayam@gmail.com_

I wish to thank Sanjeev Gupta of R.S.Prints, 40\12, Gautam Nagar, New Delhi for his invaluable help in the computerization of the book and my grand daughter Deepali Ruhela for her help in the correction of the proofs and many suggestions.

BACKGROUND STORY

Lord Shiva's Boon to Rishi Bhardwaja— Birth of Incarnation The Sai Trinity

"Thousand of years ago the great sage Bharadwaja, wishing to master all the Vedas, was advised by Indra (the King of the gods) to perform a *yagna*. Eager to have the *Shakti* (Consort of Lord Shiva) preside over it and receive her blessings, Bhardwaja left for Kailash, the abode of Shiva and Shakti, to convey the invitation. Finding them coupled in the cosmic dance, Bhardwaja waited for eight days—apparently ignored by them, although he had failed to comprehend the welcoming smile cast at him by *Shakti*.

Unhappy and disappointed, Bhardwaja decided to return home. But as he began to descend, he fell in a stroke, his left side paralyzed as a result of the cold and fatigue. Shiva then approached and cured him completely by sprinkling on him water from the *Kamandalu* (vessel). Consoled by Lord Shiva, Bhardwaja was greeted by both Shiva and Shakti, who also were pleased to attend the *yagna*.

Shiva promised the *Rishi* (sage) that they would both take human form and be born thrice in the Bhardwaja *Gotra* (lineage)—Shiva alone at Shirdi as Shirdi Sai Baba as Shiva and Shakti as Sathya Sai Baba, and then Shakti alone as Prema Sai."

Sri Sathya Sai Baba revealed this secret on 6th July, 1963 when he cured himself from a serious and dreadful disease (which he had purposefully taken over which was actually of a devotee). As a compensatory act to the above incident (where Sage Bhardwaja was paralyzed), Swami (Sathya Sai Baba) paralyzed himself on his left side. But himself being Shiva-Shakti, Shiva (his right side) cured Shakti (his left side) by the same sprinkling of water. This incident paved the way to the revelation of this secret by Swami.

Swami said that the third Prema Sai *Avatar* (Incarnation) will take place in Gunaparthi, in the Mandya District of Karnataka. Sathya Sai Baba also said that Prof. Kasturi will be the mother of Prema Sai.

Howard Murphet, in his book 'Sai Baba: Invitation to Glory', wrote that finally, Sathya Sai states, would be Prema Sai born in Karnataka (the old Mysore State), at a place between Bangalore and the city of Mysore.

On page 16 of the book '*Living Divinity*' author Shakuntala Balu had written:

'Sri Sathya Sai Baba would be has said that there will be one more Sai Avatar called Prema Sai. The third Sai will be born in Gunaparthi, a village in the

Mandya district of Karnataka. Thus, Sri Sathya Sai Baba refers not only to his past, but also to the future form he will assume as Prema Sai.'

The missions of the triple incarnations:

In his book 'Spirit and the Mind', Samuel Sandweiss, the author recounted an extended interview given by Sathya Sai Baba to the Senior Editor, Mr. R.K. Karanjia, of Blitz magazine in September 1976.

Question: Why had this task to be divided into three separate incarnations of the Shirdi, Sathya and Prema Sai Baba?

Baba: They are not separate. I have already mentioned the complete oneness of the three in the final objective of the mission . . . Their tasks and powers requisite to them differ according to the time, the situation, and the environment. But they belong to, and derive from, the same divine body (*dharma swaoop*). The previous Avatar, Shirdi Baba, laid the base for secular integration and gave mankind the message of duty as work. The mission of the present Avatar is to make everybody realize that the same God or divinity resides in everyone. People should respect, love, and help each other irrespective of colour or creed. Thus, all work can become a way of worship. Finally, Prema Sai, the third Avatar, will promote the evangel news that not only does God reside in everybody, but everybody is God. That will be the final wisdom that will enable every man and woman to go to God. The three *Avatars* carry the triple message of work, worship and wisdom.

SECTION I

The First Sai Baba
Sri Shird Sai Baba
(1838-1918)

Sri Shirdi Sai Baba's *mantra*
"Om Sai, Sri Sai, Jai Jai Sai"

Sri Shirdi Sai Baba

PROSTRATIONS TO SRI SHIRDI SAI BABA

Prostrations again and again to Sai has left his body at Shirdi and is showering blessings on his devotees.

Prostrations unto Sainath, who is the import of the *Pranava, 'Om'* and embodiment of Pure *jnana*, who is without origin and who is perfectly peaceful.

Prostration again and again to Sai who is Vasudeva, Shiva, the Supreme Soul, Govinda, who removes the distress of the devotees."

—*Sri Sainatha Manana*

1

Who is Sai Baba?

I

There are three views regarding the question 'Who is Sai Baba?'

According to Gunaji, the English translator of 'Shri Sai Satcharitra'—the original and most authentic biography of Sri Sai Baba of Shirdi.

1. Many persons who are accustomed to see things and persons superficially said that Sai Baba was a mad Fakir who lived for many years in a wornout and dilapidated masjid at Shirdi, who talked at random and extracted money in the form of *Dakshina* (cash offering) from people who went to see him.

This view is quite wrong. To a friend of Mr. R.A. Tarkhadkar who was full of tears when he was taking Sai Baba's leave at the time of leaving for Bombay. Baba said, "Why do you behave like a madman? Am I not with you there in Bombay?" The friend said, "I know that, but I have no experience of your being with me there in Bombay." Thereupon Sai Baba said that the person who thinks that Baba is in Shirdi only, has not at all seen Baba (does not know him really).

2. Some persons said that Sai Baba was a saint. The Muslims took him for one of their *Pirs* and the Hindus regarded him as one of their saints. The managers of the festivals annually celebrated at Shirdi refer to Sai Baba in their announcements as the crest jewel-best of the saints.

The view is also not correct for

3. Those who knew Sai Baba intimately and really regarded him as God incarnate. We give below a few instances:

(i) Hon. Mr. Justice M. B. Rege, B.A., High Court Judge, Indore in his foreword to "Sai Baba's Sayings and Characters" by B.V. Narasimha Swamy says:

"Baba in the flesh was, to his devotees, the embodiment of the Supreme spirit lighting the *Sadhakas* (spiritual seakers) path by his word and action." The mortal body has passed away but the 'Baba' once in it now lives in the Spirit Eternal, helping in the silent way. He often did in the flesh, the myriads of his devotees who seek solace in him.

(ii) A High Court Judge of a state in the north in his statement *"Devotees Experiences"* by B.V. Narasimha Swamy says:

"I look upon Shri Sai Baba as the creator, preserver and destroyer. I did so before his *Mahasamadhi* (passing away) in 1918 and do also now. To me, he is not gone. He is active even now.

"To me, he had no limitations. Of course when he was with us, there was the fleshy tabernacle. That was prominently brought to our notice at times. But mostly the infinite aspect of his was what remained before me. I thought of him as a mental or spiritual image, in which the finite and infinite blended very perfectly—yet allowing the finite to appear before us at times. Now that the body has been cast off, the infinite alone remains as "Sai Baba'.

(iii) Professor G.G. Narke of the College of Engineering, Poona in his statement on page 19-20 in *"Devotees Experiences"* by B.V. Narsimha Swamy says:

"I have placed Sai Baba amongst the household gods we worship daily at home. Sai Baba is God, not an ordinary *Satpurusha* (great soul). My father-in-law, Mr. Buti, my wife and my mother were all great devotees of Sai Baba and worshipped him as God.

"At an *Aarti* (worship) in my early visit, Sai Baba was in a towering passion. He fumed, cursed and threatened for no visible cause. I doubted if he was a mad man. That was a passing thought. The *Aarti* was completed in the usual way. In the after-noon (of that day) I went and massaged his feet and legs. Then he stroked my head and said "I am not mad." Lo! He is seeing my heart. Nothing is concealed from him. He is my *Antaryami*—the inner soul of my soul. I thought. Thence forward, numerous instances occurred in my own experience of his Omniscience. When he talked, he spoke as one seated in Rama, knowing all its thoughts and all its wishes etc. This is God within. I had no hesitation in deciding that he was God. I tested him at times. Each test produced the same conviction that he was all knowing and able to mould all things to his will."

(iv) The Dadasaheb Khaparde—the famous and learned Advocate of Amraoti-Berar in his introduction to 'Shri Sai Baba of Shirdi' by R.B.M.W. Pradhan (Page 3) says:

"He appeared to know the innermost thoughts of every body, relieved their wants and carried comforts to all. He fulfilled my idea of God on earth."

(v) Shri Das Ganu Maharaj in his *Stavanmanjari* (*ovi* 17) refers to Sai Baba as the Primary Cause of the universe, the Pure Consciousness, the Ever Merciful etc.

(vi) His biographer Hemadpant first referred to Sai Baba as a wonderful Saint who ground wheat, but after coming in closer contact he referred to him as God or Brahman, (18-41, 21-126).

(vii) Shirdi devotees, especially Madhav Rao Deshpande alias Sharma who was very intimate with Sai Baba and other devotees from outside always addressed Sai Baba as *Deva* (God).

We agree with all these devotees and think that they are perfectly right.

The Doctrine of the Immanence of God

Our ancient Rishis, the Seers of the Upanishads propounded the doctrine of the Immanence of God. They declared in various passages of *Brihadaranyak, Chhandogya, Katha and Shwetashwatara Upanishads* that the whole of Nature including all things and beings which is God's handiwork is filled and inspired by the *Antaryamin*, i.e., the Inner Controller and Ruler. If any illustration of proof be needed to prove this doctrine, it is Shri Sai Baba. If the reader reads carefully the *Sai Satcharitra* and other Sai Literature that is being published, he will no doubt be convinced of this doctrine and know 'The Real Sai Baba'.

During his life time (1838-1918) Sai Baba preferred not to disclose his social background and the facts and circumstances of his early life. Only to his very few close devotees he had given some hints about his background—that he was a Brahmin, his family belonged to Pathri village in Maharashtra, he was brought up for a few years by a Muslim Fakir (mendicant) and his wife, Guru Venkusha was his Guru with whom he had lived for twelve years, and he had countless births in the past and in one of them he had been Kabir—the famous saint of medieval India.

'Shri Sai Satcharitra', Sri Shirdi Sai Baba's authentic biography written originally in Marathi by Anna Saheb Dabholkar 'Hemadpant' (which was later on translated into English by Gunaji and published by Sai Baba Sansthan, Shirdi in early 19th century) gave thrilling account of the innumerable miracles, teachings and graces of Sri Shirdi Sai Baba. To all Sai devotees, this book is the most sacred scripture—their Holy Bible. In 1910 Hemadpant had sought Sri Shirdi Sai Baba's permission and blessings to compile this book and he had started doing so even during the great saint's life time. He had collected his materials from many people who had been Baba's devotees, visitors to him and his contemporaries.

Besides this treasure house of information on Sri Shirdi Sai Baba, four more books by Baba's three close devotees—*Shirdi Diary* (Khaparde), *Shri Sai Baba of Shirdi* (Pradhan) and *Shri Sai The Superman* and *Shri Sai Baba* (in Gujarati language by—Sai Sharanananda), published in 1918, 1943, 1962 and 1966 respectively, gave thrilling accounts of the life, miracles and teachings of this unique saint of Shirdi. Sri Narasimha was Swami ji, a doyen among the propagators of Sri Shirdi Sai Baba's divine life and teachings, after Baba's

Mahasamadhi, took up on himself the task of gathering the memories of Baba's devotees and visitors in 1936, and he brought the testimonies of about 80 such persons in his book *'Devotees' Experiences of Shri Sai Baba' i*n the late 1930s. He also brought out *'Life of Sai Baba'* (in four volumes) and *'Sri Sai Baba's Charter & Sayings'* in the late 1930s.

All these precious books have given very authentic and inspiring account of Sri Shirdi Sai Baba's divine incarnation. A very interesting big book *'Shri Saiche Sathya Charitra'* (in Marathi language) published in 1993 by M.B. Nimbalkar is based on *Sai Satcharitra* and some other original Marathi sources.

All these books have presented the life of Sri Shirdi Sai Baba in a rather traditional way; they have by and large, not tried to go beyond the limits of *'Sri Sachcharitra'* and not ventured to discover Baba's background and throw light on Baba's workings and his place in the Spiritual Plane or his incarnation.

II
Information on Sai Baba Emerging Since 1974

Since 1974, a number of thrilling new pieces of information on Sri Shirdi Sai Baba have come to light. They may very briefly be summarized as under:

(i) In 1974, Sri Sathya Sai Baba, the saint of Puttaparthi (Andhra Pradesh), who had as a boy of 14 in 1940 claimed himself to be the re-incarnation of Sri Shirdi Sai Baba, first of all revealed that Sri Shirdi Sai Baba was a Brahmin, his parents were Ganga Bhavadia, a boatman of Pathri, and Devagiriamma, and that he was born due to the blessings of Lord Shiva who had come to test the devotion and integrity of Devagiriamma, that he was born in a forest near Pathri and was forsaken by his mother who followed the foot prints of her husband who had become a recluse, that he was picked up by a Muslim Fakir and his childless wife and brought up by them in their house at Manwat till the age of 4, and after the Fakir's death his wife, disgusted by the strange religious behaviors of the boy 'Babu' took him to Guru Venkusha of Selu; the latter brought him up till the age of 16, that one of the jealous *Ashramites* (dwellers of Guru Venkusha's hermitage) hit him with a brick, and then the Guru immediately transferred all his spiritual powers to Babu and asked him to leave the ashram for good, and thus he ultimately come to Shirdi and later on became Sai Baba of Shirdi.

In his three discourses specially focused on the life of Sri Shirdi Sai Baba on 28 September, 1990, 27 September, 1992 and 6 October, 1992 Sri Sathya Sai Baba made further revelations about Sri Shirdi Sai Baba—that he was born on 27 September 1838.

This claim of Sri Sathya Sai Baba is not acceptable to most of the devotees of Sri Shirdi Sai Baba and these running Sri Shirdi Sai Baba's organization—'Sai Baba Sansthan, Shirdi', but all the devotees of Sri Sathya Sai Baba throughout the world, firmly believe in this claim of their Guru.

Sri Sathya Sai Baba revealed also that Sri Shirdi Sai Baba had told his devotee Abdul that he would be reborn after 8 years assuming the name of 'Sathya' in Madras Presidency.

(ii) V. B. Kher in his book 'Sai Baba of Shirdi: A Unique Saint' (1991) claimed that in course of his field research in Pathri village and Selu in 1975-76 he discovered that Sri Shirdi Sai Baba was a high caste Yajurvedi Desahatha Brahmin, his family was known as Bhusari family whose family deity was Hanuman of Kumharbawdi on the outskirts of Pathri and his parental house was No. 4-423–61 in Pathri.

3) The famous spiritual Guru Meher Baba who was the disciple of Sri Upansani Maharaj of Sakori fame, the only disciple of Sri Shirdi Sai Baba, who had seen Sri Shirdi Sai Baba, has revealed in his book 'Sai Baba: The Perfect Master', published by Meher Era Publication, Avatar Meher Baba Poona Centre, Poona in 1991 that:

"Sai Baba was not only a *Qutab*, but was the *Qutab-e-Irshad*, meaning the Chief of Spiritual Hierarchy of the Age, who brought the Formless God into form and gave him power."

A Sufi saint Zar-Zari-Zarbaksh, who lived about 700 years back at Khuldabad village near Ellora Caves in Maharashtra, had been the Master of Sri Shirdi Sai Baba in one of his past incarnations. Sufi Saint Sheikh Nizamuddin Auliya had sent Zar-Zari-Baksh with 700 followers to Deccan for spreading doctrines of Sufism in 1300 A.D.—he had died in 1302, a foot note in the book states.

Gopal Rao Deshmukh of Selu, who was popularly known as Guru Venkusha, was a *Jagirdar* (Feudal Lord) of Selu (Shelwadi village); the intensity of his religious temperament can be gauged from an incident related about him. One day while going out for a walk he looked at a beautiful woman, which gave rise to lustful thoughts in him. He at once returned home and standing before the households deity Venkatesh, pierced both the eyes with an iron poker. He lost the light of the external world. But it enhanced the inner light in him.

The widow of the fakir who had brought up the infant Shirdi Sai Baba begging from door to door and suffering insults and refusal often, sometime receiving sufficient to sustain themselves, at last arrived at the door of blind saint Gopal Rao Deshmukh (Venkusha). Evidently, the saint was waiting for the mother and son. With great respect and love he prepared a room in his own house for them to live with him permanently. When the boy was twelve years old, his mother died. All parental connection being snapped, the boy was drawn closer to the saint and he lived with him in the same house for several years. During this period the saint slowly unveiled to the boy the mysteries of the spiritual world and the boy became Gopal Rao's chief disciple. Seeing their close association, the Saint's Brahmin disciples became resentful and envious of the boy. One of them threw a brick at the boy's head; and hit him and blood flowed; but instead of hitting the boy, the stone hit Gopal Rao.

Soon after Gopal Rao's *icchamaran* (self desired death) the very next day, the young man (young Sai Baba of 16 years of age) left Shelwadi (Selu).

Sai Baba was a *'ghouse'* type of spiritual personality . . . he was in charge of World War I. As the Head of the Spiritual Hierarchy of his time, Sai Baba controlled World War I. As the war was ending, on September 28th, 1918, Sai Baba, then said to be eighty years old, had an attack of fever which lasted for two days. After seventeen days with no food, Sai Baba leaning of the shoulder of a close disciple breathed his last at 2.30 in the noon uttering *'Ah, Deva!'* (Oh God! The day was Thursday, October 15, 1918, the important Hindu holiday of Dassera.

"Sai Baba had several strange personal habits. He was a very heavy smoker and the *chillum* (Indian earthen pipe) he would pass around amongst his devotees sitting around him . . ."

(iii) According to (Late) A. Somasundaram, Founder and Honorary Secretary of Divine Centre, Markapur (District Prakasam) Andhra Pradesh, after his passing away in 1918, Sri Shirdi Sai Baba reached the spiritual plane and became the Guiding Spirit controlling the universe. In 1941 his spirit merged in God, and his mental fell on the spirit of Rishi Ram Ram who remained as the spirit controlling the universe till May 1967, and after his spirit's merger in Lord Srinivasa (Lord Vishnu), his mental fell on the Spirit of Swami Amritanandaji, who is still controlling the world from the spiritual personality Mrs. Anne Besant of the Theosophical Society was quoted by Somasundaram in his book *'The Dawn of New Era: The Vision of Master Rishi Ram Ram'* (1970)

"In a message delivered on 17.4.1942, Mrs. Annie Besant speaks about Ram Ram thus:

"Good morning. I am now happy having seen the Masters who guided us unerringly for many years. Ram Ram is the greatest of Masters, gentle as Jesus Christ, all knowing and pure, his resplendent presence is an inspiration. He is guiding humanity into the higher paths of spiritual life and he is guiding many denizens of the invisible worlds into the right path of the evolving souls. You do not and cannot measure Ram Ram's greatness by human comparison. He stands head and shoulders above many masters, and guides your vision to see unity amidst the diversities of life.

Sri Sai Baba after achieving the spiritual regeneration of a considerable cross-section of the people of India, having realized the universal self merged himself with the universal consciousness the necessary sequel. His mental fell in 1941 on Rishi Ram Ram, who was elected as the spirit guide of the world." (pp. 5-6)

In his other book '*The Dawn of a New Era and The Need For Universal Religion*' (1970) also, Somasundaram disclosed the following spiritual secret unknown to most of the people beings so far:

"The spiritual guides are disembodied spirits belonging to higher plane. Their duties are to guide the lower plane spirits in the spirit world and also persons in the earthy plane along the spiritual path. Their activities are controlled by a highly evolved spirit who is called 'The Spirit Guide of the World'. A highly evolved spirit, usually belonging to the sixth plane is nominated by the Cosmic Greatness (God) and the Fourth Plane Spirits, who will benefit the most by this guide, are asked to signify their approval. According to the spiritual sources, the recent Spirit Guides of the World were Sai Baba and Ram Ram. Apart from their arranging for religious instructions to the spirits of different spiritual planes, they have also to arrange for the spiritual education of persons in the earthly plane." (For more details, readers are referred to the interesting book '*Twenty-Six Years of Contact With The Spirit World*' by Sri V.S. Krishnaswamy, I.F.S. Retired, Madras.

(iv) Zoroastrian Yogi M.K. Spencer (1888-1958), a great spiritualist was some years attached to The Spiritual Healing Centre, Coimbatore during the 1950s. He was being guided by the Spirit Man Rishi Ram Ram since he was in his cradle. According to A.Somasundaram, who too was attached to The Spiritual Healing Centre, Coimbatore in those years, on reaching higher stages in his spiritual evolution, his (Spencer's) progress we was taken over by Sri Shirdi Sai Baba's Spirit till the last stage—God realization.

In his autobiography '*Romance of a Soul*' (1954) published by The Spiritual Healing Centre, Coimbatore, M.K. Spencer wrote as under:

". . . God ordered Ram Ram to take the soul under his special protection . . . It was Ram Ram who made him pay visits to two God-realized souls on the earth plane, viz., Meher Baba and Sri Ramana Maharishi. He took to solitude and deep contemplation and meditation connect with his Master Ram Ram and the study of Scriptures, which enabled him to write a series of books on Spiritual Philosophy and Religion published by the Spiritual Healing Centre of Coimbatore—an institution founded under the guidance of the same

Master, Ram Ram—developed the soul to such an extent that Ram Ram was ordered by Ahura Mazda to relax his teaching and to hand over the aspirant for further training and guidance to God himself." (pp. 50-51)

Let us recall that Sri Shirdi Sai Baba, having relinquished his charge as the Spirit Guide of the World in 1941 had himself merged into God—he was that God who had ordered Ram Ram to hand over the further spiritual training to himself.

Sri Shirdi Sai Baba appeared before M.K. Spencer in his meditations during 1952-53 and gave him 77 rare discourses which he recorded. Under the guidance of Sri Shirdi Sai Spirit, M.K. Spencer wrote a 2000 page typed manuscript 'How I Found God'. One hundred copies of that manuscript were printed by The Spiritual Healing Centre, Coimbatore in 1953, but before that interesting, illuminating book could be released for the benefit of the devotees, God (Sai Baba) ordered Spencer that all the copies of that book, which had been written by Spencer be burnt. This shocking incident was God's test to judge whether there had remained any grain of egoism in Spencer. The latter withstood the trust, and finally was able to achieve salvation—the highest goal of his soul, in 1957.

(v) In July 1995 an unknown person M.R. Raghunathan, a Sai devotee from Madras (resident of 22, Venkatachala Naicken Street, Komaleeswarapet (Pudupet), Madras 600002) conveyed to me the thrilling news that from ancient *Naadis* (Palm leaf records) preserved in Madras and Kanchipuram he had just discovered Shirdi Sri Sai Baba's horoscope which revealed that Sri Shirdi Sai Baba's mother Devagiriamma had been reborn as Smt. R. Seethammal "Baba Patti", ('Baba Patti' means 'Grandmother' or elderly lady connected with Sai Baba in Tamil), Shirdi Sai Baba's elder sister had been reborn as Smt. P. Rajeswari, daughter of Smt. Seethammal (who at that lived in House No. 22, III Trust Cross Street, Mandavelipakkam, Madras 600028) and Sri Shirdi Sai Baba's elder brother Ambadass has been reborn as himself (M.R. Raghunathan). He wrote to me as under on 27 July, 1995:

"I started going to Little Kanchipuram (about 80 kms from here) since March 1992 and visited the *Naadi* readers quite often for getting my predictions from Sri *Agasthya Naadi* there, also for the sake of my friends and relatives. I have been in close contact with another established Naadi Reader here at Madras ('Jothida Ratna' Dr. A. Karunakaran, Sri Sughar Agasthiyar Naadi Jothida Nilayam, 14 Mannar (Reddy) Street, T. Nagar, Madras 600017: Tel. 4348094). I was already moving close with Smt. P. Seethammal, called 'Baba Patti' (Grand mother) aged 84 years and her 54 year old daughter Smt. P. Rajeswari (wife of A.V. Padmanabhan, a retired employee of Electricity Board,

Madras, living at 22, III Trust Cross Street, Mandavelipakkam, Madras 600028) (as my mother and sister) (Brahmins and both staunch devotees of both Shirdi Sai Baba and Sathya Sai Baba).

Only then I got my first *Gnaana Kaandam* (Canto) as written by Sri Agasthiya Muni (thousands of years back), on 15.2.1993 wherein the Rishi tells that I was born to Smt. Seethammal (then Smt. Devagiriamma, the mother of Sri Shirdi Sai Baba as her first son (Ambadass), then Smt. Rajeswari (as Balwant Bai) was born after me, and Sri Shirdi Sai Baba was born to her thirdly as our younger brother. I only informed these revelations to the above mother and her daughter and their own individual predictions taken by me later on their behalf have also proved the above Sri Agasthiyar's words as true.

I have been consulting the *Naadi* centre here is Madras and I have consulted almost all different *Naadis—Maha-Siva-Vakya* (Elaborate); *Vashista, Vishwamithra, Suka Muni* (son of the great Guru Veda Vyas*), Bhoga, Pul; Plani, Koushika, Koumara*—all these are different *naadis,* and all of them confirm the things as above as true and correct . . ."

Sri M.R. Raghunathan also sent me the horoscope of Sri Shirdi Sai Baba prepared by him, based on the *naadi* revelations, in which it was mentioned that Sri Shirdi Sai Baba was born in a forest near Pathri village on 27 Sept., 1838 on Thursday, Tamil year *Vilambhi,* *Vikrama* year 1895, *Hijri* 1254 (*J. Akhir*), Month—Tamil *Purattasi, Kanya*; 13th (Tamil Date in month *Kanya*), and his parents were Sri Ganga Bhavadia (Brahmin) and Smt. Devagiriamma.

Horoscope of Sri Shirdi Sai Baba discovered by M.R. Raghunathan in 1994

Ketu	*Mangal*		*Shani*
4	5	6	7
3			8
	Rasi		
			Shukra
2			9
Lagna			*Ravi*
Chandra		*Rahu*	*Budha Guru*
1	12	11	*Guru*
			10

Star	*Pooraadam* (20th star, 3rd part)
Rasi	*Dhanus* (Sagittarius)
Lagna	(Ascendent): *Dhanus* (Sagittarius)
Exact Time of Birth	12 Hrs. 5 Min. 25 Sec. (12-5-25PM in a Forest near the village Pathri of Aurangabad District of Maharashtra)
Date	27-9-1838, Thursday (Tamil Year *Vilambhi*; *Vikrama* Year 1895; *Hijri* 1254 (*J. Akir*; Month Tamil *Purattaasi*;
Rashi	*Kanya*
Month	13th Tamil date in the month of Kanya
Father	Shri Ganga Bhavadia (Brahmin)
Mother	Smt. Devagiriamma (in this birth Smt. R. Seethamal, Madras)
Brother	Elder brother Shri Ambadass (in this birth, the writer, M.R. Raghunaathan, Pudupet, Madras-600 002)
Sister	Elder sister Smt. Balwanth Bai (in this birthSmt.P.Rajeshwari, D/o above Seethammal called as "Baba Paatti")

III
Thrilling life Story of Shirdi Sai Baba

Sri Shirdi Sai Baba once disclosed his true identity in these words:

"I am all-pervasive, all-engulfing spirit of the world and all its manifestations are none else than me. My divine nature will be revealed to the entire humanity with lightening speed. I am a nutshell, I am the Goal, Abode, Refuge, Friend, Origin, Dissolution, Foundation, Treasure-house and imperishable seed of things. I am existence and non-existence, aught and naught, is and is-not, I am the ineffable cosmic mystery."

- A keen researcher on the Baba, B.V. Kher had discovererd by his field research in the 1970s that Sri Shirdi Sai Baba most probably belonged to the Bhusari Family of the Brahmins of Pathri village and his parental house (No. 4-438-61) was situated in Vaishnav Gali. That house was later on bought by B.V. Kher and donated to the local people who formed *"Shri Sai Smarak Mandir Samiti"*. This Samiti has erected a shed and temple for local Sai Devotees to perform *aarti* (worship) of Sri Shirdi Sai Baba.
- According to the revelations discovered by (Late) M.R. Raghunathan from the ancient *Naadi* (palm leaf records) in Tamil authored by the sages lik Agusth, Suka and others, Sai Shirdi Sai Baba was actually born near

the present Pathri village, in a jungle at 12 Hrs. 5 Mts. 25 sec., in noon time of Thursday, the 27th September 1838. His father was Sri Ganga Bhavadia and his mother was Srimati Devagiriamma. His elder brother was Sri Amba Das and his elder sister was Srimati Balwant Bai. Smt. Devagriamma and Balwant Bai have been reborn and are living in Chennai as Smt. R. Seethammal (88 year old lady known as 'Baba Paatti'), Mr. M.R. Raghunathan was Sai Baba's elder brother Amba Das in his previous life.

· Pathri is now an important place. There are two trains on Central Railway line from Bombay to Selu. They halt at both Selu (Sailu) and Manwat. Pathri is about 15 kms from Selu and about 10 kms from Manwat. Tapovan Express does not halt at either of these but only at Parabhani from which Pathri is 40-45 kms distant. One can catch these trains at Manwat also if one is at *Shirdi*. There are direct State Transport buses from Bombay to Pathri, a *taluka* town.

· Sri Shirdi Sai Baba's father was a boatman. It was a poor family. Baba's parents were religious people who worshipped Hanuman, Shiva, Shakti and other gods of the Hindus. They did not have any child. Once when Ganga Bhavadia had gone to the riverside to save his boat in rainy and stormy night and Devagiriamma was alone in the house, at about 9 p.m. at first, Lord Shiva, Disguised as an old man came to her house and asked for shelter and food, then Goddess Shakti (Lord Shiva's Consort), also came there in the form of a village woman of low caste for massaging the legs of the old man. Being happy with the hospitality, good character and pity of Devagiriamm, the old man and the woman gave *darshan* as the divine couple Shiva and Parvati, and blessed her that she would have three children—one son, then a daughter and then one son, adding further, that the third child would be the incarnation of Shiva.

This divine blessing materialized in course of a few years. First, a son was born and then a daughter. When the third child was going to be born, suddenly Ganga Bhavadia developed *vairagya* (detachment with the worldly life) and decided to leave the hosue and family to become a renunciate. Devagiriamma, being a devout wife, decided to follow her husband's path; she sent both her children to her mother's home and accompanied her husband. On 27 September 1838, they left Pathri early in the morning. While they were passing through a forest, a few miles away from their village, birth pangs set in. Devagiriamma implored her husband to wait till the child was born, but he would not heed and went ahead. So Devaririamma gave birth to her third child all alone in the forest. Placing the child on the ground and covering him

43

with *peepal* leaves near the forest path around mid-day, she hastened after her husband. This child was later known as the famous Sri Sai Baba of Shirdi.

After some time, an elderly Muslim Fakir, named Patil and his wife, called Fakiri, who were returning from his in-law's house in a *tonga* (horse carriage), reached the spot where the new born baby was lying. Fakiri alighted the tonga to answer the short call of nature and then she heard the cries of the new born baby. Exited at this, she called her husband to the spot. As they were a childless couple, they thought that *Allah* (God) had sent that child for them. They took the child to their village Manwat. They named the child as '*Babu*'. They brought up the child as their own. Unfortunately, the Fakir died after four years, i.e. in 1842. The child was uncontrollable. He was doing very strange and offensive acts like visiting Hindu temples to recite the Quran and visiting the mosque to install stone *Lingam*. He sang songs in praise of and worshipped Allah in Hindu temples. Disgusted with the daily complaints of neighbors against her son, Fakiri ultimately decided to carry Babu to Sailu village and leave him there in the ashram of a Hindu saint, Gopal Rao 'Venkusha' who looked after a number of abandoned, orphaned and poor boys. He had been the ruler of that place and so his ashram was in a big building and there was no dearth of food and clothing for the inmates.

· In one of his past lives, Venkusha had actually been Guru Ramanand, the teacher of the eminent saint poet Kabir. It is said that Venkusha had a dream one night in 1842 in which Lord Shiva appeared before him and told him that he would himself be coming to his ashram at 11 A.M. the next day. So when Fakiri carrying the four year child Babu on her back all the way travelling on foot for miles, they were readily welcom and given shelter in the Guru Venkusha's ashram. She was given a room to live in. She dued after some years. The Guru loved Babu very much being highly imprsssed by his love, devotion and service, later on when Babu came to be known as a great saint Shirdi Sai Baba once he mentioned about his guru Venkusha's great love for him in his *ashram* to one lady devotee Radhabai Deshmuk.His glowing words in praise of his guru are recorded at length in chapter 18-19 of his official biography *Shri Sai Charitra*:

"I had Guru. He was great saint and most merciful. I served him long, very long; still he would not blow any *mantra* in my ears. I had a keen desire, never to leave him but to stay with him and serve him and at all cost receive some instruction from him . . . I resorted to my Guru for 12 years. He brought me up. There was no dearth of food and clothing. He was full of love, nay, he was love incarnate. How can I describe him? When I looked at him, he seemed to be in deep meditation and then, we both were filled with bliss. Night and day, I gazed at him with no thought of hunger or thirst. Without him, I felt restless. I had no other object to mediate, nor any other thing than my Guru to attend . . . He always protected me by his glance, just as the tortoise feeds her younger ones whether they are near or away on the other side of the river bank, by her loving looks."

Because of Venkusha's great love for Babu (the original name of Shri Sai Baba) the other boys of the ashram grew jealous of him. In 1854, one day, when Babu had been sent by his Guru to the forest to bring bilva leaves for worship, a group of the ashram boys beat him there and one of them hit his forehead with a brick and Babu bled profusely. The boys ran to the ashram; Babu came to the Guru with that brick. Venkusha tore his loin cloth and bandaged Babu's forehead wound. He was deeply grieved. He shed tears. He told Babu: "Now, the time has come for me to part with you. Tomorrow at 4 p.m., I shall leave this body. I shall vest my full spiritual personality in you. For that purpose, bring milk from a black cow." Young Babu went to Hulla, the Lambadi (herdman). He had only one black cow but she was not giving milk. Babu, nevertheless, came with the cow to the Guru. The Guru touched the cow from horns to tail and asked the Lambadi, "Now pull at the teats." The Lambadi's pull drew out plenty of milk and the whole of that milk was given by Venkushsa to Babu and he drank it then and there. The Guru's blessings and full spiritual powers immediately were thus passed on to the 16 years old Babu.

At the same time, the boy whose brick had hurt Babu, fell dead. His friends ran to Guru Venkusha to request him to revive the dead boy. Venkushsa asked them to request Babu for this, as all his powers had already been transferred by Venkusha to him. Babu touched the dead body and immediately he came back to life. This was the first great miracle that Sri Shirdi Sai Baba performed in his life.

Thereafter, Babu was asked to leave the ashram and go towards the Godavari river. The Guru gave Babu his old sheet of cloth and the brick which had hit him. Carrying these two things as gifts from his Guru, the young Baba (Saint) traveled on foot for several days and ultimately reached the Shirdi village, which is a few miles away from the Godavari river.

He quietly reached Shirdi and stayed under a big *neem* (margosa) tree outside the village. It was the same neem tree which we now find at *Gurusthan* at Shirdi—the place of Shirdi Sai Baba's Guru in one of his previous births. An old woman of Shirdi, the mother of Nana Chopdar, then saw the young Baba and she the portrait of him:

"This young lad, fair, smart and very handsome, was first seen under the *neem* (margosa) tree, seated in an *asana* (yogic posture). The people of the village were wonderstruck to see such a young lad practicing hard penances, not minding heat and cold. By day he associated with none, by night he was afraid of none . . . Outwardly he looked very young but by action, he was really a great soul. He was the embodiment of dispassion and an enigma to all . . ."

After about two months, one day he suddenly left Shirdi. For about four years shrouded in mystery, he wandered without disclosing his identity. During these four years, he visited a number of places, lived in some mosques, and influenced a number of people.

"I grew up in Meurgad (a place sanctified by the presence of Lord Dattatreya). When people pestered me, I left for Girnar; there too people pestered me much and I left for Mount Abu (a hill station in Rajasthan). There too the same thing happened. Then I came to Akkalkot and from there, to Daulatabad. Then I went to Pandarpur, from there came to Shirdi."

But prior to this, as per his own revelation, he walked on foot for eight days on the path from Pathri (his parental village) via Selu (Sailu), Mannoe (Manwat, where he had spent the first four years of his life in the Muslim Fakir's house), and Jalnapur; "trotting over the grass and sleeping at night in the grass", he reached Paithan, Aurangabad, where he stayed in an old mosque and guided and begged for an old Muslim Fakir for some years.

·   The Baba once disclosed to Upasani Maharaj's elder brother, Balkrishna Govind Upasani that he had seen the battle in which the Rani Laxmi Bai of Jhansi took part, as he was then in her army. (Rani Laxmi Bai was one of the foremost freedom fighters in the first Battle of Independence of the Indians with the then British rulers in 1857 and she was killed in the battle in late June in that year). It is likely that soon after her death in 1857, the Baba might have left the army service and reached Meurgad and later to Girnar, Mt. Abu Akkalkot, Daulatabad and Pandarpur as mentioned above.

From Paithan, the young Baba went towards the twin villages Sindhon—Bindhon. One noon, he was sitting in the forest near these twin villages when a Muslim landlord of Dhoopkhera village Chand Bhai Patil was passing. Seeing him sad, the young Baba addressed him by his name, called him near, did the miracles of calling Chand Bhai's lost mare and of materializing live amber and water by thrusting his tongs in the ground. These miracles of the young Baba greatly thrilled Chand Bhai Patil. He invited the Baba to his house. The Baba did not go with him, but he reached his village a few days later. At

Dhoopkheda, the curious villagers crowd became unruly and started pinching and pestering the young Baba. So, Baba became furious and started pelting stones at the crowd. Two stones hit a mad adolescent girl (who used to roam about naked) and a lame boy. They were immediately cured of their ailments by the miraculous hitting. These miracles immediately impressed the villagers. Baba stayed at Chand Bhai's house for a few days. He accompanied Chand Bhai's nephew's marriage party on bullock carts to Shirdi where the bridegroom was going to be married to Chand Bhai's sister's daughter. The carts of the marriage party halted near the Khandoba temple outside Shirdi. Baba was the first one to alight from the cart. He moved a few steps towards the Khandoba temple.

The priest of the Khandoba temple, Mhalsapati, who was somewhat friendly with the Baba when he had first come to Shirdi in 1854, welcomed him with these words, "*Ya Sai*" (Welcome Sai). This new name 'Sai' (which means Saint, Divine Father) given by Mhalsapati, was accepted by the Baba, and from that memorable day in 1858, he became known as Sai Baba.

Although Sai Baba moved to a nearby village for a few weeks, he soon returned to Shirdi and permanently settled down here. He made an old discarded mosque his home. Throughout his life, till his *Maha Samadhi* on 15 October 1918, he lived in this mosque which he had named as 'Dwarkamayi'. In the beginning, he was considered to be a cynical, half-mad *Fakir* and children used to pelt stones at him, but gradually he became the favorite of all the villagers of Shirdi and the neighboring villages.

- In his early years, he used to cure people with herbal medicines but when one patient, who was a leper, died due to the violation of food and other precautions (he indulged in sexual relations with his wife during treatment which was prohibited by Sai Baba), Sai Baba stopped giving medicines. Gradually, Dwarkamayi *masjid* (mosque) became the heart of Shirdi and the Baba did all his *leelas* (miracles), teaching and spiritual transformation of his devotees there for six decades.

He used to live on alms collected from only five specific families. He shared his food freely with his devotees as well as other creatures like dogs, cats, birds etc. His external appearance of a simple, modest, illiterate, moody, very indulgent, at times very fiery and sometimes abusive in speech and an aggressive fakir. All this was, in fact, the mask of *maya* (illusion) put on by him just to hide his real identity as God Incarnate.

However, the villagers of Shirdi and nearby places soon discovered (by experiences of his thrilling miracles and compassionate instant mysterious help) that he was no ordinary saint, but was, in fact, a divine personality of a very high order. Rarely did he declare publicly that he was God. Mostly, he uttered the name of *Allah* and advised people to remember, depend on and venerate whatever God or Goddess they had been worshipping in their families. He demonstrated that he was the incarnation of Shiva, Dattatreya (the Incarnation of the Trinity of Brahma, Vishnu and Mahesh) and that all other Gods and Goddesses were within him.

- He incessantly worked for Hindu-Muslim unity in Shirdi. Despite the then prevailing fundamentalism and opposition on the part of Muslims and Hindus, he was ultimately successful in making them appreciate and tolerate each other's faith. He taught them spirituality and morality in very simple words. During 1885, he died for three days, but again came back to life. During his sixty year stay at Shirdi, he performed many thrilling miracles. His fame spread fast from 1910 and people from far and near started coming in crowds and presenting *dakshina* (cash gifts) as demanded by him from whomsoever he wanted. During the last 10-15 years of his life, he daily received hundreds of rupees as *dakshina*, but by evening he would distribute all of it among his devotees, beggars and poor people. Before his *MahaSamadhi* in 1918, he had assured that all his miracles and grace would be available to those who would remember him and visit his *Samadhi* and *Masjid* complex at Shirdi. And rightly so, innumerable people have actually been benefiting by praying to Sri Shirdi Sai Baba and visiting Shirdi and many have witnessed the miracle of seeing him in person even now, in different forms or in his usual attire and in their dreams.
- The name of Sri Shirdi Sai Baba has been spreading very fast throughout the world. Now there are hundreds of Shirdi Sai Temples not only in India, but even in London, Los Angeles, Loredo (U.S.A.), Canberra, (Australia), Durban (South Africa), Logos (Nigeria), Mauritius, Nepal, Japan, China and recently in Russia. Some other countries may be having Shirdi Sai Temples.

He has staunch devotees not only amongst Indians but also among Germans, Americans, Australians, Africans, Britishers, Italians, Japanese etc. The name of Sri Shirdi Sai Baba and the Sai movement has been are spreading like wildfire in the world for the last thirty years. The simple village Fakir of Shirdi, which lived till 1918, has now become the object of deep veneration and adoration of countless seekers of peace, bliss and spirituality.

· The eminent mystic Meher Baba, the disciple of Upasani Maharaj,(the only disciple of Sri Shirdi Sai Baba) had seen Sri Shirdi Sai Baba in 1915. His testimony is very valuable and revealing. Accordig to him:

"You will never be able to understand thoroughly how great Sai Baba was. He was the personification of perfection. If you know him as I knew him, you will call him the Master of Creation."

· Sri Sathya Sai Baba revealed about Sri Shirdi Sai Baba as under:

"Shirdi Sai was a *Brahma-jnani*. He was the embodiment of Universal Consciousness, *Gyanswaroopa*. He was also the *Sadguru* teaching his devotees the reality and guiding them along the path of truth.

He was a *Poornavatar* (Full or Integral Incarnation of God) and possessed the attributes of Divine *Shakti* (Power) but he held them in check and did not reveal them fully. He was like a learned musician who exhibits his musical skills occasionally; he was like a gifted poet who gave voice to his verse only rarely. He was like a skilled sculptor who revealed his artistry some times.

Siddhis (miraculous power) and *Leelas* (sport) were merely outpourings of his love for his devotees. They were not meant to attract but only to safeguard and protect. He did not use them like visiting cards. He used his *Shakti* (power) only to save the devotees from distress and trouble, from sorrow and pain . . . His advent was for revealing divinity."

· Sri Shirdi Sai Baba's miracles were of many kinds—miraculous cures, removal of poverty, barrenness, warding of disease, lighting lamps with water, saving lives, forecasting future calamities, giving blessings for prosperity, his own thrilling yogic exercise like *Khand yoga*, removing his intestines and drying them in the sun and granting all kinds of boons. He would often tell people about the number of past births in which some of his close devotees had been associated with him.

His devotees and followers belonged to all religions, castes, social classes and occupational groups. Even some foreigners came for his *darshan* and they held him in high esteem. There were then about fifty contemporary saints in Maharashtra and other adjoining states. They interacted with Sri Shirdi Sai Baba by paying visits to him and many of them did so mysteriously, remaining at their places. Baba remained a celibate all his life. Although he was loving and calm, yet, at times he became furious and abusive, and some times he beat people. He was fond of smoking his *chillum* (pipe). He often danced and sang some bhajans. All kinds of village entertainers, dancing girls, musicians, acrobats, circus men, jugglers etc., often exhibited their skills at his Dwarkamayi mosque. Although he was very kind and sympathetic towards everyone in Shirdi, yet he had a towering personality and none except two very close devotees Tatya and Shama dared to take liberties with him. Some times he was humorous. Daily, he told parables and stories to instruct his devotees as also to reveal the working of spiritual laws like *Rinanubandha* (Bondage of give and take), *Sambhava* (principle of equality), *Karma* and *Punarjanma* (Action and Rebirth), unity of the souls of all creatures etc. He disliked casteism, practice of untouchability, dowry, religious conversion, religious fundamentalism, and the traditional bar on women in matters of worship and social life.

· He was a mild and tolerant incarnation of mediaeval rebel saint Kabir who boldly criticized rituals and superstitions of both the Hindus and Muslims and taught spirituality pure and simple. He once disclosed that he was Kabir in one of his past Births. But as Shirdi Sai instead of attacking the so-called superstitious beliefs and practices of the Hindus and the Muslims, he liberally allowed and encouraged each one of them to continue following his or her traditional beliefs and religious modes or worship. Thus, he promoted intrinsic and genuine communal tolerance and emotional and national integration by allowing both the Hindus and Muslims to worship him according to their respective modes of worship in the Dwarkamayi mosque. The wonderful miraculous *Udi* (Holy Ash) of his *dhuni* (fireplace) in Dwarkamayi was his regular gift to all his visitors and devotees. It was and is still considered to be a unique miraculous and beneficial substance much sought after by all devotees.

· His image as an *Avatar* (Incarnation)—a *Fakir* (mendicant) clad in rags, begging alms for his sustenance and wishing well of all creatures, his austerity and superb poise and spiritual attainments have for decades been turning millions of people into his devotees. Each day, the number of his devotees is increasing in astronomical proportions. When he breathed his last, the only property he had, consisted of 16 rupees in his pocket, some of his clothes and shoes, *chillums* and *sadka* (a wooden stick), a *chakki* (hand mill) to grind grain and a tin pot. Although, during the later years of his life, he had been daily getting hundreds of rupees as *dakshina*, so much that the British Government Income Tax department once considered to tax his daily income which, during 1916-18, was more than that of the Governor General of India. In all wisdom, they did not tax him for he was giving away all his daily income in charity, but they did tax some of the regular beneficiaries of his charity.

.   B.V. *Narsimhaswamyi*, the foremost *pracharak* (propagator) of Sri Shirdi Sai Baba, wrote these apt words on the Baba's greatness:

"Baba, however, is not a mere worker of miracles. He is a *Samartha Sadguru*. (All powerful Guru). He applies miracles or miraculous means to fill with faith and gratitude the hearts of devotees. Gratitude soon turns into love and then Baba's real work is seen. Baba purifies the hearts of all of the dross of low attachments and their consequences, and gradually raises the devotee's souls to loftier and still loftier states of being, till they finally merge into him."

IV
Information on Sri Shirdi Sai Baba (Wikipedia)

Full Name: Sai Baba of Shirdi
Died: October 15, 1918 (age 80)
Era: 19th to 20th Century
Region: India
School: Hinduism *(Advaita Vedanta)* and Islam (Sufism)

Sai Baba of Shirdi (Unknown—October 15, 1918), also known as Shirdi Sai Baba, was an Indian *guru, yogi* and *fakir* who is regarded by his Hindu and Muslim devotees as a saint. Hindu devotees consider him an incarnation of Lord Dattatreya. Many devotees believe that he was a *Sadguru*, an enlightened *Sufi Pir* or a *Qutub*. He is a well-known figure in many parts of the world, but especially in India, where he is much revered.

Sai Baba's real name is unknown. The name "Sai" was given to him upon his arrival at Shirdi. No information is available regarding his birth and place of birth. Sai Baba never spoke about his past life. Sai is of Sanskrit origin, meaning "*Sakshat Ishwar*" or the divine. The honorific "Baba" means "father; grandfather; old man; sir" in Indo-Aryan languages. Thus Sai Baba denotes "holy father" or 'saintly father".

Sai Baba had no love for perishable things and his sole concern was self-realization. He remains a very popular saint, and is worshipped by people around the world. He taught a moral code of love, forgiveness, helping others, charity, contentment, inner peace, and devotion to God and guru. Sai Baba's teaching combined elements of Hinduism and Islam: he gave the Hindu name

Dwarakamayi to the mosque he lived in, practiced Hindu and Muslim rituals, taught using words and figures that drew from both traditions, and was buried in Shirdi. One of his well known epigrams, "*Sabka Malik Ek*" ("One God governs all"), is associated with Islam and Sufism. He always uttered "*Allah Malik*" ("God is the Owner, Master or King of all)

Sai Baba is revered by several notable Hindu religious leaders. Some of his disciples became famous as spiritual figures and saints, such as Mhalsapati, priest of Kandoba temple in Shirdi, Upasani Maharaj, Saint Bidkar Maharaj, Saint Gangagir, Saint Jankidas Maharaj, and Sati Godavari Mataji.

Early years:

Little has been documented on the early life of Shirdi Sai Baba. Baba reportedly arrived at the village of Shirdi in the Ahmednagar district of Maharashtra, British India, when he was about 16 years old. It is generally accepted that Sai Baba stayed in Shirdi for some times and * disappeared for a year, and returned permanently around 1858 'long hair flowing down to the end of his spine' when he arrived in Shirdi, and that he never had his head shaved. It was only after Baba was defeated in a wrestling match with one Mouniddin Tamboli that he took up the *kafni* (long shirt) and cloth cap, articles of typical Sufi clothing. This attire contributed to Baba's identification as a Muslim fakir, and was a reason for initial indifference and hostility against him in a predominantly Hindu village. According to B.V. Narasimha Swamyji, a posthumous follower who was widely praised as Sai Baba's "apostle", this attitude was prevalent up to 1954 even among some of his devotees in Shirdi.

In India, it's a common sight to find a Sai Baba temple in any city or town, in every large city or town there is at least one temple dedicated to Sai Baba. There are even some in towns and cities outside India. In the mosque in Shirdi in which Sai Baba lived, there is a life-size portrait of him by Shama Rao Jaykar, an artist from Mumbai. Numerous monuments and statues depicting Sai Baba, which serve a religious function, have also been made. One of them, made of marble by a sculptor named Balaji Vasant Talim, is in the Samadhi Mandir in Shirdi where Sai Baba was buried. In Sai Baba temples, his devotees play various kinds of devotional religious music, such as *aarti*.

Indian Postal Service released a Sai Baba commemorative stamp in May 2008.

On July 30, 2009, the New and Renewable Energy Minister Farooq Abdullah inaugurated what has been acclaimed as the largest solar steam system in the world, at the Shirdi shrine. The Shri Sai Baba Sansthan (Trust) paid an estimated Rs.1.33 crore for the system, Rs.58.4 lakh of which was paid as a subsidy by the renewable energy ministry. It is said the system can cook 20,000 meals per day for pilgrims visiting the temple

Film and television:

Sai Baba has been the subject of several feature films in many languages produced by India's film industry.

Year	Film	Title role	Director	Language	Notes
1977	Shirdi ke Sai Baba	Sudhir Dalvi	Ashok V. Bhushan	Hindi	Also featuring Manoj Kumar, Rajendra Kumar, HemaMalini and Shatrughan Sinha. Sachin, Prem Nath
1986	Sri Shirdi Sai Baba Mahathyam	Vijayachander	K. Vasu	Telugu	Dubbed into Hindi as Shirdi Sai Baba Ki Kahani, into Tamil as Sri Shirdi Sai Baba
1989	Bhagavan Shri Sai Baba	Sai Prakash	Sai Prakash	Kannada	
1993	Sai Baba	Yashwant Dutt	Babasaheb S. Fattelal	Marathi	Also featuring Lalita Pawar
2001	Shirdi Sai Baba	Sudhir Dalvi	Deepak Balraj Vij	Hindi	Also featuring Dharmendra, Rohini Hattangadi, Suresh Oberoi
2005	Ishwarya Avatar Sai Baba	Mukul Nag	Ramanand Sagar	Hindi	Composite movie drawn from Sagar's Sai Baba (TV series).
2010	Malik Ek	Jackie Shroff	Deepak Balraj Vij	Hindi	Expected release in 2008. Also featuring Manoj Kumar, Divya Dutta,Zarina,Rohini Hattangadi, Zarina Wahab and Anup Jalota as Das Ganu.

A new film in the life of Shirdi Sai Baba is being made by the devotees of Sri Sathya Sai Baba.

2

Main Events in Sri Shirdi Sai Baba Avatar's Life

27.9.1838:	According to ancient Tamil *Naadi* records at Chennai.
1838-42:	Was born in forest near Pathri village at 12 Hrs, 5 Min. 25 Sec. Noon, was brought up by a Muslim *Fakir* Patil and his wife Fakiri at Manwat.
1842:	The Fakir's wife left the child Babu in the charge of Guru Venkusha at Sailu.
1842-54:	Was brought up after birth and instructed by Guru Venkusha in his Ashram at Sailu.
1854:	Departure from the Ashram in 1854 with Guru's blessings; the Guru also died the same day.
1854:	First visit to Shirdi, stayed there for about two months.
1854-58:	Period of *Agyatvas*: (unknown wanderings) —visited various places doing various jobs; —lived with Bade Baba at Aurangabad; —lived with Fakir Akbar Ali at Ahmed Nagar; —moved with other Fakirs and Hindu saints; —visited Shivagaon Pathodi and asked Gadge Maharaj for bread. —served in the army of Rani Laxmi Bai of Jhansi in 1851.
1858:	Chand Bhai Patil met him in jungle near the twin villages Sindhon-Bindhon: Baba showed him his lost mare, materialized live amber and water for his pipe. Visited Chand Bhai Patil's village Dhupkheda, three days after meeting him in the forest.
1858:	Reached Shirdi (second time) with Chand bhai's nephew's marriage party; Mhalsapati addressed him as *"Ya Sai"* (Welcome Sai), he assumed the name 'Sai' from that time.
1858:	Went to Rahata village, stayed in *Chawdi* (resting place in village for visitors) there for some days; wanted to stay in Rahata permanently, but soon decided to come back to Shirdi.

1859:	Visit of Saint Gangagir, who said of him to the villagers of Shirdi, "He is a precious gem."
1861:	Occupied an old forsaken mosque and named it *Dwarkamai*. Many villagers and children teased him, pelted stones at him, considering him to be a mad Fakir.
1873:	Saint Bidkar Maharaj visited Baba.
1881:	Mahadev Rao Deshpande, Shirdi village Primary School teacher, accepted Baba as his Guru. Baba nick-named him as 'Shama'.
1886:	Severe attack of Asthma on Baba; Baba's *Prana* (life) left his physical body for three days entrusting it to the watch of Mhalsapati.
1889:	Arrival of Abdul as servant-devotee of Baba from Fakir Aminuddin of Nanded.
1890:	Baba went to live with a pseudo Guru Javar Ali at Rahata; villagers of Shirdi persuaded him and Javar Ali to return to Shirdi; Javar Ali was efeated in a spiritual contest by Saint Jankidas of Shirdi and so he fled away from Shirdi.
1891:	Nana Saheb Nimonkar first met Sai Baba at Rahata village.
1892:	On Diwali Day Baba did the famous miracle of lighting his Dwarkamai *masjid* (mosque) lamps with only water when oil was refused to him by the village grocers. This miracle spread his fame far and wide.
1904:	Baba's great miracle 'Jamner incident': Baba sent Aarti and *Udi* (holy ash) with Ramgir Bua for Mainatai, daughter of Nana Saheb Chandokar at Jamner, materialized a horse carriage and servants to take Ramgir Bua from Jalgaon station to Nana Sahib's residence in night to be delivered to Mainatai at the time of her painful delivery.
	Baba appeared miraculously (in his other body) at Pallachi near Coimbatore with Sanyasi Thangavel Gounder; gave *darshan* to hundreds of villagers there for two days; blessed Rajamma Gounder, (later on named as Shivamma Thayee) a 15 year old married girl, niece of Sanyasi Thangavel Gounder, and spoke to her in Tamil.
1908:	Baba gave *darshan* as a Sadhu to Chandrabai Borkar at Kopargaon.
1909:	Fakir Baba (Baba's first disciple at Aurangabad) came to stay with Baba in Masjid and lived there till Baba's *Mahasamadhi*.

1909:	Baba appeared in the form of Lord Rama in Dwarkamai Masjid to a doctor devotee of Lord Rama.
1909:	H.S. Dixit met Baba at Shirdi and became his ardent devotee.
1909:	From 19 December 1909, the ritual of worshipping Baba and taking out his procession from Masjid to Chawdi was started by his devotees which is still continuing at Shirdi.
1910:	Dabholkar met Baba; Baba gave him the name of 'Hemadpant' and later on permitted him to write his biography *'Shri Sai SatCharitra'.*
1910:	Foundation of Dixitwada was laid on 10th February 1910; completed in April 1911.
1910:	Baba's *Shej Aarti* (Night worship) on every alternate day was started.
1910:	Baba's famous miracle of grinding wheat in Masjid and getting its flour sprinkled on the boundary of Shirdi village to prevent plague entering the village.
1910:	Baba stopped cooking *Prashad* (*Handi* Food) in Masjid due to very large number of devotees coming there by then.
1911:	Visit of Upasani Maharaj to Baba on 27 June.
1911:	Baba assumed the form of three-headed child Lord Dattatreya in Dwarkamai; witnessed by Balwant Kohojkar and others on Dattatreya Jayant day at 5 PM.
Dec. 1911:	Visit of a noted Muslim Saint Durvesh Sahib to Baba; was cordially treated by Baba.
25th Jan.1912:	Death of Baba's ardent devotee Megha, Baba wept and shed tears while putting flowers on his corpse.
1912:	Visit of Chinna Krishna Saheb who became his great devotee.
1912:	Visit of Sagun Meru Naik.
1912:	Renovation of Dwarkamayi *masjid*; noted services done by three carpenter brothers Kundaji, Gawji and Tuka Ram.
1914:	Visit of famous singer Khan Sahib Kasim Khan (father of now famous singer Hirabai Badodekar), his party and wife Tahera and daughter Gulab Kavali *(Hirabai Badodekar)* to Baba; they sang a number of *Bhajans* of Kabir and *Abhangs* of Tuka Ram in a music session before Baba and hundreds of villagers in the night till 2 A.M.; were blessed by Baba with silver coins and *burfi* sweets.
1915-17:	Training of Upasani Maharaj under Baba's guidance at Shirdi in Khandoba Temple.

1915:	Visit of young Parsi spiritual seeker Mehrun (Meher Baba); Baba directed him to become Upasani Maharaj's disciple.
1916:	Arrival of a 3½ year old abducted and abandoned child Narayan with pilgrims to Baba; Baba welcomed and looked after him till his *Mahasamadhi* (death); he became famous as Sai Narayan Baba who had been given the power to materialize Baba's hot *Udi* (ash) and cure people.
1916:	Baba asked his devotee G.C. Narke to beg food for Baba attired in his European suit, in order to teach him the lesson of egolessness.
1917:	Famous politician and spiritual seeker Lokmanya Tilak met Baba on 19 May 1917; Baba told him, *"Ja, jap, Swaraj aata"*. (Go, mediate, Independence follows).
1918:	Baba sent food offerings and Rs. 250 to Fakir Samsuddin Mia and a garland of Sevanthi flowers to Faqir Banne Mia conveying the message of his *Mahasamadhi* in the near future giving its exact date, in June or July 1918, through Kasim, son of Bade Raba and Imambhai Chote Khan.
28 Sept. 1918:	Baba developed high temperature; still he went out to beg alms.
8 Oct. 1918:	Baba gave *mukti* (Liberation) to an ailing tiger brought by a band of Fakirs to Dwarkamai *masjid* and then got it buried near the masjid.
15 Oct. 1918:	Baba achieved *Mahanirvana* at 2.30 p.m. It was Tuesday.

Spread of Sri Shirdi Sai Baba's Fame

Sai Baba's popularity and teachings spread from 1858 when he settled down in Shirdi. His spiritual movement has since then been growing in the world.

First Stage

(a) From 1858 to 1886

Baba came to Shirdi in 1858. His fame gradually spread. "Baba's main work was that of a *Samarth Sadguru* who had to diffuse religion and help the good and remove the evil that oppresses the good. Even before 1886, he was possessed of vast powers used for this purpose. In 1886, he had a small body of worshippers who might all have been benefited both temporarily and spiritually by reasons of *Poorva rinanubandha* or present contact.

(b) From 1886 to 1908

Baba passed away in 1886 but returned after three days. "He had to get back into the same body to work out the same remaining portion of the present life". During this time, the Baba's name and fame spread in Maharashtra.

(c) 1908-1918

During this time, the Baba's fame spread in South India; most of his prominent devotees came to him from southern states and also from Gujarat and even northern states; most of his widely known miracles took place; Hindu-Muslim unity was fused through secular worship by both the communities in Dwarkamai: lots of crowds came there, offerings of cash, food and other articles were given to him and they were distributed by him among devotees and the poor ones. Due to the publicity done by Das Ganu and Upasani Baba, Baba's name and fame spread far and wide.

Second Stage (1920s-30s)

Shirdi became known all over India and Sai literature was created by Das Ganu, Dabholkar, H.S. Dixt etc. and *Sai Leela* magazine was started. There was little crowding during this period. The number of persons approaching Sai Baba at Shirdi was small on ordinary occasions.

Third Stage Sai (1940s)

The Sai Baba movement flared up in the thirties and forties and it attained All India character and drew thousands instead of hundreds to Baba's feet. The Baba's presence outgrew Shirdi and was felt in the various temples that were built for him and in the *bhajan* halls, even in the homes.

Fourth Stage 1950s-1960s

Spread of Sai Baba's name throughout the country and other parts of the world. Due to the writings of Narasimhaswami, Shirdi became known all over.

Fifth Stage 1980s—till now

Many propagated the name, fame and message of Shirdi Sai Baba, e.g. Sri Sathya Sai Baba, Sri Narayan Baba, Smt. Sivamma Thayee, Sai Jeevi Radhakrishnaji, Sri B.V. Kher, Sai Das Baba, B. Uma Mahesware Rao, Paras, etc. Many Sai Temples, organizations and journals were established all over India and in some foreign countries.

Now, Baba's popularity as the foremost *Avatar* of the Kali Age is at its highest peak all over the world. Shirdi Sai Temples and Shirdi Sai websites have been established. Sai Baba Samadhi Mandir Complex has been renovated by the Sai Baba Organization of Shirdi.

3

Charismatic Personality of
Sri Shirdi Sai Baba

Sri Shirdi Sai Baba lived till the age of 80. From 1858 till his *Samadhi* in 1918 he lived in Shirdi. Physically he never moved out of a radius of 10 kms or so of Shirdi. His life was that of a Fakir (humble holy saint). He put on white tattered clothes, ate whatever was given in alms and brought by his devotees and lived in a small old mosque to which he gave the name *'Dwarkamayi'* (Mother Dwarka) Dwarka was actually the capital of Lord Krishna's Kingdom about 5200 years ago. He lived like a Muslim Fakir, but he was born as a Hindu. He led a simple, godly life. He always uttered the words *"Allah Malik"* (God is the Master), although he himself was God incarnate. He puffed tobacco *chillum* (pipe), ate whatever was put in his begging tin (mug). He freely shared his food with dogs, cats, birds and his devotees without any distinction, considering all souls to be equal and worthy of being treated with kindness. Although he appeared to be illiterate and never signed his name, yet he knew Sanskrit, Tamil and many other languages. He could recite and explain verses from the Gita and other holy scriptures correctly and authoritatively. He was very kind and affectionate. He treated everybody with utmost love and compassion. At times, he flared up in anger and even abused, scolded and beat people.

He was *Trikaldarshi*—one who could see and tell the past, present and future of every creature, not only of men and women, but even of animals, insects, birds and water creatures. There are so many incidents and stories popular about him which clearly and authentically tell us that he knew the actions of people and creature who came in contact with him or under the umbrella of his grace in the past 72 or even more lives. He could predict anybody's future. He cured people of their physical, mental, socio-economic and other problems merely with his blessings and by the gift of *Udi* (*Vibhuti* or holy ash)—the sacred ash of his *Dhuni* (fire place) established by him in the Dwarkamayi mosque. He was fond of gardening and cooking for his devotees. Some times he danced in the mosque. He often witnessed rural sports, dances and music sessions held before him in the mosque. He was a wonderful saint

60

having all powers of an omnipotent, omnipresent and omniscient *Avatar* (incarnation). He did innumerable miracles, most important of which were lighting the lamps of his mosque with water when oil was denied to him by the local shopkeepers; warding-off diseases; curing people of their illness and misfortunes; giving the boon of children to barren women; saving his devotees from fire and other calamities; appearing before his devotees in dreams, in their meditation and in other forms and helping them; giving *Nirvana* (*Mukti* or liberation) to departed souls and creatures of the animal kingdom etc.

He lived and operated solely in Shirdi which was then a very small village, quite far from the hustle and bustle of life- a simple village of Maharashtra but people from many parts of the country came to see him and receive his blessings and Godly intervention.

Baba had no love for any perishable article. His only possessions were a tin mug for collecting alms, a pair of shoes, some smoking pipes and a grinding wheel. He did not care for honour or dishonour. He spoke freely and frankly with all people. he watched the acting and dances of *nautch* girls and heard *gazals*. Still, he moved not an inch from *Samadhi*.

His *durbar* (court) was imposing. He had a vast store of stories and parables which he told his disciples daily, still he swerved not an inch from his vow of silence. Most of the time, he kept his eyes closed and sat silent.

He was meek, humble, and egoless and pleased all.

In the early days, he wore a white turban, a clean *dhoti* (loin cloth) and a long shirt. He then practiced medicine in the village, examined patients and gave medicines. He was always successful and became a famous *Hakim* (doctor). He always sat erect in meditation; sometimes after a bath and at other times, without one. People greatly benefited by having a *darshan* (glimpse) of Baba. Some became hale and hearty; wicked people were changed into good ones. Leprosy was cured in some cases. Many got their desires fulfilled, some blind men got back their sight and some lame ones got their legs.

According to Professor Charles S.J. White of the Department of Philosophy and Religion at the American University, Washington D.C., Shirdi Sai Baba was in the Nathpanthi tradition of Guru Gorakhnath. In his words:

"Sai Baba's religious practices blended Hindu and Muslim practices . . . He moved into a tiny, unused mosque which became his abode for the rest of his life. There he performed a kind of Hindu ritual with lights and incense. He kept a fire burning perpetually in a *Dhuni* (and his followers keep it burning even today) in the manner of a Nathpanthi Pir. His rituals included both Muslim *Namaz* (Arabic *Salat*) and Hindu prayers and offering. From obscure origins, he rose to a commanding position as a spiritual master and object of worship for a polymorphuous body of devotees: Hindus, Muslims, Parsees and even Christians. Sai Baba was a celibate remaining in one place performing miracles and admonishing his disciples and keeping a fire perpetually burning in *Dhuni*. Therefore, it would not be unreasonable to assume that he was following customs already sanctified in the Nathpanthi tradition with its own degree of Hindu-Muslim assimilation . . . We note too, that dogs, which iconographically accompany Dattatreya or figure in Kabir legends, find their counterparts in the iconography of Sai Baba. To the function of Guru, ascetic and saint, Sai Baba adds that of avatar, as many of his followers consider him to be the main incarnation of God in this age."*

White, Charles S.J., "The Sai Baba Movement: Approaches to the Study of Indian Saints", *The Journal of Asian Studies*, Vol. XXXI, No. 4, August, 1972, pp. 863-878.

According to Justice P.K. Mukerjee of Calcutta High Court: "He (Sai Baba) was unassuming, retiring, shy and unobtrusive and yet the most dynamic and titanic force that made itself felt like the air we breath, and by which we transform overselves every minute." (Speech at Sri Sai Samaj, Calcutta on 29 September, 1968).

4

Miraculous Powers of Shirdi Sai Baba

It is vividly mentioed in all books and articles that Shirdi Sai Baba had miraculous powers. In his mosque, water jars were kept in mosques for people to wash their feet before entering the sacred precincts. In the dusk, one Diwali villagers saw Baba take water from the jars and pour it into his lamps. Then he lit the lamps and they burned. They continued to burn, and then the oil mangess of Shirdi realized that the fakir had turned the water into oil. In consternation they fell at his feet, and prayed that he would not put a curse on them for the way they had treated him.

This was the first miracle Sai Baba performed before the public in Shirdi and it was the match that lit the fire which became a beacon drawing thousands of men to him from afar. Many became his devotees. He used his miraculouos powers to cure their ailments, to help them in their day-to-day problems, to protect them from danger wherever they happened to be, and to draw them towards a spiritual way of life.

Many people found their sense of values changing. Some surrendered themselves entirely to the divine will which they saw in Baba, gave up their worldly lives and came to live at Shirdi as close disciples. Sai Baba taught them according to their needs and capacities. Learned pundits who taught him illiterate found that he could discourse on spiritual philosophy and interpret the sacred writings of India more profoundly and clearly than anyone else they had ever known. But always he led his disciples along the *Bhakti marga*, the radiant pathway of divine love, self-surrender and devotion.

Baba's devotees loved Baba's all actions. Many of them always felt spiritually benefited by his talks, stories and teachings. They forgot their pains, their cares and their anxieties. They felt completely safe and the hours passed unnoticed in blissful happiness. One devotee, a Parsi woman wrote: "Other saints forget their bodies and surroundings, and then return to them, but Sai Baba was constantly both in and outside the material world. Others seem to take pains and make efforts to read the contents of people's minds, or to tell them their past history, but with Sai Baba no effort was needed. He was always in the all-knwoing state."

Many pieces of thrilling information are current among Sai devotees and in many books. One object of the fire he kept burning always at the mosque was to provide a ready supply of ash. This he called *Udhi* or *udi*, which he used for many kinds of miraculous purposes, particularly for curing ailments. The miracles he performed cover the full range of *siddhis* (supernormal powers), as expressed in such spiritual and yogic classics as the *Srimad Bhagavata* and Patanjali's *Yoga Sutras*.

Many times he proved to his devotees that he knew what they were thinking and saying and doing when hundreds of miles away from him. Frequently in times of crises he appeared wherever he was needed, either in his own form or apparently in some other body—a beggar, a hermit, a workman, a dog, a cat or something else. There was plentiful evidence that he could project himself through space and take any material form he chose. Those who were in the best position to know, his nearest disciples, had no doubt whatever on this point.

Baba gave vision to people, as for instance, visiting Tamil Brahmin Vijayanand who was dubious about going into the Moslem mosque. From outside the mosque the Brahmin saw Sai Baba as the God-form he worshipped, Sri Rama. So convincing was this vision of Rama that he rushed in and fell at Baba's feet. Other types of miracles include the giving of protection at a distance—protection against accident, plague, ill-fortune and imminent death; the granting of issue to those who were childless or desired to have a son; appearing to people in dreams with advice and help in their problems.

Like Jesus, Baba was able to cast out evil spirits from those obsessed and cure the most terrible diseases, such as blindness, palsy and leprosy. For instance he allowed Bagoji, a man with advanced leprosy, to come and shampoo his legs. People were afraid that Baba would himself be infected, but on the contrary Bagoji was completely cured of his leprosy only scars and marks remaining.

According to the eminent Sai devotee and author, V.B. Kher's Sri Shirdi Sai Baba possessed all the following 23 *Siddhis* (Powers):

Eight Great Siddhis

(1) *Anna*: The reduction of one's form to an atom.

(2) *Mahima* or *garmia*: To make the body weighty or heavy.

(3) *Laghima*: To make the body light excessively and beyond what is natural.

(4) *Trapti*: To acquire objects of sense performing to the respective organs.

(5) *Prakashya*: To see and know invisible things in the other world.

(6) *Ishita*: To stimulate bodies and creatures; to have control over natural forces.

(7) *Vashita*: To achieve supremacy over the senses.

(8) *Yatkamshadavasyati*: The power to obtain joys in the world effortlessly, by mere willing.

Six Medium *Siddhis*

(1) *Anoormimattvam:* Hunger, thirst, grief, information/stupefaction/delusion/confusion of mind, *moha* (attachment), old age and death affect the body injuriously.

(2) *Doorsharavanm*: To hear, sitting at one place, speech from howsoever distant a place may be.

(3) *Doordarshan*: To see, sitting at one place, events/things in all the three worlds.

(4) *Manojava*: The body travels at the speed of mind at any place as one desires.

(5) *Kamaroopa*: To assume at once any form of desire.

(6) *Parakayapravesh*: To enter into another body dead or alive, temporarily leaving one's own body.

(7) *Swachhadamrutyu*: To die at one's own will, death having no control over him.

(8) *Sahabridamdarshanam*: To see the sport of gods in heaven and capacity and powers to participate in it.

(9) *Ajneprathihatagatih*: One's command and movement have no obstruction and stoppage.

Little *Siddhis*

(1) *Trikalajnatvam*: The knowledge of past, future and present.

(2) *Advandvam*: To be beyond the control of the duality of pleasure pain, cold-heat, soft-very hard.

(3) *Parachittadyabhijhata*: To be tell about another's dream or to know his mind.

(4) *Pratishtambah*: To stop the effect of fire, wind, water, weapen, poison and the sun.

(5) *Aparajayah*: Not being defeated by anybody; being victoriouos everywhere.

Sai Baba had all these 23 *Siddhis* and some others not mentioned above, like *Khandyoga*.

—(*Shri Sai Leela*, Shirdi, March 1990)

5

Shirdi Sai Baba's *Darbar* (Court)

—T.S. Anantha Murthy

In Sai Baba's Dwarkamayi *masjid* is found his grace instantly flowing and problems solved. Since at no other place in the entire universe such perennial assurance fructifies, for no one, other than the gracious saint Sri Shirdi Sai Baba has given such a grand assurance, Shirdi has become the epicenter of the Sai devotion and not only devotees but non-devotees also from India and many foreign visit this holy place with great expectations and reverence.

Long before 1910 A.D., Sri Sai Baba converted a small village like shirdi into a divine or spiritual centre and he himself was the Divinity presiding there. Every day, hundred of men and women surrounded him and prayed for his benediction and got what they desired. Those who went there resided in small *wadas* of the hamlet hoping to earn Baba's grace. They kept themselves busy from morning to night in performing various acts of worship, prayer, study of spiritual literature or some kind of *'sadhana'* (spiritual persuit). They became holy thereby. In such an assemblage of Sai-devotees, there was no difference made on the ground of caste, community, race, religion or sex. The reason why every one behaved in such a cosmopolitan or brotherly spirit was that Sri Baba told them that they were all his children that they should therefore love one another and that his grace was obtainable only if his devotees treated all human beings and all creatures with humanity, sympathy and fellowship. Khaparde's diaries help us to get a mental picture of this unique feature of Sri Sai Baba's spiritual durbar.

Sri Baba knew all Hindu yogic secrets and practices and he allowed Hindu mode of worship of himself. But his outward appearance was that of a Mulslim. His *'kafni'* or long robe, open at the chest, the his loose *dhoti* tied below the waist and the *'kerchief'* tied on his head proclaimed that he was a fakir of that religion. More than all, he uttered *'Allah Malik'* now and then and this habit of his was also in correspondence with the Muslim custom. When he blessed devotees, he would say that *'Allah Malik'* would grant such and such a prayer. He encouraged Muslims together round him and recite Holy Koran in his presence. Further he showed special consideration to old and pious Muslims, who had gone on a pilgrimage to Mecca and come back. Khaparde's entry in this diary under date 15.12.1911 makes mention of an incident which illustrates Sri Baba's love of such Mecca-returned Muslims. A fakir known as Durvesh Falke lived at that time in another *masjid* of Shirdi and he had returned after visiting Mecca. Sri Baba was very considerate to Durvesh Falke. Khaparde saw Sri Baba sending every day a plate of food to that Durvesh and he has mentioned it in his diary. Sai Baba's ears were found pierced at the lobes. The holes in the lobes of Baba were visible and so it was guessed that he had Hindu parents. Piercing the lobes of a child is a Hindu custom. Children of Muslims do not have such marks on the lobes of their ears. Moreover, Sai Baba was not circumcised at all. His devotees discovered this fact, because he had once stood naked in the masjid. Though he lived in a *masjid* (mosqe called Dwarkamayi) disregarding objections by local Muslims, he maintained an ever-burning fire called *'dhuni'* and he fed the fire himself by putting faggots of dry wood into it. He purchased wood for that purpose. Sometimes, he blew a conch, which made the sound of *Aum* or *Om*. Last but not lest he allowed his Hindu devotees to worship him as God or Lord Shiva or as Lord Krishna and so on. Khaparde noticed all these characteristics of Sri Baba and made a record of them in his historic diaries. Khaparde further tells us that those who worshipped Sri Baba in the mosque, were not ordinary simple village-folk but included pious and orthodox and learned Brahmins. Those Brahmins worshipped Sri Baba in the customary Hindu style and his *pooja* consisted of *'arghyam'*, *'archanam'*, *'vandanam'*, *'pada-sevanam'*, *'naivedyam'* and *'karpoora-arati*, as the final act of worship. Sri Sai Baba submitted himself to all such acts of homage and Hindu worship. What, in particular, attracted the attention of Khaparde was that all classes of Hindus of every denomination jointly took part in worshipping Sri Baba and there was also the usual ringing of the bell. Sri Baba ate meat dishes sometimes when he took food with Muslim fakirs. He ate food cooked with fish also. He sometimes ate food touched by dogs, cats and sweepers and he did not think that the food touched by them was unfit or unclean. His Hindu devotees and his Brahmin devotees ignored such habits of Baba and yet they had no hesitation in declaring that he was their Supreme God or Deity. But a few devotee considered him to be a *'Satpurusha'* or a *'Mahapurusha'* endowed withal spiritual qualities mentioned in the sacred Hindu books. His extraordinary power of omniscience and his love of all human beings and animals and his utter sense of resignation to the will of God, whom he called *Allah Malik* confirmed this view about him. He asked learned Brahmins, who visited him to study such books as *Bhagavatam, Bhagavadgeeta, Panchadas Ramayana, Yoga Vasishtha, Ramayana* and so on, he advised them to study those books in their lodgings after observing customary rules of personal cleanliness and ritual. Such was Sri Sai Baba's cosmopolitan or all-embracing outlook and mission. He desired men and women of all strata of society to become spiritually enlightened and he attracted them all to his *durbar* (court), which he held in a humble masjid without ostentation or publicity. Khaparde has enabled us to arrive at the above mentioned conclusions having thus been given a general idea of Sri Sai Baba's spiritual mission and *durbar*.

Sri Sai Baba sat on a thick seat and leaned on a bolster. He sat very near the entrance of the *masjid,* close to the *'dhuni'.* His attendants now and then fed that fire by putting pieces of dry wood into it. Devotees would be sitting round him and some of them would fall at his feet in veneration and beg for his grace. He would then pick up a little ash or *'udi'* from the fringe of the *dhuni* and give it to the supplicant and say that Allah Malik would cure all troubles of the supplicant. His old practice of giving herbs to sick people had long been stopped and its place had been taken up by the practice of giving a pinch of *'udi'.* The *'udi'* thus gifted by Sri Baba was considered by every recipient to be a real medicine or talisman or as a 'cure-all'. It was deemed to be so effective as to cure all physical diseases if a little of it was swallowed with some water. It was also considered to be a talisman the posserion of which on the devotee's person, would protect him from all hostile forces and would further help him to achieve success in any endeavour. It was deemed to be the repository of Sri Sai Baba's power. Khaparde discovered these facts within a few days after obtaining his first *darshan* of the saint. Khaparde saw devotees invariably presenting to Sai Baba such articles as garlands, fruits, pieces of fine cloth, sugar candy etc. Though he did not wear on his person any clothes except a long white cotton robe and a strip of cloth tied below his waist as a *'dhoti'* devotees gave him such things and he accepted them just to give pleasure to the donors. Khaparde saw that Sri Baba welcomed all persons with a smile indicating endless patience and universal benevolence. Sai Baba was most certainly established in desirelessness. But yet, he seemed to have one desire, namely that all persons should visit him and become objects of his love and grace. His *'sankalpam'* (determination) was the force or magnet, that attracted distressed people to his feet. Since his *'durbar'* was open to all, without any distinction, there were no door keepers to prevent any one from entering. A man like Bala Ganpat Shimpi suffering, from malarial fever and shivering, could run into the *masjid* and fall at Baba's feet and pray for a cure of his longstanding malady. The leper, Bhagoji Sindia, stinking with his wounds, could freely enter Baba's presence and beg to be cured. Like-wise, the ignorant and the learned had free access to him. Thus Sri Baba was a spiritual King holding his *durbar* (court) in a masjid. He demanded a few rupees as *'dakshina'* from those, who visited him. They paid it with pleasure and humility, because they were sure that they would receive from him in return both spiritual and temporal benefits, which no wealth or cash could buy elsewhere. We may justly state that the *'dakshina'* asked for by Sri Baba, was a kind of "tribute", which he, as a spiritual King had the right to levy and receive from his subjects. The money received by Sai Baba were spend away immediately for the most charitable or necessary purposes. The lighting of the lamps and the burning of the *'dhuni'* were both for public good. His only personal need was a small quantity of tobacco for smoking his clay pipe. Except the pipe, he had no personal needs. His simple meal was no problem at all, for he begged whatever was necessary from a few houses. He seemed to have endless store of energy. He paid little attention to what he ate for sustaining his physical body. In one word, Sai Baba sat in the masjid as a 'GIVER' of boons or precious knowledge. He was never a receiver of any worldly goods. That which he received was only *'alms'*. He received it humbly as a fakir or a beggar. He depended only on God whom he called *Allah Malik*, for his existence and well-being.

Sai Baba's *darbar* began, as sitnessed by Khaparde, very early in the day, Sai Baba got up from his bed long before day-break. It appeared that he never slept at all in the usual sense of that word. As soon as his devoted attendants noticed that he was sitting on his seat, they would convey the news to other devotees, who would have, by then, gathered in the courtyard of the masjid or the chavadi. It has already been stated that he slept on alternate nights in the chavadi which existed about half a furlong from the masjid. The assembled devotees would cry *'Jai Jai'* and enter the masjid or the chavadi as the case may be. Accordingly to the story narrated in chapter 37 of *Sri Sai Satcharitra*, the worship of Baba began at the chavadi also on the 10th of December 1909 and it was continued till he passed away. Baba's worship under the roof of the masjid had been started nearly fifteen years previously. The early morning *'arati'* of Sri Baba was called *'kakada-arati'*. We may understand it to have been a from of *'Suprabhatam'*—dawn worship ritual done in many famous temples like the Triupati temple. *'Kakada-arati'* consisted of doing *'pranams'* to Sai Baba and of giving to his hands a few fresh flowers and then waving lighted lamps or camphor in front of him. Though two or three long-standing devotees alone took part in doing *'kakada-arati'*, yet all others stood around and raised shouts of *'Jai Jai'*. Their joy consisted of seeing him and obtaining his *'darshan'* at the break of a new day. He was a living God to them and to all the residents of Shirdi. They therefore exhibited their joy by assembling before day break and performing *'arati'* to him.

He slowly got up from his seat, holding the arms of his immediate attendants by way of support. He had become a heavy figure when Khaparde saw these events in 1910 and his legs seemed to have lost their strength by that time. He therefore required the supplementary support of his attendants to stand up from his sitting position. He would then slowly walk out and to the masjid, if he had started on that morning from the chavadi. If on that particular morning, he had started from the masjid, he would slowly walk rewards the Lendi garden, which was situated at some distance. In 1910 when Khaparde saw that garden it was full of trees. When Sai Baba walked towards the garden, he had to pass through some lanes. His devotees followed him. They followed him in a regular regal style. One devotee held an ornamental umbrella over Baba's head. This umbrella was 'chatra'. Another attendant held a similar mace and walked behind Baba. Some others held 'chamara' (peacock feathered fan) and waved it now and then. Casual visitor and some resident of the locality would also join the procession. If Baba had started on that morning from the chavadi, this destination would be the masjid. Though the distance between the chavadi and the masjid was just forty yeards, yet his devotees took him in a slow regal procession and frequently shouted 'Jai', Jai' vociferously. As witnessed by Khaparde, the ardour with which devotees performed their allotted duties during Sai Baba's morning walk was astounding. Their ardour amazed Khaparde as he admits it in his diary. Sri Sai Baba did not wear any foot-wear at all. He walked barefoot. So, the members of his retinue too walked barefoot, some ahead of him and some behind him. There were houses and *wadas* between the chavadi and the masjid. Men and women residing in the adjacent tenements came out of their dwellings when Sai Baba's morning procession passed by. They saluted Sai Baba with great devotion calling him 'Deva' (God). When he reached his destination, the members of his retinue dispersed and deposited 'chamara' and the mace and such other articles of paraphernalia in a house reserved for that purpose. In addition to such daily morning procession of Sri Sai Baba, there used to be special or occasional procession as also. On some feast-days, Sri Baba used to be taken by his devotees along the lanes of Shirdi, in a procession observing the rules of royal etiquette described above. Those occasional processions of Baba gave great delight not merely to the devotees taking active part in them but also to the entire neighbourhood. All communities of people rejoiced to see him walking in such a royal style. Sai Baba too seemed to enjoy the simple but devoted enthusiasm of his humble adorers. It appeared that he desired thereby to enhance their 'bhakti-bhava' towards him.

On some rare dyas, Sai Baba would be carried in a silver planquin by his devotees along the lances of Shirdi, attended by his retinue. When Baba's processions were taken out during nights, as, for example for the masjid to the chavadi, his attendants carried burning torches and lamps on addition to the other articles such as 'chamara'. Those torches and lamps were obviously necessary to shed light in the dark lanes. Sometimes, Sai Baba took part in such functions silently and sleepily as though he was not interested in such proceedings. But, on most occasions, he would he smiling and talking to devotees round about him, as though he too was enjoying the fun and frolic of it. It was obvious to all devotees and new comers that Sai Baba was indeed supremely indifferent to all notions of display or grandeur. He was essentially a begging, homeless fakir whose only wealth was his childlike trust in the omnipotence his God, whom he called *Allah Malik* and whom he remembered at all times. From the diaries of Khaparde, we can find out the devotion of devotees, who habituality or occasionally took part in the procession of Sri Sai Baba. During his stay in Shirdi for nearly hundred days, Khaparde too took active part in the procession described above. Sometimes, his wife and he marched behind Sai Baba's procession. Khaparde refers several kinds of worship of Sai Baba such as 'noon-arati' a 'Seja aarti' and so on. 'Seja-arati' meant night-worship just before Sai Baba retired to sleep.

Khaparde's diaries begin with the description of the events which he saw on 5.12.1910. They end with his experiences of 19.3.1912. In his diary under date 6.12.1910, he says that for the first time in his life, he saw the great saint walking from the masjid towards the Lendi garden with an embroidere umbrella held over his headed by some devotee. On the night of the same day, Khaparade saw Sai Baba starting from the masjid to the chavadi for resting there during that night. According to his description, the night-procession of Sri Baba was impressive. In addition to the state-umbrella, held aloft over Baba's head, several mace chavaries, decorated fans and burning torches were being carried by numerous Sai-devotees. Baba walked slowly holding the arm of a young devotee. The religious fervour of the throng of devotees thrilled the imagination of Khaparde. Khaparde had never before witnessed such a scene. He had never before seen such a deification of a living 'Guru' or 'God'. Dovotees, who carried maces and chavaries, were attired in special uniforms and caps, which dazzled on account of bright lights carried in the procession. It appears that some rich Sai-devotee living in Bombay had specially sent such dazzling apparel, so that mace-bearers could wear them during nights. Khaparde noticed that there was no fixed time-table for either the beginning or the ending of such processions at that period of time. If Sri Baba rose from his seat at the masjid and indicated by his gesture that he was ready to start, his immediate attendant called out. Then other devotees standing in the courtyard and outside take up positions assigned to them and stand in a line holding the umbrella and other paraphernalia.

If, on the other hand, Sai Baba was inclined to sit very late in masjid, the processionists would be singing *bhajans* (devotional songs) till then. Khaparde noticed that the part or role to be played by Sai-devotees was more or less fixed and that there were was no confusion or rivalry amongst the attendants of the 'noon-*arati*' and '*seja-arati*' also. In those days, the function of doing '*arati*' so Sri Sai Baba with camphor was a duty allotted by Baba himself to the Brahmin devotee Megha. If, for any reason, Megha went late to fulfil that duty, the worship of Sai Baba would wait till he arrived. Sometimes, the mid-day *arati* would be started late. The result of such delay was that visitors like Khaparde, who took part in it, waited at the masjid till it was finished and then went back to their lodgings and then took food, Sai Baba would not stick to any time-table at all. As a rule, he would distribute '*prasad*' and give '*udi*' only after 'noon-arati'. Devotees, who desired to get them from his hands had to wait indefinitely. The general rule was that male-devotees should stand separately from women-devotees, during Sai Baba's worship. But, sometimes, Sri Baba would direct that women-devotees alone should be present within the masjid when his worship was being conducted. On such occasions, male devotees stood onside the masjid and watched the '*pooja*' from a distance. Khaparde tells us that the witnessed such a procedure on 31.12.1911.

After taking mid-day meal, Sri Sai Baba smoked his *chillum* (pipe) sitting alone on his seat. After doing so, he walked out and roamed aimlessly, here and there according to his moods. Khaparde saw residents of Shirdi falling at Baba's feet, when he walked near them, he would either ignore them or talk with them according to his pleasure. When Sai Baba walked in that manner through the lanes of Shirdi Village, he sometimes waved his hand in all directions and uttered some words, which no body could understand. After thus spending a few minutes, Sai Baba returned to the masjid and sat on his usual seat. There after noon session of his '*durbar*' commenced. Visitors entered the masjid and sat down after prostrating to him. Baba sometime sang if he was in a jovial mood. He used to sing a very clear tones as remarked on page 181 of Sai-Charita. One paragraph of Hemadpant's biography describes the '*durbar*' of Sai Baba. emadpant informss as under:

"In the *Durbar* of Sri Sai Baba, many personalities appear and play their part. Astrologers come and give their predictions. Princes, poor men, nobleman, sannyasis, yogis, songsters and others come and obtain *darshan* of Sai Baba. Even a scavenger comes in, bows and says that Baba is his father and sits down, jugglers and nomads, the blind and the lame, Natha-panthis and dancers, merchants and others come and play their part and then go away."

Khaparde describes Sai Baba's afternoon *durbar (audience)* in which dancing girls danced and exhibited their beauty. The girls sang as they danced. Sai Baba and others watched such dancing on many days. On 12.1.1912 and the day following, such dancing took place. After the girls had danced and exhibited their art, Sai Baba called each of them to his side and gave them *'udi'* and directed them to depart.

One more important point has been referred to by the late Mr. Khaparde. He saw Sai Baba taking a bath during one afternoon. That was done near a well. Sri Baba did not then allow any one to go near him. On some days Sai Baba would be very serious from morning to night or he would talk occasionally just a few words. On some other days, Baba would be smiling throughout the day and dance within the masjid, while the devotees looked on with delight. Khaparde adds that it gave him and the other members of the congregation great pleasure when such scenes were witnessed.

Khaparde informs us that Sai Baba's moods were unpredictable. One day when Khaparde and other devotees were actually doing *'pooja'* of Baba in the masjid, Baba suddenly flew into a fit of anger and threw away the plates of flowers kept near him. Khaparde could not understand why the saint had behaved in that manner. However, after some minutes, Baba became normal then Mhalsapati's son Martand boldly went near Sai Baba and said, 'Baba, we have not yet finished our usual *'pooja'*. You have thrown away the plates of flowers. I request you to permit us to do at least the *'arati'*. On hearing those words of Martand, Sai Baba laughed heartily and said, "All right, do *'arati'* and finish soon'. Then, one Sitaram performed the day's *arati* quickly and the noon worship came to a close. This unusual event took place on 18.1.1912, according to the diaries of Khaparde.

The events of 19.1.1912 described by Khaparde are important and instructive. They relate to a poor Brahmin devotee Megha, who has been referred to in the previous pages. The happenings of that day are not fully described in the English *Sai Satcharitra* by Gunaji. They are graphically told by Khaparde in his diary under date 19.1.1912. With gratitude to that author, I reproduce here the entire story as narrated by him on that very day. He wrote thus:

'Dixit Kaka told me that Megha had died at 4 a.m. on the night of the previous day. When I saw Sri Baba entering the chavadi for taking rest, I was myself holding an ornamental fan and standing near him. He then told me that Megha would die soon. It has happened accordingly. Baba was sad on the morning of 19.1.1912, when I went for his *darshan* at the time of *'akkad aarati'*. He did not even open his eyes. He did not even show his face to us. He did

73

not glance at us as he used to do. Arrangements were made for the cremation of Megha's dead body. Sai Baba came near just when the body of Megha was being brought out of the *wada*. I heard Sai Baba loudly lamenting the death of that young man. Sai Baba's voice of sorrow was so touching and it brought tears to my eyes and to the eyes of others too. Sai Baba followed the dead body till the bend of the main road was reached and then he walked away in some other direction. Even when he was walking away, Sri Baba's words of lamentation could be distinctly heard by me. From a distance, he was waving his hands and swaying them as though he was bidding good-bye to the dead Megha. When the dead body was lying down on the mound, Sai Baba came near and touched it on the head, chest, shoulders and feet. We were all glad that Sai Baba had touched and blessed that dead youth. I then recollected how Sri Baba had foretold Megha's death.

After recording these details relating to Megha's death, Khaparde has told us that Baba appointed Bapusaheb Jog to do the duty of *'arati'* which was till then being done by Megha. Thus, the diaries of Khaparde are graphic descriptions of Sai Baba's acts and words which are important for any biography of that saint. In another entry, Khaparde has told us that Sai Baba got angry at the lady devotee called Radha Krishna Ayi, because she had, without permission, washed his clothes. That lady was so vexed at Baba's words of anger that she closed the doors of her room and shut herself in. However, Sai Baba's anger did not last long. On the very next day, he became kind and jolly and danced and sang like a boy in front of Khaparde and others. On seeing Sai Baba dancing in that jovial manner, Khaparde recollected how Lord Sri Krishna, used to sing and dance at Gokul in former ages. Such is the description given by Khaparde about Sai Baba's spiritual mission, as he saw in 1912.

In the foregoing paragraphs, I have referred to some instructive episodes which throw light on Sai Baba's *leela*, by way of supplementing what I have gathered from Khaparde's diaries, I will now turn my attention to the 17th chapter of Gunaji's book, where a fuller description of Baba's worship by his devotees can be found. I will abridge what Gunaji has said in it and describe the different kinds of worship, which had become a daily feature in Sai Baba's career on earth. It runs thus:

Sai Baba's habit of sleeping one right at the masjid and of sleeping on the next night at the chavadi was continued almost to the end of his career. From 12.12.1901, his devotees began to do *pooja* (worship) to him at the chavadi also. It was an innovation made or introduced on that historic day. The chavadi was then an old building having two rooms. Baba's devotees had furnished it according to their fancy, though he told them that he did not need any cot, couch and such other appurtenances. Sai Baba would be taken from the masjid to the chavadi in the following manner:

When night advanced Baba's retiring time arrived his devotees assembled in the courtyard of the *masjid*, which had been improved and widened as described before. Devotees started doing 'bhajan'. They gathered there in the space between the 'ratham' and the *tulasi* plant which was growing there. Some of them held musical instruments such as *Tal, chiplis, Khartal, Mridang, khanjari, chol* and harmonium. Some held burning torches in their hands. Some would tie buntings and flags at the corners of the masjid compound where many lamps would be kept burning. Sai Baba's horse Shyam-karna was decorated with trappings and brought to the gate. All devotees could cry 'Jai, Jai' at frequent intervals. The leader of the procession was Tatya Patel. He went into the masjid and reported to Baba that every thing was ready for the ngiht-procession. Holding Tatya's arm, Baba would then slowly get up from the seat and walk out of the masjid. Baba wore his usual *dhoti* (loin cloth) and over it, a *kafni* (a loose robe). In his hands, he carried his *satka* (stout wooden stick). He carried also a packet of tobacco and a clay pipe. Over his robe, he wore also a loose cotton cloth. When he thus emerged out of the masjid, Tatya would put over Baba's body one gold-embroidered shawl. Baba would then put out one lamp till then burning in the *masjid premises*, with his right hand by way of signifying that he had moved out of it. That acts of his marked the start of the night journey. At that moment, all musical instruments would be played by those who had them in their hands. Some crackers too would on some nights be ignited and loud noise would thus be created by young boys. Many devotees sang Baba's glory and among those singers many women too could be seen singing. Volunteers, clad in uniform walked in front to clear the way. Baba slowly walked holding the hand of Tatya. On his two sides, deevotees held *chavaries* and fans and moved forward. Sometimes, they fanned him by way of doing service. While Tatya held one arm of Baba, his other arm was held by Mhalasapati. Babusaheb Jog held the royal umbrella *(Chatra)* over Baba's head and moved alongside. Baba's decorated horse slowly walked at the head of the procession and added dignity to the show. At the rear, many devotees sang *Hari-nama* (God's name) and Baba's 'nama' (name) and kept pace with the moving procession. Within a few minutes, the street-corner, where the chavadi was situated, would be reached. Baba stood for a while at that corner. Then the processionists would all halt in their respective places. During those few minutes, he made some gestures with his hands and waved them in all directions. His face would suddenly shine with trasnscendental glory. On seeing it, devotees raised cries of joy. Then, Kakasaheb Dixit would come out of the chavadi carrying a silver plate full of flowers and how those flowers slowly on Baba's head and shoulders till the plate was empty. During those moments, Mhalasapati, would dance on the road as though he was possessed by some spirit. After dancing in that way, Mhalasapati would again hold Baba's hand and lead him towards the steps of the chavadi. Various instruments would be played when Baba ascended the four steps of the chavadi. By then, the interior of the chavadi would have been decorated suitably. The mud-roof of the chavadi was covered up with a white ceiling cloth. Ornamental mirrors were hung or the walls. Lamps were lighted in all the corners. Tatya entered the chavadi first and spread Baba's couch and arranged the pillows properly and begged Baba to sit on the couch and lean on the bolster. Baba graciously obeyed Tatya's words. After Baba sat down comfortably, Tatya would place a cloth called 'angavastram'. First of all, a crown was placed on Baba's head. Then, numerous garlands and sometimes jewels would be put round Baba's neck. Devotees would, one after another, go near him and put marks on his forehead with sandal paste and draw lines horizontally and put a mark in the middle. That was considered by them to be a 'Vaishnava-mark'. Sai Baba silently submitted himself to this kind of worship, because he loved those who took part in it. With such sandal-paste marks and with garlands, the facial expression of Baba looked grand or splendid. When he was thus being worshipped, the state umbrella was ceremoniously held over his hand by Nana-saheb Nimonkar. Then, after such worship, Bapusaheb Jog washed the feet of Baba with water by way of 'arghyam' and the washing of the feet took place when Baba kept his feet in a large silver plate, after arghyam, Jog smeared Baba's arms with sandal paste. Finally, tambul (betel leaves) would be offered to him and he was thus slowly chewing betel leaves, the assembled devotees prostrated before him one after another with typical humility. When they did so, others held the maces and fans, which had been kept on the floor. Then, Shyama prepared the chillum of Baba and gave it to Tatya's hands acccroding to regulated custom, which was as follows. Tatya ignited the chillum with the help of a match-stick and smoked it for a second or two to find out that it was well and fully ignited. After Tatya was satisfied that the chillum was fully lit up, he affectionately handed it to Sai Baba, who thereupon smoked the chillum (clay pipe for smoking) for some minutes with joy spread on his face. Baba then gave the chillum to the hands of Mhalasapati with a direction that the latter should also smoke it. Mhalasapati, the earliest of Sai-bhaktas from the point of time, had been given this rare privilege. He enjoyed the pipe for a short-while and according to custom, he passed on the same chillum (for smoking) to the other devotees, who were present during the night-function. Those devotees smoked the same pipe one after another. This practice indicated the extraordinary intimacy between the great Saint and his *bhaktas* (devotees). The bonds of love between them were delightful to watch and see. Khaparde was filled with wonder on seeing such a sight. The night-worship of Sai Baba did not end even after his *bhaktas* had smoked his chillum, in the manner described above. One more humble *'seva'* remained to be done. That took place as follows:— Bapusaheb Jog gave a few fresh flowers to the hands of Sri Baba for smelling and enjoying their fragrance. Though this act was simple, yet it indicated the desire of the *bhaktas* to give a chance to Baba to enjoy the fragrance of flowers. Baba smelt those flowers affectionately and said that the smell was excellent. He was such s desireless *Maha-purusha*; but yet he made a show of enjoying the fragrance of flowers. When a biographer contemplates on such *'Sai-leelas'*, all that he can say is that Sri Baba was enjoying the exhibition of love by his humble devotees, whose destiny it was to serve him in that manner. After Baba had smelt the flowers, the same Jog performed the last *'karpoora-arati'* by waving a plate containing burning camphor in front of the Master. Jog alone prostrated once again and stood up. This was the last act of *'seja-arati'* (which means night worship). Then, all devotees left Baba's presence and went to sleep in their lodgings. Then only one devotee remained with Sri Baba. That fortunate man was Tatya. Tatya stood for a while to find out if Baba had any particular order to communicate to him. Generally, Baba had nothing to say. So Tatya said, 'Baba, may I go?' Sai Baba then said, *'Oh, Tatya, you may go if you like. But, come here now and then to guard me during the night.'* This was Baba's usual remark or formula for sending away Tatya from his presence. Tatya then said 'yes' and walked away from the room. Tatya went away to his own house to sleep. The night *durbar* (or *seja-arati*) of the great saint came to an end in such an extraordinary manner. Sai Baba then stood for while alone in that room. He then prepared his own bed. That act was also unusual. He spread fifty or sixty chaddars, one above the other and made a very soft bed. He lay down on it and rested alone merging his mind in Allah Malik. Such was the play or *'leela'* of the merciful saint.

Now I will describe how the original *'urus'* and *Ram Navami* celebrations of an earlier period had developed. Till about 1897 A.D., there was no public celebration of any kind and the Saint's mission of mercy was limited to the men and women giving in the immediate neighbourhood of Shirdi, Rahata and Nimgaon. Individual devotees living in those places obtained his *darshan* at the masjid, made their prayers, paid some *'dakshina'* when he asked for it and secured his benediction and *'udi'* and went away. In the year 1897 A.D., his devotees decided to start some public function so that people of remoter regions might obtain his *darshan* and benediction. The idea of *'urus'* was first conceived by a devotees called Gopalrao, who had, through Sri Baba's grace, obtained a son. On enquiry, he found out that the celebration of 'urus' required the sanction of the collector. Such sanction was also obtained through the grace of Baba. The zeal and hardwork of Gopal Rao, Tatya Patel, Dada Kote Patel and of Shama (Madhavaro Deshpande) and of Mhalasapati and others bore fruit. The urus was a Muslim celebration. Sai Baba desired to foster friendly feelings between Hindus and Musssalmans of the locality. So he advised his devotees to start urus on a Ramanavami Day. Many outsiders were expected to take part in it. Shirdi had then only two drinking-water wells. Water of one of them was unfit for use. So, devotees mentioned above, begged Sri Baba to use his power and make that disused well fit for supplying drinking water. Baba went near that well and put flower into it. The power of Sai Baba was such that the well-water became clean and fit for human consumption.

The 'urus' had to be begun with a flag-procession according to time-honoured custom of the surrounding villages. Likewise, holding of wrestling matches was also considered to be part of 'urus'. A Muslim devotee of Baba lived at Ahmadnagar and his name was Anna Kasar. He agreed to supply the required number of flags. He too had obtained a son through the grace of Sai Baba. Nanasaheb Nimonkar also supplied some ornamental flags. Some shops were opened to sell articles to visitors. Anna Kasar also arranged for many wrestling matches between Hindu and Muslim wrestlers. When these arrangements were completed, the festival of Ramanavami (Lord Ramna's birth Annivrerary) arrived.

On the morning of Ramanavami Day (Lord Ram's birthday), Hindu devotees and Muslim devotees of Sri Baba assembled at the masjid. After obtaining Sai Baba's permission, they carried respective group-flags in joint procession through the streets of Shirdi accompanied by band and play of music. After the procession, they brought the flags into the masjid and with Sai Baba's consent, took them over the roof of the masjid. This was called the 'flag-procession'.

On the night of the same day, those Hindu and Muslim devotees of Baba again gathered at the masjid. With Baba's permission, they started another procession called Sandal procession. It was a function that could be undertaken only during nights. The leader of that procession was known as Amir Shakkar. This man also had become a great devotee of Sri Baba. Muslim devotees of Baba had sandal paste in broad plates. Some others had plates containing burning incense. Carrying such plates on their head or hands they walked through the streets of Shirdi. Since it was a night function, some others carried burning torches in their hands. They too walked with the rest; Hindus too joined that procession. But they carried nothing in their hands. At Sri Baba's direction, the Hindus also accompanied the Muslim plate-bearers and walked along the streets of Shirdi. After the procession ended, all of them returned to the masjid. Muslim devotees threw sandal paste first on the nimbur or niche of the masjid and then sprinkled some paste on the body of Sai Baba also. Then, all of them dispersed. During the evening, wrestling matches took place and winners were duly declared and honoured. Thus, the two communities had, under Sai Baba's guidance, cooperated fully in all functions of the day. The whole affair was known as 'urus'. The holding of 'urus' became an annual function from that year and it is continuing even now, at Shirdi. In 1918 A.D. also, this 'urus' was held under the patronage of Sri Baba. Till now, there has never been any quarrel, dispute or fight between the two communities at Shirdi, because Sri Baba had taught them to maintain intimate friendship among all classes of people of the locality. In former times Tatya Patel and other Hindus mentioned above were taking the leading role in such functions. After a lady-devotee called Radha-Krishna Bai had become a permanent resident of Shirdi; she introduced new features into the two processions described above. In particular, she introduced the custom of feeding of the poor as part of the 'urus' function. She became also the custodian of the paraphernalia of the functions. It has already been stated that 'urus' began on the day of Ramanavami. One day previous to Ramanavami Day, she took permission of Baba and cleaned and whitewashed the masjid and its surroundings. She did that work without taking any one else's help. She worked throughout the night to facilitate her work of cleaning. Sri Baba slept on that night in the chavadi. Such cleaning and whitewashing used to become necessary, because the 'dhuni' was always burning in the masjid and the smoke emitted by burning faggots turned the walls ugly and dark. When Sri Baba was resting at the chavadi, Radhakrishna Bai, single handedly removed all moveable articles from the masjid and kept them safely in the courtyard. Then, she first swept it. Then, she whitewashed all the walls twice and made them white. She then replaced the moveable things in their respective places within the masjid. She then made a report of what she had done to Sri Baba and went to her lodgings she and some others cooked large quantities of food at her residence and at about noon poor-feeding took place under the personal supervision of Sai Baba. After all the poor had been fed, Radhakrishna Bai used to send some articles of food to Sai Baba. He would sit alone in the masjid and eat a little. It was only occasionally that Baba allowed others to eat food with him. Till about 1912, the 'urus' used to be held at Shirdi in the simple manner described above. They were being celebrated on a large scale or on a small scale, depending on the number of people, who took part. In 1912 A.D., significant changes were introduced in respect of that function, I will describe those changes below.

At the outset, it must be borne in mind, that the function 'urus' took place on the day of Ramanavami. A new Sai-devotee Krishnarao Jogeswar Bhishma took part in the 'urs' of 1912 A.D. in Shirdi. He thought that the 'urs' function should be converted into *Ram Navami* feast celebration and that the Incarnation of Sri Rama should be duly rememebered and properly celebrated on that day. He consulted Kaka Mahajani and other oldest Sai-devotees. All of them welcomed his suggestion and went to Sri Sai Baba and told him that they would hold it in such a way as to describe the story of Sri Rama's Incarnation at Ayodhya. Sri Baba gladly gave his consent and told his devotees that the Incarnation or *avatar* (incarnation) of Sri Ramchandra on that day mgith suitably be enacted in the masjid. Accordingly, necessary preparations were made.

This happened in the morning of Ram Navami day of 1912. All the Hindu devotees of Sri Sai Baba assembled at the masjid. The premises had been suitably cleaned up and white washed according to old custom. The morning was bright and devotees arrived with articles of worship. The leader of the group was the above mentioned Krishnarao Jogeswar Bhishma. He and his friends decorated the premises by tying green mango leaves and bunches of flowers. A cradle was brought and placed at Sri Baba took a garland of flowers and placed it in the cradle. That act signified that Shri Rama had taken birth as a baby and was lying in the cradle. Thus, the glad tidings of Shri Rama's birth was announced symbolically. But, the story of the birh of Shri Rama had to be sung by some one by means of 'Hari-katha' or 'kirtan'. Sri Baba selected the above mentioned K.J. Bhishma himself as the 'kirtankar' for the function. Then, Sri Baba himself put a garland on the neck of Bhishma and directed the latter to begin the 'kirtan'. He got ready to do so. He required some one to play ont eh harmonium while he sang. Then, Sri Baba put another garland on the neck of another devotee called Kaka Mahajani and directed the latter to play harmonium. Thus, *kirtan* (singing of religious songs) of Rama's birth started in the masjid under the presidentship of the Saint himself. All the devotees raised a chorus of joy. The 'kirtan' ended after some time. Then, the devotees threw *gulal* powder on each other and on Shri Rama's Incarnation had been celebrated at the masjid in the usual Hindu style. People danced and sang songs just as they would do at their houses. Just then, a trouble started. Some devotee had, in his enthusiasm thrown *gulal* (colored powder) on Baba and some particles had fallen into Baba's eyes and caused pain in the eye. Sri Baba shouted with anger and abused the devotees standing near him. Some of them began to run away in fear. But older devotees knew that Sai Baba would become calm within minutes. They stayed on and encouraged others to sit quietly. The merciful saint became calm again as they had hoped. Then, the customary 'pooja' and 'arati' of Sai Baba were conducted in the masjid with flowers, incense and so forth. The food offered as 'naivedya' to Baba was left in the masjid so that he could eat it when he got the mood to do so. By then, it was past noon, Assuming that Ramanavami had been duly celebrated, devotees tired to remove the decorated cradle from inside the masjid. But, Sai Baba asked those devotees to keep the cradle for one more day within the masjid. Sri Sai Baba said, "Leave the cradle here. We will celebrate *Krishna Jayanthi* or *Krishna Janmasatami* (Birthday of Lord Krishna) here tomorrow". Accordingly, devotees dispersed.

On the next morning, at the same time, devotees gathered at the masjid to celebrate the birth of Lord Shri Krishna. In the same cradle, an earthen pot containing parched rice mixed with curd was kept to signify the birth of Lord Sri Krishna. It was then suspended by means of a string so that all devotees could see it from a distance. The cradle had been decorated in an attractive manner. Bhishma, the devotee mentioned above, was directed by Baba to perform a *"kirtan"* for celebrating the birth of Sri Krishna. Mahajani played on the harmonium just as he had done in the previous morning. After the *kirtan* ended, the curd-mixed rice was distributed as 'prasad' (consecrated eatable) to all the assembled there. Then, the worship of Sri Baba started. He sat on his usual seat and devotees worshipped him by means of 'arghyam', 'vandanam', 'naivedyam' and so on. The final *arati* was also done. On those two days of *Jayanti* celebrations, the customary flag-procession in the morning and the customary sandal-procession of the evening were also held in the usual style. From that year, the 'urus' at Shirdi was being celebrated year after year in the manner described above. Its name too was changed from 'urus' to 'Ramanavami Jayanti' celebration.

From the next year, that celebration included other functions such as 'nama saptaha' and 'parayana' and so on. Such functions began on the 1st of *Chaitra* month. It may be noted here that such additional functions were included. In *Ramnavami* celebrations at the instance of Radhakrishna Bai, whom all devotees honoured and called 'mother'. 'Nama Sankirtan' required the cooperation of many like-minded devotees and through the grace of Sai Baba, they came forward and conducted *Nama saptaha* for an unbroken period of 7 days beginning from the 1st of the *Chaitra* month. From the next year, the function of kirtan was permanently added as parts of *Ramnavami Jayanthi celebrations*. In 1914 A.D., the famous 'kirtankara' namely Das Ganu Maharaj conducted the *kirtan* of Sri Rama's incarnation. It was at Sai Baba's special command that Das

81

Ganu became permanently associated with the celebrations. He would always visit Shirdi every year to take parts in *Ramnavami* celebrations. These facts illustrate that the benevolent Sai Baba was interested in fostering the feeling of *Bhakti* (devotion) in the minds of his ever-growing devotees. On account of such religious celebrations at Shirdi, that hamlet prospered and its inhabitants lived happily. Sai Baba's rich devotees gave him many costly articles such as a silver palanquin, a horse, beautiful pictures, big mirrors and so on. He did not need them at all but the devotees felt that the Saint's *durbar* should be suitably equipped with such marks of Royalty. Ordinarily, about 5000 devotees gathered at the masjid for taking part in Ramanavami celebrations. But, on some occasions, their number increased to 75,000. Through the grace of Sri Sai Baba, no epidemic broke out in any year of those celebrations. Such is the long story of the masjid becoming the centre of *Ram Jayanthi* and *Krishan Jayanthi* celebrations.

6

Full significance of Sri Shirdi Sai Baba

—S.P. Ruhela

Sri Shirdi Sai Baba is being worshipped throughout the world today by millions of people. There are over a dozen journals and many books exclusively devoted to him published and there are many Sai institutions or organizations in the world. No one correctly knows how many Shirdi Sai temples are there in India and abroad, but this much is known to us that there are such temples in almost every town in India and there are such temples in foreign countries. It is a visible Sai miracle that inspite of the fact that there is no central global Shirdi Sai organization for the propagation of Sri Shirdi Sai Baba's name, countless self-inspired devotees take upon themselves the responsibility of strating organizations, temples, welfare activities in the name of Sri Shirdi Sai Baba. Countless people visit Shirdi every day seeking Baba's blessings although Baba attained Mahasamadhi in 1918, and there numbers are increasing each year.

Spite these facts, this is a fact that most of the devotees and even those managing the Shirdi Sai Baba temples of Sri Shirdi Sai Baba do not really know about the full and true form of Sri Shirdi Sai Baba

A number of books have come out mentioning about the past births or past incarnations of Sri Shirdi Sai Baba. This should interest all Sai devotees. Thus, it has been revealed that he was the incarnation of Dattatreya, he was the incarnation of Shiva, in the Bhakti period of Indian history he was born as Kabir—the great iconoclast who hit hard the superstions and dead rituals of the Hindus and Muslims and preached the essence of spirituality and *bhakti (devotion)*; in one incarnation he was the same Muslim Fakir who had blessed the fugitive Emperor Humayan that he would be blessed with a son at Umarkot who would be a great ruler of India; the same Fakir had then advised Mukund Brahmachari of Kashi, who in his next birth was born as Emperor Akbar about whose secularism, *Deen Ilahi* and proclivity towards Hindus and spirituality a lot has been written in countless books. *Shri Sai Satcharitra* mentions many stories of past births of Baba in which he and his devotees of Shirdi Avatar days had lived together in the same family, locality, valley, were kinsmen etc.

These past incarnations of Sri Shirdi Sai Baba must also be great relevance to all his devotees in order to appreciate the crucial fact that he did not suddenly emerge as an Avatar in the 19th century; as a matter of fact, for countless births he had been a pilgrim on the path of spirituality and had been spreading divine knowledge and promoting love and communal understanding among people and compassion towards all. As Avatar at Shirdi, it was the culmination, the highest achievement of his soul as a saint or Godman on our planet earth.

After his *Mahasamadhi* (death) on 15 October, 1918, what happened to him? This a very large percentage of Sai *pracharaks* (spirited program) and devotees do not know and do not care to know, and they are content with the rituals and fossilized knowledge. It is time to know about Sri Shirdi Sai Baba's Spirit after his *Mahasamadhi* event.

As a keen and long time researcher in the Sai phenomenon, fortunately I have discovered two very important relevations about which most Sai devotees do not know anything:

1. Shirdi Sai became the *'Spirit Guide'* of the world immediately after his *mahasamadhi* (death) in 1918 and he occupied this high position in the higher plane till 1941, and Rishi Ram Ram, a great Spirit succeeded him as the Spirit Guide of the world.

2. Thereafter he merged into God and became the God Almighty. The following are the three most startling and hither to unknown evidences of these two great spiritual mysteries about Sri Shirdi Sai Baba:

1. On 17 April, 1942, Mrs. Annie Besant, the well known pioneer of the Theosophical movement in India, announced as under publicaly:

"Good morning, I am now happy having seen the Masters who guided us unerringly for many years. Ram Ram is the greatest of Masters, gentle as Jesus, all knowing and pure, his resplendent presence is an inspiration. He is guideing humanity into one higher path of spiritual life.

Sri Shirdi Sai Baba, after achieving the spiritual regeneration of a considerable cross-section of the people of India, having realized the universasl self merged himself with the Universal Consciousness, the necessary sequel. His mentle fell in 1941 on Rishi Ram Ram, who was elected as the spirit guide of the world."

2. In a book *'Twenty-six Years in Contact with the Spirit World*, V.S. Krishnaswami, I.F.S. (Retired) published from decades back, it was mentioned:

"According to the spiritual sources, the recent Spirit Guides of the World were Sai Baba and Rishi Ram Ram. Apart from arranging for religious instructions to the spirits of different spiritual planes, they (Spirit Guides) have to arrange for spiritual education of persons in the earthly plane."

(Quoted in: Somasundaram, A., *The Dawn of a New Era: The Vision of Master Rishi Ram Ram*, 1970, p. 45.

3. In the First Sai Devotees Convention in 1971, the following extract had been published in the Souvenir:

"MINOCHER SPENCER, a Parsi, a seeker of truth used to receive instructions from a departed saint Ram Ram. The Saint (Ram Ram) one day revealed himself to Spencer and told him, "I have told (instructed you in spirituality) so far. But for further guidance you pray to Sai Baba."

The *Sadhaka* (Spiritual seeker) Spencer has left a book entitled *"How I Found God"* and therein he narrates about the daily lessons he took from Sri Shirdi Sai Baba who used to appear to the devotee (him) in Astral Body; besides Sai Baba had given him messages from 3.11.1952 to 18.2.1953.

In that matchless and thrilling book '*How I Found God*' Spencer has himself recorded that from his cradle days he was under the spiritual care and guidance of Rishi Ram Ram, a great Spirit of the Spirit world, he was spiritually trained by Rishi Ram Ram till 11th May 1949, when the utter handed over the change of his spiritual training and efforts to God-realization to Sri Sai Baba, the God Almighty, the highest Spirit controlling the entire universe.

Before that on 10th April 1949 Rishi Ram Ram had told M.K. Spencer:

". . . I have taken you to the very end of the journey. It is now for God to take you in in. (page 209).

The same day the Master put Spencer's case before Sai Baba, the God Almighty, whom the Parsis call Ahura Mazda, at the time of the transfer on 11 May 1949 the Master told him, "I am handing you on to him (Sai Baba) for he has the final authority to liberate your soul, and not I. (p. 260) and also that "I shall now await the happy day of your transformation which you will achieve through Sai Baba who is the greatest in the whole celestial hierarch." (p. 261)

In the foreword to this monumential book M.K. Spencer's cousin Homi S. Spencer, who was imself a great spiritualist of his time, commented as under:

"The position of this socalled Sai Baba in the Celestial Hierarchy becomes quite definitely clear as the story unflolds itself. First of all it shows by numerous incarnations that Sai Baba is the God himself in his '*Sakari*' (or Manifest) aspect of Asho Ahura Mazda Ameshaspand—a fact which is emphasized over and over again not only by Baba himself but also by Rishi Ram Ram and several other Celestial beings of pre-eminence in the Celestial Hierarchy (like Jesus Christ, Lord Krishna, Lord Buddha etc.)." (p. 32)

On 18th May 1949 Rishi Ram Ram told the Yogi M.K. Spencer:

"I reveal to you this secret. God is manifesting to you in the shape and form of Sai Baba. Bow down to him in utter devotion. To put it in the words of Homi (H.S. Spencer) he is asho Ahura Mazda Amshaspand. He is Amashaspand as well as God.) when he manifested himself he is amshaspand. You have heared him. You will also soon see him." (p. 276).

At a later stage, Sai Baba, the God Almighty told his pupil M.K. Spencer, "It is not a question of mere self-realization but a realization of God with all the mystic powers added for superconscious work on a large scale on your earth plane." (p. 411)

Sai Baba, the God Almighty, took Spencer's soul out of his body in September 1949. On 25th September 1949 Sai Baba revealed to him:

"I took out your soul without putting you into trance . . . The soul passed away from your body and came back in a minute and that minute was terrible for you. It was I who in that one munute's gap sustained you by my invisible force and power." (p. 393-394)

Rishi Ram Ram commented upon this as under and told Spencer:

"It is not a joke to take out the soul when the body is in living condition and in full consciousness and to bring it back quite safe and sound. No Master can do it. It is only Sai Baba alone who can do it and by so doing he has manifested to you his tremendous power and at the same time shown you what he actually is. He is your God whom you worship day and night. He is your Ahura Mazda Amshaspand who has taken the form of Sai Baba for the simple reason and no other that you have his picture in yoru altar room. He can take any form." (p. 394)

Zoroastrian spiritualist Yogi M.K.Spencer in his book 'How I Found God' vividly described Sai Baba as God, his great divine powers and how ultimately he showed himself to him. In his message recorded on page 471 Sai Baba clearly confirmed this:

". . . God has taken the form of Sai Baba and when you see him face to face it will be the exact copy of the picture you have in your alter room."

Ultimately Sai Baba, the God Almighty, helped him in God-realization. On 13th December 1957, the Ahura Mazda (God as the Zoroastrians call Him) as Sai Baba gave this most assuring message to M.K. Spencer for all of us to note and rejoice:

"I am God and I am going to save your world from destruction."

All this highly authentic spiritual revelation, which has hither to remained undisclosed as per God's plan, should now enlighten all that Sai devotees and *pracharaks* all over the globe, and convince them and make them feet greatly happy to discover that by their worshipping Sri Shirdi Sai Baba they are on the right track—they are worshipping not only Sai Baba as *Avatar* but also Sai Baba who is now the God Almighty—the highest of the Celestial Hierarchy in the highest of the planes of consciousness.

The foregoing factual position about the full reality of Sri Shirdi Sai Baba—that he is not merely an *Avatar* who was with us in this earthly plane during 1838-1918 but now God, the Almighty, the very Ahura Mazda of Parsis and Allah of the Muslims and the God of the Christians, binds all of us to a number of commitments.

4. It is now our responsibility to see that we seriously heed and follow his messeges—not only the words he spoke as his teachings as recorded in *Shri Sai Satcharitra, 'Devotee Experiences of Shri Sai Baba, Sai Baba's Charters and Sayings*, and many books on his Avataric career and mission, but more than them we should pay heed to the divine mysterious messages from Sri Shirdi Sai Baba as God from the highest spiritual plane as received by his chosen great contemporary devotees like (Late) Sri B. Umamaheswara Rao of Guntur, Dr. K.V. Raghav Rao of Hyderabad, Prof. P.S. Verma (Acharya Purshotamananda of New Delhi and some others, which have been very carefully recorded by them just on receiving them in their meditation and dreams, and which are full of highest spiritual truths, wishes of God Sai Baba and what we must do to liberate ourselves in this very life. A book 'Sai Baba of Shirdi—A God'. written by Bapatula Hanuman Rao and translated into English by Ram Chasndra Rao *et al,* published by Sai Leela 0rganization in four parts, convincingly proves that Sri Shirdi Sai Baba is God who walked on earth.

We find that there is an unplecedented tide of enthusiasm among Sri Shirdi Sai *pracharaks* and devotees to organize *kirtans,* establish Shirdi Sai temples, do *seva* activities, write books articles, poems, founding Sai organizations, installing Sri Shirdi Sai's statues, organizing *Sai Sandhyas* (eveing devoted to mass singing of songs in praise of praise of Sai Baba), *Langar* (community dinner) and do all these and more including national and international conventions and the like.

Sri Shirdi Sai Baba taught mutual harmony, secularism of the highest order, integration love, piety, justice, *shraddha* (faith) and *Saburi* (patience) and a host of other high values. As Avatar at Shirdi till 1918 and then as God Almighty, he has been deeply concerned about bringing in an era of one religion—the religion of humanity. His rare 77 messages (Discourses) dictated to and most carefully recorded by Yogi M.K. Spencer in *'How I Found God'* clearly advise the inhabitants of this earthly plane;

- to move "from darkness into light",
- to realize that "renunciation is the essence of spirituality",
- to "remain true to yourself and work your way to spiritual heights discarding all that is gross and carnel",

- to "make life the cornerstone of your life", to realize that "Truth alone will survive",
- to "break the chain of *maya* (Illusion) with the hammer of selfconsciousness",
- to "destroy sin with the hammer of God's name",
- to realize that "As you sow, so shall you reap",
- to know that God realization is the goal of life, not earthly happiness."
- Baba says: "Don't make life a tomb of woe and wantonness. Rise from the graveyard of sickness and sorrow, both of mind and soul, and climb the altitude of high thoughts and aspirations, to free you from the maddening temptations of your world and it vagaries. Keep away from the shore of dead sea apples. Clinch pure gold and not putrid flesh. Kindle the light of your heart with the flame and fire of God's Love and Light and you will safe in your march from the earth on to the realms beyond." (From: *How I Found God*), and many such spiruirual gems.

Let us take stock of the contemporary global situation. We find that the world is suffering because of so many dissensions and racial, social, cultural, economics and political conficts, jealousies and disjunctive and dysfunctional tendencies which have made the life of human beings everewhare very insecure. Religions have disappointed humanity because of misdoings of many fundamentalists, fanatics, hypocrites, money-loving and power-hankering saints, *yogis* and *acharyas* who rarely see eye to eye even among themselves and do not feel shy in condemning each other publicly. In such social and religious context of the contemporary world, Shirdi Sai Baba alone comes upto the expectations of the masses of the world as the ideal Godman who epitomizes simplicity, spirituality, love and genuine concern for all creatures of the highest order. The world is fad up with all those who teach religion, morality, spirituality and *yoga* and the like in enchanting words but crave for worldly properties, publicity, political patronage and all the pleasures and luxuries of the modern life. Sri Shirdi Sai Baba, therefore, impresses us most. Baba's simple teachings are without any trappings of complicated philosophy and his grace can be easily available to all.

5. Famous Sai devotee and spiritual healer D.H. Jagtag from Chennai has rightly written:

"Saints are rarest. Lesser saints are maximum in number. Lesser Saints lapse into meditation, forget their physical realm, pass through the subtle realm and stay steady at the mental realm, the creative plane of all worlds invisible and visible. There they get charged with powers divine latent in them and all in all beings. Salvine the prenatal and natal impulses embedded in them and also in all beings from the every vibrating Cosmic Morhogenic field and descend to the Earth Realm to work out graciously and mysteriously the plan of the spiritual revolutionary, the Universal Mind. But the lesser saints have to lapse into meditation at distant intervals to resume their unfinished task.

Contrarily, Shirdi Sai Baba, the rarest of the rarest was excercising dual (Over Soul and Casuled Soul) Consciousness simultaneously in all beings and in inanimate and animate objects without any need to lapse into meditations.

The Oversoul deals with Harmony with the Universal Mind. The capsuled soul is veiled and handicapped by the physical ego which is a hindrance to the evolving souls.

Allah Malik Shirdi Sai Baba is not only but also is omnipresent, Omnipotent, Omniscient, Omni bountiful, Omniplentitude, and Omnimerciful."

—D.H. Jagtap
(Courtsey: *Shirdi Sai Leelamruta*,
April-June 2011 issue)

D.H. Jagtap is an ardent and highly blessed unique devotee of Sri Shirdi Sai Baba. He has for many years been doing miraculous healing of thousands of people invoking the name and grace of Sri Shirdi Sai Baba free of cost in camp at different places where-ever he is invited by Shirdi Sai organizations or groups of Sai devotees. The testimonies of hundreds of people cured by him with the special healing power bestowed on him by Sri Shirdi Sai Baba are regularly reported in the issues of the English Quarterly magazine 'Shirdi Sai Leelamruta' which is published and freely distributed by 'Sai Deep', I, Loganathan Street, Tambran (West), Chennai—600045 (Phone 22261670).
Sri D.H. Jagtap can be contacted on:
Tel.: 044-22294719, Mobile: 09841586849
E-mail: jagtapsai@rediffmail.com

Important Books on Sri Shirdi Sai Baba

Sai Baba of Shirdi has been a great influence on literary mindscape of those who were inspired by his life and philosophy. He has been written about in volumes and bookshops are agog with Sai Literature Books on Sai Baba are immensely popular among poeple of all faith and tradition. The life philosophy and all the things that were linked to this epoch-making saint and guru has been the treasure trove for writing books that are always in demand. Here are some of the important works that are written on Sri Shirdi Sai Baba different authors:

* *108 Names of Shirdi Sai Baba*, compiled by Vijaya Kumar.
* *Ambrosia in Shirdi*: 101 Experiences of Devotees when Sai Baba was Embodied, and 100 Experiences of Devotees after Sai Baba's Samadhi in 1918, by Ramalinga Swamy.
* *Shri Sai Satcharita* (Enlarged Edition), by G.R. Dabholkar.
* *The Blossom of Praise to Shri Sainath*, (Shri Sainath Stavan Manjari), by Das Ganu.
* *Children's Sai Baba*, by D.L. Parchure.
* *Devotees Experiences of Shri Sai Baba* (Statement of 81 devotees most of whom had Seen Sai Baba), by B.V. Narasimhaswami.
* *Golden Words of Sri Sai Baba of Shirdi*, by Ramalingaswamy.
* *Guide to Holy Shirdi*, Shri Sai Baba Sansthan.
* *Gurus Rediscovered: Biographies of Sai Baba and Upasani Maharaj of Sakori*, by Kevin R.D. Shepherd.
* *The Incredible Sai Baba* (The Life and Miracles of a Modern Saint), by Arthur Osborne.
* *Introduction to Sai Baba of Shirdi*, by B.V. Narasimhaswami.
* *The Life and teachings of Sai Baba of Shirdi*, by Antonio Rigopolous.
* *The Life and teachings of Sai Baba of Shirdi*, by T.S. Anantha Murthy.
* *Life History of Shirdi Sai Baba*, by Ammula Sambasiva Rao, Sterling.
* *Life of Sai Baba*, by B.V. Narasimha Swamy ji.
* *A Mission Divine* (novel on Shri Sai Baba), by R.S. Junnarkar.
* *Pictorial Sai Baba*, Sri Sai Baba Sansthan.
* *Sai Baba: Master*, by Acharya E. Bharadwaja.
* *Sai Baba: The Perfect Master*, edited by D.N. Irani.
* *Sai Baba: The Saint of Shirdi*, by Mani Sahukar.
* *Sai Baba of Shirdi* (Pictorial), by Indira Anantha Krishna.
* *Sai Baba of Shirdi: A Unique Saint*, by M.V. Kamath and V.B. Kher.
* *Sai's Help*, by B.V. Narasimhaswami.
* *Santakathamrita*, by Das Ganu, 1903
* *Shirdi Darshan* (Pictorial), Sri Sai Baba Sansthan
* *Shirdi Diary* of the Hon'ble Mr. G.S. Khaparde (events between 1910 December and 1918 March), Shri Sai Baba Sansthan.
* *Shirdi Sai Baba: An Epic*, by Basavaraj Gunaki.
* *Sree Guru Charita*, by Gangadhara Saraswati.
* *Shri Sai: The Superman*, by Swami Sai Sharan Anand
* *Shri Sai Baba*, by Swami Sai Sharan Anand.
* *Shri Sai Baba of Shirdi*, by Rao Bahadur Moreshwar W. Pradhan.
* *Sri Sai Baba's Charters and Sayings*, by B.V. Narasimhaswami.

* *Sri Sainath Sagunopasana*, by K.J. Bhishma.
* *The Eternal Sai*, by S. Maneey.
* *Sai Baba: The Perfect Master*, Complied from writings by Dr. A.G. Munsif
* *The Spiritual Philosophy of Sri Shirdi Sai Baba* by Uma Maheswar Rao.

7

Sri Shirdi Sai Baba's Teachings

I

Sai Baba did not deliver long or abstract discourses. Whatever he said was expressed in a very brief, simple and straight-forward manner. All his teachings were very simple; they were the most essential substance or essence of all the scriptures of Hinduism and Islam.

A content analysis of all his teachings, his devotees conversations with him, his outbursts, his miracles and his oft repeated words and stories of previous lives and all such materials recorded by his devotees in his lifetime in their memories enable us to identify the following main spiritual themes, concepts or key ideas:

Teaching of Sri Shirdi Sai Baba:

(1) *Rinanubandha:* (Bondage of Give and Take)

Nobody comes to us in this life, unless he or she has to take from us or give us something as debt repayment. Therefore, Baba's teaching was to always treat him with due courtesy whoever comes to us in this life.

(2) *Saburi* (Patience) and *Shraddha* (Faith)

We must have faith in our *Guru* (Master). We must venerate and obey our *Guru* and serve him with all our devotion. Then we must have patience, for everything takes time to happen, to materialize. These two were the oft-repeated pet concepts of Baba to all his devotees. He assured all his devotees: "If you look to me, I look to you." He blessed all those who had faith and dedication.

(3) *Samarpan* (Total Surrender)

We must have the attitude of total surrender towards our *Rama* whose *Kripa* (kindness) alone can lighten the load of our past *Karmas* (actions), who alone can lead us to salvation. He explained: "Surrender restores the balance or harmony of *gunas* that was upset when the separate existence of the *Jiva* (individual soul) commenced. Surrender is brought about when the feeling of the devotee towards his Guru gets intensified."

(4) *Sambhava* (Equality)

"See God in all beings." This was taught by Baba to his devotees on many occasions. Once he said:

"Take pity on me like this. First give bread to the hungry and then eat yourself. Note this well. The dog which you saw before meals and to which you gave the piece of bread is one with me, so also are other creatures (cats, pigs, flies, cows etc.) one with me. I am roaming in their forms. He who sees me in all these creatures is my beloved. So, abandon the sense of duality and serve me as you did."

(5) Detachment

Baba taught again and again: "Let the world go topsy turvy; you remain where you are."

(6) *Dakshina* (Donation)

Baba used to accept and sometimes even ask for money. One earns merit by doing so.

(7) *Integration*: Being a genuine Universal Master, Sai Baba tried his best to bring Hindus, Muslims, Parsees, Christian and followers of other religions to the ultimate and supreme realization that all are essentially one and that is the very basis of intrinsic unity and integration.

(8) *Simplicity:*

Sai Baba led a life of simplicity. He preached simplicity in eating, dressing, worship, behaving and in all human relations. He preached: "Do not be deluded by worldly honour. The form of the Diety should be ever devoted to the worship of the Lord, let there be no attraction for any other thing; fix the mind in remembering me always, so that it will be calm, peaceful and care-free."

II
Sri Shirdi Sai Baba's Divine Words of Wisdom

1. Action *(Karma)*

   "This *Deha Prarabdha* (present fate) is the result of the *karmas* (actions) done by you in the former births."

2. Assurance

   "If a man utters my name with love, I shall fulfil all his wishes, and increase his devotion. If he sings earnestly of my life and deeds, I shall be set him in the front, back and on all sides."

3. Beauty

   "We are not to bother about the beauty or ugliness of a person, but to solely concentrate on God who underlines that form."

4. Charity

   "The donor gives, i.e., sows his seeds, only to reap a rich harvest in future. Wealth should be a means to work out *Dharma*. If it is not given before, you do not get it now. So, the best way to receive is to give."

5. Contentment

   "One must rest content with one's lot."

6. Dakshina

   "The giving of *Dakshina* (reverential gift) advances *Vairagya* (non-attachment) and thereby *Bhakti* (devotion)."

7. Death

   "No one dies; see with your inner eyes. Then, you will realize that you are God and not different from him. Like worn out garments, the body is cast away by God."

8. Disillusion

   "Whenever any idea of joy or sorrow arises in your mind, resist it. Do not give room to it. It is pure disillusion."

9. Destiny

   "Whosoever is destined to be struck, will be struck. Whosoever is to die, will die. Whosoever is to be caressed, will be caressed."

10. Discrimination

    "There are two sorts of things—the good and the pleasant. Both of these approach man for acceptance. He has to think and choose one. The wise man prefers the good to the pleasant, but the unwise, through greed and attachment, chooses the pleasant and thereby, cannot gain *Brahma Gyana* (Self-realization)."

11. Devotee

    "He who withdraws his heart from wife, child and parents and loves me is my real lover (or devotee) and he merges in me like a river in the sea."

12. Devotion

"Knowledge of the Vedas, or fame as a great *jnani* (learned scholar), or formal *bhajan* (worship)—these are of no avail unless they are accompanied by *Bhakti* (devotion)."

13. Differences

"People differentiate between themselves and others, their properties with other's properties. This is wrong. I am in you and you are in me. Meditate on the self with the question "Who am I?""

14. Duty

"Unless a man discharges satisfactorily and dispassioniately, the duties of his station in life, his mind will not be purified."

15. Egoism

"Who is whose enemy? Do not say of anyone that he is your enemy. All are one and the same.

16. Equanimity

"Let the world go topsy-turvy, you remain where you are. Standing or staying at your own place, look calmly at all things passing before you."

17. Exploitation

"Nobody should take the labour of others gratis. The worker should be paid his dues promptly and liberally."

18. Feeding

"Know for certain that he who feeds the hungry, actually serves the food to me. Regard this an exomatic truth."

19. Food

"Sitting in the *Masjid* (mosque), I shall never, never be untrue. Take pity on me in this manner: first give bread to the hungry and then eat yourself. Note it well."

20. Forbearance

"Our *Karma* is the cause of happiness and sorrow. Therefore, put up with whatever comes to you.

21. God

"God lives in all beings and creatures, whether they be serpents or scorpions. He is the greatest puppeteer of the world and all beings, serpents, scorpions etc. obey his command.

22. God's Gifts

"What a man gives, does not last long and it is always imperfect. What my *sarkar* ((Master, God) gives, lasts to the end of life. No other gift from any man can be compared to his."

23. God's Grace

"You must always adhere to the truth and fulfil all the promises that you make. Have *Shraddha* (faith) and *saburi* (patience). Then, I will always be with you wherever you are."

24. God's Will

"Unless God wills, nobody meets us on the way; unless God wills, nobody can do any harm to others."

25. God's Will:

"Unless God wiils, no one meets us on the way. Unless God wills, no body can do harm to others.

26. Greed:

"Where there is greed, there is no room for thought of meditation of the *Brahman*. Then, how can a greedy man get dispassion and salvation?"

27. Guru

"Stick to your own Guru with unabated faith, whatever the merits of other gurus and however little the merits of your own."

28. Guru's Grace

"The mother tortoise is on one bank of the river and her younger (meditating upon) their mother. The tortoise's glance is, to the young ones, a downpour of nectar, the only source of sustenance and happiness. The relationship between the *Guru* and the disciples is similar."

29. Humility

"Humility is not towards all. Severity is necessary in dealing with the wicked."

30. Happiness

"If others hate us, let us take to *Nama japa* (Chanting God's Name) and avoid them. Do not bark at people, do not be pugnacious. This is the way to happness."

31. Help

"If someone begs and if it be in your hand or power to give and if you can grant the request, do so. Do not say "no". If you have nothing to give, give a polite negative reply but do not mock or ridicule the applicant nor get angry with him."

32. Hospitability

"No one comes to us without *Rinanubandha* (some previous bond of give and take). So when any dog, cat, pig, fly or person approaches you, do not drive it or him away with the words *"Hat-Hat" "Jit-Jit"*.

33. Inquiry

"Always inquire: Who am I?"

34. Introspection

"We must see things within ourselves. What good is there in going about asking for this man or that for views and experiences?"

35. Liberation

"Service at the feet of the *Guru* is essential to attain *Moksha* (Liberation)."

36. Lust;

"A person who has not overcome lust can not achieve (realize God)."

37. Name Chanting:

"If you chant, *"Raja Ram, Raja Ram"*, your mind will attain peace and you will be benefited immensely."

38. Non-possession

"Everything belongs to us for use. Nothing is for us to possess."

39. Omnipresence

"I am not confined within this body of three and a half cubic height; I am everywhere. See me everywhere."

40. Oneness

"The dog which you saw before meals and to which you gave the piece of bread is one with me, so also other creatures (goats, pigs, flies, cows etc.) are also one with me. I am wandering in their forms. So abandon the sense of duality and serve me as you did today (by feeding that dog)."

41. Poverty

"Poverty is the highest wealth and superior to the Lord's Position. God is brother of the poor. The *Fakir* (mendicant) is the real emperor. Faqirship does not perish, but an empire is soon lost."

42. Quarrel

"If anybody comes and abuses you or punishes you, do not quarrel with him. If you cannot endure it, just peak a simple word or two, or else go away from that place. Do not battle with him."

43. Questioning

"Mere questioning is not enough. The question must not be put with any improper motive or attitude to trap the *Guru* and catch mistakes in the answer, or out of idle curiosity. It must be put with a view to achieve *Moksha*."

44. Reality

"Brahma" (God) is the only 'Reality' and the Universe is ephemeral and no one in this world, be he son, father or wife, is really ours."

45. Self-Realization

"The idea that "I am the body" is a great disillusion and attachment to this idea is the cause of all bondage. Set aside this idea and the attachment therefore, if you want to reach the goal of self-realization."

46. Service

"*Seva* is not rendering service while retaining the feeling that one is free to offer or refuse service. One must feel that he is not the master of the body, that the body is that of the *Guru* and exits merely to render service to him."

47. Sin

"Inflicting pain on others by body, mind and speech is sin, the reverse is merit, good."

48. Support

"Come what may, stick to your support, i.e., *Guru* and ever remain steady, in union with him."

49. Surender

"It is my special characteristic to free any person who surrenders completely to me, who worships me faithfully and who remembers me and meditates on me constantly."

50. Truth

"You should always have truth with you. Then, I will always be with you, wherever you are and at all times."

51. Unity

"Rama and Rahim were one and the same; there was not the least difference between them; . . . You ignorant folk, children, join hands and bring both the communities together, act sanely and thus you will gain your object of national unity."

52. Vissitudes of Life

"Gain and loss, birth and death, are in the hands of God. But how people forget that God looks after life as long as it lasts."

53. Wisdom

"Whoever is bestowed with the kindness of God does not speak much. But the absence of God's kindness makes one speak unnecessarily."

8

Sai Baba's Sai Baba's Unique Samadhi Mandir at Shirdi

Baba's supreme popularity and the phenomenon of wide spread SaI faith and devotion is due to the fact that Baba is easily approachable for answering of our prayers even though the degree of one's faith is intense or slender. Baba is ever compassionate father/mother in this scientific space age. Being established as 'Universal Master' he has harmonized all religions and faiths and demonstrated the oneness of God, and affirmed that all paths lead to one goal i.e., 'God', as expounded by Lord Krishna in the Bhagavad Gita.

Similarly Shri Rama Krishna Paramhansa realized the oneness of God in all faiths and emphasizes the truth in a simple, significant simple as follows:

"As one and the same material viz., water is called by different people by different names—one calling it water, another *'Vari'* a third *'Aqua'* and another *'Pani'*, the one *'Sat-Chit-Anand'* (Existence-knowledge-Bliss Absolute), is invoked by some as 'God', by some as *'Allah'*, by some as *'Hari'* and by others as *'Brahman'* etc.

In the beginning Baba's influence and glory spread slowly, but his message spread far and wide soon, as clearly pointed out by Arthur Osborne—the great propounder of Ramana Maharashi's philosophy of 'Self-enquiry (Who am I?). He says that 'Sai Baba does not accord with the modern conception of a Saint—i.e., that is, that he should lead a decorous life, not performing too many or too starling miracles and should expound his teachings in philosophy, on which the scholars can write thesis. There are different view points of a mountain peak from its base, a master may turn his light on any one or another of the paths leading upto it. Such paths illumined by various masters may cross as they wind up the mountain side, so that the short-sighted geographer may think that they run in opposite directions, btu the master knows the summit, and knows that all paths and there." (*Incredible Sai Baba*, page. 7)

Though Baba seemingly left his mortal coil in 1918 He is ever present as before, as the very sight of Samadhi Mandir of Baba at Shirdi brings that experience. Persons of diverse religions come and receive his grace and blessings. He exhorted all to follow their respective personal religions and conscientiously observe their tenets. He did not found a new religion or sect. His Samadhi Mandir is a shrine of Universal Religion for all for their salvation.

Paramahamsa Sathyananda Saraswathi Founder Sivanand Ashram, Munghyr, Ganga Darshan (Bihar), spoke as follows on 12th-14th March 1989 at Shirdi:

"The *Samadhi* of Sai Baba who has been heralded as an *Avatar*, was the first Thirtha I visited in Maharashtra. It is said that just not the temple but the entire town of Shirdi resonates with the spiritual vibrations of the great saint Sai Baba. Sitting at the eternally lit *Dhuni* (fire place) to Baba I did feel a strong spiritual energy field which could only have been created by the *'tapasya'* and *vairagya* of a *Mahapurusha* (great man)."

- Scientists in order to testify the reason for so much of surging crowds thronging at Shirdi, put minute and powerful electronic cameras at Samadhi Mandir at Shirdi and they found that 3 lakhs and more rays are emanating from the *Samadhi* at every second. (Revealed during *Sai Leela* contributors meet held on 4th & 5th March, 1990 at Shirdi). This cannot be seen by our naked eyes, just like 'X' ray, Micro ways, T.V. waves—only true devotees can have a glimpse of them. Those of receptive pure hearts, can know by their inner vision.

- Lord Sai also promised that "whoever ascends the steps of his *masjid,* named by him as *'Dwarakamayi'*, all his sufferings will come to an end." Baba also stated: "If anyone hurts another, I am hurt. If you are unkind to anyone, I am pained." With such words Sai Baba has exhorted his devotees to look upon all equally. His love was universal. He protects his devotees like a tortoise for its young ones. The means to get such protection is one pointed devotion and singular surrender. Baba has a place for all—the man in sorrow and difficulties, the one who seeks worldly advancement, the seeker of knowledge.

- Whether the Devotee was a Hindus, Muslim, Parsi, Christian, Brahmin or *Shudra* (low caste), Sai Baba looked upon all with equal vision and tried to lighten the burdens of all alike. Service was his creed and he sacrificed his life for his cause. The blessed biographer of Baba, Hemandpant in *Sai Satcharitra* expressed that Baba did not expect anything from his devotees expect constant remembrance, unflinching faith and devotion. If I am asked what I would suggest to one who wishes to find out how (not having met Sai Baba in flesh) could make himself a devotee of Baba and get his help, my answer will be that he should sit whole-heartedly and try to pour his heart in love to Sai Baba. It is not essential that he should go to Shirdi for that purpose—though Shirdi associations are undoubtedly helpful; all that he should do is to transcend his senses and concentrate with love on Sai Baba. He would surely reach and obtain help of Sai Baba—to obtain all that he is fit to achieve and receive."

• Sai Baba Temple: The Second Richest Temple in India

Sri Sai Samadhi Mandir at Shirdi is said to the second richest temple in India next to Sri Venteswara Temple at Tirpati. It visited by at least 20000 people on an average daily and on Thusdays and festival days their number swells to more than a *lakh* (hundred thousand). They come from all over India as well as from many foreign countries and they belog to all social classes, social statuses, occupations professions, religions and cultural backgrounds. voluntarily offer *dakshina* (customary gift or donations) to the temple and Dwarkamayi in the name of benevolent and gracious Sai Baba in belief that Sai Baba will kinldly fulfill their wishes and solve their all kinds of problems. Many offer their donations in gratitude to Sai Baba since their serious problems have already ben solved by hisd miracuilous grace. Thus the temple has been receiving huge income from devotees and visitors.

- The Press Trust of India released on its web site *http;// ndtv.com/aticle/ India-irdi-, saibaba—temple—has—ornaments—worth—over—rs—* . . . the following infomation on 8th January, 2013:

Shirdi Saibaba temple has ornaments worth over Rs.50 crores

The famous Saibaba temple at Shirdi in Maharashtra, one of the richest shrines in the country, has ornaments and jewellery worth Rs.50,53,17,473 and a tootal fixed deposits worth Rs.6,27,56,97488 as on March 31 last year, including investments in Kisan Vikas Patra.

The ornaments and jewellery worth has increased by Rs.11,04,50,335 as compared to figures of year ended on March 31, 2011, which was total of Rs.39,48,67,138.

Similarly, the total value of fixed deposits, investments in Kisan Vikas Patra (KVP) is of Rs.23,34,00,000 at end of last fiscal year against Rs.40,84,00,000 (KVP) of previous year (March 31, 2011), according to the annual report of the Sai Baba Trust, Shirdi which was constituted by teh Government of Maharashtra for smooth functioning of activities in 2004.

The fixed deposits with various nationalized banks have increased by Rs.1,38,06,28,921 during the financial year of 2011-12, the yearly report, which was tabled during the Wintr Session of State Legislature in late December 2012, said.

Gold worth Rs.9,20,55,539 was added to its kitty during the year 2011-12 from the existing value of Rs.27,95,27,935 (March 31, 2011).

However, there were no additions of gold coins and gold pendants during 2011-12.

The Trust has foreign currency on hand worth Rs.17,05,137.

It was spending Rs.76,74,26,961 on various charity work (grant in aid) including Rs.45 crores towards development of proposed airport at Shirdi and for hosting Sai Bhajan Sandhya (musical evening) in London at an expense of Rs.24,69,239, the report said.

The temple has received total donations during the year to the tune of Rs.2,06,14,96,152 including Rs.1,60,45,78,233 from charity boxes (both cash and kind), the report added.

- **Daily Programme at Sai Baba Samadhi Mandir, Shirdi**

Time	Programme
4:00 AM	Temple opens
4.15 AM	*Bhupali*
4:30 AM-05:00 AM	*Kakad Aarti* (morning)
5:00 AM	*Bhajan* in Saibaba Mandir
5.05 AM	Holy Bath of Shri Sai Baba (*Mangal Snaan*) in Samadhi Mandir
5:35 AM	*Aarti "Shirdi Majhe Pandharpur"*
5:40 AM	*Darshan* begins in Samadhi Mandir
11:30 AM	*Dhuni Pooja* with rice and ghee in Dwarkamai
12:00 AM-12:30PM	Mid day *Aarti*
4:00 PM	*Pothi* (Devotional reading/Study) in Samadhi Mandir
At Sunset (20 min.)	Dhoop Aarti
8:30-10:00 PM	Devotional Songs in Samadhi Mandir and other Cultural Programmes (if any)
9:00 PM	Chavadi and Gurusthan closes

9:30 PM	In Dwarkamai water is offered to Baba, a mosquito net is hung and the hanging lamp is lit
9:45 PM	Dwarkamai (the upper part) closes
10:30 PM-10:50 PM	*Shej* (night) *Aarti*, after this, a shawl is wrapped around the statue in the Samadhi Mandir, a Rudraksha mala is put around baba's neck, Mosquito net is hung, and a glass of water kept there
11:15 PM	Samadhi Mandir closes after night Arati

Abhishek Pooja Timings

1st Batch	7.00 am to 8.00am
2nd Batch	9.00am to 10.00 am
3rd Batch*	11:00 am to 12:00 pm
Depends on Crowd Note: amount payable for *Abhishek Pooja* is Rs 101/-only	

Satyananarayan Pooja timings

1st Batch	07.00 a.m. to 08.00am
2nd Batch	09.00 a.m. to 10.00 am
3rd Batch	11.00 a.m. to 12.00 pm
4th Batch*	01:00 p.m. to 02:00 pm
5th Batch*	03:00 pm to 04:00 pm
*Depends on the crowd	

Palanquin Program is arranged on every Thursday at 9.15 pm
Darshan Line will be closed during

1) after Noon *Arati*   -   11:15 a.m. to 1:00 p.m.
2) After *Shej Aarati*   -   10:00 p.m. Onward
3) *Dhuparati*   -   Half hour before *aarati*

9

Sri Shirdi Sai Baba's Closest Devotees

Among Sri Shirdi Sai Baba's closest devotees were Madhava Rao Balwant Deshpande whom Sai Baba gave the name 'Shama'; Tatya Kote Patil, Kashi Ram Simpi, Appa Kulkarni, Narayan Govind Chandorkar (popularly called Nana Saheb), Hari Om Dixit, Abdul, Rao Bahadur Hari Vinayak Sathe, Gopal RAo (Bapu Saheb Buty), Kaka Mahajani, G.S. Khaparde, Bayja Bai, (who used to feed Baba, Baba used to call her *Mami, (maternal aunt),* and say that their relationship dated back to many previous lives), her son Tatya Kote, Radha Krishna Aai, Das Ganu (who popularized Baba's name through his devotional songs), Rajamma (Shivamma Thayee) Upasani Maharaj etc. Some of them have reincarnated:

(1) It has been heard that Abdul, a trusted servant of the Shirdi Sai Baba, who used to serve and sometimes cook for him and read out Quran before him, has now reincarnated as one Mr. Ken, a Canadian, of Japanese birth. This information was revealed by Sri Sathya Sai Baba.

On 23rd June, 1998, one Sai Dass (K.C.I. Retd.), 78 years old Sai devotee from Sai Kutir, Sabarmati, Ahmedabad (Gujarat) wrote to me that when he visited his daughter's store 'Vicky Stores' in Gervard Street in Toronto (Canada) one evening in 1984, then that person "Mr. Ken, his wife Sendra, cousin brother and a German girl approached my daughter for a vegetarian hotel. In the store, he saw a Shirdi Sai photo with *Shivaling* and Cobra with the right hand raised in blessing . . . After that, they came to see me and the first time there was discussion about Gayatri Mantra:

This full letter is reproduced in my book *'New Light on Sri Shirdi Sai Baba'* (1999).

(2) Shama has also incarnated in the form of an American boy studying in India. Mlahasapathy, who gave the name 'Sai' to Baba on second coming to Shirdi in 1858 as a young *Fakir* and who was his closest devotee till his *Mahasamadhi* in 1918, has reportedly ben reborn as Ranjit Kumar Trehan of Malsiya village (36 kms from Jalandhar) in Punjab. He has been rendering valuable social service rural areas with extraordinary devotion and zeal. The story of his dedicated sevice of the village folk was beautifully recorded by researcher Sarla Joshi in one of her books.

(3) A Muslim *jagirdar* (feudal Lord) Chand Bhai Patil of Dhoopkheda village, who witnessed the first miracle of the young Baba when his lost mare was found by his miraculous information a few days before his coming to Shirdi, with the marriage of party of his nephew, and who had been Baba's life long devotee, has been reborn as a Muslim. He became a smuggler and joined the service of the smuggler-king Haji Mastan of the Western coast. He was involved in smuggling operations, but his young God-fearing wife, afraid for his life, regularly prayed to God to reform her husband. Once Shirdi Sai Baba's Spirit form overpowered him when he was trying to smuggle in gold and other contraband articles in the high sea of Arabian Ocean and guided him to Sai Baba temple. Ultimately, he reached a Shirdi Sai Temple and vowed to end his ways as asked by Baba. Again he fell into evil ways, but again the Spirit of Shirdi Sai Baba took charge of him and directed him to come and see Sri Sathya Sai Baba at Puttaparthi and, finally, he reformed himself into a law-abiding and peaceful citizen a few years ago. The story of the transformation in Chand Bhai Patil's present incarnation due to Baba's compassionate grace was recalled by an ex-student of Sri Sathya Sai Institute of Higher Learning in the Summer Course on Indian Culture and Spirituality, Brindavan, Kadugodi (Bangalore) in the divine presence of Sri Sathya Sai Baba in June 1992, and heard by the author there.

(4) One Madhav Dixit, who as a boy had seen Shirdi Baba with his H.R. Dixit and another lady Sharda Devi called 'Pottu Boddu, who had seen Sai Baba and to whom Sai Baba had confided that he would be reborn as 'Sathya Sai Baba', lived for the rest of their life at Sri Sathya Sai Baba's Prasanthi NIlayam and Vrindavan ashram respectively.

(5) The Raja of Chicholi state was a devotee of Sri Shirdi Sai Baba. The Baba had visited his house in a tonga sent by the Raja. His widow was informed by Sri Sathya Sai Baba that in his previous incarnation as Shirdi Sai he had visited her house and given a *lot* (a metal pot) to her husband. The Rani became Sri Sathya Sai Baba's ardent devotee and gifted that *tonga* (horse carriage) to the Sri Sathya Sai Muslim of Spirituality in Prasanthi Nilayam. It can be seen by visitors to that Museum even now.

The story of the lives of Madhav Dikshit and Sharda Devi 'Pottu Boddu' is mentioned in M.N. Rao's book *'You are God'* (Sai Towers Publishing, 1998 pp. 45-47. Puttu Bothi's article on her life appeared in *Sathya Sai: Avatar of Love* (1992, pp. 56-60), a publication of Sai Prasanthi Society, Hyderabad. It is heard that she will be reborn to be the father of the third Sri Baba—future Prem Sai Baba in Gunapartha village in Mandeya Distirct of Karnataka state.

106

10

Sri Shirdi Sai Baba Movement: The Trends

While there are over 150 books and countless articles on Sri Shirdi Sai Baba available today, most of them deal with his divine life as Avatar, teachings and miracles. His most important contribution to humanity as a unique architect of Integration of the hearts of all communities, particularly the Hindus and the Muslims who had then lots of mutual misunderstanding, apprehension, distrust and conflicting socio-cultural and religious moorings, have not yet been explored and presented.

In my book '*Sai Shirdi Sai Baba: The Unique Apostle of Integration*' (2007), this unique contribution of the immortal Fakir of Shirdi, not only to the social and emotional integration of the Indians but also to the Atmic Integration of the whole of mankind and to the ushering in an era of global awakening, universal love and harmony, co-existence and peace has been highlighted. All the nations of the world can learn a lot from this unique and most successful experiment of integration done by Sri Shirdi Sai Baba at his Dwarakamayi *masjid* at Shirdi during 1858-1918.

1. Where else, except in the divine personality and role-functioning style of Shirdi Sai Baba, do we find located in one person the vibrant elements of Krishna's superb magnetism of love and knowledge of the reality of self, Buddha's compassion and piety, Adi Shankar's *Advitism* and the zeal for the fight against sectarianism and strict orthodoxy, Kabir's unconventional scathing attack on bigotry and obscurantism, Tulsi's devotion to Lord Rama (one's chosen God), and the divine outpourings of love for the divine as that of the great integrators like Mira, Chaitanya, Nanak, Purandardasa, Thyagaraja, Kanakdasa, Tukaram, Ramdas, Narasi Mehta, Ramanand, Nayanar Eknath, Namdev, Manikkayakchekak, etc., the mysticism of Ramkrishna Paramhansa and the love, brotherhood and service taught by Christ, Mohammed, Mother Teresa, Dalai Lama, Baba Amte and the like and the philosophical musings of Ramana Maharishi, Sri Aurobindo and many saints of other religions and countries. Sri Shirdi Sai Baba epitomized the quintessence of the high values and ideals taught by the world's greatest religious and spiritual masters of all religions and and in history.

2. A Canadian Sai devotee and researcher, Marianne Warren, in the her doctoral thesis *'Unraveling the Enigma—Shirdi Sai Baba in the Light of Sufism'*, has pointed out that while Dabholker (Hemadpant) in his original book *'Shri Sai Charitra'* in Marathi, had repeatedly acknowledged Sai Baba's Muslim Fakir status, Ganaji's (his adoption of Dabhodkar's book), it transpires, had the effect of giving a further Hindu gloss of Sai Baba. In Shirdi almost all the worship prayers and rituals are now according to the Hinduism, whereas during Sai Shirdi Sai Baba's life-time, Hindus, Muslims and others were freely allowed to offer their prayers and observe their religious rituals worshipping him in the Dwarakamayi masjid.

A keen social observer Prof. T.K.N. Unnithan, Former Professor of Sociology and Vice-Chancellor of the University of Rajasthan, had acutely felt and complained that the Muslims are now not allowed to offer their prayers and read Quran in the Sai Baba Temple at Shirdi. The descendents of Abdul Baba had brought this fact to the notice to the Chairman of Shri Sai Baba Sansthan, Shirdi to very kindly accommodate the wishes of the Muslims also and let them worship in the Sri Baba Temple at least once a week but it had little effect. Prof. Unnithan told this to me personally when he came to meet me at my house about 6-7 years back.

3. However, devotion towards Sri Shirdi Sai Baba has been tremendously increasing throughout the world—more and more books, articles, poems and religious songs are being written on him, more and more journals are being published, websites devoted to him are increasing, and Sai temples are coming up in many parts of India and in foreign countries. The spiritual philosophy of Sri Shirdi Sai Baba is influencing more and more people in the world.

With great expectations, thousands of people visit Shirdi every day and most of them indeed feel the presence of divinity there and find peace and happiness. The Sai Baba Sansthan is doing excellent work for the providing facilities to the visitors. It is spending crores of rupees every year on various social services. It manages accommodation facility to hundreds of visitors and runs an excellent canteen that provides sumptuous vegetarian Indian food at very low cost to visitors. There are other facilities like reading room, hospital, homeopathy dispensary, school, polytechnic, reading room, and permanent exhibition of Sai Baba's photographs and personal effects. Shirdi was a very small village in the interior of Maharastra till the mid-20th century but now it has grown into an important town connected with road, train and air travel and costly hotel facilities. The Sai Baba Samadhi temple and the whole complex has been renovated has been renovated and modernized. Visitors find peace, happiness and spiritual enlightenment here.

However, in the last 15 years, some social problems have been observed in Shirdi by visitors and commented upon by keen social observers. Subha Varma in her Hindi article published in *Saptahik Hindustan* on 22 November, 1992 had mentioned "the menace of lottery ticket sellers, beggars, brokers and pick pockets in Shirdi". A number of houses near the Dwarkamayi and Chawadi have been converted in to private hotels or lodging houses having tiny, dirty and impoper rooms some of which are unfit for any decent visit or to live in as they have unsatisfactory sanitation facilities. Finding cheap unaffordable accommodation is a great problem for poor and middle class people. Hotels are costly, although a number of Sai devotees and rich people like Ramani of Chennai and some others have built free or low rent rooms for the pilgrims but still it is very difficult for the visitors to find place in Shirdi. The Sai sansthan has provided hundreds of rooms and sone inns are coming in villags around Shidi but findind cheap and good accodation is very difficiult for the vistors on Thursday, Sunday and all festival days.

4. Although Sri Shirdi Sai Baba's divine name and fame has been spreading like wild fire throughout the world and more and more people are becoming his, yet, unfortunately, several undesirable and controversial views and practices have also creeped in due to a number is over-enthusiastic and self-seeking *Sai pracharaks* and organizers of Sai activities in India which must not be ignored.

5. Some *Sai pracharaks* are posing themselves as *Guruji, Sai Sewaks,* or plenipotentiaries of Sri Shirdi Sai Baba and they are not only expecting but encouraging devotees to touch their feet and getting themselves worshipped along with Sri Shirdi Sai Baba. There is now a growing fashion to organize *Jagran* (night long devotional singing) type of *Sai Keertans* is public on a grand scale, in homes and in public places, singing all sorts of devotional songs on the tunes of popular filmi songs, *Kawallis* and the like, collecting lots of donations from door to door and paying not only thousands but even more than one lakh rupees to professional film singers invited to the Sai Baba *jagrans*. The so-called organizers give special blessings to the rich hosts or organizers and even sing Punjabi style *Badhaiyan* (song of congratulations). This creates inferiority complex, unhealthy spirit of competition among devotees who are rich, middle class as well as poor person."

- (Late) Nimbalkar, devotee had observed: "If a Sai Baba temple is constructed lot of money pours in. Therefore, a number of Sai Baba temples are being constructed all over India and in foreign countries also. Since it is not possible for every one to visit Shirdi frequently, it is good to construct Sai Baba's temples in one's area by installing Sai Baba statue therein. But in some places exact replica of Sai Baba Samadhi is constructed in front of the statue which is not correct, because his body is interted in Shirdi only, *dhuni* also is established. Simple devotees are misled and offer their money and devotion in abundance at these places.

- A myth is being perpetuated that Sri Shirdi Sai Baba was *Ayonijic*, that he was never born of a woman, although the eminent Sai*Pracharak*, Sri Narasimha Swamiji had in 1896 itself, termed it as illogical and untenable.

- The Sai Baba Sansthan, Shirdi, had in 1994 a publicnotification *The Hindustan Times* (New Delhi) daily of 3 May, 1994 mentioning that the action of one of their trustees—carrying around with him "fake *padukas* (shoes) of Sri Shirdi Sai Baba was a fraud" on the religious and mental sentiments of all devotees. At many places, false *padukas* of Sri Shirdi Sai Baba are often displayed and money collected fraudulenty. Some years back another cheat from Shirdi was heard to be fradulently exhibiting a fake *kafni* (long shirt) of Sai and collecting a money from ignorant Sai devotees and others publickly in North Indian devotees by befooling them.

- The nuisance of threatening and tempting chain letters of Shirdi Sai Baba are sent by some anonymous *pracharaks*, often by fixing inadequate or no postal stamps on the envelope, continues unabated I too have received several such letters in English and Hindi.Sri Shirdi Sai Baba would have certainly never appreciated any *pracharak* to send much chain letters far and wide. This only shows that some over-zealous *pracharaks* are doing more harm than any good to the cause of spreading Sri Shirdi Sai consciousness in the world.

- In some Sai temples a lot of politics and financial impropriatic have been going on for some years. Shocking news about some of them were published in newspapers and some journals devoted to Sai Baba which exposed them. The Editor-in-Chief Ramesh Khanna of Neel Kanth Publications, H-89, Lajpat Nagar—I, New Delhi-110024, has in recent years exposed in his articles the wrong doings of certain persons formerly connected with Sai Baba temple in Shirdi, those hailing from Shirdi, and certain self-seeking and undemocratic office bearers of the management committee of a Sai Baba temple in New Delhi, and some highly egoist self-styled 'prominent Sai devotees, *pracharaks* and *Sai Bhaian Samrats* (Kings of Sai devotional music),' and those certain ccontroversial persons who have been involved in corrupt and deceitful

110

practices and petty politics who have been bringing bad name to Sai Baba movement. Some court cases relating are said to be going on now.

Such ugly features of the Shirdi Sai Baba movement in India in recent years are regrettable, Most of the Sai devotees in India earnestly wish thaty such wrong practices should be eliminated. Sai Baba'great ideals and teachings should be followed by all who really seek to have his divine grace and lead a noble life in their present birth and future births. Hypocricy, duping others by invoking the holy name of Sri Sai Baba and improper motives and actions to show off and earn wealth by unfair means will not not help anyone ultimately. Sai Baba's main dictum "As you, so shall you reap" must be always kept in mind by every one.

11

Sri Shirdi Sai Baba's Miracles

During his 60 years stay at Shirdi, Sri Shirdi Sai Baba from 1958 to 1918 performed countless miracles, the details of which are recorded in the books of his contemporary devotees like Das Ganu, Dhabholkar, Pradhan, Khaparde, Meher Baba etc. I have compiled in my book *'Divine Grace of Sri Shirdi Sai Baba*—Thrilling Experiences of Sai Devotees in the Post-Samadhi Period (1818-1997), as many as 169 incidents of Sai Baba miracles were experienced by them in their lives, and my Hindi book *'Sri Sai Baba ke Divyas Chamatkar'* (2007) has mentioned many more recent ones. They reveal the omnipotence, omnipresence and omniscience of Sri Shirdi Sai Baba.

Countless miracles done by Sri Shirdi Sai Baba experienced by his devotee are being spread all over the world and more of them are coming to our knowledge each day in books and on various Sai Baba websites of the internet daily. They are true and increase one's faith in the divinity of Sai Baba and no one should have any doubt about them. Three of them wwhich have come to my notice are mentioned here.

1. An American lady tourist took a photo of Sri Shirdi Sai Baba's statue at his Samadhi Mandir in Shirdi in March1999, but in in place of the face of the Baba's statue his real image came in the print. She gave it to the principal of Sai School, Bamanpalli near Puttaparthi (Andhra Pradesh) who was an ardent Shirdi Sai devotee. He later on gave it to Maria Aragous, an ardent devotee of Sri Shirdi Sai Baba and who is Spainish publisher of books (Her firm is *Ed.l'Ermit, Traverserra De Diet*, 62, Barcelona, Spain) She sent a copy of that miracle photo to me in November 1999 as she knew me, being the publisher of the Spanish version of my book *'Sri Shirdi Sai Baba:The Universal Master'*, sent a photo copy that rare and minaculous photo to me, in mid-November, 1999.

2. An old Zorastrian Mr. Dinshaw J. Buxey, who introducing himself as a close acquaintance of Yogi M.K. Spencer and his cousin brother Homi S.Spencer's family in Mumbay had sent the following Sai miracles known to him for my information and publication:

- H.S. Spencer's father was captain of Parsi cricket team in Bombay.

1900. Here is a Sai miracle of ashes in Bandra (Bombay) where also Spencer lived. I used to visit (his) house during 1955-1980.

There was a burnt photo of Sai.

I could never ask. We were too busy with his Zoroastrian books, which have not seen the light of day. Someone wrote from Europe, books are with Brill, you can't do better than that. The books went to 100 Universities, but Zoroastrian centres have not heard of it. Now he was ill. I was on his bed, got on opportunity to ask his most devoted sister Putlibai, and this is the story she told me.

I will try to put it in her own words—may Sai help me:

"A friend brought the photo. I never believed, but kept it. I heard about ashes . . . and then . . ."

(I interrupted—when did the photo get burnt? How?—and why kept?)

"I am coming to it, dear boy . . . have patience . . ." she said.

"We had a big shepherd dog . . . devoted to us . . . year 1946 or 1948 (I don't remember exact year she said) . . ." he was dying on this very bed in pain.

I was touching him, patting him—my eyes fell on photo . . . small lamp beneath . . ."

I said, can you, Sai Baba, do something?

The light shot up . . . photo caught fire . . . I screamed . . .

I left dog, put out flames with bare hands."

(now ashes on her hands)

dog whined as she left him.

She rushed did not think even as she petted him . . . that Sai ashes are on her hand . . . and now on dog . . . pain left . . . dog passed away peacefully . . .

and Homi, on other bed, in pain . . . echoed Meher Baba's words (I saw him as a child in 1937 at Sunderbai hall took stool, put on stage-crossed legs-looked at him as devotees greated him, he'd give me a wink)—"You cannoi understand Ari Shirsi Sai Baba's greatness.

- **Sai Baba's second miracle in my life**

I am not a liar. Ever since, as child, I read Sri Ramakrishna, that truth, is our support—I have clung to it.

Cheated in business, (perhaps past *Karma*, perhaps not knowing how to do business—Karmic reaction). I had no money for plumber, and removing 100 times, up and down, toilet marble heavy top-got hernia. Dr. Bhamgara of Nature Cure Institute, Marine Drive (now closed) diagnosed it. Having no money, I want to Charak Clinic where Dr. Telang confirmed it operation means death.

I phoned to my ex-office, Dr. Beck & Co. Ltd. (a Mahindra and Mahindre concern then, later bought by BASF group, now part of multinational Schenectady group of USA), which I helped started. The operator Ludi could not believe her ears, that it was me. (I had found a brilliant chemist, and competed with them—with disastrous financial results, as I was told I have to study character in the business partner or boss, not chemistry; I had to look up the word, "character" in son's dictionary).

I heard her say, "Bane, Buxey on line." "Impossible". I heard him say. "I tell you it is he . . ." Pause . . . silence . . . "yes, sir." timid voice replied.

I gave him straight: "Bane, take me to Shirdi". Please, silence.

Perhaps he was being tactful. I was no longer his boss, and I was asking for the company car—my old car. "Sir" he said, "you are in no position to travel", and then knowing my attachment to him (since childhood) he gave it to me straight: "Pray mentally."

I put phone down.

Later, I went to Dr. Kriplani downstairs. "Who told you you had hernia? . . ." To cross-check—I went to Dr. Telang and asked him "How you can make such a mistake . . . ?"

"I never do . . ."

"Take out your clothes . . . Who cured?

He sereamed, "This is NOT the condition in which you came."

I breathed a sigh of relief and one word, Thanks.

It was Sai Baba's miracle that I was cured at that time.

12

Miracles Grace of Sri Shirdi Sai Baba in My Life

—S.P. Ruhela

- **Shirdi Baba Sai Shirdi saved my life in 1997:**

On 28th February 1997, I felt great pain in my chest to 6 A.M.I intensely prayed to Shirdi Sai Baba, "Baba, kindly save my life as I have still several pressing family responsibilities to discharge and I wish to write some more books on You." I took Baba's holy *udi* (ash) and slept at 8 A.M. I got up after four hours feeling weak. But I then dictated six pages of the Hindi translation of my book *'Sri Shirdi Sai Baba: The Universal Master'* to my former student who as taking my dictation daily.

During that time I received the phone call from my daughter-in-law Dr.Saryu Ruhela, Lecturer in Physical Education, from her house in another sector of this city, enquiring about my health. When I told her about my chest pain and heavy sweating in the last two nights, she said that these were symptoms of heart trouble and so I should immediately reach our family Dr.Rakesh Gupta of Sarvodaya Hospital in Faridabad for check up and she assured me that she too would be reaching there soon to see me. I at once drove my car to the hospital. I was immediately examined by the doctor. He said that I had indeed suffered two serious heart attacks. He was shocked and surprised to know from me how I had reached the hospital all alone driving my car all the several miles which was very risky. On his advice I was at once shifted to the Cardio wing of the nearby Sun Flag hospital for heart treatment there. After my initial treatment there for 15 days, I was advised to go to the famous Escorts Heart Institute in South Delhi. My angiography was done there and it was found that my arteries/veins were 90% blocked. I was told by the doctor that the heart operation might be needed and I should be ready for that. I was advised to report to the doctor after 7 days. I was extremely worried and shaken for the fear of heart operation as it might be very risky and very costly which I could not afford. So all the time I prayed to Shirdi Sai Baba to kindly have mercy on me and my family and save me from the ordeal of heart operation. On the next date of appointment reported to the doctor who had done my

Angiography, I expressed to him my grave fear and worry for undergoing heart operation.

He then examined my angiography film again and its report very carefully and then reassuringly said, "Heart operation is not done in all cases. Do not worry; you need not undergo heart operation. I am prescribing certain medicines, dietary precautions and daily walk for you. Follow this course. You will be O.K. in some months." By these words of the doctor, I was greatly relieved and felt indebted to Shirdi Sai Baba for this miracle and then I solemnly promised to Him in my heart that I would like to devote the remaining years of my life in hi service by writing and editing books on Sai books on Sai Baba phenomena and spirituality. Since then I have been doing so without heart problem andin spite of so many difficult problems of my life. The grace of Sai Baba has enabled me do so.

- **Baba inspired and miraculously helped me in writing a number books on him and his second incarnation Sri Sathya Sai Baba, Value education and Sociology of Education.**

In January 1994, I had received a letter from the a Sai devotee T.R.Naidu of Khargpur and then again his second letter in September 1994 from him from Hyderabad after he had shifted there. He was unknown to me but he had read my earlier books on Shirdi Sai Baba. He informed me about the great spiritual book "*How I Found God*" by Yogi Spencer. I had the privilege of editing and condecing that 1394 page book into 500 pages and get it published by New Age Books, a prominent publisher of books on Spirituality, and brought to the notice of spiritual seekers in the world.

Yogi Spencer's book '*How I Found God*' is a wonderful and unique record of how Yogi Spencer ultimately achieved his soul's ardent wish in three human births to find God. He could indeed succeed in it by undergoing the rigorous unique spiritual training provided by Spirit Master Rishi Ram Ram and by Shirdi Sai Baba as God interlaced with the occasional encouraging talks of great Spiritual Masters Jesus Christ, Krishna, Buddha, Raman Maharishi, Mehar Baba and Maitriya.

I firmly believe that it was solely due to the unique miraculous grace of Sai Baba that such great privilege was bestowed upon an insignificant man like me. The Hindi translation of this rare book entitled 'Maine Ishwar ko kaise paya' has also now in 2013 been done by the eminent Sai devotee and my esteemed friend and former colleague Acharya Purshottamananda (Prof. P.S.Verma). I am still quite unaware of Shri Shirdi Baba's mysterious divine plan as to when and how this Hind version will be published and by which blessed publisher, but I believe that it will be published by Sai Baba's grace in near future.

It was just by chance but it was as a mysterious divine plan of Sri Shirdi Sai Baba that I unexpectedly met an unknown spiritualist Swami H.D Lakshmana of Bangalore in an evening of July 1992 in the second class compartment of K.K. Express train, in which I was traveling to reach Puttaparthi—Sri Sathya Sai Baba's famous *ashram*. Swami Lakshmana boarded it from Manmad and entered the same bogey and sat on the seat just near me. He was then returning from his pilgrimage to Shirdi with a small band of his close devotees to his home town Bangalore. After silently watching me for some hours he started conversing with me and in course of our conversation he suddenly closed his eyes for a few minutes and said to intuitively in a low voice: "Just now I have got the divine intuition that you are the blessed son of Saraswati—the Goddess of Learning. You are presently thinking of writing a book on Sri Shirdi Sai Baba. In it you should highlight Sri Shirdi Baba's unique status and role as the 'Universal Master.' which aspect has so far not been projected by most of the writers on him so far. Sadguru Sai Baba's wishes so and this is his divine assignment for you. Would you accept it with pleasure?" I readily accepted it with great pleasure. Then he said to me," Please meet me at my home-cum-temple of Banashankari Devi (Goddess Parvati—the Consort of Lord Shiva) in Bangalore. My address is:

Aadi Shankara and Dattatreya Adhyathmik Bhakti Mandali,
No.52," Sri Manjunatha Degula".
14th "B' Main Road, 2nd Stage, 2nd Phase,
(Behind Nandini Theatre) West of Chord Road,
Mahalakshmipura, Bangalore—5000860)

When you will be coming to Bangalore from Puttaparthi after some days on your return journey to New Delhi in order to take the K.K. Express from Bangalore Junction, please come my place and stay with me for the night.I shall then perform special worship of Goddess Banashankari Devi for obtaining her blessings on you for the successful completion of this new project of writing this book. Then you should return to your place and there you should prepare the tentative Table of its Contents and then bring it to Shirdi on the mutually agreed auspicious day in the next month (August}. I would reach there and we both shall together pray at the Sai Baba's Gurusthan and Sai Samadhi Mandir to seek Sai Baba's blessings on your book project."

Thus I travelled to Bangalore and reached Swami Lakshmana's place—in the noon of 24thJuly. he was very glad to receive me and soon we soon started talking.n course of our talks, he casually mentioned about a great local woman *Sanyasin* saint Shivmma Thayee who was then 102 year old and was known as then known to be the only surviving ardent and oldest devotee of Shirdi Sai Baba. She had been privileged to see Sai Baba as early as in 1906 when she was only 15 year old She had visited Shirdi many times till 1917 i.e., one year before Baba shed his mortal coil. He had given her the new name Shivamma Thayee when she had been left alone and deeply frustrated by great tragedies in her life—her husband had deserted her due to her being highly spiritual and unworldly and soon remarried, and then her only adult son along with his wife and son had unfortunately died in motor cycle accident and thus she was rendered totally homeless and helpless. In 1917 Sai Baba instructed her to go and settle down in Bangalore. For many years she was just homeless with no acquaintance with any body, confined to a forsaken corner in Bangalore and survived on begging alms till in 1944 one pious soul donated his surplus land to her and built for her a modest "Sai Baba Ashram' in Roopen Agrahara, Madiwala locality in Bangalore.

Hearing this, I became very impatient to go to meet her immediately and so Lakshamana Swami asked one of his devotee to take me on his motorcycle to meet her in the afternoon before 5 P.M. to seek her blessings for the success of the project of writing the book 'Sri Shirdi Sai Baba: The Universal Master' so I was greatly impressed and fascinated by her her highly advanced age and spirituality and simplicity. I wished to interview her and for that she asked me to come next day at 10 A.M. She very graciously allowed me to interview her in depth for over four hours. Swami Lakshman and two local Tamil devotees, who were luckily present there, acted as Tamil interpreters. She spoke in her mother tongue Tamil fluently and they translated her narrations into English for me and my queries in English into Tamil for her to reply. Thus I was privileged to write and bring out the book '*My Life with Sri Shirdi Sai Baba—Thrilling memories of Shivamma Thayee*" in 1992. It has been translated and published in Japanese, Hindi and Tamil languages subsequently and the glory of Shirdi Sai Baba and Shivamma Thayee has been spread world wide.

As prophesied and blessed, I was able to write my book '*Sri Shirdi Sai Baba: The Universal Master*" and get it published in 1995 and republished in 2007 by another publisher and it has been selling all over the world. By Sai Baba's miraculous grace I was privileged to write these two importent books in 1994-95.

In mid-1995, I received a letter dated 27th July, 1995 from an unknown Sai devotee M.R. Raghunathen, a retired clerk from the Madras informing me that he had discovered Shirdi Sai Baba's rare horoscope from the renowned over 2000 years old palm leaf *naadi* book of fure predictions in the lives of individuals by the ancient sage Agastya, which was in the possession of Dr Karunakaran, *Naadi* Astrologer of Sughar Agastyar Naadi Jyothida Nilayam, 14, Mannar (Reddy) Street, T. Nagar, Madras. That rare ancient *naadi* revealed that his (Sai Baba's) mother Devagiriamma had re-incarnated as Tamil Brahmin lady Seethamma, then popularly known as Baba Patti (84 year old) and Sai Baba's elder sister Balwant Bai had slso incarnated as P.Rajeswari (54 year old) ass the only daughter of Baba Patti, who was married but childless and they both were then living in Rajeswari's Rajeswari's retired husband A.V.Padnabhan's House Nno. 22, III Trust Cross Street, Mandavallikam, Madras—600 026.

This horoscope written by Sage Agastya thousands of year back also revealed that Raghunathan had been Shirdi Sai Baba's elder brother Ambadass in his past birth. It further showed that Sai Baba was born on Thursday, the 27th September, 1838 in the Tamil year of *Vilabhi, Vikram samvat* 1895, in the Tamil month of *Pruattassi*, His Rasi was *Dhanus* (Sagittarius) at12.05 and 25 seconds in the noon of that day. His parents were Ganga Bhavadia and Devagiriamma of Pathri village. The Horoscope of Sri Shirdi Baba has been given in an earlier chapter of this book.

Shri Raghunath sent me these thrilling highlights of Sai Baba's horoscope and urged me to travel to Madras to personally verify these rare fact by meeting the famous *naadi* astrologer Jyothda Ratna Dr.Karunakaran and them—Baba Patty and Rajeswari, if I wanted to do so as an earnest researcher and committed writer on Sai Baba. His letter was very motivating to me as I was really eager to collect these rare facts which were thereto unknown to the Sai devotees all over the world; they are still not known to over 99% Sai devotees. I soon reached Madras and met Raghunath and the naadi reade Dr,Karunakatran and then interviewed Baba Patti and her daughter Rajeswari at their house on 27th November, 1995. Later on I wrote a small pocket size beautifully illustrated book 'Shirdi Sai Baba's Mother and her Re—incarceration' reporting the full interview, which was later published in 1998 by Aravali International (P) Ltd, New Delhi-110020. This again Sai Baba's unique miraculous privilege granted to me. I consider it to be my pious duty to apprise these rare facts about Sri Shirdi Sai Avatar to all His devotees before my death. Wither any body believes in them or not, it does not bother me. I am grateful to Sai Baba for giving me the rare fortune of discovering them and publicizing them. Sri Sathya Sai Baba's revelations about Shirdi Sai Baba's home village, prarents and day, date and the place of his birth (forest near Pathri) tallied with the particular revelations Sage Agustya's *naadi* horsoscope of Shirdi sai Baba but surprisingly the devotees of these both Sai Baba have not bothered to know their stunning similarities. So I consider it to be my pious duty to apprise these rare facts about Sri Shirdi Sai Avatar to all His devotees before leaving this world,. Wither any body believes in them or not, it does not bother me, it is my commitment as an earnest social scientist and researcher and writer on the unique Sai Baba Trinity phenomenon.

By Sai Baba's miraculous grace, blessings and help only that I could write/ edit these books on Shirdi Sai Baba in spite of my ill health and severe and financial and agonizing family problems in the last 21 years without any body's financial support:

- *Sri Shirdi Sai Baba Avatar,* 1992.
- *My Life with Sri Shirdi Sai Baba* (Shivamma Thayee),1992.
- *What Researchers say on Sri Shirdi Sai Baba,* 1994.
- *Sri Shirdi Sai Baba:The Universal Master.* First published and then in 1994.
- *Sri Shirdi Sai Baba:El Maetro Universal* (in Spanish), 1994.
- *Shirdi Sai The Supreme,* 1997.
- *Thus Spoke Sri Shirdi Sai Baba* (Compiler: B.Uma Maheswar Rao of Guntur, 1997.
- *Divine Grace of Sri Shirdi Sai Baba,* 1997.
- *Divine Grace and Recent Predictions* (Spiritual experiences and utterances of Prof. P.S. Varma), 1999.
- *Divine Revelations of a Sai devotee* (Spiritual experiences and utterances Prof. P.S,Varma, 2000.
- *Communications from the Spirit of Shri Shirdi Sai Baba*—Unique messages received by the compiler in meditation from Sri Shirdi Sai Baba from the Spiritual Plane (Compiler B. Uma Maheswar Rao of Guntur, A.P.),1998.
- *Shri Shirdi Sai Baba and His Teachings* 1998, (Compiler: M.Rajeswar Rao of Hyderabad).
- *New Light on Sri Shirdi Sai Baba,* pp.159: 1999.
- *Sri Shirdi Sai Baba Bhajan-mala* (in Roman, 1998.
- * *Sai Ideal and the Sai World,* (containing also the 41 unique postings of eminent Sai devotee Ram Nathan of Sarangpur (West Bengal) in his unique 'The Sai Graph Mail'. pp.96),: 1999.
- *The Divine Glory of Sri Shirdi Sai Baba,* pp. 126: 1998.
- *Hamre pyare Sri Shirdi Sai Baba,* (in Hindi) 1999.

- *The Immortal Fakir of Shirdi*—Sai Baba as seen by His contemporary devotees, 2000.
- *The Spiritual Philosophy of Sri Shirdi Sai Baba* (Complied by B.Uma Maheswar Rao of Guntur),1998.
- *Shirdi Sai Speaks to Yogi Spencer in Vision.*, 1998.
- *Divine Revelations of a Sai devotee* (Spiritual experiences and utterances Prof.P.S.,Varma) pp.270:2000.
- *The Eternal Sai* (Complier Maneey of Banglore),2001.
- *Sri Shirdi Sai Baba: The Unique Prophet of Integration*, 2004.
- *The Eternal Sai* (Complier Maneey) 2001.
- *Sri Shirdi Sai Baba: The Universal Master*, 2007.
- *Divya Sai Sandesh* (Rare Discourses of Sri Shirdi Sai Baba as God received by Yogi M.K.Spencer (in Hindi), 2007.
- *Sri Shirdi Sai Baba ke Divya Chamatka*, pp. 2007.
- *Grace of Shri Shirdi Sai Baba,*:2013.
- *Maine Ishwar ko Kaise paya* (In Hindi) (To be published in near future)

- **Shirdi Sai Baba is miraculously helping me to survive in the most difficult years of my post 2007 life and live with poise.**

I believe that due to my unknown bad *karmas* (actions) in my previous births the last six years of my life have been very difficult and painful. In September 2008 I had suffered a serious attack of paralysis but Sai Baba miraculously helped in recovering my health considerably within three years. I have been able to resume my studies and writing work. I can now work on my computer for some hours daily although it is not possible for me to walk, travel and speak. My devout and spiritually minded wife suffered thrice bone and hip fractures and she had to undergo a major operation and transplantation of steel rod in her leg and she is still suffering pain in her limbs and weakness, but by the grace of both Shirdi Sai Baba and Sathya Sai Baba's she discharges all her family duties with poise and patience and continues to be my sole support in my old age. Besides these, we have been surrounded by some other grave problems since 2008, but Sai Baba has been saving us and giving us ample courage and strength to face them and not get disheartened and but keep on having *Shraddha* (Faith) and *Saburi* (Patience). By Baba's grace and miraculous help last year I came to know about "*SAI AMRITVANI*" composed by B.K.Bassi, A1/42 Panchsheeel Enclave, New Delhi-110017, and I could get this small book from the eminent Sai devotees Ashoka Gupta and Veena Gupta of Flat No.19, Pocket - B, Siddartha Enclave, New Delhi—110014 (Mobile 98688905). I have got this wonderful and effective pious melodious Shirdi Sai Prayer song downloaded from the web *site www.saiamritvani.com.* I enjoy listening to it and feel very much relaxed and peaceful in the midst of all the humdrum of life. I have been able to maintain my peace of mind and equilibrium is the evidence of Sai Baba's miracle in my life.

13

Pilgrimage to Holy Shirdi

Now Shirdi is a very sacred, powerful and important place of pilgrimage in India. One can visit this holy place easily. It is a well developed town now, connected by bus routes. The K.K. Express from New Delhi to Bangalore passes through an important Railway Station called Manmad. A number of trains from Bombay and Delhi also pass through this station. Shirdi is only about 58 kms from Manmad. Buses and taxis are easily available to reach Shirdi. The distance of Shirdi from some important cities is as under:

Mumabi—266 kms	Nasik—122 kms
Hyderabad—610 kms	Surat—373 kms
Nagpur—618 kms	Jalgaon—233 kms
Ahmednagar—83 kms	Delhi—1166 kms
Pune—207 kms	Sholapur—312 kms

These are arrangements for boarding and lodging made by the Shirdi Sai Sansthan.

Daily Programme at Shirdi

The *Kakad Arti* is performed in the early morning at 5.15 a.m. From 6 a.m. to 7 a.m., the *Samadhi* and idol are washed and clad ceremoniously. Records of *Sai Geet* and *Mangal Sahnai* are also played at this time. Then, individual *Abhisheks* are started at 7.30 a.m. The collective *Abhishek* starts at 11 a.m. The noon *Arati* takes place exactly at 12 noon. Nobody is allowed to go up to the idol or the *Samadhi* after this *Aarti* (worshiping by waving a burning candle clock-wise around the face of a living Godly personality, or a deity's picture or statue, bridegroom to honor them). Then, there are programmes of singing, *bhajan* and *kirtan* in the afternoon. At 6.30 p.m. (Sunset hour), it is time for Arti again, followed by *kirtan* or *bhajan* till 10 p.m. and the last *Arti* i.e. *Shej-Aarti* takes place at 10 p.m. The mosquito net is let down over the idol and the *Samadhi* after the *Aarti* and Lord Sri Sai Baba is deemed to have gone to sleep.

On Thursday night, there is a procession of the *Palki* and the *Padukas*. Five gunshots are fired at the time of the procession. Mike arrangements are made at the time of the *Aarti* and other programme of the day.

Important Places at Shirdi

1.   Samadhi Mandir

The construction of the *Samadhi Mandir* was started by Baba's ardent devotee Sri Buti during Baba's lifetime, with a view to have a temple of Sri Murlidhar. When the construction was almost complete, Sri Sai Baba said that he would stay there. After Sri Sai Baba attained *Nirvan* (liberation from physical body, death), his mortal remains were buried in that temple. The white marble pavement on the *Samadhi* was made later. The marble statue prepared by the famous sculptor, Sri Talim, was installed by the side of the *Samadhi* in 1954. The spacious hall in front of the *Samadhi* was also paved with marble tiles later on. People, coming for *darshan* first come into the hall, which is decorated with photos of the saints and devotees of Sri Sai Baba. The statue of Sri Sai Baba in a seated posture is such that it appears to be looking at every devotee coming for *darshan* in the hall. In a room on the leftside of the hall, the articles used by Sri Sai Baba are displayed for public view. There is a cellar below the rooms on the right, where valuables are kept. There is a gallery on the first floor and several other rooms, which can be used by the devotees. The rooms on both sides of the hall are used to office the management. These are a well-paved open space in front fo the hall with a stage for *kirtan, prasad* distribution etc. A lot of renovation and new construction has been done in recent years. New construction and addition have been made recently.

2.   Dwarakamayi

This was an old Masjid named 'Dwarakamayi' by Sri Sai Baba himself. He would spend his day here, sitting on a big stone, which is still preserved. A portrait of Sri Sai Baba, painted during his life-time, is also kept here. In front of the portrait, is the sacred *dhuni* (fire) kindled by Sri Sai Baba. This has been kept burning since then. A grinding stone, bathing stone, a wooden pillar, *chulha, padukas* and *Tulsi Vrindavan*, which were used by Sri Sai Baba, are all maintained here. The *rath* and palanquin are also kept here in a small room. The *Udi*, taken out from the ever-burning *dhuni*, is used by the devotees as miraculous ash.

3. Chavadi

Sri Sai Baba used to rest at this place, which is to the east of *Dwarkamai*, on every alternate night. A number of portraits of deities have been exhibited here since the days of Sri Sai Baba. A wooden plank and a wheel chair sometime used by Sri Sai Baba are also kept here. Ladies are not allowed to enter that part of the Chavadi, where Sri Baba's portrait is kept on an altar, respecting longstanding practice.

4. *Gurusthan*

This is the place of Sri Sai Baba's *Guru* in one of his previous births. Sri Sai Baba used to sit here under the *Neem* tree, the leaves of which lost their bitterness due to the grace of Sri Sai Baba. Incense is burnt here day and night in a pot, in front of the Mandir, wherein, Lord Shiva's Pindi and Nandi are installed and the *Padukas* of Lord Sri Sai Baba are also kept.

5. Lendibag and Nandadeep

Lendi *nalla* flowed through this land and there was a burial ground at the place. Sri Sai Baba dug a well here and drank its water. Now, the Lendi *nalla* has been filled and a garden laid there. A *Nandadeep* has been kept burning there since the day of Shri Sai Baba, who used to sit here on a *par* (stone otla) near the *Nandadeep*, below the *Neem* tree. This *par* has been renovated and maintained. A new *Datta Mandir* has been built in the garden in front of the *Ashwattha* tree. The place is very calm and quiet. A guest house is built in the *Lendibag* for dignitaries visiting Shirdi. The *Samadhi* of the horse *Shamsunder*, who used to bow to Sri Sai Baba in his lifetime and thereafter to the *Samadhi* every day until its death, is also here. The *Samadhis* of devotees Abdul Baba, Nanavalli, Bhau Maharaj and Tatya Kote are at the entrance of the *Lendibag*. These have been renovated.

6. Khandoba Mandir

This is a small emple situated on Ahmednagar-Kopargaon road. It was at this temple that Sri Sai Baba was first greeted by Sri Mhalsapati with the words, *"Ya Baba"*.

7. Mahadev Temple, Shani Mandir and Ganesh Temple

These three temples have been built in a line. The *Mahadev Mandir* is very old and a statue of a tiger has been installed behind Nandi. There is a *Dhuni* in the *Shani Mandir* also. The Ganesh temple is also very old.

A calm and peaceful atmosphere is maintained at all these places.

There is one *Keshav Mandir* and *Mangal Karyalaya,* built beyond the road on the eastern side. Devotees can perform marriages and thread ceremonies in the Mangal Karyalaya. New buildings have been constructed in the campus of the Sansthan.

14

Prominent Shirdi Sai Temples & Centres in the World

Sri Shirdi Sai Baba's name and fame has spread all over the world. There are countless Shirdi Sai Baba temples and centres in India and in a number of foreign countries. Given below are the prominent ones among as far as known to me:

- Shirdi Sai Baba Temple, Shirdi (Maharashtra)
- Nag Sai Baba Temple, Coimbatore (Tamil Nadu)
- Sri Bahrava Sai Baba Temple, Bharat Nagar, Chennai
- Shirdi Sai Baba Temple, Kolhapur (Maharashtra)
- Shirdi Sai Baba Temple, Sholapur (Maharashtra)
- Shirdi Sai Baba Temple, Khar (West) Mumbai (Maharashtra)
- Shirdi Sai Baba Temple, Mylapore, Chennai
- Shirdi Sai Baba Temple, Bharat Nagar, Chennai
- Shirdi Sai Baba Temple, Lodi Road, New Delhi
- Shirdi Sai Baba Temple, Shirdi (Maharashtra)
- Shirdi Sai Baba Temple, Sector 16A, Faridabad
- Shirdi Sai Baba Temple, Chandigarh
- Shirdi Sai Baba Temple, Sector 25, NOIDA (U.P.)
- Shirdi Sai Baba Temple, Sector 40, NOIDA
- Shirdi Sai Baba Temple, Gurgaon (Haryana)
- Shirdi Sai Baba Temple, Agra, Chippitola, Agra (U.P.)
- Shirdi Sai Baba Temple, Aligarh (U.P.)
- Shirdi Sai Baba Temple, Shirdi (Maharashtra)
- Shirdi Sai Baba Temple, Jaipur (Rajasthan)
- Shirdi Sai Baba Temple, Kukas, Jaipur (Rajasthan)
- Shirdi Sai Baba Temple, Bank Colony, Hyderabad
- Shirdi Sai Baba Temple, Moradabad (U.P.)
- Shirdi Sai Baba Temple, Bareilly (U.P.)
- Shirdi Sai Baba Temple, Sapnawat (U.P.)

- Shirdi Sai Baba Temple, Shirdi Sai Temple, Shastri Nagar, Meerut
- Shirdi Sai Baba Temple, Illford,(U.K.)
- Shirdi Sai Baba Centre, Forida, Inverness (U.S.A.)
- Shirdi Sai Baba Temple, 45-16, Robinson Street, Flushing, New York
- Shirdi Sai Baba Temple, Bronswick, New Jersey (U.S.A.)
- Shirdi Sai Baba, Ambers Creek, Flushing, Pittsberg (U.S.A.)
- Shirdi Sai Baba Temple, Chicagoland, Hampshire (U.S.A.)
- Shirdi Sai Baba Temple, Hurlington House, Nathan Road, Tsim Tsa Tsui, Kowloon, Hongkong

There are many Shirdi Sai Baba Temples in Himachal Pradesh, U.P., Andhra Pradesh, Tamil Nadu, Odissa and other states in India and in foreign countries like Mauritius but we do not know their exact addresses yet. Many of these temples have been started by the efforts of Sathpathi ji who is a highly inspired *pracharak* (promoter) of Sri Shirdi Sai Baba.

Important Shirdi Sai Baba Organizations

* All India Sai Samaj Mylapore, Chennai. (T.N.)
  Sai Publications, Red Cross Road, Civil Lines, Nagpur (Maharashtra).

* Dwarakamayi Publications, Hyderabad-500033. (A.P.)

* Sri Bhagwati Sai Sansthan, Panvel-410206 (Maharashtra) (Sai Sevak Narayan Baba, Spiritual Head).

* Sai Foundation India, New Delhi-110060: H-353, New Rajinder Nagar.

* Sai Prachar Kendra, S.C.F. 18, Sector 19-D, Chandigarh-160 019.

* Sri Sai Spiritual Centre, T. Nagar, Bangalore-560 028.

* Sri Sai Samaj, Picket, Secunderabad (A.P.)

* Sri Sai Baba Sansthan, Shirdi (Maharashtra)

* Sri Sai Samaj Calcutta, P-113, Lake Terrace, Calcutta-700 029.

* Sai Sudha Trust, Shirdi Sai Baba Mandir, Garkhal, Kausauli (H.P.)-173 201.

* Sai Bhakta Parivar, 91, Napier Town, Jabalpur (M.P.).

* International Pragya Mission, Saket, New Delhi-110017. (Swami Pragyanand, Founder President).

* Akhil Bhartiya Shirdi Sai Bhakti Mahasabha, Hyderabad. (M. Rangacharya President).

* Akhanda Sainama Saptaha Samithi, B/3/F-15, Krupa Complex, Ananda Bagh, Hyderabad-500 047. (A.P.) (D. Shankariah, Secretary).

* Shirdi Sai Baba Web Site Organization
  182, West Melrose Street, Suite No. 4,
  South Elgin, 1L 60177, U.S.A.
  Phone: 847-931-4058
  Fax: 847-931-4066
  Web: http://www.Saibaba.org
  E-mail: maildrop@Saibaba.org
  (Mukund Raj, Web Site Administrator)

* Shirdi Sai Temple
  46-16, Robinson Street, Flushing,
  New York (U.S.A.)
  Tel: (718) 3219243

* Shirdi Sai Baba Sansthan of America,
  4625, Summerset Country,
  Richwater Township, New Jersey-08807 (U.S.A.)
  Tel.: (908) 3061420

* Shirdi Sai Foundation Centre,
  4901, Pleasant Grove, Inverness,
  Florida—34452 (U.S.A.)
  Tel.: (352)—8602181

* Sai Foundation, Kenya (Africa)
  P.O. Box 41409, Nairobi, Kenya)
  E-mail: "ushmid@africaonline.com

* Shri Shatha Shruga Vidhya Samasthe (R)
  Magadi Main Road,
  Bangalore—560079, (Phone: 3486044)

* Shirdi Sai Baba Satsang,
  KBRS Bldg., Near Velu Mudaliar Dispensary,
  Kamaraj Road, Bangalore—560042
  Phone Off.: 5300225, Res.: 5300116

* Shri Saibaba Sansthan Trust
  PO: Shirdi Tal. Rahata Dist. Ahmednagar, Maharashtra State, India
  Phone: +91-2423-258500 (30 lines)
  Fax No.: +91-2423-258870, P.R.O. Office +91-2423-258770
  E-mail: saibaba@sai.org.in
  URL: http://www.shrisaibabasansthan.org/ & http://www.sai.org.in/

* "International Sri Sai Consciousness Foundation Centre"
  Venue: "Sri Sai Sharanalaya" Premises
  II Main, Nagarabhavi Main Road
  Sanjeevini Nagar, Moodalapalya
  Bangalore—560 072

* Shirdi Sai Baba Old Age Home Educational Trust
  Plot No. 124, 4th Main Road, Sundara Babu Nagar,
  Veppampattur, Thiruvallur Dist.
  Ph.: 044-27620950, Cell: 9840081877

* All India Akhanda Sai Nama Seva Samithi
  A.K.S. Shruthi, Flat No. S-18, Second Floor, 63, K.K. Road, Venkatapuram,
  Ambattur, Chennai-600 053, Tel.: 044-2657 3496
  R. Radhakrishnan (Sai Jeevi) Chief Patron

Journals Devoted to Sri Shirdi Sai Baba

1. *Sai Chetna* (English), Chennai, Sri Sai Baba Spiritual & Charitable Trust, Injambakkam, Chennai-600 041.
2. *Sai Kripa*, (English & Hindi). New Delhi-110003) Shri Sai Bhakta Samaj, 17, Institutional Area, Lodhi Road, New Delhi.

3. *Sai Kripa*: (Hindi) New Delhi: Sai Kripa Sansthan, A-16, Naraina II New Delhi-110 028, (Editor: Dipli Tuli).

4. *Sai Padananda*, Bangalore-560 028: Sri Sai Spiritual Centre, T. Nagar, (Editor: R. Seshadri).

5. *Sai Prabha* (English & Telugu). Hyderabad-500 027: H.No. 3-5-697/A, Telugu Academi Lane, Vittalwadi, Narayanguda.

6. *Sai Sudha*, All India Sai Samaj, Mylapore, Chennai (T.N.).

7. *Sai Sugam* (English & Tamil), Sri Shirdi Bhairava Sai Baba Temple Trust, 6 Bharath Nagar, Neel Kattabi Road, Madipakkarm, Chennai-600091.

8. *Shri Sai Leela* (English & Hindi), Bombay-400 014: 'Sai Niketan', 804-B, Dr. Ambedkar Road, Dadar.

9. *Sri Sai Avatars*, (English & Bengali). Calcutta-700 029: Sri Sai Samaj, Calcutta, P-113, Lake Terrace, (Editor: S.M. Bannerjee).

10. *Sri Sai Divya Sandesh*, (English & Hindi). (Distt. Raigarh): Sri Bhagawati Sai Sansthan, Plot No. 400/I, Near Railway Station. Panvel-410 206.

11. *Sri Sai Spandan*, Hyderabad-500 872: Self-Analysis Institute, 402 Raj Apartments, B.H. Society, Kukatpally (A.P.)

12. *Shradha Suburi* (English & Hindi). 702, 7th Floor, Plot No. 9, Yash Apartment, Sector 11, Dwarka, New Delhi (Editor: Ruby Sharma)

15

Shirdi Sai Baba Websites

- Annababa.com
- Baba's Eleven Promises
- From Shirdi Sai to Sathya Sai
  By Sharada Dev
- Life History of Shirdi Sai Baba
  By Sri Ammula Sambasiva Rao—Online book
- My Meeting with Baba of Shirdi
  By Shivamma Thayee
- OSaiBaba
- Reincarnation of Shirdi Sai Baba
- Sab-ka-malik-ek
- Sai Aarati and Bhajans
- Sai Baba of Shirdi
- Sai Baba Temple, Shirdi
- Sai Bharadwaja
- www.Saidrbarusa.org
- Shri Sai Baba Sansthan, Shirdi
- Shree Shirdi Sai Sansthan Sydney, Australia (The first Temple in Australia dedicated to Shirdi Sai Baba)
- Shri Saibaba Sansthan, Shirdi
- Shirdi Sai and Sathya Sai are One and the Same
  By Arjan D. Bharwani
- Shirdi Sai Baba.com
- Shirdi Sai Baba Website
- Shirdi Sai Baba Site
- Shirdi Sai Baba on the World Wide Web
- Sai Baba Guru Srinath
- Shirdi Sai Organization
- Shirdi Sai Baba—Hindi Literature
- Shirdi Sai Jalaram Mandir
- Shri Saibaba Sansthan, Shirdi
- Sri Gurucharitra

- Sri Sai Baba of Shirdi
- Sri Shirdi Sai Baba Temple
- The Sai Baba of Shirdi
- The Shirdi Sai Avatar
- http://www.saibaba.website.org
- http://www.saibaba.org
- http://www.admn@saibaba.org
- http://www.saijanmasthan.com
- http://www.floridashirdisai.org
- http://www.saidarbarusa.org
- http://www.saimukthi.com
- http://www.saipatham.com
- http://www.saibaba.org
- http://www.shirdisaitemple.com
- http://www.saileela.org
- http://www.saisamidhi.org
- http://www.saimandir.org
- http://www.shirdi.org
- http://www.shirdibaba.org
- http://www.shirdisaibaba.com
- http://www.templeofpeace.org
- http://www.srisaimarggam.org
- http://www.theshirdisaimandir.com
- http://www.shrishirdisaicanada.org
- http://www.shidisainath.org
- http://www.saisamsthanusa.org
- http://www.baba.org
- http://www.saibaba.us
- http://www.saishrddhasaburi.org

16

Sainath Give Me Assurance
(A devotee's prayer)

Look up to me, and I will look up to you
As assured by Sainath which is not new,
Yet, I request for Sai-assurance, the following few.

Sainath give me the assurance of your love,
So that I serve you with full warmth and love,
When I am amidst people with hate and deny love.

Sainath give me the assurance of your generosity,
So that I serve you with full zeal and intensity,
When I am faced with severe financial scarcity

Sainath give me the assurance of your humanity,
So that I serve you with full humility,
When I experience the near and dear ones cruelty.

Sainath give me the assurance of your mercy,
So that I serve you with full courtesy,
When I am endangered and you come in emergency.

Sainath give me the assurance of your protection,
So that I serve you with full concentration,
When I am working under constant tension.

Sainath give me the assurance of your nobility,
So that I serve you with full serenity,
When I am prone to more than one calamity.

Sainath give me the assurance of your humbleness,
So that I serve you with utmost fondness,
When I flare up and am unable to retain consciousness.

Sainath give me the assurance of your justice,
So that I serve you without any prejudice,
When I feel most harassed at my office.

Sainath give me the assurance of yoru presence,
So that I serve you with clear conscience,
When I fall prey to easy temptations thereby losing patience.

Sainath give me the assurance of winning a Sai-gem,
So that I serve you justifying my name of a gem,
When it is difficult even to acquire one costly gem.

Sainath give the assurance of you granting me promotion,
So that I serve you with complete surrender and devotion,
When my superiors in all fields are bent on suppression.

—(Ms) N.B. Sanglikar
C/o. *M.A.C.S. Research Institute*
Law College Road, Pune 411 004
Sai Leela (Journal)

17

The 108 Divine Names of Sri Shirdi Sai Baba

(*Om* is the name of God)

1. *Om Shri Sainathaya namah.*
   (*Om* obeisance to Shri Sai Nath)
2. *Om Shri Sai Lakshminarayanays namah.*
   (*Om* obeisance to Shri Sai Nath who is Narayana, Consort of Goddess Lakshmi)
3. *Om Shri Sai Krishna-Rama-Shiva-Maruityadirupaya Namah.*
   (*Om* obeisance to Shri Sai Nath, the manifestation of Lord Krishna, Ram, Shiva, Maruti & others)
4. *Om Shri Sai Shes-shayine Namah.*
   (*Om* obeisance to Shri Sai Nath, the Manifestation of Lord Vishnu resting on the thousand headed snake)
5. *Om Shri Sai Godavri-tata-sidhi-vasnih namah.*
   (*Om* obeisance to Shri Nath, who made Shirdi on the banks of river Godavari his abode)
6. *Om Shri Sai Bhakta-hridalayaya Namah.* (*Om*, obeisance to Shri Sai Nath who dwell in his devotees hearts)
7. *Om Shri Sai Sarva-hrinnilayaya Namah.*
   (*Om* obeisance to Shri Sai Nath who dwells in the hearts of all beings)
8. *Om Shri Sai Bhuta-vasaya namah.*
   (*Om* obeisance to Shri Sai Nath who is in the hearts of all living creatures)
9. *Om Shri Sai Bhuta-Vhavishyad-bhava varjitaya namah.*
   (*Om* obeisance to Shri Sai Nath who does not allow the thoughts of past and future to torment the mind)
10. *Om Shri Sai Kata-teetaya namah.*
    (*Om* obeisance to Sri Sai Nath who is beyond the limitations of time)
11. *Om, Shri Sai Kataya namah.*
    (*Om* obeisance to Shri Sai Nath who is time incarnate)
12. *Om Shri Sai kalkalaya namah.*
    (*Om* obeisance to Shri Sai Nath who is the Lord of eternity)

13. *Om Shri Sai Kal-darpa-damanaya namah.*
(*Om* obeisance to Shri Sai Nath, who has destroyed the pride of death)
14. *Om Shri Sai Mrtyunjayaya namaha.*
(*Om* obeisance to Shri Sai Nath who has conquered death)
15. *Om Shri Sai Amartyaya namah.*
(*Om* obeisance to Shri Sai Nath who is immortal)
16. *Om Shri Sai Martyabhaya-pradaya namah.*
(*Om* obeisance to Shri Sai Nath who grants freedom from the fear of death)
17. *Om Shri Sai Jivadharaya namah.*
(*Om* obeisance to Shri Sai Nath who is the support of all living beings)
18. *Om Shri Sai sarydharyaya namah.*
(*Om* obeisance to Shri Sai Nath who is the support of the Universe)
19. *Om Shri Sai Bhaktavana-samarthaya namah.*
(*Om*obeisance to Shri Sai Nath who grants power to his devotees)
20. *Om Shri Sai Bhaktavana-pratigyaya namah.*
(*Om* obeisance to Shri SaiNath who has vowed to protect his devotees)
21. *Om Shri Sai Anna-Vastra daya namah.*
(*Om* obeisance to Shri Sai Nath, the bestower of good health and freedom from diseases)
22. *Om Shri Sai Dhana-mangalya-pradaya namah.*
(*Om* obeisance to Shri Sai Nath, who grants wealth and happiness)
23. *Om Shri Sai Riddhi-Siddhi-daya namah.*
(*Om* obeisance to Shri Sai Nath who bestows psychic and spiritual powers).
24. *Om Shri Sai Putra-mitra-kalatrabandhu-daya namah.*
(*Om,* obeisance to Shri Sai Nath who grants sons, friends, spouse and relatives)
25. *Om Shri Sai Yoga-kshaema-vahya namah.*
(*Om* Obeisance to Shri Sai Nath who undertakes the responsibility of providing for and sustaining the devotees)
26. *Om Shri Sai Apad-bandhavaya namah.*
(*Om* obeisance to Shri Sai Nath who protects his devotees like friends)
27. *Om Shri Sai Marga-bandhava namah.*
(*Om* obeisance to Shri Sai Nath who is a companion on life's path)
28. *Om Shri Sai Bhukti-mukti-svargapavarga-daya namah.*
(*Om* obeisance to Shri Sai Nath who is the bestower of worldly pleasure, salvation, heavenly bliss and ultimate beatitude)
29. *Om Shri Sai Priyaya namah.*
(*Om* Obeisance to Shri Sai Nath, the beloved)

30. *Om Shri Sai Priti-vardhanaya namah.*
(*Om* obeisance to Shri Sai Nath who provides capacity for boundless love)

31. *Om Shri Sai Antaryamine namah.*
(*Om* Obeisance to Shri Sai Nath who is familiar with the innermost secrets of heart)

32. *Om Shri Sai Sahhidatmane namah.*
(*Om* obeisance to Shri Sai Nath who is symbol of truth and pure consciousness)

33. *Om Shri Sai Nityanandya namah.*
(*Om* obeisance to Shri Sai Nath who is the embodiment of eternal bliss)

34. *Om Shri Sai Parama-sukha-daya namah.*
(*Om* obeisance to Shri Sai Nath who bestows supreme happiness)

35. *Om Shri Sai Parmeshwaraya namah.*
(*Om* obeisance to Shri Sai Nath, the Supreme Lord)

36. *Om Shri Sai Bhakti-Shakti-Pradaya namah.*
(*Om* obeisance to Shri Sai Nath who grants strength for devotion)

37. *Om Shri Sai Gyana-vairagya-daya namah.*
(*Om* obeisance to Shri Sai Nath who is the bestower of knowledge and freedom from worldly desires)

38. *Om Shri Sai Prema-Pradaya namah.*
(*Om* obeisance to Shri Sai Nath, who grants love)

39. *Om Shri Sai Sanshaya hirdaya-daurbalyapapa-karma-vasana kshaya namah.*
(*Om*, obeisance to Shri Sai Nath who removes doubts, human weakness and inclination to sinful deeds and desire)

40. *Om Shri Sai Hridaya-granthi-bhedkaya namah.*
(*Om* obeisance to Shri Sai Nath who unbinds all the knots in the heart)

41. *Om Shri Sai karma-dhvansine namah.*
(*Om* obeisance to Shri Sai Nath who destroys the effects of past evil deeds)

42. *Om Shri Sai Shuddha-sattvasthitaya namah.*
(*Om* obeisance to Shri Sai Nath who inspires pure and pious thoughts)

43. *Om, Shri Sai Gunatita-gunatmane namah.*
(*Om* obeisance to Shri Sai Nath who attributes is endowed with all wirtues and yet transcends them all)

44. *Om Shri Sai Ananta-kalyana-gunaya namah.*
(*Om* obeisance to Shri Sai Nath who has limitless virtuous attributes)

45. *Om Shri Sai Amita-parakramaya namah.*
(*Om* obeisance to Shri Sai Nath who has unlimited Supreme power)

46. *Om, Shri Sai Jayine namah.*
(*Om* obeisance to Shri Sai Nath, who is the personification of victory)

47. *Om Shri Sai Durdharshakshobhyaya namah.*
(*Om* obeisance to Shri Sai Nath who is unchallengeable and impossible to defy)

48. *Om Shri Sai Aparajitaya namah.*
(*Om* obeisance to Shri Sai Nath who is unconquerable)

49. *Om Shri Sai Trilokeshu Avighata-gataye namah.*
(*Om*, obeisance to Shri Sainath, the Lord of three worlds whose actions there are no obstructions)

50. *Om Shri Sai Ashakya-rahitaya namah.*
(*Om* obeisance to Shri Sai Nath for whom nothing is impossible)

51. *Om Shri Sai Sarva-Shakti-Murtaye namah.*
(*Om* obeisance to Shri Sai Nath, who is the Almightly, the Omnipotent)

52. *Om Shri Sai Suroopa-sundaraya namah.*
(*Om* obeisance to Shri Sai Nath who has a beautiful form)

53. *Om Shri Sai Sulochanaya namah.*
(*Om* obeisance to Shri Sai Nath whose eyes are beautiful and whose glance is auspicious)

54. *Om Shri Sai Bahurupa-vishva-murtaye namah.*
(*Om* obeisance to Shri Sai Nath who is of various form, and is manifest in the form of Universe itself)

55. *Om Shri Sai Arupavyakatya namah.*
(*Om* obeisance to Shri Sai Nath who is formless and whose image cannot be bound in mere word)

56. *Om Shri Sai Achintaya namah.*
(*Om* obeisance to Shri Sai Nath who is inconceivable and incomprehensible)

57. *Om Shri Sai Sookshmaya namah.*
(*Om* obeisance to Shri Sai Nath who dwells within every minute creature)

58. *Om Shri Sai Sarvantaryamine namah.*
(*Om* obeisance to Shri Sai Nath who dwells in all souls)

59. *Om Shri Sai Manovagatitaya namah.*
(*Om* obeisance to Shri Sai Nath who is the familiar with the thoughts, speech and past of the devotees)

60. *Om Shri Sai Prema-murtaye namah.*
(*Om* obeisance to Shri Sai Nath who is the embodiment of love and affection)

61. *Om Shri Sai Sulabha-durlabhaya namah.*
(*Om* obeisance to Shri Sai Nath who is easily accessible to his devotes but inaccessible to the wicked)

62. *Om Shri Sai Asahaya-sahayaya namah.*
   (*Om* obeisance to Shri Sai Nath who is the supporter of the helpless)

63. *Om Shri Sai Anathanatha-decna-bandhave namah.*
   (*Om* obeisance to Shri Sai Nath who is the protector of the unprotected and the kinsman of the destitute)

64. *Om, Shri Sai Sarva-bhara-bhric namah.*
   (*Om* obeisance to Shri Sai Nath who takes over entire burden of all)

65. *Om Shri Sai Akannaneka-karma-sukannine namah.*
   (*Om* obeisance to Shri Sai Nath who himself is the non-doer yet inspires others to perform numberless virtuous deeds)

66. *Om Shri Sai Punya-shravana-keertanaya namah.*
   (*Om* obeisance to Shri Sai Nath hearing about whom and speaking of whose glories, is an act of religious merit)

67. *Om, Shri Sai Tirthaya namah.*
   (*Om* obeisance to Shri Sai Nath who is the embodiment of all holy places)

68. *Om Shri Sai Vasudevaya namah.*
   (*Om* obeisance to Shri Sai Nath who is the incarnation of Lord Krishna i.e. Vasudeva)

69. *Om Shri Sai Satam gataya namah.*
   (*Om* obeisance to Shri Sai Nath who guides the devotees on the noble and cirtuous path)

70. *Om Shri Sai Sat-parayanaya namah.*
   (*Om* obeisance to Shri Sai Nath, who is fully dedicated to truth)

71. *Om Shri Sai Loknathaya namah.*
   (*Om* obeisance to Shri Sai Nath who is the Lord of the Universe)

72. *Om, Shri Sai Pavananghayanamah.*
   (*Om* obeisance to Shri Sai Nath whuo is pure and free form sins)

73. *Om Shri Sai Amritanshave namah.*
   (*Om* obeisance to Shri Sai Nath who is ambrosial)

74. *Om Shri Sai Bhaskara-prabhaya namah.*
   (*Om*obeisance to Shri Sai Nath who is lustrous like the sun)

75. *Om Shri Sai Brahmacharya-tapashcharyadi-suvrataya namah.*
   (*Om* obeisance to Shri Sai Nath who has adopted celibacy, sceticism, devout austerity and other spiritual disciplines)

76. *Om Shri Sai Sathya-dharma-parayanaya namah.*
   (*Om* obeisance to Shri Sai Nath who has taken to truth and righteousness)

77. *Om Shri Sai Siddhesvaraya namah.*
   (*Om* obeisance toi Shri Sai Nath who is the incarnation of Shiva i.e. Siddheswar)

78. *Om Shri Sai Siddha-sankalpaya namah.*
    (*Om* obeisance to Shri Sai Nath whose determination prevails)
79. *Om Shri Sai Yogeshvaraya namah.*
    (*Om* obeisance to Shri Sai Nath who is Yogeshwar i.e. incarnation of Lord
    Shiva & Lord Krishna)
80. *Om Shri Sai Bhagavati namah.*
    (*Om* obeisance to Shri Sai Nath who is the Divinity)
81. *Om Shri Sai Bhakta-vatsalaya namah.*
    (*Om* obeisance to Shri Sai Nath who is full of love for his devotees)
82. *Om Shri Sai Satpurushaya namah.*
    (*Om* obeisance to Shri Sai Nath the virtuouos, pious & venerable one)
83. *Om Shri Sai Purushottamaya namah.*
    (*Om* obeisance to Shri Sai Nath who is the incarnation of the Supreme i.e.
    Lord Rama)
84. *Om Shri Sai Sathya-tattva-bodhakaya namah.*
    (*Om* obeisance to Shri Sai Nath who is the preceptor of the essence of truth)
85. *Om Shri Sai Kamadi-sad-vair-dhvansine namah.*
    (*Om* obeisance to Shri Sai Nath who destroys all worldly desires i.e. lust,
    nager, greed, delusion, ego and envy)
86. *Om Shri Sai Abhed-anand-anubhav-pradaya namah.*
    (*Om,* obeisance to Shri Sai Nath to the bestower of the bliss arising from
    oneness with God)
87. *Om Shri Sai Sama-Sarva-mata-sammmataya namah.*
    (*Om,* obeisance to Shri Sai Nath who preaches that all religions are equal)
88. *Om Shri Sai Dakshina-murtayenamah.*
    (*Om* obeisance to Shri Sai Nath who is himself Lord Dakshinamurti i.e.
    Shiva)
89. *Om Shri Sai Venkateshharamanaya namah.*
    (*Om* obeisance to Shri Sai Nath who is remains merged in Lord
    Venkateshwara i.e. Vishnu)
90. *Om Shri Sai Adbutananta-charyayanamah.*
    (*Om* obeisance to Shri Sai who is Divine and is ever engrossed in blissful
    meditation)
91. *Om Shri Sai Prapannarti-haraya namah.*
    (*Om* obeisance to Shri Sai Nath who eradicates the distress of those who
    take refuge in him)
92. *Om Shri Sai Sansara-sarva-duhkha-kshaya-karaya namah.*
    (*Om* obeisance to Shri Sai Nath who destroys all the calamities of the world)

93. *Om Shri Sai Sarvavit-sarvato-mukhaya namah.*
(*Om* obeisance to Shri Sai Nath who is omniscient and omnipresent)

94. *Om Shri Sai Saravantar-bahih-sthitaya namah.*
(*Om* obeisance to Shri Sai Nath who exists everywhere and in everything)

95. *Om Shri Sai Sarva-mangala-karaya namah*avde.
(*Om* obeisance to Shri Sai Nath who is the bestower of auspiciousness)

96. *Om Shri Sai Sarvabhista-pradaya namah.*
(*Om* obeisance to Shri Sai Nath who established amity and harmony amongst followers of diverse religions leading to a common path of virtue)

97. *Om Shri Sai Samarth Sadguru Sainathaya namah*h.
(*Om* obeisance to Shri Sai Nath who is the most powerful and the Supreme Guru in Spiritual life).

98. *Om Shri Sai Dakshina-murtayenamah.*
(Om obeisance to Shri Sai Nath who is himself Lord Dakshinamurti i.e. Shiva)

99. *Om Shri Sai Venkateshharamanaya namah.*e
(Om, obeisance to Shri Sai Nath who remains merged in Lord Venkateshwara i.e. Vishnu)

100. *Om Shri Sai Adbutananta-charyayanamah.*
(Om, obeisance to Shri Sai who is Divine and is ever engrossed in blissful meditation)

101. *Om Shri Sai Prapannarti-haraya namah.*
(Om obeisance to Shri Sai Nath who eradicates the distress of those who take refuge in Him).

102. *Om Shri Sai Sansara-sarva-duhkha-kshaya-karaya namah.*l
(Om obeisance to Shri Sai Nath who destroys all the calamities of the world)

103. *Om Shri Sai Sarvavit-sarvato-mukhaya namah.*
(Om obeisance to Shri Sai Nath who is Omniscient and Omnipresent)

104. *Om Shri Sai Saravantar-bahih-sthitaya namah.*ro
(Om obesisance to Shri Sai Nath who exists everywhere and in everything)

105. *Om Shri Sai Sarva-mangala-karaya namah.*
(Om obeisance to Shri Sai Nath who is the bestower of auspiciousness)

106. *Om Shri Sai Sarvabhista-pradaya namah.*
(Om obeisance to Shri Sai Nath who grants all desires)

107. *Om Shri Sai Samarasa-sanmarya-sthapanaya namah.*
(Om, obeisance to Shri Sai Nath who established amity and harmony amongst followers of diverse religions leading to a common path of virtue).

108. *Om Shri Sai Samarth Sadguru sainathaya namah. and*
(Om obeisance to Shri Sai Nath who is the most powerful and the Supreme Guru in Spiritual life).

SECTION II

The Second Sai Baba
SRI SATHYA SAI BABA
(1926-2011)

Sri Sathya Sai Baba's *Gayatri Mantra*:

*"Om Sayissvaraya Vidmahe, Sathya Devaya,
Dheemahi Tanna, Sarva Prachodayat."*

We realize Sri SathyaSai Baba as the Supreme Lord, we meditate on the Lord
Sathya—the embodiment of trancedental truth We pray for norishing Love of
his grace and protection!. Let Peace reign Supreme.

5.00 भारत INDIA

2013

सत्य साईं बाबा SATHYA SAI BABA

Commemorative stamp released on the occasion of
Bhagavan Sri Sathya Sai Baba's 88th Birthday.

18

Sri Sathya Sai's Name

Sai like an incantation
confers on me the benediction of *Pranava*—
the first word the cosmos heard.
When I run my mind's eye
on my chosen form—
rather short than tall
the crinkly hair the deep-changing complexion
the eyes showering compassion
the lips forming words of wisdom
or communicating though not parted,
conjointly with your glance
wart and all as I recall-
the same that one time
had looked at me
as though from a shadowy limbo
all now abuzz and agog,
pulsating with a newly released energy:
The blue-throated Shiva
holding the Ganga in his matted braid,
bearing *kodanda* on his shoulder
and a quiver of glistening arrows on his back Rama,
the slayer of the ten-headed Ravana,
and casting his spell with the ambrosia of flute melody
or trampling upon and subduing
the fire-belching hooded serpent
Krishna, the lover and the destroyer.

—P.P. Sharma

19

Why I Have Incarnated

—Sri Sathya Sai Baba

➢ "In order to turn men away from the bylanes of immortality and injustice, greed and envy, on to the royal road of *sadhna*, through gentleness; "In order to interpret the spiritual heritage of man that has been distrorted and dilated during the intervening ages; "In order to demonstrate the validity of truth, righteousness, peace and love as instruments for individual and social progress; "In order to infuse confidence and contentment in the hearts of the good who are struck by fear and anxiety; I, the Lord has incarnated at Puttaparthi."

➢ "I have come to light the Lamp of Love in your hearts, to see that it shines day by day with added luster. I have not come in behalf of any exclusive religion. I have not come on a mission of publicity of a sect or creed or cause, nor have I come to collect followers for a doctrine. I have no plan to attract disciples or devotees into my fold or any fold. I have come to tell you of this unitary faith, this spiritual principle, this path of love, this duty of love, this obligation of love."

➢ "My power is immeasurable, My truth is inexplicable and unfathomable,"

➢ "I am the primodial cause for the entir cosmos, I am '*Adi Shakti*'. I am the fundamental energy for the entire moving and non-moving creation."

20

Divine Life of Sri Sathya Sai Baba Avatar

—S.P.Ruhela

Eight years after Shirdi Sai Baba left his mortal coil, exactly as prophesied by him, his next incarnation took place, on 23 November 1926. He was born as Sri Sathya Sai Baba. He is the combined *Avatar* of Lord Shiva and his consort Shakti. He was born in Puttaparthi village in the house of Pedda Venkappa Raju, and his mother was Eswaramma. He was born in an ordinary lower middle class family of Raju Kshatriyas. Both Shirdi Sai Baba and Sathya Sai Baba have been born in the lineage of the ancient sage Bhardwaja who had secured a boon from Lord Shiva and Shakti about 5600 years ago. Right from his birth, Shri Sathya Sai Baba was performing innumerable kinds of miracles, not only of creating *Vidhuti* (Holy ash), rings, ornaments, statues, pictures, sweets, fruits, medicines, etc., but curing the most acute cases of heart disease, cancer and other diseases and misfortunes of people. All the powers of the universe were contained in his palm.

You must have heard stories of fairies and messengers of God in the holy scriptures like the *Puranas* and the Bible, describing the miracles and you probably dismissed them as improbabilities, figments of imagination or materials created by illogical religious writers of ancient times to influence or amuse readers.

Till April 2011, we had amidst us Shri Sathya Sai Baba. He was the *puranavatar* or integral incarnation of God. he possessed all the attributes and powers of God. Whatsoever he wished in his heart that must immediately materialized. Holy ash, (*Vidhuti*) and all kinds of articles as wished by him, instantly appeared in his right palm and he used to give them to his devotees to cure them, console them, bless them and encourage them to make more and more efforts for their moral and spiritual upliftment. He materialized rings, lockets, ornaments, statues of gold, silver and other metals, photographs, rosaries *rudraksha* beads, Cross, sweets, sugar candy, fruits, books, pens, watches and many other kinds of things and gave them away to the visitors without asking for anything but devotion and love towards the chosen God of the person concerned. Once, he even materialized a live monkey on the persistent request of a foreigner. He brought back life in the dead bodies of a number of people;

the cases of the resurrection of at least three persons Robert Cowan, Radha Krishna and Bose are on record. More than ten million people belonging to different religions, races, nationalities, occupations and professions are believed to be his staunch devotees and followers; none can estimate the exact number of people in the world who believe in him. Scientists have accepted the Baba's most astounding miracles which defied all lawses of nature.

The life of Sri Sathya Sai Baba is an inspiring story. His detailed biography has been written by Prof. N. Kasturi in four volumes of 'Sathyam Shivam Sundaram'. Kasturi's most interesting books 'Loving God' and 'Prasanthi—Pathway to Peace', Ra Ganapati's scholarly book 'Baba: Sathya Sai (in two parts) and two highly readable and comprehensive small books—'Bhagawan Shri Sathya Sai Baba: Avatar of Our Age' published by Sri Sathya Sai Prakashan, Guwahati, and 'Avatar Gatha' (in Hindi) published by Sri Sathya Sai Books and Publications Trust, Prasanthi Nilayam, are the best publications on the life of the Baba. There have been many hitherto unknown things about the life of the Sai Baba in this incarnation but the Baba graciously disclosed them in some of his discourses. Now, we have almost complete information regarding his life. We shall present it very briefly, leaving out the details and retaining only the essentials.

Family and Parentage

-   Born in Raju (Kshatriya) family of Puttaparthi village.
-   Lower middle class agricultural family having religious, musical and literary traditions.
-   Father Sri Venkappa Raju, mother Srimati Eswaramma. They had five children:

    (1) Shesham Raju (Son)
    (2) (Late) Venkamma (Daughter)
    (3) Parvathamma (Daughter)
    (4) Sathyanarayana Raju (Son)—Later on he was known as Sri Sathya Sai Baba.
    (5) Jankiramayya (Son). He was a local politician and social worker and also a Trustee of Sri Sathya Sai Baba Trust in Puttaparthi.

-   Sai Baba's great-grandfather, Kondam Raju was an expert of ancient Hindu scriptures. He built the temple of Lord Krishna's consort, Sathyabhama, in Puttaparthi village, after seeing her in his dream.
-   Sai Baba's grandfather, Sri Venka Avadhoot, had renounced the world.

- Sri Venkappa Raju lived in thatched hut on a small piece of land in Puttaparthi, Sri Sathya Sai Baba was born in it. In 1979, it has been converted into a Shiva temple which is now visited by Sai.
- The Baba's father Sri Venkappa Raju was noted for his epic roles played on the village stage.

Birth

Sri Sathya Sai Baba was born at Puttaparthi village on Monday, the 23 November 1926, at 9.06 a.m.

Childhood

- Was a loving, gentle-natured, kind and sober child with extraordinary intelligence.
- Kind to birds, animals, poor people, other children.
- Liked only vegetarian food; did not kill or trouble birds and animals.
- Insisted on giving food to beggars and poor people even at the age of 4.
- Mostly lived in the household of a neighboruing elderly Brahmin lady Subamma and ate vegetarian food cooked by her.
- Fond of singing, dancing, cooking, worship, teaching children, religious and moral values and worship, playing on the bank of Chiravadi river near the village.
- Would materialize fruits, sweets, toffies, rubber, pencil etc. miraculously for his peers in the village, on the river bank and on the hill where a tamarind tree was turned into "*Kalpavraksh*" (Wish-fulfilling tree) by him.
- Studied in the village primary school. At 10 he formed a local *Bhajan Mandali* of his peers, to sing songs in devotion to Lord Vitthal of Pandharput.
- After completing primary school, he went to school at Bukkpatanam, about 3 miles away; used to go on foot.

Adolescence

Life at Kamlapur (Andhra Pradesh)

- Joined middle school at Kamlapur, stayed with elder brother Seshama Raju's wife's brother's family there; had to do house-hold chores like bringing wood from the jungle which was at quite a distance and water from a far off well many times a day, in heavy pitchers, but he never complained to any one for it.

- Was a good student, respected by students and teachers; fond of songs and dramas; was made the monitor of the class; English teacher asked the class to write some sentences on the glory of India; Baba wrote: "Consisting of high mountains, large rivers with many branches and many plains, India is beautiful with all these grand contents."

- One miracle done in class: Teacher Kondappa punished Sathya Narayan Raju (Baba) for not copying some thing in class by asking him to keep standing up on a bench till the end of the period: the period ended, the teacher wanted to get up from his chair but was stuck to it. Another teacher Mehboob Ali saw this; he politely asked Raju to get down from the bench and then the teacher Kondappa was released by the chair.

- Miraculously created stationery items, sweets, fruits etc. for his classmates.

- Enthusiastically served as a Boy Scout in a fair and cattle show at Pushpagiri, went there on foot due to poverty.

- Had only one pair of Scout shirt and knickers, which he washed and ironed daily; did not like to accept the gift of another shirt from his rich class mate.

- Also wrote some small songs and poems for money, for Kote Subanna Store and other shopkeepers for the publicity of their articles in the market.

- Wrote original dramas 'Navyug' &'Choopinatalu Cestara?' (Are your actions not unlike your professions?) for school children.

- Lived in poverty and deprivation at Kamlapur, bearing all inconveniences.

Life at Urvakonda:

- Elder brother was appointed as a Telugu teacher in the High school at Urvakonda; Baba was admitted to the school, stayed with the brother and did all kinds of household chores.

- His divine personality started influencing the Headmaster Lakshmipati, teachers and villagers and school students; the Headmaster used to touch his feet in the closed office room every day.

- Led the school prayer every day; was the most popular singer and a bright student.

- Once he was scolded by his brother's brother-in-law when he sat on a wooden revolving chair in his house and was asked to get down; he replied, "A day will come when I will sit on such a chair made of silver like an Emperor and you will live to see that day." Seven years later, the prophecy of the Baba came true; Rani of Chincholi presented a silver chair; Baba asked that relative who was also present at that time to unwrap it at Prasanthi Nilayam ashram.

- On 23 May 1940 a big poisonous scorpion bit the Baba's toe. He became ill with much pain; was cured, but started behaving abnormally. Various treatments were tried, at last a witch doctor (necromancer) was called to Puttaparthi, who shaved off his head and made a cross with a sharp knife and applied irritating juicy medicine on it. His head was swollen and gave him a lot of pain. He got cured after some days, but his laughter in the company of unknown spirits persisted.

- One 23 May 1940 at his village Puttarthi he miraculously materialized sugar balls, sugar candy and flowers before some people. A crowd gathered around him and some jealous one complained to Sathya's father Pedda Venkappa Raju who rushed in, full of anger, and threatened to beat him with a stick asking "Who are you—God, ghost or lunatic?" Sathya replied politely, "I am Sai Baba. Mine is Apasthamb Sutra. I belong to Bhardwaja Gotra. I have some to save you from dangers. Keep your houses clean and pure." When asked to prove his divinity then and there, he asked a person standing there with jasmine flowers in his hands, to give those flowers to him. He took the flowers and threw them on the ground; the flowers fell in such a manner that 'SAI BABA' was written by them in Telugu, the Baba's mother-tongue.

- In October (first fortnight), Sathya and his elder brother were invited by Ramaraju, Chairman of Bellary Municipal Committee, to spend the Puja holidays in his company; Baba and about 50-60 people in a party were taken to see the old ruins of Hampi and the Virupaksh temple. Sathya did nto enter the temple feigning stomach-ache. The party went inside the temple; to their surprise, they found the real life image of Sathya on the statue of the God Virupaksh instead of Virupaksh. His brother sent some one to verify whether Sathya was still outside the temple; he was there as well as in the temple. This miracle convinced his brother and some others of his divinity.

- The Municipal Chairman of Bellary, Ramaraju, presented a gold collar pin to Sathya to wear on his shirt as a token of his love and veneration on 20 October 1940. It was lost in Urvakonda; Baba composed a poem on its loss and sang it himself:

"October 20th was Monday,
Retiring from Hampi, the Baba was going to school.
The (gold) collar pin was lost and couldn't be found.
That was the day of transformation.
The loss of the pin was the cause of the big change;
The links with worldly ties have gone,
The pilgrimage to Hampi also served its purpose,
Freedom from Maya was attained."

That very day Sathya renounced his home. He returned to his brother's home halfway from school, threw aside his books at the porch, and spoke to his sister-in-law:

"I am no longer your Sathya. I am Sai. I am going. I don't belong to you. *Maya* (illusion) has gone. My devotees are calling me. I have my work. Give up all your efforts to cure me. I am Sai. I do not consider myself related to you."

This historical event of Baba's renunciation of the worldly ties took place on 20 October 1940, Baba was 14 years old at that time.

Therefore, he went to sit in the garden of his devotee Anjayalu and sat on a rock amidst trees. A crowd assembled. He sang the first prayer, teaching everyone to sing it throughout their lives:

"*Manas bhaj re Guru charanam*
Duster bhavasagar tarnam."
"Meditate in thy mind on the feet of the Guru.
This alone can take you across the turbulent
sea of worldly existence birth after birth."

- Three days passed in worship led by him. A photographer came to take a photograph of Sathya Narayanan Raju seated in the garden. He wanted to remove a crude stone that was right in front of him but Sathya did not agree. The Photographer took the picture and later on, the stone became an image of Shirdi Sai Baba in the photograph.
- In the evening, the Sathya's parents came to see him, mother Eswaramma entreated him to come back to stay in their village of Puttparthi; he agreed to live in Puttaparthi forsaking all worldly ties.
- On his departure from Unvakonda, his two classmates, who used to sit on the same bench with him, became mentally ill sand died due to estrangement from Sathya.

- He generally lived in Subamma's home giving *darshan*, blessings, articles and *vidhuti* created by him to the devotees who came to him. He gave moral and spiritual sermons.

  He (Baba) was invited by many devotees to Bangalore, Mysore etc. There, he gave evidence of being the reincarnation of Shirdi Sai Baba, and cured and blessed many devotees, even the rich and princely ones, by his miracles.

- The young Baba started wearing coloured (yellow, orange and then blood red coloured long robe) presented by his earlier devotees; later on he stopped accepting them.

- The Baba gave visions of various Gods and Goddesses including Shirdi Sai Baba to his parents, sisters, Subamma and many other devotees.

- In 1941 (at the age of 15 years) the Baba operated a duodenal ulcer with instruments mysteriously materialized. He performed many unbelievable miracles. He prophesized that Puttaparthi would be the spiritual centre of the world which would draw millions of people towards him; none believed it then.

Adulthood of Baba

- Baba shifted to Patta Mandir (Old Temple) built in 1944.
- Baba's fame grew; elder brother Seshma Raju's letter asked him to shun the company of all sorts of rich and princely persons coming to him and the likelihood of his name being spoilt; Baba's historic letter of 25 May, 1947 (at the age of 22). His reply was:
- "I have a Task: To foster all mankind and ensure for all of them lives full of *anands* (bliss). I have a Vow: To lead all who stray away from the straight path, again into goodness and save them. I am attached to a 'Work' that I love: To remove the sufferings of the poor and grant them what they lack. I have a reason to be proud, for I rescue all who worship and adore me, aright.
- I will neither give up my mission nor my determination. I know I will carry them out. I treat the honour and dishonour, the fame and blame that may be the consequence, with equanimity.
- No one can comprehend my glory, whoever he is, whatever his method of inquiry, however long his attempt.
- You can see yourself the full glory in the coming years. Devotees must have patience and forbearance".

Since 1947, the Baba has emerged as the Universal Master.

- Inauguration of Prasanthi Nilayam (Abode of Peace) Ashram on Baba's 25th Birthday on 23 November 1950; it has grown into a big township, the real "Spiritual Heart of the Universe".
- In 1953, the Baba brought back to life one devotee V. Radhakrishna, whose body had started decomposing at Prassanthi Nilayam. In 1971, the Baba brought back to life an American devotee Cowan after his death in Chennai. Many great miracles have been done by the Baba so far, besides innumerable cures, materializations etc.
- In 1957, the Baba presided over 'All India Divine Life Convention' at Venkatgiri; his eminence as a truly divine power was instantly established among learned pundits of ancient scriptures of that time.
- Established a hospital on a hill behind Parasanthi Nilayam in October 1957.
- Went on a tour to North India on 14 July 1947: visited Delhi, Rishikesh, Sivanand Nagar (where he cured and blessed Sivanandji), Mathura, Sri Nagar performing miracles, blessing thousand of people and recharging the *Jyotirlinga*.
- Inaugurated *Sanathana Sarathi*, spiritual journal from Prasanthi Nilayam, (edited by Prof. N. Kasturi for about two decades); now published in many languages, including English.
  On 29 June 1959, a Banyan tree was planted by Baba on a hill behing Prassanthi Nilyam. He placed a thick copper plate materialized by him under it about 15x10" in size, to serve as a meditation tree for devotees.
- On 7 June 1961, Baba visited Badrinath; consecrated the *Netralinga* there.
- On the first day of *Dushera* festival he declared that he had come to propagate *Sathya, Dharma, Shanti* and *Prema* (the first two were the concerns of rama and the last two were the concerns of Lord Krishna.
- Baba's biography *Sathyam, Shivam, Sundaram* (First volume) by Prof. N. Kasturi was released by Baba.
- The Baba's declaration: "My Birthday festival will not be marred by any dispiriting news, you will get positive news." The Chinese, who had attacked India's eastern borders and entered it, started mysteriously withdrawing from the mid-night of 22-23 November, 1962.
- 20 June 1963, the Baba took an himself serious disease of a devotee and suffered for eight days.

- On *Gurupurnima* day, 6 July 1963, the Baba's declaration of being the combined incarnation of Shiva and Shakti, and disclosing that Sri Shirdi SaI Baba was Shiva's incarnation, while the next incarnation of Prema Sai Baba would be purely Shakhti's incarnation.

- Establishment of Prasanthi Vidvamaha Sabha and the All India Academy of Vedic Scholars.

- On 23 November 1964 (on his 34th Birthday) the Baba made the great declaration:
  "I am Sai Nath, Lokanath, and Annathnath, the same God who saved Gajendra (Elephant in the mythological story), the saintly boy Dhruva, poor Kuchela (Lord Krishna's classmate Sudama), and helpless Pralhad, son of demon king Hiranyakashyap."

- During *Dushera* Festival of 1965, *Veda Purusha Saptaha Jnana Yagya* was performed; the Baba as Yagyapurusha, offered to the sacred flame precious stones materialized by him; a video film *'Aura of Divinity'* shows those scenes.

- On 16 May 1968, the First World Conference (and Second all Indian Conference) was inaugurated by the Baba at Bombay.

- 30 June 1968 to 14 July 1968: the Baba's visited East Africa. blessed devotees of African and Indian origin in Kenya and Uganda; visited Nairobi, Kampala and other places; even Idi Amin, the then Chief of the Army, who later became the Dictator of Uganda, came to meet him. Visit arranged by Dr. C.G. Patel, the Baba's ardent devotee.

- In 1972, the first summer course on *'Indian Culture and Spirituality'* was organized under the Baba's guidance at Whitefield.

- Sai Baba's discourses were published by Sri Sathya Sai Books and Publications Trust, Prasanthi, Nilayam.

- Educational institutions were started by the Baba: College for Women at Anantapur; Boy's College at Whitfield; Colleges for Women at Jaipur and Bhopal.

- Establishment of Sri Sathya Sai Institute of Higher Learning, Prasanthi Nilyam in 1982 (Deemed University, as recognized by the University Grants Commission).

- Baba was Chancellor of the SSIHL since its inception till his death in April 2011.

- A number of schools and colleges for boys and girls have been started in different parts of India. In foreign countries also, devotees have started such schools to teach the Sai ideals to their children. A Planetarium was started at Prasanthi Nilayam.

- Baba launched a global movement of "EHV" (Education in Human Values).
- *Sri Seva Samitis* were started in about 100 countries of the world. Now there are countless such *Samitis*.
- November 1991: Celebration of Golden Jubilee of the Baba's declaration of Avatarhood, Fifth World Conference of Sai Organizations, about one million people came to witness these historic events at Prasanthi Nilyam in November 1990.
- On 23rd November 1990 (65th birthday) the Baba's announced that a rupees 200 crores worth hospital would be inaugurated by him on his next Birthday in 1991:

  "Whether it is a heart bypass operation, a kidney transplant, a lung operation, brain surgery, everything will be done free." This unique hospital started functioning on 22nd November 1991.
- The Baba was always blessing and giving *Vidhuti* and other presents of articles materialized by him to innumerable spiritual leaders, saints, philosophers, politicians, educationists, businessmen, diplomats, judges, doctors, scientists as well as millions of other devotees in the world. His influence as a greatest spiritual master of the universe in the modern age, just like that of his previous incarnation as Sri Shirdi Sai Baba has been acknowledged world-wide.

Since 20 October 1940, Sri Sathya Sai Baba had been declaring repeatedly and emphatically saying that he was God incarnate and all the Gods and Goddesses known to mankind were subsumed in him. He has not only declared but convincingly proved to millions of people that he was omnipotent, omnipresent and omniscient incarnation of God possessing all powers and attributes. He often said that all people are god, but the people did not know this whereas he knew that he was God. He tried to transform mankind using his instrument of love and teachings of selfless service and that was how he won the hearts of people of all cultures, religions and social strata of society in the modern of science, technology and democracy.

Baba or Swami as he is addressed by all his devotees emerged as the greatest Spiritual Teacher of mankind, teaching the highest universal values. He was the true synthesizer of all religions, races and nationalities of man in the universe by the divine charisma of his magnetic personality and his words of love, wisdom and compassion. As prophecied by him in the historical letter to his elder brother on 25th May 1947, it is only due to his divine personality and unfolding of his predetermined mission that the unknown obscure hilly village of Puttaparthi of the 1930s has today become the spiritual heart of the whole world the international pilgrimage for Hindus, Christians, Sikhs, Zorastrians, Muslims, Buddhists and other religions and sects. The divine plan of his mission declared by him in abolescence was:

- First sixteen years as *Bal Leela* (Miraculous plays of childhood)
- 16-32 year as *Mahina Kal* (Period of Divine Glory enfoldment)
- 32 onwards, *Dharmsthapan* (Establishment of righteousness)

His life plan has worked out like this. He passed away on 24th April, 2011.

As a tireless worker, working from down to dusk, he was engaged in giving *darshan*, blessings, personal guidance—directing the affairs of the University and other institutions of his *Ashram* and mission, meeting people coming from far and near and spreading spiritual waves throughout the world. He did not teach any new religion to his devotees. He tried to inculcate love and unity among the followers of all religions. He wanted to make his devotees real men and women who are like God, not animals. He said that to receive his blessing, we should do two things: (a) whatever religion we follow and Gods or Goddess we worship, we must continue to do so with sincerity and intensity; (b) we should have real love for all people and creatures of the world and we should serve them. "Service of men is service of God"—this is his main teaching. He laid utmost emphasis on the four great values of truth, righteousness, love and peace, chanting the names of Gods and Goddesses, on singing their names in *Bhajans* or *Kirtans* (devotional songs).

He founded a unique organization called "Sri Sathya Sai Seva Organization", which has its branches in over 180 countries of the world and millions of his devotees have for decades been rendering selfless service and help to thousands of poor, distressed and helpless people in many countries through the local units of Sri Sathya Sai organization. He runs his big, modern and peaceful Prasanthi Nilayam ashram near his native village Puttaparthi. He also runs a university level institution called "Sri Sathya Sai Institute of Higher Learning of which he was the Chancellor. He established a highly sophisticated super speciality hospital called the "Sri Sathya Sai Institute of Higher Medicine" at Prasanthi Nilayam in 1991, in which the most complicated treatment and operations of heart, brain and other vital organs of the body are done totally free of cost to all people poor and rich alike. A similar Super Speciality Hospital was started by him at Whitefield, Bangalore, in November 2000. The Baba has launched a number of movements and projects like EHV (Education in Human Values), Village Adoption

Programme, *Narayan Seva* (Feeding the poor people), popularization of *Bhajans* and *Nagarsankirtan* (Community singing while walking in the locality), establishment of a unique spiritual museum called the *"Sri Sathya Sai Sanatan Sanskrit Eternal Heritage Museum"* at Prasanthi Nilayam. He was always trying for the upliftment of moral and spiritual levels of mankind through his ever-flowing discourses which emphasize the five most essential values— *Sathya* (Truth), *Dharma* (Righteousness), *Shanti* (Peace), *Prema* (Love) and *Ahimsa* (Non-violence). He was the Master of the Universe, the great "Cosmic Emperor", the most unique Incarnation of God that mankind has ever seen.

He had declared that the whole universe was in his palm:

I was Rama, I was Krishna; it was I who had sent Christ to the world; I am the Incarnation of Lord Shiva and Shakti. Actually, I am *Sarvadevtaswaroopam* (All Gods and Goddess rolled into this form of mine)."

His whole life span as an *Avatar of Kali yuga* is dedicated to the noble mission of awakening spirituality in mankind and for that he taught that according to the great ideals of all should lead their lives according to the great ideals of truth, righteousness, peace, love and non-violence.

In the thousands of years old history of human civilization, such a matchless great incarnation of Gods has not taken place as the incarnation of Sri Sathya Sai Baba. Baba had rightly declared:

"No *Avatar* has done this before—going among the masses, guiding them, consoling them, uplifting them, direction them along the path of *Sathya, Dharma, Shanti and Prema.*"

"I rescue all those who worship and adore me. I will never give up those who attach themselves to me."

Sri Sathya Sai Baba assured the mankind that whatever may happen, he would save the good souls and his devotees throughout the world from all calamities. He stressed that they must follow his teachings, serve others and work for the welfare of those who are poor and distressed and try to improve their present lives, so that their future may also improve.

Sai Baba was the real form of Saraswati (Goddess of Learning), Lakshmi (Goddess of Prosperity) and Durga (Goddess of Destruction and Protection). He gave his most learned discourses in a very simple and enchanting language. He related stories from all religions and lives of great prophets and righteous people. he authored over a dozen books on the essence of spirituality. Although he received formal schooling only upto class VIII, yet he was very learned and a mine of knowledge and virtues. He sang devotional songs in his unique melodious and forceful voice which has been enchanted millions of devotees and casting an indescribable spiritual spell on them instantly. He recognized the importance of modern science and technology and prescribes that a judicious blending of modern science and traditional spirituality should be used for ensuring the welfare and progress of mankind. For fulfilling the purposes of his avataric role, he used all the techniques and methods at his command—miracles, *upadesh* (teaching), social service, chanting God's names, appearing in his devotees dreams and giving messages of guidance to people in many ways.

He was seen present at two places at the same time. He left behind some concrete evidence of his visit to devotees homes. Countless people throughout the world chant his name in worship. They very firmly believe that he is Shiva, Shakti, Vishnu, Brahma, Allah, Vaheguru, Zoroaster or whatever form of God any section of human beings venerate. He led mankind towards the Golden age—the *Satyuga* (Age of Truth). Sri Sathya Sai Baba left his mortal Coil on 24th April, 2011 at 7.30 A.M.

A number of ancient scriptures and religious books—*Markendeya Puran, Agasthyandi, Sukranadi, Sukanadi, Bhrigu Samhita, Jaimani, Mahabharatha, Bible, Mehdi Moud, Bihar-ul-Anwar* (of the Shia Muslims), indirectly or directly, had prophesied the coming of this great miraculous incarnation of Sri Sathya Sai Baba. Many more ancient palm leafy nadis have in receny years been collected and published by his famous devote Vasantha Sai of Tamil Nadu who stresses that Baba has not really departed from the world in April 2011, but he is still very much there with us all in his spirit form loking asfter the welare of all these who remember him and following his five teachings of univrersal values and and do selless sevice to, and he may reappear any time, and definitely he will reincarnate as the third Sai Baba—who would be known as Prema Sai Baba in the laster half of the present 21st century itself and many of us who are young will surely be privileged to see him, serve him and blessed by him in their present birth.

Sri Sathya Sai Baba was indeed a unique superman in this world whose mission to uplift humanity—morally, spiritually and materially will ever be remembered in this world.

21

The World with Sai

Early childhood and youth

1936   10 year old Puttaparthi boy Sathya mobilized young village boys to form the Pandhari Bhajan group. They sang and danced to inspiring songs of God's glory composed by Sathya.

1938   12 year old Sathya wrote and directed the play, *"Cheppinattu Chesthara"*, that instructed the village folk to do as they say by harmonizing their thoughts, words and deeds.

1940   20th October Avatar Declaration Day: 14 year old Sathyanarayana Raju revealed his divine identity and life's mission. He taught his first bhajan, *Manasa Bhajare Guru Charanam*.

1946   Baba visited Ooty, Hyderabad and Tirupathi, drawing thousands to his unique personality and riveting message.
        Muslims from neighbouring villages started revering Baba. He assured them full freedom to follow their faith to receive his grace.

1947   25th October: Baba delivered the first-ever public speech in Karur, near Trichy in Tamil Nadu, starting the tradition of his nectarine discourses which he used to give to the Tamalians especially on festive occasions.

Baba at 22 strengthens his mission

1948   The first devotee from Argentina Adelina Del Carril de Guiraldes visited Baba, marking the sowing of the Sai movement seeds in Latin America.
        Foundation laid for Prashanti Nilayam—the Abode of Highest Peace that would in future become the spiritual capital of the world.

1950   On Baba's 25th birthday, 23rd November 1950, Prashanti Nilayam Mandir was inaugurated.

1957	Baba presided over the 9th All India Divine Life Convention in Venkatagiri, a landmark event aimed at reviving the glory of Indian culture and spirituality a decade after the end of British colonialism. Swami Satchidananda was the Organizing Secretary.
1958	From his 32nd year, Baba began to guide humanity with a clear message through the medium of regular pubic discourses. In the same year, the Ashram's monthly magazine *Sanathana Sarathi* was started to spread Baba's message of loving service across the country and overseas. Baba wrote five series of articles under the titles *Prema Vahini, Dharma Vahini, Dhyana Vahini, Prashanti Vahini and Sandeha Nivarini*, in simple spoken Telugu. Sanathana Sarathi continues to be published monthly in English, Telugu, Tamil, Malayalam, Kannada, Marathi, Gujarati, Bengali, Hindi, Assamese, Sindhi and Nepali.
1960	The first volume of Baba's biography *'Sathyam Shivam Sundaram'* by historian Professor Kasturi was published, offering a well-researched and comprehensive account of Baba's life.
1961	*Veda Purusha Jnana Saptah Yagna* was inaugurated during Dashera. Experts discoursed on the university of the Sanathana Dharma as a harmonious way of life.

Baba at 36 Reveals a World Plan

1962	The first Panamanian visited Baba and was conquered by his love instantly. He carried the Sai message back to Panama and soon the Sai Centre was established there.
1963	Ramchand Chugani from Japan visited Prashanti Nilayam for the first time.
1964	Australian Howard Murphet met Baba in Madras intrigued, fascinated and curious, he investigated and studied the Master, his miracles and message. In 1971, Murphet published Sai Baba—Man of Miracles, a book that introduced millions to Sai.
1965	American Dr. John Hislop was drawn to Baba. He would later play a pivotal role in taking Sai message to the USA and setting up the American Sai organization.
1966	Opal MaCrae, a famous writer and social worker from USA, came to Prasanthi Nilayam and presided over the Hospital Day celebrations. Russian-born American citizen living in Mexico, Indra Devi was directed to Baba by a clairvoyant and later by

the Murphets. A renowned yoga teacher, Indra Devi lectured extensively across America, introducing her students to Baba and his message. Same year, Norwegian Alf Tideman Johanessan met Baba in Bombay after being guided through Shirdi Sai. His experiences led many more seekers from around the globe to Sai.

1967   20th-21st April. The All India conference of office bearers of all the organizations bearing Baba's name was held at Madras, in his presence. Also present were delegates from Hong Kong, China, Japan, East Africa, Sri Lanka and Norway. The Sai movement was acquiring an international profile.

Baba at 42 Brings the World to Bharat

1968   12th May: Baba inaugurated Dharmakshetra, the Sai hub in Bombay. The event coincided with the First World Conference. Devotees from Ceylon, Singapore, Manila, Kuwait, Dubai, Casablanca, Mombasa, Nairobi, Kampala, Arusha and Malta, Hong Kong, Fiji, Tehran, Tokyo, West Indies, Peru, Brazil and the Pacific and Atlantic coasts of America attended.

At the same conference, Charles Penn, an American pilot, had his first-ever physical darshan of Baba. Prior to this, Charles had had the fortune of connecting with Sai in meditation, thus creating a bond, even without any physical contact.

30th June: That was Baba went to East Africa, and that was his only foreign visit. Bob Raymer of Los Angeles was part of the entourage. Upon return, Raymer brought about a wave of Sai information to California.

November   Richard Bock, Founder President of Pacific Jazz & World Pacific Records and his wife, Janet came to Baba after a brief introduction about him from sitar maestro Pundit Ravi Shankar and yoga teacher Indra Devi. Richard recorded Swami's talk and *bhajans* that lasted for over 45 minutes and this tape became the first long-playing record of his *bhajans* to be released in India and the West. The Bocks were to record several films on Baba that became a valuable resource for introducing millions more in English speaking countries to the glory and message of Sai.

1969   Miss Ravaneau became the first person to visit Sai from Honduras. She returned home to start a Sai organization

Age of Sai Literature Dawns

1970   Age of Sai literature dawns
              This decade marked the beginning of Sai Literature. Books on
              spirituality by Baba and others about his life, miracle and message
              began to pour in.
1971   Frederick Muller, London published Howard Murphet's Sai Baba:
              The Man of Miracles. Murphet was to write three more books on
              Baba later on. Inspired by 'Sai Baba: The Man of Miracles', Arnold
              Schulman, an American playwright screen-writer, producer,
              story-writer, and novelist wrote the book 'Baba', which was
              published in New York.
              Sai Centers were started in parts of USA, including Elsie Cowan's
              Sathya Sai Book Centre in Tustin, California.
1972   Sai awareness in Hong Kong started by a devotee named Shastri.
              The movement had its simple beginnings in the office of
              Dorothy Plant where people would like to play *bhajans* on a tape
              recorder, they also started there Sai consciousness that was gaining
              momentum in Latin America.
May: Baba visited Gujarat, and at the same time, a local newspaper,
              'Nava Kaal' was running a series of articles on Sai's Miracles. The
              editor Sri P.K. Sawant enquired from Baba, about his miracles
              that raised controversies, and published Sai's answers in the paper.
              Baba's answers silenced the critics and satisfied the skeptics.
October: Hollywood Sai Centre was inaugurated owing to the tireless efforts
              of Indra Devi—'The First Lady of Yoga in America' and her
              associates who had brought Sai Baba's name to America.
              Hilda Charlton of New York moved to India to experience Bhagwan
              Baba. She had many pupils, and through her letters to them about
              Baba, she inspired many to take the path of self-realization.
              Phyllis Krystal, learnt about Sai Baba. In decades to come, she
              was to write several books that have guided, inspired and healed
              thousands of Westerners with the balm of Sai love and teachings.
              After visiting Prashanti Nilayam, B.R. Sachdev of Thailand
              celebrated Baba's birthday in his house in Thailand. This attracted
              a number of people including Mr. And Mrs. Sanger, who soon
              started *bhajans* in their house also.
1973   The first Mexicans, Dr. Luis Muniz and his wife Gail traveled
              to Puttaparthi and were blessed with an interview. Upon return,

they started a Sai Centre in Mexico and 37 years later the centre is the hub of the noblest social outreach programs, reaching to the unprivileged, educating thousands in character education and bringing about a transformation in teens through loving guidance.

1974   The Sai Organization of America was started with John Hislop as its President. This organization soon emerged as the engine of the Sai movement outside of India.

The first Bolivian Ramiro Sotello Murillo visited Baba as did Arlette Meyer who had been translating books on Bhagawan into Spanish. The latter returned to start a Sai Centre in Venezuela.

1975   Sai movement started in Kobe, Japan *Bhajan*-singing and *seva* *(service)* were the major activities.

Hiru Bharwani was the first Indonesian to visit Puttaparthi. The Indonesian Sai movement was thus born.

Sai movement was born in Switzerland when a visionary Dr. Ali Hussein, had his first *darshan* of Bhagawan Baba. The dedicated Hussein family pioneered the Sai work in Europe.

Dr. Samuel H Sandweiss's first book '*Holy Man and Psychiatrist*' was published. It chronicled the experiences, observations and conclusions of the Americans Psychiatrist as he came to investigate Baba's powers against the touchstone of Western Psychiatry and Science. Dr. Sandweiss's description of his spiritual awakening as he came closer to Sai, as well as his ability to relate it with devotion and humor, accounted for the books worldwide success.

After returning from the second world conference in Prashanthi Nilayam, Beuno Wesner set up a small Sai Centre in Nuremberg, Germany and the number multiplied in the coming years.

The first glimpse of Sai Movement started in New South Wales, Australia as Lyn Penrose came into contact with the Murphets and learnt about Baba.

1976   Howard Murphert's second book *Sai Baba: Avatar, A New Journey into Power and Glory,* was published. This book contains Murphet's further spiritual adventures plus an exceptional array of uplifting Sai stories and miracles.

1977   Shanthi Nilayam was inaugurated in Hong Kong leading to greater Sai spiritual activities.

1978   John Hislop's first book '*Conversations with Bhagawan Sri Sathya Sai Baba*' was published in California. For many, this has been an introductory book to Bhagawan Baba.

Enrique Garrido, became the first Chilean to know about Bhagawan through a hermit called Pablo. The hermit said to him, "Sai Baba is the only one in this age capable of liberating anyone."

1979   A couple from Peru, Mr. and Mrs. Bravo Figueroa traveled to India to ask Bhagawan permission to set up a Sai Centre in Peru.

The first Sai Centre was started in Guatemala by a couple named Augusto and Balbina Ansueto.

As a result of Indra Devi's persistent efforts to create awareness about Sai at all her Yoga retreats in various countries, a Sai Centre blossomed in El Salvador.

1980   A residence in Strathfield, Australia was converted into a Sai centre and was officially inaugurated in Guru Purnima that year.

The first Sai Centre was formed in Argentina. Devotees Ananda Giri and Monica Zokotoscky had brought the word about Baba to Argentina. The first Sai Centres were opened this year in Beunos Aries and then Cordoba.

First Sai Centre in Chile began adding momentum to the Sai movemnt in Latin America. A group of devotees got together to sing *bhajans* in Taipei, Taiwan and soon started feeding the poor as well.

1981   Loraine Burrows started SSSEHV in Thailand.

American pilot Charles Penn published his first book on Bhagawan, *'My Beloved'*.

The New South Wales Sai Centre of Australia established by Heidi Gulyas became affiliated with the World Council of Sai Organizations.

Costa Rican Minister of Finance Rigoberto Martinez and his wife came to Baba. On return they started study circles and bhajans in Costa Rica inspiring friends Mireya Mendez and Guilermo Hidalgo to join their efforts to spread Sai mission in Costa Rica.

1982   Three important books on Sai glory and message were published: N. Kasturi's autobiography *'Loving God'*, Phyllis Krystal's *'Cutting the Ties that Bind'* and Howard Murphet's *'Sai Baba, Invitation to Glory'*.

Spreading Sai Awareness Through The 1980's

1983   *Bhajans* started in Dhammasthan in Chulalongkorn University, Bangkok.

The formal Sathya Sai Organization in Australia was established when Mr. Indulal Shah, Chairman of the Sathya Sai World Council, visited Australia in April 1983.

The Sri Sathya Sai Books and publication Trust was established on 19th June. Aimed at fostering human values through Baba's noble teachings via various publications spread over different media, SSSBPT has been relentlessly on the task over the past quarter century, serving as a lifeline between Prashanti Nilayam and the world. (*www.sssbpt.org*)

1984   A handful of devotees from Taiwan returned home to further strengthen the Taiwanese Sai movement after Baba granted them a group audience in Prashanti Nilayam.

1985   The Sathya Sai Foundation of Bangkok was registered during the 60th year of Sai Advent. Four important Sai books were also published: Charles Penn's *'Sai Ram'*, John Hislop's *'My Baba and I'*, Samuel Sandweiss' *'Spirit and Mind'* and Phyllis Krystal's *'Sai Baba: The Ultimate Experience'*.

1986   Charles Penn's final book *'Finding God'*, was published. Here, he relates his life-long search for God and his road to Sathya Sai Baba.

1987   Sathya Sai Organization was formed in Puerto Rico.

1988   After the Sai Centre had firmly established in Uruguay, the devotees unified to take up more service activities at old age homes, helping poor and impoverished Children of the streets, started regular food and clothing drives.

1990   Sai Foundation of El Salvador swung into full service mode, rebuilding a Catholic church and providing disaster relief in the aftermath of an earthquake. The movement became even more service driven.

1991   The first major European Service project was organized and was continued until 1995. Led by the Austrian Sathya Sai Organization, its main purpose was to help alleviate the suffering of the people in former Yugoslavia, an area struck by civil war.

The first public conference was held in the Sai Centre of Dominican Republic.

1992   The first *Sri Sathya Sai School* was established in a very poor community in Vila Isabel, in Rio de Janeirc Brazil. It has served as an inspiration and a model for the founding other Sai Schools in the country, such as the Sai Schools in Recife, Goiania, Ribeirao Preto and Minas Gerais.

1995	9th July Inauguration of Sai Kulwant Hall Prashanti Nilayam to accommodate up to 20,000 devotees at a time for Baba's daily *darshans*.
1997	*A Compendium of the Teachings of Sathya Sai Baba*—Compiled by Charlene Leslie-Chaden: An exhaustive guide to Baba's teaching on all possible topics was published.
	July: Thousands of youth from hundreds of countries attended the I world Youth Conference at Prashanti Nilayam.
1999	Sri Sathya Sai International Centre at New Delhi inaugurated. (*www.saidelhi.org*)
2001	Inauguration of the ashram's new Books and Publications Division in Prashanthi NIlayam. (*www.sssbpt.org*)
2001	23rd November Radio Sai Global Harmony was launched from Prashanti Nilayam. Renowned scientist Padmashree Dr. G. Venkataraman leads this project taking Baba's message of love and harmony to the world via internet, World Space radio, and ezine Heart-to-Heart. (*www.radiosai.org*)
2003	Congregational prayers began in China and community service also started.
2005	November SSS 8th World Conference on the theme 'Unity, Purity, Divinity' held in Prashanti Nilayam.
2006	November The Sri Sathya Sai World Foundation started.
2007	Over 6000 youth from 85 countries attend Sai World Youth Conference on the theme 'Ideal Sai Youth—Messengers of Sai Love' in Prashanti Nilayam.
2008	Sri Sathya Sai Wrold Education Conference on the theme 'Sathya Sai Education in Human Values' was held in Prahanti Nilayam.
2009	Sri Sathya Sai International Centre for Medical Service established with its main hub in Los Angeles, USA.
2010	November Sai Sathya Sai 9th World Conference held in Prashasnti Nilayam.

Courtesy: *The Times of India* (New Delhi), 2010)

22

Who is Sri Sathya Sai Baba?
Testimony of the Modern Day Masters

—R.D. Awle

One of the greatest saints of this century was a woman named Ananda translates as 'Bliss-permeated Mother'. There's a photo of her, standing Yogananda, in *'Autobiography of a Yogi'*. She was so pure and filled with widely considered to be a Divine Incarnation herself: there seemed to be God, and her words were truth itself. According to one of her closest devotees she had often been asked, "Who is this Sathya Sai Baba? For many years she never gave an answer. In the last year of her life, this question came up again, and this time she gave the following response:" This body will speak on to this question only once; don't ask again. Sathya Sai Baba is the most powerful incanation ever to come to the Earth. And there won't be another at His level for another for sixty centuries.'

That amazing testimony was recently strengthened for me recently when I went to one of Anandmoyi' Ma's ashram in the Himalayas. When I shared the preceding quote with a Swami there, he said that Andamoyi Ma had then added, "It's no wonder you keep hearing about Sai Baba. He is the *Avatar* of this *yuga* (age)!"

Other Saints have given similar testimony. Shortly before he left his physical body, Paramahansa Yogananda wasa approachd by oner of his close American disciples, a women. "Master", she said, "I know you are leaving your body. You must take me with you. You are my God!"

"Nonsense." replied Yogananda, "God is God. I am your Guru."

"But Master, if you leave without me, I will commit suicide!"

"Enough of the foolishness! God himself is now incarnate on Earth, in Sai Baba in South India. When I leave you are going to live with him." (His prediction proved correct after Yogananda's death, that devotee spent the rest of her life at Sai Baba's ashram.

Mata Amritanandamayi (also known as Ammachi), herself considered to divine mother, was once asked, "Who is Sai Baba?" She replied, "*Avata*r. Perfect from birth."

On the day after Sai Baba's birth (November 23, 1926), Sri Aurobindo, another saint of 20th century, broke a long period of silence to announce,

"Twenty-fourth November the descent of Krishna into the physical. A power infallible shall lead the hearts kindle the Immortal's Fire, even the multitude shall hear the voice at this point that his announcement of Krishna's physical re-embodiment birth of Sathya Sai Baba.

Mother Krishnabai, the self-realized disciple of Swami Ramdas told her devotees, "Sai Baba is an Avatar, a full incarnation of Krishna and Shiva together in one form!"

Swami Satchidananda, the enlightened sage who currently runs an *ashram* in Kerala was I asked about the allegations against Sai Baba. He replied, "Forget that He is God!"

Karunamayi (also known as Vijayeshwari Devi, considered by many to be the Goddess Saraswati recently told one of her close devotees, "Sai Baba and I (herself) are both watching over you." Apparently she also knows who Sai Baba is.

Yogi Ramsuratkumar made it clear on numerous occasions that Sai Baba Is an incarnation of God.

Shiva Balayogi, another of the great Gurus of the last century, was once asked about Si Baba. He replied, "Sathya Sai Baba is an *Avatar*."

Master El Moya and Master Kuthumi, two of the great Ascended Masters the Theosophical Movement also declared Sai Baba to be an *Avatar*, Howard Murphet, in his book *"The Light Will Set You Free"* the Master Sai Baba is carrying the Divine consciousness in the world today."

Maitreya, the mysterious Master who has been miraculously appearing at various places around the globe throughout the last two decades, has said throiugh his spokesman Benjamin Crème) that Maitreya is the planetary *Avatar* while Sai Baba is the Universal Avatar.

23

Sri Sathya Sai Baba: The Cosmic Ruler

—S.P. Ruhela

"In the centre of the earth is a place called Puttaparthi,
The embodiment of the Atma made its advent.
While mankind was seeking knowledge of science
A University came into existence here.
People of all nations gathered here to experience
peace and joy,
Millions of virtuous aspirants and adepts have filled this place.
The Sai Lord has come to teach the world love and the truth
of all religions,
Sathya Sai has incarnated as embodied Love to shower joy on all."

—Sri Sathya Sai Baba

Bhagwan Sri Sathya Sai Baba of Puttaparthi (Prasanthi Nilayam) in Andhra Pradesh attract devotees attracted eager devotees and visitors from all parts of the world as he had claimed to be incarnation of God in many of his discourses and songs, and his devotees entirely believe in him. On the other hand, many critics, spiritual seekers and devotees of Sri Shirdi Sai Baba whose incarnation he was have their doubts on his claims. Hundreds of books have been written on him by now. Every author of a book on him thinks that he has understood the reality of Sri Sathya Sai Baba, but is it a fact? For Sri Sathya Sai Baba has at many times said that no one can understand his reality as a divine personality, whatever methods one may employ to do so.

I have been an humble devotee of Sri Sathya Sai Baba since I had his first *darshan* in April, 1973. During the last 40 years, I have visited his holy place Prasanthi Nilayam at least 50 times—and have had the rare opportunity to get private interview with him four times. I have read almost all significant books written by him and written on him in English and Hindi, researched on him extensively and have written many books on him. I have had a number of very happy and as also some unpleasant experiences in his ashram.

170

In this chapter I have tried to present an objective analysis of Baba's divine mystery in a proper methodological perspective, based on my study, observations and understanding to the best of my comprehension skills. Future scholars and researchers may further improve upon and perfect intellectual profile of this great divine personality whom most people believe to be God or *Branmand Nayak* (Cosmic Emperor).

II. Sri Sathya Sai on his Own Reality

A close perusal of Baba's life history reveals that when he was a boy of 14 in 1940 he first revealed that he was Sri Shirdi Sai Baba's incarnation. Then in the 1960s he declared that he was '*Sarva-devta-swaropam*' (All Gods and Goddesses rolled into One. Then he further declared specifically that he was the combined incarnation of Shiva and Shakti—the second Sai in the Sai Trinity. There-after he claimed that he is the same Lord Vishnu who had saved Prahlad, Dhruva, Kuchela and Gajraj (the legendary Elephant).

"He alone is a real man whose thoughts, words and deeds are in perfect harmony.

How can he be a genuine man when his mind is divorced from speech and deed,

And all the three are not in harmony?

When to save Prahlada, the Supreme Person came,

The attributes and qualities which were assumed,

When to save the elephant, the Lotus eyed (Vishnu) came;

The attributes and qualities which were assumed

When to save the boy Dhruva, he came from Heaven;

Now, with all the attributes, all the qualities has come

He whom the gods adore, the refuge of the rejected,

The Lord of all the worlds, the Lord of infinite glory,

As all existence, as all knowledge and all bliss in one form embodied,

As Puttaparthi Sathya Sai, the overlord of all that is."

—Sri Sathya Sai Baba

In his discourses he had broadly hinted that he is the God, the Cosmic Ruler—*Brahmand Nayak* or *Sironayak*. In one of his songs he sang thus, "*Sathya Sa bina Bhagwan nahin*" (There is no God other than Sri Sathya Sai). He spoke of his divine Kingdom thus:

"You are all in the Kingdom of Sai

You are all in Sai's home,

You are all in Sai's light,
I will bless you, I will bless you this holy night,
That is your right."

(Baba's discourse on Christmas, Dec. 25, 1989)

III. The Various Approaches to the Study of Sri Sathya Sai's Reality

As a social scientist I think, these may be the possible approaches or perspectives to study the reality of his divine personality:

(1) Religious Approach: All devotees have or are expected to have full faith, blind faith in their Guru, Prophet or deity. Accordingly, a staunch Sai devotee will surely have full faith in Baba's declarations about his supreme divine stature. This approach does not allow the devotee to reason out things, but just to believe in them.

(2) Philosophical Approach: Those following this approach use logic and other philosophical concepts and do comparative analysis *vis-à-vis* Sri Sathya Sai phenomenon.

(3) Comparative Approach: By comparing Baba with other saints, Godmen or Prophets, one will try to determine his place among them objectively.

(4) Sociological Approach: This requires empirical study of the social reality—his charismatic personality, his mission, his *ashram* set up and functioning, his relations with his family members, functionaries, devotees, politicians, etc., and his social impact rituals, practices, celebrations etc. etc., all of which constitute his *Maya* or outer manifestation.

While this approach should help an objective researcher to a great extent to unravel his mystery, it can not, I feel, do so fully, for a mystic phenomenon can not be fully understood by probing the externals only.

What should then be the correct approach? Instead of any one approach only, a judicious mixture of all these approaches should help us.

In one of his very important discourses in 1989 Sri Sathya Sai Baba had thrown valuable light on this methodological dilemma and suggested the proper approach to study his divinity.

According to him:

". . . .There are three types of proofs (or approaches) for arriving at the truth. One is Direct Perception (*Pratyaksh Pramana*). Today every man relies on this kind of proof. For everything he seeks evidence of direct perception or experience. He is not prepared to accept anything which is not amenable to the proof of direct perception. This is really a sign of ignorance. Direct perception is associated with many afflictions. For instance, when the eye is free from any disease it recognizes the different colours in their true forms. This is the basis of authority of direct perception. What happens when the eye is afflicted by jaundice? Everything appears yellowish. No other colour can be perceived. How then can we trust the evidence of the eyes? All evidences based on the perception of the sense organs is vitiated by this effect. When the sense organs themselves are subject to change, how can they be regarded as infallible indicators of absolute truth? Senses which are liable to change cannot be the means to arrive at the unchanging reality.

The second type of proof is based on Inference (*Anumanam*). You infer the presence of fire on a hill when you see smoke going up from it. But you cannot be sure whether it is smoke going up from a fire or a cloud of water vapour. Without seeing the fire, to infer its existence from smoke is likely to be wrong. Conclusions based on inference can not be the stamp of certainty.

The third type is *Shabda Pramana*, the authority of the spoken word. This type of proof is related to what a person, who has had a direct experience of something, says about it. The authority of the Veda is based on this concept. It has to be accepted as such.

'*Shabda Pramana*' (proof based on spoken word) is of two kinds: '*Vedic Pramana*' and '*Loukik Pramana*'.

'*Loukik Pramana*' is not concerned with spiritual truth. It cannot explain God. Only '*Vedic Pramana*' (Vedic Testimony) seeks to describe God. The *Brahmand Nayak* declares: '*Sastra yonivatvaah*'—the Divinity can be known only on the authority of the scriptures. What is the meaning of the *Sastra* (Scripture)? Sastra is that which conveys to the ear what is not audible otherwise. It brings back to the memory what has been forgotten."

This logical analysis of the approaches done by Baba is crystal clear and very helpful to us. It shows that the prevailing approach of the social and physical scientists—that of relying on empirical evidence alone—is infact not the correct or perfect one to study divinity. Evidently, few among the social scientists and physical scientists who have ventured to study Sri Sathya Sai Baba have tried to study Baba's divinity using this *Vedic Pramana* approach.

IV. The Vedic *Pramanana* (Proof) about God

1. In the *Rig Veda*, the Supreme God has been described as the Cosmic Emperor in these important verses:

*"The God is definitely pure, omnipotent; he purifies all; he has golden voice; he is worthy of Darshan. Such God bestows great prosperity on his devotees by removing their three kinds of afflictions—spiritual, physical and mental."

(*Rig Veda*, M. 7.S.7:7)

"O God endowed with prosperity, you as *Senapati* (Commander-in-Chief), protect us from all sides and rule over us as you subject; so your glory and strength are great. O God, kindly bless us that living in your kingdom and following your orders we may be advancing in the direction of progress."

(Rig Veda, M.8.S.6:26)

"O devotees, you should worship the Supreme God who is *Vishwanarayana* (Leader of the Universe), omnipresent in the entire cosmos, whose great powers and great fame are the spiritual happiness of human beings and whom sky, earth and all men and women living here praise.

In several other verses of the Rig Veda, these qualities of the Supreme God— the Cosmic Emperor—have been mentioned: he protects; he removes misery; he gives wealth, motherly love, wisdom, happiness, peace; he teaches *Brahma Vidya* (Spiritual Knowledge); he shows correct path to the ignorant ones; he gives us result of our actions; he removes the darkness of *Agyan* (ignorance); he removes fear; worshipping him gives *eswarya* (prosperity) to the learned ones; he is omnipresent, omnipotent and omniscient; he is the Ruler of the Cosmos.

2. In *Bhagavad Gita*, Lord Krishna declared that God incarnates from age to age to protect the virtuous and destroy the evil doers. When God incarnates as a *Purna Avatar* like Lord Krishna, he has 16 attributes (*kalas* or phases)—five he shares with human beings and other animals; the five doors of perception i.e., sight, hearing, smell, taste and touch. Another four he shares with human beings—mind, heart, intelligence and *turyavastha* (transcendence or intuitive experience).

Seven characteristics exclusively of his as *Purnavatar* (Full incarnation of God) are:

(i) Power to give grace or reward for effort which fails to be regarded though it has come from the deserving;

(ii) Power to give '*anugraha*' (Special Grace) whether the receiver merits it or not;

(iii) Power to create a new way of life in society, new state of consciousness in individuals or new objects;

(iv) Power to destroy what is evil;

(v) Power to assume a form which, whenever it is recalled mentally or in the presence of a photograph, results in the immediate spiritual presence, sometime even physical of the *Avatar* himself, affording a solution to the problem that the beholder has in mind;

(vi) The assumption of a name that has a similar potency.

3. Several scriptures of other religions like Christianity, Islam, Sikhism and others have also identified the attributes of the God Almighty who comes as godman, incarnation, master, *sadguru, akal purush* or the superman. The well known medieval Indian saints like Kabir, Nanak, Namdev, Tulsi, Surdas and modern saints like Rama Krishna Paramhansa, Aurobindo, Ramana, Yogananda, Bhaktivedanta and several others have given valuable insights into the attributes of God as *Brahman Nayak* (The Cosmic Emperor).

4. In a masterpiece work '*Godman—Finding Spiritual Master*'* Sant Kirpal Singh, a wellknown spiritual master, has enumerated the following twelve criteria or attributes of a *Sadguru (Divine Master) or Avatar*:

(i) In his presence, the mind grows docile and feels anchored. How can we get the company of such a one by looking at whom the ever-restless mind gets lost, and life impulses warm upon the soul? The beloved Master makes a true friend, and bestows God intoxication.

He sheds around him rays of purity, saturated with dignified humility, which exert a powerful influence upon the *jives* (living beings). His words are charged with spirituality and drag the soul into the beyond and administer a kind of living intoxicating exhilaration. If he were to disclose his secrets, my very soul would swiftly soar Godward. Steady gaze at his forehead and eyes reveals peculiar light which gives a pull to the soul and momentarily gathers up the all pervading sensory currents, and one feels his being in higher consciousness.

(ii) He is a Prince of Peace, and is above the pairs of opposites. His association releases in us current of bliss and benediction. He dispels all thoughts of antagonism and rivalry, and gives instead, equipoise to the soul, leading, gradually to the Godhead. In whose company one feels blessed, in the Master of Truth. He purifies the mind and grants salvation to the soul.

(iii) He is completely filled with the power of *ojas* (the fruit of chastity), and his forehead shines with Godly Light. One is irresistibly drawn by the magnetism of his charged words. From his eyes a peculiar light shines forth, which like an osprey paralyses the mind. He works like a leaven and quickens life in the desert of the mind.

With his lynx eyes, his gaze can penetrate deep into the feelings and emotions of a person; and he adjusts his instructions according to times and individual needs. The physical encasement (body) of a *jiva* or soul is for him just like a transparent glass jar; though he can easily detect what is thereon, he never exposes it to public view, and keeps his experience of each to himself. Whoever goes to him, whether a beetle or a wasp, gets sweet fragrance as from a flower. In the House of the Master, everything is in abundance, and each gets what he wishes for. Every person who contacts a Master Soul receives spiritual impressions which, in course of time, are bound to fructify. From the very moment an individual meets a Master, better times are assured to him.

(iv) A *Sant* or *Satguru* is verily the Son of God. He has genuine love alike for persons of all religions, nationalities and countries. He sees the light of God in all. His appeal is, therefore, universal to all mankind.

- "All are born of the same light, and as such there is no difference between man and man. O Nanak! People of all denominations flock into the fold of the Satguru. He was all-merciful and all-knowing. He treats all alike, and does the work of all who have faith in him."—Nanak

- He neither destroys the old church nor sets up another church of his own. He was master of Truth and does not care to what sect or creed a person may belong. All that matters is spiritual aspiration, for that alone befits a *jiva* for the Master's Path.

- "When one revels in *Shabd* or Word, he forget all about himself. For the intelligent there is but One Path, no matter be he a *Pundit* or a *Sheikh*."—Kabir

- He fearlessly talks of the Spiritual Path that lies within each one of us, in spite of our religious differences. One who is able to establish contact with such a master is in fact a veritable pilgrim on the path, and gets the greatest benefit from him. Maulana Rumi, therefore, savs:

"Should ye be anxious for a pilgrimage, ye must take for a guide and companion any experienced pilgrim, no matter whether he be a Hindu, a Turk, or an Arab. Care not how he may look but see only that he is competent and knows the Path.

We have, after all, not to establish any worldly relationship with the Master. All that we need from him is spiritual instruction and guidance, and if he can give us that, it should be considered enough."

(v) Master saints are the manifestation of Godhead. As heavenly truths dawn on them silently and subtlely, so do their instructions work quietly, and sink into the very depths of the jives without any word of mouth. A *Sheikh* (Master), like God, is embedded in the formless Beyond, and he imparts his teachings without uttering a single syllable. The instructions of the master are in a language that is speechless and can neither be imparted by word of mouth nor by word recorded.

- "Why do ye not understand my speech? Even because ye cannot hear my word."—John 8:43
- Tongue of thought is his only instrument. It is a matter of inner experience for the spirit.

Maulana Rumi says:

"Soul is of the same essence as that of God; it is God epitomized, and can express itself without any outer aid (like organs of speech). In the teaching of the Masters, physical senses are not of much avail. Everything is done automatically despite the senses.

One sees without eyes, hears without ears, walks without feet, acts without hands, and talks without tongue; for this is just like Death-in-Life.

O Nanak! It is then alone that one can know the Cosmic Will and meet the beloved."

This (human body) is the exact replica of *Brahmand* (universe). The same spirit is working on both the microcosm and the macrocosm. We cannot see, feel, and be one with the Cosmic Spirit unless we establish harmony and come in touch with the spirit within us.

Until the embodied spirit becomes disembodied and rises above the sensual plane, it can hardly hamonise itself with Universal Spirit.

Nevertheless, our quest for God or Universal Spirit is all the time on the physical plane. We try to discover God under the bowels of the earth, on the snow-capped mountains, in the waters of the sacred rivers, and on desert sands; in manmade temples and mosques. In churches and synagogues; hence we fail to find him.

If we know the inner path in the body, we can hope to experience and feel the influence of the great power within. But this inversion or conversion is not possible without the aid of an adept in *Para Vidya* (Science of the Soul), for he alone holds the key to the kingdom of God and his words act as an open sesame that fling open the secret door.

Just peep within as instructed by the Master, and thou shalt find within thyself a veritable temple of God.

(10) The teachings of Master souls are perfect, and their findings are as verifiable as in any other exact science.

This experience and realization is, however, quite different from book learning and intellectualism, nor is it a figment of an obsessed brain, as some think.

The saints always talk with conviction and authority, for their utterances come from the depths of their souls. Their knowledge is neither derived from books nor based on hearsay testimony. They directly give us first-hand experiences of their own, in pure, unalloyed and unadulterated form. Again, they never ask for blind faith and acceptance on authority. On the contrary, each aspirant is asked to personally verify the result for himself.

Truth is that which must be experienced at once, and not after ages, no matter how slight that experience may be in the first instance. The Masters see things through to their very roots, and then talk.

Nanak sees God right before him.

Sri Ramakrishna, being questioned by Naren (later known as Swami Vivekananda) about seeing God, replied, "Yes, my child! I have seen God as I see you."

In fact, all Master souls have actual experience of the Godhead and they revel in his light and life and in a way become conscious co-workers with him. Shamas-i-Tabrez says: Better by far it is to see God with one's own eyes and the hear the Voice of God with one's ears.

He never keeps his followers in delusion about the inefficacy of outer pursuits. His cardinal tenets centre around one thing: contact with, and devotion to Shabd alone. The manifestation of ceaseless music within is a gift of a Master Soul.

"O Nanak! Whoever contacts the perfect Master hears within himself the Divine Melody."

Satguru is every engrossed in *Naam* (repeating *the Lord's holy name*), and like a master pilot safely ferries bonafide aspirants across and leads them back to the kingdom of God lost within them.

"One dyed in the colour of Naam is Satguru and, in Kali Yuga, he acts as Captain of a ship."

He who confides and resides in him is carried across and finds truth manifested in him.

(11) A Master soul at times does uncommon things that may appear baneful to ordinary individuals. This he does to keep the worldly-minded away from him, as one would do in the case of flies so that they will not obstruct the way of true aspirants.

A *darvesh* (man of piety) needs no *darwan* (gateman);

Yes, he does need one, to keep the dogs of the world away.

An evil tongue or slanderer does work as a *darwan* (gate keeper) for *darveshes* (saints) so that the worldly-wise are kept out of the way.

In the biography of Bhai Bala it is on record that once Guru Nanak said:

"In *Kali Yuga* many Saints or manifestations of God will come down, for the good of suffering humanity."

Bhai Ajita questioned:

"Master, will you tell us how we would know a perfect Saint; what would be his expression and how shall we recognize him?"

The Master replied:

"Whenever a Saint appears, some leaders of society, religious bigots and caste-ridden individuals, talk ill of him. Rare indeed are those who go to him. The rank and file slander both the Master and his disciples. The people in general engage in outer pursuits, like reading scriptures, offering public prayers in churches, temples and mosques, and recitation of *mantras*, etc. They will not practice *Surat Shabd Yoga* by tuning with the primal Sound Current. When such conditions predominate, I will come time and again to revive the Path of the Masters and link people with *Anhad Bani*.

(12) With the advent of a saint, the refreshing showers of spirituality flood the dry and parched hearts *encrusted* with the dust of ages. Everyone who comes to him, whether a devotee or a sinner, derives benefits in his own way and gets solace from him. Many a robber, murderer and highwayman has had a complete transformation in his company. Like a master washerman, he cleans our souls through and through of all impurities, bodily, mental and causal; until they shine forth in primal glory and become luminous and living selves.

We find in a saint a living embodiment of selfless love and sacrifice. His appeal is universal and directed to the soul of man. The aspirants in thousands congregate around him and are benefited by his teachings.

(13) A saint is truly a son of God and shares with him all his powers. His long and strong arm embraces the universe, and his helping hands extend to all parts of the world. Distance has no limitation for him. His saving grace miraculously works wonders in strange and unpredictable ways, and people escape unscathed from many a tense and hopeless situation, even from the jaws of death.

Master of earth and the heavens, he guides the spirits in their homeward journey through spiritual regions, and his lustrous form ever keeps company with the pilgrim soul as it transcends the body.

Maulana Rumi says: "The hand of a master Soul is in no way shorter than that of God. It is in fact the Hand of God himself. Yes, it stretches across seven skies and inspires spirits with hope and confidence. These are just a few of the innumerable signs that indicate a saint."

"An *aulia* (superman) has in him wonderful powers and possibilities, which a man of piety alone can see and experience."

The glory and greatness of a Godman becomes more and more manifest to a spirit as it crosses over bodily and mental limitations and proceeds onward in his company. The lustrous form of the Master in ever with him now wherever he may be, guiding his footsteps both within and without, answering all his questions, the sole arbitrator of this destiny—his very Saviour. It is at this stage that a person gets firmly established in him sand cries out, The Master is ever with me, for now he realizes the truth of the Master's sayings:

Everyman, I will go with thee and be thy guide:

"In thy greatest need to be by thy side."

The world of full of people who profess to be Masters and teachers of mankind. But all those who hanker after pelf and power, name and fame, cannot possibly play the role and perform this arduous duty, and one must try to avoid such false prophets, who are no less than treacherous revening wolves in the garb of lambs.

"It never pays to test and try a genuine Master. His very presence will of his own accord magnetize the mind."

V. Attributes of an Ideal Ruler

The desirable qualities, powers, duties and policies of an ideal Ruler or Emperor were described in ancient scriptures like *Manu Smriti* by Sage Manu, *Ramayana* by Sage Valmiki and Tulsidas, *Mahabharata* by Veda Vyas and *Arthshastra* by Chanakya, etc.

In *Manusmriti*, Manu mentioned that the emperor should be powerful, religious, wise and expert in *niti* (policies). In *Ramayana*, there is a reference that Rama, when in exile, was approached by his younger brother Bharata. He advised Bharata how he should rule Ayodhya in his absence. Sri Sathya Sai Baba devoted his one full discourse on this very theme on the Ram Navami Day on 9 April, 1995.

According to him, Rama advised how Bharata's government should be carried out, "Have the ministers only persons of character and virtue. Give no place to selfish persons. Do not allow anyone given to vices like gambling and drinking to wield authority. Entertain only those who command the esteem of the people and who are respected and loved by the people. You must have daily conferences with them or with such ministers. Your talks should be in private and no outsider should know anything. Don't employ women as ministers. You must revere the parents, the preceptors and all elders. If any person misbehaves within your kingdom, do not punish him. Banish him. That will be punishment enough."

In *Shanti Parva* or *Bhishma Kanda*, the octogenarian Bhishma lying on the bed of arrows sermoned to the Pandavas as to what should be the qualities and role strategies of an emperor and how the kingdom should be administered by him. Similarly, the Prime Minister of Dhratarastra Vidur's book *'Vidur Niti'* described the desirable qualities and strategies of an ideal emperor. Kautilya's *Artha Shastra*, a well-known treatise on statecraft, Kautilya (Chanakya) described how a ruler should administer with the help of *dharma, niti,* cleverness, able ministers, secret services, strong armies and the overall policy of centralization in administration. A *Chakravarti Samrat* (A Great Emperor) should not only be strong and able, he should rule his subjects with religiousity, compassion, justice and firmness and forever seek to expand the frontiers of his kingdom. Moral and spiritual values should guide all his actions as an emperor. Rules of the ancient times like Janaka Maharaj (father-in-law of Lord Rama), Yudhisthira (eldest son of the Pandavas), Lord Krishna, ruler of Dwaraka, Chandra Gupta Maurya and Ashoka have been the ideal emperors whose examples were worthy of emulation by other kings.

VI. Sri Sathya Sai as the Cosmic Ruler

It is in the context of these scriptural evidences about the criteria of incarnation and ideal emperor we venture to analyse the reality of Sri Sathya Sai Baba. He is God's incarnation and he is virtually the Emperor of Puttaparthi ('*Puttaparthi Samrat*'). Sai is the *Chakravarti Samrat* of Puttaparthi, his Sai kingdom established in the hearts of millions of people of all religions and races, is extended throughout the world. His name and fame as the unique Master of the Cosmos has spread all over the universe. He was known not only as an able administrator, but the greatest preceptor or Guru of mankind as well as the greatest judge of the conduct of his subjects.

The innumerable evidences gathered by Sai devotees and researchers of various disciplines, as reviewed in my book '*In Search of Sai Divine*', amply bear out that Sri Sathya Sai Baba meets all the above-mentioned criteria of God's incarnation and an ideal *Chakravarti Samrat* laid dawn in the Vedas and other ancient scriptures of the Sanathana Dharma and also those of the other world religions.

VII. Sri Sathya Sai as God

Sri Sathya Sai Baba has revealed that God is the supreme authority presiding over the three authorities responsible for creation (Brahma), protection (Vishnu) and dissolution (Shiva):

". . . The first aspect to be recognized is *Shristi* (creation of the cosmos). What is involved in it should be understood . . . . The principal authority responsible for the creation is known as *Brahma*. He is incharge of all that is related to creation. Next comes protection. What has been created has to be fostered and protected. The authority responsible for this is called Vishnu. After growth comes the stage of dissolution. There is an authority responsible for laying down the rules for dissolution and enforcing those regulations. This authority is called *Easwara* (Shiva) . . . There must be someone who presides over these three functionaries, like the Prime Minister in the Cabinet . . . There is a supreme authority presiding over these three. This supreme authority was called by the *Bhartiyas* (ancient Indians) as *Bhagavan* (God). Members of different faiths have given different names to this authority. The term that is most widely sued in this context today is God. Bhagavan refers to the one who governs all the three functions—creation, protection and dissolution.

In the word 'GOD' you have three letters: G, O, D. The letter G refer to 'Generation' (or creation). O refers to organization (that is, keeping creation going). D stands for destruction.

. . . God is permanent witness. He has no attributes. He has no specific form. He can assume any form. The attributeless Divine has attributes also.

. . . The divine cannot offer what is not there. He will not take away what is one's due. He lets the respective deities carry out their functions according to rules. Hence he is called the Embodiment of Dharma. The Lord will not interfere in the functions of the different deities. He lets Brahma, Vishnu and Eswara carry out their respective functions. As he remains a witness, he is described as the embodimnt of *Dharma* (Rightousnes) and Truth.

. . . The cosmos is governed by the three principal deities. I am letting you into a secret. So far as creation is concerned, propitiate *Brahma* and establish links with the deity. As regards protection, establish links with *Vishnu* (by propitiating him). With regard to destruction, establish association with Easwara (Siva). However if your heart is totally pure, you can establish direct connection with God. You need not approach the less deities. For this, there is way. That is the establish a direct link with God, heart to heart."

. . . The Overlord (*Sironayakam*) who is above these three is God. He can overrule the Trinity. How? By mitigating the magnitude of the consequences of *Karma* (action). He can counteract any kind of situation. That is the Divine prerogative of God. He can create anything, protect anything. He creates and brings about its dissolution."—*Sanathana Sarathi, April, 1995*, pp. 83-89.

The countless mind boggling miracles done by Sri Sathya Sai Baba, which reveal his divine powers of creation, preservation and dissolution, amply prove that he is the Sironayakam—Overlord, above Brahma, Vishnu and Mahesh. The whole universe was held in his hands; innumerable devotees have experienced this fact.

VIII. Sri Sathya Sai as *Chakravarti* (Grand) Emperor

As the *Chakravarti* emperor, who ruled from his Prasanthi Nilayam ashram at Puttaparthi, Sri Sathya Sai controlled his millions of devotees, world powers and other forces by his mysterious divine powers of omnipotence, omnipresence and omniscience, his words of advice and command and through the code of conduct enforced by him. He controlled the subjects of Sai kingdom spread all over the world in two ways—externally through a network of the units of Sri Sathya Sai Seva organization and internally through his direct contact with each of his devotees in the universe.

He was all powerful in wisdom, knowledge, Sri (glory), fame, wealth, power, moral and spiritual strength, niti (strategies), and abilities of administering his vast empire. He was a unique sovereign emperor; all control was vested in his hands. Although he was all powerful, he functioned within the *maryada* (normative limits) enforced upon him by himself as divine incarnation. His strategies were—love, instruct, guide, persuade, chastise, and persuade people to do self-realization. He did not punish the erring ones. He just turned them out of his Prasanthi Nilayam ashram for some year if he was displeased with them.

How he administered his Prasanthi Nilayam *Ashram*? He himself once said he did each and everything. All powers were centralized in his hands although there is a truth and the whole organizational set-up of selfless devotee workers and Sevadal (volunteers). There is a Secret Intelligence Service in his ashram, called PSS (Prasanthi Security Service) run by retired Police and CID officials and Sevadal specially trained to deal with criminals, undesirable people and unwanted devotees who were suspected to be against Sai Baba and the Sai mission. They reported all things secretly to the Central Organization daily.

The State Presidents also kept on reporting on various kinds of activities of Sai devotees and others to Baba through their written reports and oral communications from time to time. The *Sevadals* (volunteers) were posted in the market outside the *ashram* and in the Puttaparthi village to keep silent watch on people and maintain law and order and peace. Many ruling politicians at the centre and in the states in India were Baba's ardent devotees, and so at just his nod or even without it—just in his name, all things were smoothly got done in administrative matters of law and order and procurement of necessary facilities for the Sai Kingdom.

The economy of the Sai Kingdom is known to be very sound. In his previous incarnation as Sri Shirdi Sai Baba he used to ask for *Dakshina* (cash offering). In this incarnationhe does not ask for any *dakshina*. There are no cash collection boxes anywhere in the Sai's capital or anywhere in his vast spiritual empire in the whole world. Countless people wished to donate or offer cash and all kinds of things to the adorable Cosmic Emperor Sri Sathya Sai Baba and his mission, but he did not accept from every one. He acceptd contributions from only those whom he considered to be pious and well-intentioned. There has been continuous flow of offerings from rich devotees in India and abroad, made with utmost humility. It was heard that Crores of rupees are received by the Sai Trust every year. Proper accounting of the funds received and spent is kept. It was known after his passing away on 24th April, 2011 that the worth of of Sai *empire* at Puttapatrthi was as stimated to be Rs.4000 crores as reported by the *Times of India* daily of 25th April, 2011, It was heared during his life time that Sari Sathya Sai Baba himself used to sign all cheques. Baba did not give any money to his relatives, nor did he spend anything on his own. He led a very simple life and needed no money to be spent on him. His left behind a lot of wealth. All funds received by him and the Trust were to be scrupulously used for construction of buildings, running of schools, colleges, university, hospitals, etc., and organizing the various functions and other activities of the Sai organization.

There is a unique system of *Sevadal,* service rendered by Sai devotees of all the states of India to Baba's ashram in turns for two weeks every year. These volunteers—both men and women, come on their expenses and render highly dedicated voluntary service to Baba's ashram in the belief that their services will be duly rewarded by the Cosmic Emperor by granting them Mukti (liberation) from the bonds of births and deaths. Even after his leaving * call on 24th April, 2011, the sevadals frm the different states of Indius have been coming to do voluntary service in Prasnthi Nilayam Puttapatherty complec round the year ith the firm coinviction in their hearts that Sri Sathya Sai Baba is virtually there and is watching eacvh and every thought and action of every one soi every one must be aslert and very conscious to abide by the code of conduct baed on th prestine values of Truth, Righgteousness, Peace, Love andf Nonviolenc.

The relationship of the Cosmic Ruler at Prasanthi Nilayam with his devotees was unique. He did not sit on a throne all the time like emperors. He openly gave *darshan* to thousands of devotees and visitors to his *ashram* by walking among them in the morning and evening during *darshan* time. Any devotee sitting there could have a very brief dialogue with him when he came near the place where the devotee was seated. Anyone could hold a letter in hand at that time, and he took some of the letters from the devotees. Any one could send him a letter or telegram. He granted interviews people selected by him and heard their problems and gave his word of advice, and also gave them his miraculously created objects for their welfare—objects created instantly by his divine powers. Although there is a formal organization established by him which organizes all affairs of the ashram, including the arrangements for *darshan*, yet Baba's contact with each one of his devotees or subjects of his empire was inner and direct. Several devotees have in their memoirs revealed that Baba's love for all his devotees is genuine. He was very gentle and loving usually, however at times he was stern-looking or angry. He did not compromise on moral principles and spiritual values. He was a great upholder of moral and spiritual values. He used a judicious mix of his divine powers of omnipotence, omnipresence and omniscience and worldly wisdom to see that his mission succeeds in all respects. He propagated his spiritual and social service mission vigorously, but usually did not criticize or comment on other Godmen, saints or Gurus and missions. But he did not spare his critics and eschew no words to condemn them as the descendents of Ravana, Shishupal, Kauravas and the like. Usually he was calm but when he gives discourses, words come out of his mouth endlessly like a torrent revealing spiritual secrets and expounding the glories of great incarnations and glory and secrets of spiritual life. None could ask him a question—so overwhelmed and awed one became in his divine presence. He did not invite suggestions or comments from his visitors or well wishers like a democratic leader; his role-functioning style was essentially that of an autocratic leader having an enchanting charisma. When he spoke, doubts of his devotees were solved. While all people comes for a few moments have his darshan and only those selected by him can have private interview with him, at his own will, people in power or high dignitaries in politics, government and important foreign personalities could have direct access with him. Usually he kept himself aloof from political and social controversies in the country or the world. he mainly confined himself to spiritualism moral teaching and social service. His discourses were and are still published in the *Sanathana Sarathi*, monthly issued

185

from his Ashram. Some of the articles in this magazine were written by foreigner devotees also. His popularity among the foreigners was enormous. People of all faith were coming towards him. Although a number of people in the world do not believe in Baba and some envious ones even criticized and talked shallow of him, Baba like sun was always showing his grace on all people. In his Makar Samkriti discourse in early 1995, Sri Sathya Sai Baba spoke as under:

"If you wish to experience oneness, you have to see the cosmos through the glass of spiritual oneness (*Ekakatma-bhava*), otherwise, the world will appear as a bewildering multiplicity because you will be seeing it through the glasses of the three Gunas—*Satva, Rajas, Tamas*. Put aside these three glasses. Wear the glass of "*Ekaatmabhaava*". Thus, the feeling of unity in Spirit. Love is one. The Supreme is one though the wise call it by many names. The divine has to proclaim this unity when God comes in human form and lives and moves among human beings. The Divine Incarnation (Sri Sathya Sai) has no likes or dislikes. He has no distinction of "mine" and "thine". He is beyond praise or censure. How, then, should the Divine (in human form) conduct himself? Everyone should understand this. Many bemoan the fact that Swami Sri Sathya Sai Baba does not speak to them despite their frequent visits. "Is Swami angry with us?" They ask. These are not mental aberrations. They are due to total ignorance. Such questions arise in their minds only when they have not understood Swami's real nature. I have no antipathy towards anyone. I do not hate anyone. All are mine. And I belong to everybody. But in dealing with devotees, I have to behave like a doctor who prescribes a specific diet for each patient. For instance, there is a patient suffering from diabetes. He should not consume sweets. If a devotee feels, "I enjoy sweet, why should the Sai Mother deny sweets to me", the answer is that it is for his own good. If Swami did not have the patient's well-being in view, he would let him suffer by giving him sweets. It is out of love for the devotee that she Sai Mother denies sweets to him. Swami adopts these different regimens in the interest of curing the devotees ailments.

There are others with a different kind of grievance. For instance, the students often complain that Swami does not talk to them because he is angry with them. I have no anger towards anyone. Whether you believe it or not, I do not know what anger means. But, occasionally I appear as if I am very angry. This is unavoidable because without such assumed behaviour on my part, the students will not heed my words. I tell them to behave in a certain way. Some students heed my words and try to act upto them. Some others go against my injunctions. In such a situation, I have to ensure respect for my words. Of what use is it to speak to those who attach no value to my words? I don't intend to devalue my words.

Truth is the life of the plighted word. My words bear the imprint of truth. I cannot depart from truth. I don't intend to devalue my words? I don't intend to devalue my words.

Truth is the life of the plighted word. My words bear the imprint of truth. I cannot depart from truth. I don't speak to those who attach no value to my words. This should be realized by those who complain that Swami does not talk to them. When people heed my words, I am ready to help them in every way and confer happiness on them. I do nothing for my own sake. This is my truth."

*A book 'Students with Sai: Conversations 1991 to 2000' published in 2010 categorically shows that Baba's spiritual kingdom was governed by him with the value of love, truth, peace, righteousness and nonviolence. Perfect cleanliness, purity, nobility, unity and divinity were his distinctive traits. Despite his omnipresence, omnipotence and omniscience and constant insistence on morality, human values and egolessness, sometimes minor intrigues, petty politics, ego-clashes and jealousies were seen in the behaviours of his organizational bosses and devotees which sometimes surprised and pained many. This confused many who asked: "How can this be when the Cosmic Emperor is there in full command of his empire". But let us not forget that in the Cosmic drama, the divine **leela** (sport) of the *Lord*, all these things also have a part. The fact that a murder attempt on Baba's life was made, some murders and thefts, etc., have happened in *Baba's ashram*, which is the spiritual heart of the world, should be understood in proper perspective Baba had himself explained that all these things are the universal phenomena; they can happen anywhere, the law of karma operates all the time everywhere. He elaborated as under:

"In the great drama of cosmic life, the Cosmic Director, God is also an actor. The Cosmic play is governed by certain rules and regulations. Because he is the Almighty, God cannot behave in an arbitrary manner. His actions have to be in accordance with his role in the cosmic play. There are certain rules as to how one should act according to his whims just because he is all-powerful . . . The Creator has to conform to the rules laid down by him for creation.

Not recognizing this truth men, who are involved in worldly ways, ask a question as to why in certain situations God did not use his limitless powers to avert certain untoward situations. These arise out of a narrow conception of things, without understanding how the Divine operates. They are concerned only about themselves and their interests. they ask: "Here is sacred temple. How would something unholy occur in such a place? They see things from a narrow perspective. They do not realize that for God the entire universe is his temple.

So, whatever happens anywhere, happens in God's temple. The Cosmos is the form of God (Vishnu). God is immanent everywhere in the cosmos . . . When things are seen with this broad perspective, it will be recognized that anything can happen to anyone at any place or any time."

-Sanathana Sarathi, August, 1993

Although he had a vast influence on the politicians in India and abroad and he advise them often, yet he did not seem to chastise them for all sorts of corruption and crisises created by them or thriving under them. In appeared that he was giving everyone a long rope. He let them bear the consequences of their actions. Although he spoke of love and compassion and millions were drawn towards him to seek his love, he was really not moved by their plight, for he knew their past actions and as a judge he had to administer justice to them. He usually do not interfere in the working of their destiny, but sometimes he was moved and interfered in it and granted his grace. Although as the Cosmic Master, he could turn sky into earth and *vice versa,* yet he usually acted within the limits imposed on himself by him as Godman. For many decades his daily routine did not change—the same routine of morning and evening darshan and bhajans.

He did not encourage ritualism, hackneyed traditions and cultural myopia. He constantly emphasized belief in God, devotion faith in himself as the Cosmic Emperor, universal brotherhood and universal values of truth, righteousness, peace, love and non-violence.

He was open-minded. He recognized no difference on socio-cultural grounds. He allowed women equal participation in all religious, spiritual and socio-cultural activities. He commanded authority by his unblemished and great moral example as an ideal person. He advised all to do *Naamsmaran,* social service and work for the betterment of human society. However, he did not attack social evils in the Indian society as passionately as Kabir Swami Dayanand, Karve and many other social reformers did. He prescribed higher moral and spiritual values and tries to uplift the humanity.

IX. Epilogue

This realistic analysis should make it clear that Sri Sathya Sai Baba met all the criteria of the Cosmic Emperor as presented in the Scriptural testimonies of the *Vedas* and other scriptures of the *Sanathana Dharma* and ancient religions of mankind. He earnestly and emphatically urged that we as his devotees should believe in his following declaration and consider it to be our great fortune that we have been born when this most unique Avatar descended on earth to usher Golden age for the mankind:

"The same Supreme Being who saved Prahalada by appearing from the pillar and punishing his demonic father, the same Supreme Being who came to the rescue of Kuchela, the same Being who descended from Vaikuntha to save Gajendra, the Lord of the elephants, has now come to the world as *Satchihanandamurthi*, presiding over the hearts of all as Puttaparthi Chakaravarthi.

". . . You should realize that I have come to remind you of your reality, that in fact, everyone of you is an embodiment of *Satchitananda* (God)."

According to Aurobindo:

"The inner fruit of the Avatar's coming is gained by those who learn from it the true nature of the divine birth and the divine works and who, growing full of him in their consciousness and taking refuge in him with their whole being, *manmaya mam upasritah*, purified by the realizing force if their knowledge and delive red from the lower nature, attain to the divine being and divine nature, madbhavam. The Avatar comes to reveal the divine nature in man above his lower nature and to show what are the divine works, free, unegoistic, disinterested, impersonal, universal, full of the divine light, the divine power sand the divine love. He comes as the divine personality which shall fill the consciousness of the human being and replace the limited egoistic personality, so that it shall be liberated out of ego into infinity and university, out of birth into immortality. He comes as the divine power and love which calls men to itself, so that they may take refuge in that and no longer in the insufficiency of their human wills and the strife of their human fear, wrath and passion, and liberated from all this unquiet and suffering may live in the calm and bliss of the Divine. Nor does it matter essentially in what form and name or putting forward what aspect of the Divine he comes; for in all ways, varying with their nature, men are following the path set to them by the Divine which will in the end lead them to him and the aspect of him which suits their nature is that which they can best follow when he comes to lead them; in whatever way men accept, love and take joy in God, in that way God accepts, loves and takes joy in man."

The most famous American Reincarnation expert Wayne Peterson believes in the incarnation of Sai Baba. He is a retired US diplomat, a very spiritually highly evolved human being and who is a world renowned spcialist on 'Reincarnation' who has led Transmission Meditation groups for many years, is the author of a very stunning book 'Extraordinary Times, Extraordinary Beings' (Website *http://www.waynepterson.com*). In this book he has mentioned about Sai Baba (Sri Sathya Sai Baba (Internet *file://Wayne Peterson, Sai Baba and Maitreya.htm)* that a spirit knwon as Ahtun Re—'the a spirit being

channeled through Kelvin Ryerson, who has solved many reincarnation cases',
had explained to him that all great spiritual beings, such as Jesus, Mohammad,
Buddha, Moses, Baba Sri Siva, Sai Baba and Maitriya, all work together with a
common purpose to help humanity evolve spiritually. Although Wayne Peterson
had never met Sai Baba yet the experienced Sai Baba's miraculous power. He
happened to unexpectedly receive a remarkable miracle photo of a parrot on Sai
Baba's shoulder.

24

The Cosmic Power and The Universe

—Liut. (Retd.) M.L.Chibber

Many people in India and abroad enquire, "Who is Sai Baba? Why are millions being attracted from all over the world to visit him in ever increasing numbers?" The questioners include genuine spiritual seekers, skeptics some who are flippantly curious and a few who are plainly hostile to what they call Indian godmen. This article attempts to share with the reader a few random experiences related to these questions and the supplementaries that are raised.

The Messiah of New Age

Those who are not familiar with the Indian spiritual heritage but are genuine spiritual seekers of God are all attention when they are informed that he is a man of *infinite wisdom*. This is so because *infinite wisdom* is one of the descriptions of God, and it goes down far better than the word 'Avatar', with which only a few in the West are familiar.

The teachings of Bhagavan Baba appeal immensely to people because of their universality. A teaching that makes a major impact on everyone relates to his mission of moving mankingto the new age that he calls the *Vishwa Parishad* (world community or global village). The blueprint that he articulates for the new age touches most people very deeply. It does so because in it they find an echo of their own faith. In just four lines, he has distilled the essence of all the faiths and philosophies that have gripped the minds of men since the dawn of history:

> *There is only one nation, the nation of mankind;*
> *There is only one religion, the religion of live;*
> *There is only one language, the language of the heart;*
> *There is only one God and he is omnipresent.*

This writer can never forget the reaction of a well-known Muslim clergy-man who is deeply involved in the violent unrest in Kashmir. His face became red. He literally jumped up from his seat and said, "General Sahib, this will happen, it has to happen." He felt very happy when the writer informed him that it was already happening at Puttaparthi, where people from more

191

than 150 countries were coming in ever increasing numbers to sit, sing and pray together at Prasanthi Nilayam. Nowhere else in the world are devotional songs dedicated to the founders of all faiths jointly sung by a congregation, as it happens in the presence of Bhagavan Baba. When a serving Pakistani Brigadier heard the above four lines, his spontaneous comment was "But, General, that is the gist of Quran Sharif". It indeed is, as it is of the Bible and the Gita.

Energy, Consciousness and Cosmic Power

In 1997, there was a special team of the British Broadcasting Corporation in India to make a film on the country after 50 years of independence. The writer happened to meet them when they were filming his regiment. A technical person of the team happened to sit next to the writer at lunch. Someone on the table made a mention of Bhagavan Baba. The BBC man intervened and said, "I had heard so much about him in England that I specially flew out to visit him. But I was so put off by his devotees that I returned disappointed. They deify him as God. how on earth a mere man can be God? It is ridiculous." A few things about Bhagavan Baba that were explained to him that made a visible impact on him are worth recounting. Performed with the Divine Hands on 25th August 1999 a model of the proposed building was placed before Bhagavan when he visited the site on 24th September 1999. The construction work started in November 1999. Bhagavan inaugurated the building on 18th November 2000 on the eve of his 75th Birthday.

Built adjacent to the hill on which the huge Hanuman statue is located, the building is a landmark in itself and an imposing structure in the Prasanthi Nilayam valley. It is 75 feet in height and has seven levels. It occupies an area of nearly 11,000 sq. ft. at the ground level and a total built-up area of 20,000 sq. ft. it has a very unique Stupa which is 36 feet in height and has lotus at two levels—at the base and nearing the top. It is surrounded by five swans which depict the five human values. From the centre of the lotus at the upper level rises the divine finger supporting the entire universe.

This grand edifice is unique in the history of mankind in many ways. As commented by Bhagavan, this will be a 21st century marvel. The architecture itself is a fusion between the East and the West. Although the roof appears like a Chinese pagoda, it has components of European architecture. Two domes of Moorish architecture have been constructed using a high technology material—titanium. The arches on both sides are Gothic, a style followed in the early Christian Era. The Koi pool in front is of Chinese origin, but very popular in Singapore and Malaysia.

It houses various types of exhibits depicting the Life Mission and Message of Bhagavan Sri Sathya Sai Baba to present a glimpse of the Divinity of the Poornavatar. The exhibits are divided into seven sections, each dealing with one aspect of the Avatarhood and bringing out various qualities and contributions of the Avatar, as one amidst us, but beyond us. The exhibits meander through different levels located at different heights and take the visitor from the dawn of creation to the modern age as outlined through the message of Bhagavan Baba.

A brief outline of the exhibits within the building is given below:

1. Unmanifest Manifests

   This section deals with the creation of the universe which arose from the will of the Divine "To Love Myself". It depicts the various incarnations of the Lord giving a prelude to the present incarnation. The presentation has been done by specialists connected with Hollywood.

2. The Coming of Sai Foretold

   The prophesies on the Advent of Sai Avatar from different parts of the world and different scriptures are laid out in this section.

3. This section covers the childhood and various Leelas of the Avatar. The Fullest Beauty aspect of the Avatar (as described in the scriptures) gives the incidents of Swami's childhood which bring out the latent Divinity of the Lord. This divine beauty draws millions to him.

4. Glory of the Divine

   This section depicts the Fullest Splendour Power of the Avatar—the Mahima Phase of the Avatar as told by him. Devotees gather to receive Divine Blessings in the form of Vibhuti, rings, pendants, chains etc., representing his omnipotence. His omnipresence is experienced through the various manifestations in far off places although he is physically not present at those places. His omniscience is felt even in his access to the subconscious (dream) state of individuals.

5. From Information to Transformation

   The Most Complete Wisdom aspect of the Avatar (the *Bodhana* Phase of the Avatar). The purpose of all these is to bring about "Individual transformation", through teachings that transcend the barriers of language, culture and nationality. The universal teachings, presenting the most complex philosophical teachings in a simple language, attract both the "*Paamar*" (the layman), and the "*Pundit*" (the scholar) alike.

6. Global Transformation

   This portion deals with the undiminished fame aspect of the Avatar. How the teachings can help in individual transformation through *Namasmarana* (chanting Divine Names), selfless service, personal Sadhana, practice of Human Values in daily living, etc., are depicted through Multimedia as well as Models and other presentations.

7. Expansion of Love

   The Infinite Vairagya aspect of the Avatar, "the Vishwarupa Darshan", in more common parlance, is presented in his expanding love through those coming in contact with him and service to mankind rendered by his devotees all over the globe.

8. International Exhibition

   This is an offering at the Lotus Feet of the activities carried out all over the world by Sri Sathya Sai Organization.

9. Books Stall

10. Mini Theatre

11. Presentation of Different World cultures with the Help of Exhibits from Different Countries

Devotees from all over the world placed at his Lotus Feet this unique piece of architecture on the eve of Bhagavan's 75th Birthday and the 7th Sri Sathya Sai World Conference in November 2000. We pray to Bhagavan to shower his divine blessings on this project for the benefit of the mankind.

The one teaching of Bhagavan Baba around which all his teachings and activities revolve is to make us understand that everything in the seen universe including human beings is a temporary from of the Cosmic Power called God. The ancient spiritual scientists of India working in the laboratories of their minds analysed this Cosmic Power and found that it had three characteristics:

Sat meaning Truth which implies indestructible permanence. Energy and love are two facets of it. Chit meaning Consciousness. *Ananda* meaning Bliss.

The three characteristics of the Cosmic Power named God are as inseparable as transparency, wetness and liquidity of a pure glass of water. Bhagavan Baba explains this in the following simple words: "In this drama of the universe, there are only two actors, who play a million roles: Jada and Chaitanya (meaning Sat and Chit or Energy and Consciousness)."

It means that everything in the universe that we can perceive is a permutation and combination of energy and needed level of consciousness. The existence of the Cosmic Power called God and the fact that everything we can perceive including ourselves is a temporary form of the same becomes crystal clear when we ponder over the following two explanations.

The *first* explanation is an extract from Bhagavan Baba's address on 22nd June 1995 after he inaugurated Laser Laboratory in Sri Sathya Sai Institute of Higher Learning, Prasanthi Nilayam Campus:

"Students, before trying to understand Divinity, try to understand the universe itself. What is meant by *Vishwa Swarupa* (the real form of the universe)? the universe is made up of galaxies, stars, the sun and the moon. The emptiness within that is known as Vishwa Swarupa. There, in the emptiness, are studded galaxies and constellations. Man, after considerable investigation, has discovered things about matter and energy. But in My view, there is nothing like matter in this universe. Everything is a temporary form of energy and is suffused with it. In one instant, this energy is turned into matter. In another instant, it is energy again. This energy destroys the previous matter. It creates new matter. This is called the nuclear process."

In simple language, *Bhagavan* Baba had explained the real form of the Cosmic Power called God (in Sanskrit, *Vishwa Swarupa* is an appellation for God) as also the great discovery by Einstein that matter and energy are interconvertible. Now let us examine what an eminent scientist has said about the universe.

The second explanation is given in the following extract from the book entitled 'Wholeness and Implicate Order" by Professor David Bohm, in which he discusses the totality of existence including matter and consciousness as an unbroken whole:

"Empty space contains an immense background of ultra high energy (zero-point energy of wavelength 10 cm^{-32}), and matter, as we know it, is small, quantized wave-like excitation on top of this background, rather like a ripple on a vast sea. One cubic centimeter of this zero-point energy is very far beyond the total energy of all matter in the known universe . . . What we perceive through senses as empty space is actually the plenum (the real universe) which is the ground for the existence of everything, including ourselves. The things which appear to our senses are derivative forms and their meaning can be seen only when we consider the plenum in which they are generated and sustained and into which they ultimately vanish."

If we could see a rock, a plant, a bird or a man through a microscope of quantum physics, we would see only a pulsating mass of protons and electrons and within them quarks, leptons and leptoquarks doing Tandav Nritya (the cosmic dance) of Siva. After listening to all this the BBC young man kept quiet but his body language did speak, "Gosh, I never thought of God in those terms." At this stage, another person sitting on the table butted in, "I have heard a lot about the miracles that he performs. Which is his greatest miracles?"

Bhagavan Baba's Greatest Miracle

The greatest miracles of Bhagavan Baba is to transform people and make them realize that not only Service to Man is service to God but it is also the source of great happiness; that it is the simplest way to reach the goal of experiencing our own Reality. Most people who come to his presence experience an inner urge to change for the better, to serve and to share. This miracle is visible in thousands of Seva Dal volunteers around the world who willingly and lovingly give their time and energy to serve.

He changed people by saturating them with boundless love. He comforted and consoled those in distress by taking on their problems; he heals the afflicated who came to him with faith in God; he offers succour to the poor and lonely. He did all this with a basic purpose. And that purpose was is to inspire people and to motivate each one to embark on an endeavour to achieve the goal of human birth. This goal is to become worthy of God's grace, to achieve permanent happiness by under-standing and then actually experiencing that *I am*

25

Uniqueness of Sai Avatar

—A.V. Gokak

An *Avatar* (Incarnation) symbolizes the descent of God on the earth in human form. The Bhagavat Gita states that whenever the unrighteous ride on the crest of the wave, God appears on the earth to establish the rule of law and righteousness. The world is becoming a veritable battlefield on account of economic, political and ethnic tensions. Swami has come as an Avatar at this critical juncture in the history of humanity. He counsels, helps, commands and stands by as a friend and a well-wisher of all, so that people may discard the evil, take to the right path and reach the goal. He talks of the role of an Avatar in his own characteristic style: "The Avatar comes to bring the kingdom of heaven to earth as well as to build the kingdom of heaven within the individual human heart."

A New World Order

Bhagavan (God) Baba wanted to transform the individual as well as the world with his spiritual revolution based on the five luminous pillars of Sai philosophy—Truth, Righteousness, Peace, Love and Non-violence. Bhagavan Baba has innumerable devotees all over the world and these belong to different professions and diverse spheres of life. Ministers, Members of Parliament, diplomats, philosophers, poets, clerks and officials are all devotees of Swami. Bhagavan Baba used their services for building up various institutions that foster these values for bringing about social and spiritual revolution in society.

Bhagavan Baba wanted to re-establish *Sanathana Dharma* for the transformation of mankind. He was therefore making efforts to educate the people about the greatness of Indian culture and philosophy by interpreting the Vedas and the Upanishads in a manner in which they can be easily understood by modern man. His discourses had an electrifying effect on the audience and are a very important aspect of the spiritual revolution that he is brining about.

Re-establishment of the Vedas and the *Shastras* was the most important mission of Sathya Sai *Avatar*. He said that his task was not merely to cure and remove individual misery. To quote him, "The removal of misery and distress is incidental to my mission. My main task is the re-establishment of the *Vedas* and the *Sastras* and to reveal the knowledge about them to all people."

Bhagavan Baba's message and values are not only for India, but for the whole world. The *Sarva Dharma* emblem of all major relions) is the best indicator of the all-encompassing character of his message and philosophy. The symbols of Hinduism, Islam, Christianity, Zoroastrianism and Buddhism, the five major faiths in the world, find a place in the emblem. The most fascinating feature of this emblem is that it is not an indicator of the establishment of a new religion as Bhagavan's goal is not to start another religion but to elevate the level of human consciousness. He never asks devotees to give up their respective religions. He asks them to adhere to their respective religions. He tells the devotees ". . . Continue the worship of your chosen God along the lines already familiar to you and you will find that you are coming nearer and nearer to me, for all names are mine and all forms are mine."

Role of the His Avatarhood

Bhagavan (God) Baba explains the unique role that he has come to play in the present crisis-ridden world. He distinguishes his role from that of Rama and Krishna, who had to kill one or more individuals, who could be identified as enemies of the righteous way of life and thereby restore the supremacy of virtues. In today's world, all are tainted by wickedness and there is a big question as to who will survive if the Avatar decides to uproot wickedness. Therefore, he says that he has come "to correct the intelligence (Buddhi) by various means." He counsels, helps, commands and stands by as a friend and a well-wisher of all, so that people may discard the evil, take to the right path and reach the goal.

Bhagavan Baba makes another important distinction between his role and that of Rama and Krishna. Rama came to establish Sathya (Truth) and Dharma (Righteousness). Krishna came to foster *Santhi* (Peace) and *Prema* (Love). However, now, *Bhagavan* says, "all these four values are in danger of being dried up. That is why the present *Avatar* has come."

He has given a very clear idea of the worldwide role he has come to play. He says, "I have come to inscribe a golden chapter in the history of humanity, wherein falsehood will fail, truth will triumph, virtue will reign. Character will confer power then—not knowledge or inventive skills or wealth. Wisdom will be enthroned in the councils of nations."

The miracles of *Bhagavan* Baba remind us of the miracles performed by Jesus. Bhagavan in his discourse on Christmas Day in 1972 referred to Jesus's statement. "He who sent me will come again" and then declared that Jesus was referring to *Bhagavan* Baba himself! In response to a question by a devotee, Bhagavan confirmed that he is what Western Christians call Cosmic Christ.

Brotherhood of Man and Fatherhood of God

Bhagavan has already become a unifying force in the world and has followers from the Arctic to the Antarctica, thanks to his charismatic personality and universality and catholicity of his outlook. Bhagavan Baba's Mission is to achieveworld unity and bring the Golden Age on the earth. He said, in age of his New Year Messages, "In a very short time, all the people of the world are going to be united. India, Pakistan, America, Russia and Japan are considered as separate from each other. Very soon, there would be unity among all these countries. Even those whom we consider our worst enemies are going to become our best friends." He said that very soon, we would witness "Brotherhood of Man and Fatherhood of God."

26

Sri Sathya Sai Baba, The Divine Alchemist

—Tina Sadhwani

It has been said that at every turning point and every great epoch of the earth's existence there has often been one extraordinary being standing at the leading edge of light, unraveling the consciousness in which the transcendent descends into the physical, in which the cosmic pulse of the universe converges to a point, to a singularity that is at once human with its manifested boundaries, as well as suprahuman, displaying its infinite capabilities. Both heaven and earth have collaborated in the sacred alchemy of such a creation and in the divine birth of such an extraordinary being. In the language of the Hindus, such a sacred being is referred to as the *Avatar*. He is the direct, super-conscious descendent of the same force that shapes the universe and renders it its harmonies and balance. He symbolizes the unity of all existence and the pinnacle of the divine intelligence that is diffused in all things.

To many around the world who have experienced him, Sri Sathya Sai Baba, was the living embodiment of such a force and spiritual descent, that unifies all the planes of existence, from the cosmic to the planetary and finally to the individual, guiding humankind to the next state of evolution, signifying the ultimate transformation and alchemy of spirit and opening us to the possibilities of a higher dynamism, a higher principle by which we may actualize our own greatest potentials. He therein points us to our own hidden depths for the divinity of which he is an extension is immanent in every one of us. As he says himself that we all are integral parts of the same omnipresent reality in which we are all inseparably connected, from which we all emanate and to which we all return. To recognize that we are vibrations of the same sacred essence however demands a sense of freedom of perception that uplifts us from the narrow precepts of our own mind.

The work of Sathya Sai Baba on this planet aims at sustaining harmony and balance that transforms the earth-consciousness in more life-affirming ways. He declared that he had come to restore India to her former spiritual glory and to spread the message and light of spirituality to the whole world. his work spans both the spiritual and physical realms providing the vehicle and the means by which Sathya (the truth of being) and dharma (the universal balance and cosmic order) are re-established. The evolutionary task that Sai Baba faces therein plummets his active energies right into the global eye of the storm, into the universal nexus that perpetually grinds the forces of light against the forces of darkness. Howard Murphet, an author who had deeply studied and personally witnessed the spiritual phenomenon that is Sai Baba had said in his book 'Walking the path with Sai Baba that "there is no doubt, of course, that Sathya Sai Baba is very active and extremely dynamic in the world of men. He is not the withdrawn yogi, spending his time in meditation. He is essentially the doer, the one who joins battle with the dark forces that rise sharply against the power of light he brings."

Sathya Sai Baba's illuminating light and selfless service has indeed reached out to and uplifted millions of people in the world. His devotees all around the world, in turn have been zealously dedicated to voluntary service towards uplifting humanity. His charitable organizations and networks have established super-speciality hospitals with state-of-the-art technology that provide all services, including open-heart surgeries for free. These hospitals have been a boon and refuge to lakhs of people from over 500 villages and poverty stricken areas in India Baba's social welfare programmes have constantly worked at providing free quality medical care to all. He has also established schools providing comprehensive education from kindergarten to post-graduate level, with all tuition made available for free. Every year these schools yield the finest graduates of India who excel not only in superior academic intelligence but are grounded in strong values of self-discipline, integrity and spiritual wisdom. There are also many Sathya Sai Baba schools operating in other countries and over five hundred schools in the world utilizing Baba's 'Education in Human Values' curriculum. In addition to this Sathya Sai Baba has created vast water supply systems and canals for draught-stricken areas in South India that now provides water to millions of people. These are all standing testimonies to the power of Sathya Sai Baba's love, reinforcing his benevolent vision of making healthcare, education and water available for free to all.

Moreover, Baba has also brought back the ancient and illuminating wisdom of the Vedic era back into our lives as he reminds us in his own words "My love towards the Veda is equaled only by my love towards Humanity . . . Every human being must revere the Vedas. It is the very foundation of life. The welfare of the nation and the prosperity of the world are dependent on the Vedas . . . The Vedas are a means of establishing a link with the Divine."

Sai Baba has essentially been a constant source of love, wisdom and inspiration to millions of people in the world, guiding them consciously as well as subconsciously through troubled times. Yet these are only some of the visible and tangible aspects of his selfless work, while the vaster range of his divine activities operate in transmuting the deeper regions of the world-soul.

Nonetheless, despite his far reaching positive influences, Sathya Sai Baba has often been criticized by rationalist organizations, cynics and others as a spurious and bogus miracle worker who capitalizes on the superstitions and blind ignorance of the masses. The blind masses that absurdly range from the common man to world famous cricketers like Sachin Tendulkar and Sunil Gavaskar, to eminent award winning doctors like Devi Prasad Shetty and Dr. N. Rangabashyam to superlative business entrepreneurs like Noah Samara (CEO Worldspace) and Sunil Bharti Mittal (Chairman and Managing Director of Bharti Telecom) to former presidents like Francisco Flores (of EL Salvadore) and A.P.J. Abdul Kalam (of India) to top echelons from the world of finance like Duvvuri Subbarao (RBI Governor) and K.R. Ramamoorthy (ING VYSYA Bank Chairman) to Royal Families like that of the King and Queen of Nepal, Princess Astrid of Belgium and Raja of Venkatagiri to Former Chief Justice of India—Justice Ranganath Mishra to Civil Aviation Minister—Praful Patel to Hard Rock Café founder—Isaac Tigrett and many more, to name only a few, who have all (for over sixty years) been drawn from various parts of the world and from diverse backgrounds to this controversial so-called magician.

Traveling across the continents and the vast stretches of space, simply to witness a man perform magic tricks would seem rather irrational and impractical an act to expect of such eminent personalities. Moreover, most of the people who are now Baba's devotees experienced his miracles and transformative blessings long before they even heard his name.

Sathya Sai Baba's power is indeed the power of divinity and his magic is in simple words the magic of love that binds and unifies. However, the alchemical processes that Baba engaged in, be it spellbinding magic, powers of materialization, unconditional love or selfless service can only be fathomed by a mind that has raised itself high enough to apprehend the mysterious workings of the Cosmic Mind. Mystic-sage Sri Aurobindo, in his understanding of the operations of a higher supreme reality affirms that "what is magic to our finite reason is the logic of the Infinite. It is a greater reason, a greater logic because it is more vast, subtle, complex in its operations: it comprehends all the data which our observation fails to seize, it deduces from them results which neither our deduction nor induction can anticipate because our conclusions and inferences have a meager foundation . . . If we observe a happening, we judge and explain it from the result and from a glimpse of its most external constituents, circumstances or causes; but each happening is the outcome of a complex nexus of forces which we do not and cannot observe, because all forces are to us invisible—but they are not invisible to spiritual vision of the Infinite."

The divided mind that subsequently divides life and the world into natural and supernatural, into reason and faith, into god and creation, or spiritual and material therein takes the limits of its perception and dichotomies of its thought for the limits of life. The sharp opposition made by rationality and reason against that which it cannot accommodate into its finite vision it dismisses as the delusions of another's mind. However, "the most glaring shortcoming of rationalists", says author Bill Aitken, "is their habit of leaving love out of the equation. Their approach is cerebral and misses out on ordinary human emotions. The rationalists use Sai Baba to attack what is in fact their main enemy—the freedom to cherish the world of Spirit."

This universe of space, time, galaxies, stars, life, mind, material objects and myriad beings can indeed be conceived of as a well contrived mathematical formula, a mechanical operation of mere physical forces and equations that can be rationally defined. But it can equally be conceived of as a divine symphony, a single magnanimous living entity, a magical phenomenon and synergy of cosmic proportions that can only be known as intimately and as inexplicably as a lover knows that rapture of love, a dancer knows the ecstasy of dance, a musician knows the power of universal harmonies or a mother knows the joy of creation, for such is the mystical nature of the power and love of Sathya Sai Baba, in the grasp of which we are indelibly and forever transformed.

"I have come to reconstruct the ancient highway to God; to instruct all in the essence of Vedas, to shower on all this precious gift; to protect Sanathana Dharma, the Ancient Wisdom and to preserve it. My mission is to serve happiness and so I am always happy to come among you, not once but twice, thrice as often as you want me. To set right those who have taken to the wrong path and to protect the good, I will be born again and again. I have come to light the lamp of love in your hearts, to see that it shines day by day with added lustre"

—Sathya Sai Baba

27

85 Years of Divine

I

A Saga of Love and Service to Mankind

The entire life of *Bhagavan* since his very childhood was a saga of selfless and unconditional love and service to mankind. It is difficult to find another Avatar or prophet or a noble soul who could give love and do selfless service to so many millions in his lifetime. There are millions of people who would vouchsafe the truth of this statement as they have actually experienced his love, blessings, grace and bounty. He meticulously practiced the maxim, "Love All, Serve All" all his life. The entire worldwide Sai Organization set up by him is guided by this most simple and most profound principle. All his life, he exhorted one and all to follow this principle and make their life sublime. This is the basic principle which can divinize man. Therefore, he exemplified this in his own life.

All the service institutions set up by Bhagavan are based on this divine principle. Two General Hospitals at Prasanthi Nilayam and Whitefield (Bengaluru) and two Super Speciality Hospitals set up by him at Puttaparthi and Bengaluru, where best treatment is provided totally free to the poorest of poor, stand testimony to his abiding love for mankind. Added to it is mobile hospital which provides loving medical services to a large number of villagers at their doorstep. Such medical services on the model set by him are being made available to a large population of needy masses in India and overseas countries by respective Sai Organizations through medical camps and hospitals. This in itself is a stupendous task when we consider how many millions benefited from it.

Bhagavan's all educational institutions also provide free education from K.G. to Ph.D. Sri Sathya Sai Institute of Higher Learning which he set up in 1981 was adjudged by a U.G.C. team as the crest jewel of education system and a model for value-based education. A Peer Team of the National Assessment and Accreditation Council (NAAC) established by the University Grants Commission of India accredited the Institute at the highest (A++) level among Indian universities.

The Peer Team felt, "This Institute stands out as a crest jewel among the university education system in the country and this model is worthy of emulation by the institutes of higher learning in the country and elsewhere." Elaborating on the purpose of setting up the Institute, Bhagavan said to the students, "This Institute has not been established just to prepare you for earning degrees. The main purpose is to help you cultivate self-knowledge and self-confidence so that each of your can learn self-sacrifice and earn Self-realization". He gave the concept of *Educare* to enable the students to manifest their inner virtues and moulded them into his own image so that like him, they became the epitomes of selflessness, service, sacrifice and spirituality and put these values into practice in their house, community and workplace. "My entire property consists of my students. I have offered myself to them", he said. He invested his time and effort in his students and made them men and women of sterling character. "Of what value is the acquisition of all knowledge in the world if there is no character?" he remarked. The campuses of the Institute at Prasanthi Nilayam, Brindavan, Anantapur and Muddenahalli and numerous other Sri Sathya Sai schools, colleges and institutes in all parts of the world follow the high ideals set by him and turn out men and women of high character from their portals. Thousands of students who received free quality education from his institutions would no doubt cherish the ideals set by him and will bring about a silent transformation in society.

Rayalaseema region in which Puttaparthi is located is drought-prone area. Scarcity of water was not the only problem; there was excess of fluoride in water which caused diseases and deformations in those who drank it. Looking at the magnitude of the problem, successive governments could not devise any scheme to solve it even after five decades of Independence. God is the refuge of those who have no other refuge. Seeing the sad plight of refugeless millions, Bhagavan took up Anantapur Water Project in March 1995 and completed it in a record period of 18 months, bring relief to a population of 9.5 million. The then Prime Minister of India P.V. Narasimha Rao inaugurated the first phase of the project in a grand function at Prasanthi Nilayam, on 18th November 1995. Citing the example of this project in their Ninth Five Year Plan document, the Government of India started. ". . . Sri Sathya Sai Trust has set an unparalleled example of private initiative in implementing a project on their own, without any State's budgetary support, a massive water supply project, with an expenditure of Rs. 3,000 million to benefit 731 scarcity and fluoride/salinity-affected villages and a few towns in Anantapur district of Andhra Pradesh in a time frame of about 18 months". On 23rd November 1999, the Government of India released a postage stamp and a postal cover in recognition of the pioneering service rendered by Bhagavan Sri Sathya Sai Baba by providing safe drinking water to the rural masses.

Bhagavan's subsequent water project provided water to 320 villages of Medak and Mahaboobnagar districts, and 220 villages of East and West Godavari districts of Andhra Pradesh. These water projects benefited a total population of 18 million people of nearly 1,500 villages. Chennai Water Supply Project which provided water to the residents of this metropolitan city and fulfilled their long-felt need was another great social service venture of Bhagavan to relieve the suffering of the people, especially poor people.

Truly, the work done by Bhagavan is unparalleled in this history of mankind, and he will always live in the hearts of millions who received his love, benediction and grace in some form or the other.

II
A Love Supreme

Two decades shy of India's independence, in a remote village in Andhra Pradesh mother Easwaramma and Shri Venkamma Raju welcomed their fourth child Sathyanarayana. No one envisaged how this happy family event would impact the destiny of the human race. Eight and a half decades later, in the weeks leading to November 23, 2010, seekers from Argentina, Japan and New Zealand to Zambia, Russia and Slovenia, as well as every country and continent in between are streaming into Puttaparthi, the birthplace of Bhagavan Baba and the seat of his ashram—Prashsant Nilayam.

Trains, planes and automobiles brought in countless pilgrims from all over India and the world, among them simple village folks, grateful patients of his free hospitals, beneficiaries of his umerous social uplift projects in 125 countries from around the globe, scholars, seekers, policy makers, young and the elderly, Indians and foreigners, to celebrate the 85th birthday of a very blessed presence in their lives.

Today, Baba's gospel of pure, unconditional love expressed through selfless service has been warmly embraced by all races, religion, cultures and age groups, creating a global movement of secular humanism sans barriers. What compels millions to undertake long journeys, at great cost and inconvenience to attend an event to invitations were sent out to? Some call it the sweet draw of his sacred persona while others compare it to witnessing the coronation of Lord Rama or the enlightenment of the Buddha or receiving the Sermon on the Mount from Jesus.

Through his unprecedented philanthropy, Baba has demonstrated that human values are the missing link in the chain of good governance and harmonious social order. All of these have been chronicled in the publication supplement 'Beacon of Love', which is available online at www.sriSathyasai.org.in. We invite you to view it as a prelude to the "The Universal Sai", which chronicles the global impact of Bhagavan Baba's all encompassing love.

Come, join this journey of love from I to we to him, by breaking out from our self-imposed limitations and living out our divine destinies.

Love Without Borders

"God is Love, Love is God, Live in Love" says Bhagavan Baba. Today, his life and message can best be summed up as Love *sans* borders.

In a historic letter dated May 25, 1947, the then twenty year old Baba had declared: "I have a Task—to foster all mankind and ensure everyone lives a life full of bliss . . . to remove the sufferings of the poor and grant them what they lack." In fulfilling this vow, Baba was working continuously to bring about the joyous experience of love and compassion to humanity everywhere. Within the past 7 decades, his mission has grown to unparalleled proportions globally.

The celebrations to mark Baba's 85th birthday began a year in advance, from October 2009. The period had seen his love draw pilgrims from 107 countries and 28 India states to Prashanti Nilayam to offer their homage in person.

This global gratitude comes from those who have transformed into noble citizens by following Baba's call to express unconditional love as service to fellow beings. Explaining this uniqueness of Baba's appeal, Dr. Michael Nobel, former Chairman of the Board of the Noble Family Society says, "What I find particularly attractive about Sai Baba's teachings is that he doesn't care what religion you belong to. Instead he gives a simple Golden Rule: Do what is good. Don't do what is bad. Love everyone."

Active in 125 countries, the International Sai Organization conducts regular community outreach projects around the globe. These include educational, service, medical and spiritual activities. There are no membership dues or public appeals to raise money in any chapter of the Sai organization.

End of Education is Character

The universal values of Truth, Peace, Love, Right Conduct and Non-violence form the common platform for all Sai education projects around the world. Sai schools, weekend SSE classes and institutes for training teachers are growing around the world.

Sai Schools" achievements

South America has more Sathya Sai schools than any other continent. Brazil alone has five. It is astonishing to hear the stories of transformation of orphans into useful citizens.

In the Republic of Columbia, a group of volunteers and over 250 teachers trained in the SSEHV program work to transform the lives of abused children in poor communities.

The Satha Sai School in Ndola, Zambia, has been nicknamed the 'Miracle school' by locals for its ability to turn round street children into well-rounded individuals. It won the Business Initiative Directions (BID) award, a prestigious international award at the 22nd International World Quality Commitment (WQC) Convention in Paris, held on 30th May, 2005.

SEAMEO and UN-HABITAT have declared the Sathya Sai School in Thailand as a 'Centre of Excellence'. Upon the request of the Ministry of Education, Thailand, over 20,000 teachers in the country have received training here. The school also trains educators from different parts of the world in "Human Values-Based Water Education". This unique program based on Baba's teachings has been adopted by the United Nations. The Sathya Sai School in Toronto, Canada has been ranked a topper among 2,742 elementary schools in Ontario by the Fraser Institute for its academic achievement.

Sai Global Health Mission

That first Sathya Sai Hospital, established in Puttaparthi in 1956, has blossomed into a Sai healthcare network of two super specialty hospitals and two general hospitals, mobile hospitals, and international medical camps, all providing state-of-the-art primary to tertiary health-care totally free of cost around the world.

Sai Net of Protection

Disease prevention has been a major focus of the Sai Organization in all its medical work. Sai Organizations in Africa, Indonesia, Laos and India have distributed mosquito nets impregnated with insecticide in malaria endemic areas. In Kenya alone, over 85,000 nets have been distributed, reducing the incidence of malaria by more than 50%. Also, mass immunization, environmental hygiene and education in healthy living through lifestyle changes are an integral part of such preventive health programs.

Service to Man is Service to God

Sai volunteers across the world participate in a variety community service projects and disaster relief work. They serve homeless shelters, soup kitchens and food banks at the community level. Clothing, blankets, toiletries, school supplies and groceries are also provided for needy families. Frequent visits to hospitals, elderly homes, orphanages and prisons are regular outreach activities of Sai Centres internationally.

Disaster Relief

In the wake of disasters, such as Hurricane Katrina and the Tsunami of 2004, the volunteers of the Sai Organization are often among the first to arrive and offer help to the afflicted. Sai volunteers worked round the clock to provide seven days after the earthquake in the midst of widespread destruction continues to this day with relief and rehabilitation to the victims of the massive earthquake that struck the Republic of Haiti of gallons of potable water, built homes and cleaned roadways for Haitians. The work that on 12th January 2010. Between 19th January and August 2010, under the guidance of Baba, they provided free medical treatment to over 34,000 people, served more than 150,000 hot meals, supplied thousands began the discipline, determination and dedication that has become the hallmark of Sai volunteers.

At the invitation of the Myanmar government, the Sathya Sai Baba Central Council of Malaysia, along with volunteers from Singapore and Thailand, undertook the monumental task of building a village with 51 new homes, a temple and a school, for the victims of the tropical storm "Nargis' that hit the Ayerawaddy Delta region of the capital city of Yangon, This village was later christened as the Sri Sathya Sai Baba Village and inaugurated on 21st December 2008. The devastating Indian Ocean tsunami in 2004 killed approximately 230,000 people in 14 countries. Sai Organization rushed immediate relief to victims in Thailand, Indonesia, Sri Lanka and Malaysia, providing medical aid, drinking water, groceries and cooked food to the afflicted. Three mosques, 108 houses, and four large water tanks were also built in Jogjakarta, Indonesia. The Sai Organization of Malaysia received the prestigious Malaysian Humanitarian Award in 2006 for its timely and large-scale relief work.

Water Projects

As part of its efforts to combat the serious water shortage that exists in Africa and parts of Asia, the UN adopted a "Human Values-based Water Education Approach" proposed by the International Sathya Sai Organization. This initiative imparts vital information on water conservation, sanitation, and hygiene. Over the years, the Sathya Sai Organization has completed 12 water projects in El Salvador in Central America providing safe drinking water for about 2,000 families. The Sai Centre of Yogyakarta, Indonesia has built 90 wells to provide clean water to more than 300 families in the community of Gunung Kidul where the wells are called 'Yayasan Sri Sathya Sai Baba'.

The One and Only Religion of Love

Baba says, "Let all the faiths exist; let them flourish and let the glory of God be sung in all languages and in a variety of tunes . . ." As a result of Baba's secular outlook Prashanti Nilayam has become the pilgrimage destination of the world. From Iranians who come to celebrate the holy month of Ramadan in Baba's presence, to the Christians who converge at Prashanti Nilayam for Christmas, a multi-faith calendar fills the ashram schedule. Be it Buddha Poornima, Chinese New Year, Shivratri or Yom Kippur, thousands arrive daily to peace of the sacred precincts.

The 2005 Interfaith Conference held in Prasanthi Nilayam, saw participants from Islam, Buddhism, Jainism, Christianity, Judaism Zoroastrianism and Hinduism who were unanimous in their prayer which neatly sums up the focus of the Sai Organization across the globe: May all the beings in all the worlds be happy!

The SAI VIP Villages

In the year 2000, the United Nations declared its eight main millennium development goals (MDG) that would lift more than 500 million people out of extreme poverty, restoring their dignity and aspirations to fulfill the human potential. According to Dr. Kalyan Ray, former Head of the UN HABITAT's Water and Sanitation Department, "Though the overarching goal of the MDGs is tackling extreme poverty, water provides an entry point for action in achieving most of these goals."

On July 28, 2010, the UN adopted a resolution to recognize access to clean water and sanitation as a human right. Even as countries set about to achieve the goals there is a sustainable model that has been functioning successfully in South India. The Sai Water Project in East and West Godavari Districts of Andhra Pradesh was followed by medical camps for tribals in the hamlets that had remained untouched by modern civilization and isolated from the rest of the world. Soon it expanded to provide medical, social, economic and holistic benefits as well. The project not only delivered drinking water but also proved that human beings can be motivated to action as much by values as by economic benefits. These initiatives were the precursors to Baba's announcement of the Sri Sathya Sai Village Integrated Programme (SSSVIP) on March 20, 2007. Immediately the 25 hamlets in East Godavari District, which were already receiving drinking water supply from the Sai Project, were selected for a pilot project.

The need for SSSVIP (Sri Sathya Sai Village Improvement programme)

The SSSVIP addressed the holistic needs of each villager, nurturing the family unit as the foundation. The eight main components of the SSSVIP are: infrastructure, employment, education, medical and health, social, spiritual and individual care.

Within a span of three years, the SSSVIP has extended to 1,300 villages across India and continues to grow. What is common among these villages is that essentials such as hospitals, schools, industries, banks or even post offices are beyond reach, majority of the population lives below the poverty line, and several of the government's welfare schemes have not touched these areas. Once a specific village is identified, a basic survey is conducted to assess the common and individual needs and the components are prioritized accordingly.

"An important aspect of the SSSVIP is counseling and emotional support. It may not be possible to solve all their problems, but the volunteers listen to the residents and provide emotional support, as well as counsel them. The emphasis is not just on material resources, but also on the healing power of love without proselytizing, "explains Mr. V. Srinivasan, the All India President of the SSS Seva Organization. In line with Baba's Universalism, the program does not discriminate between the beneficiaries on religious. Caste, community or socio-economic grounds. Further, "It empowers the villagers to get involved", says Dr. Ram Manohar, the SSSVIP's National Coordinator.

Showing the way

Testimonials of the program's success are many. Nine-year old Vignesh waves his thin arms in excitement and struggles to stand up and welcome the guests to his two-room house at Maagaral village in Tamil Nadu.

Vignesh was a healthy child till he was seven months old. Constant epileptic seizures and lack of medical attention rendered him physically and speech disabled. Vignesh now has a new found hope in a pair of new calipers and the encouragement to walk daily with support. Volunteers of the Sai organization talk and play with him on their visits to the village. They also chaperone his mother to his physiotherapy that has been arranged in Chennai.

Elderly Yagatha of the same village was malnourished and living alone. She is now a beneficiary of "Amirtha Kalasam" program, which ensures her monthly groceries and toiletries. In the Kanchipuram district of Tamil Nadu, the SSSVIP addressed nutritional and ecological concerns by planting thousands of drum sticks, papaya and curry leaf saplings for 700 families.

Earlier on in 2004, the Sai volunteers of U.P. and Uttarakhand successfully implemented a hydro-electric project at Pakhari, a village with 50 households in the Gharwal Hills. With technical inputs from IIT Kanpur, the project generates 5000 watts power from a small river.

In East Godavari District, the tribals had adopted shift cultivation, cutting down the forest trees to grow their produce. Food was scarce. Villagers, including children were consuming toddy to overcome hunger. The Sai sevadals provided seeds to raise kitchen gardens, taught the children to bathe daily, clip their nails and comb the hair. They worked with the teachers in the nearby school and organized medical camps. Now, the children in the 25 hamlets are completely free from alcoholism are completely free from alcoholism and at least 50 per cent for the women no longer consume toddy. The Government has been motivated to lay roads to all the hamlets which few knew existed prior to the Sai Water Project. As the world approaches the 2015 deadline for achieving the Millennium Development Goals, India has proven that SSSVIP is a viable model that builds trust and confidence, motivating people and authorities towards public participation and shared responsibility for the goal of community development.

Education: Transforming Through Truth

Richard Mohan of Coimbatore, sending his daughter to the weekly Sathya Sai Education (SSE) classes has been a blessing. "My daughter now understands and appreciates the importance of prayer and our [Christian] customs", he says. A non-formal, yet highly effective mode of education, SSE or Bal Vikas is the brainchild of universal teacher, Bhagavan Baba, whose vision of education goes beyond more eradication of illiteracy or acquisition of degrees. Defining noble character as the desired end of education, Baba stresses education must equip the learner for life and not merely for a earning a living. For the past 42 years, he has been filling the vacuum in the education system not just in India but also around the world through a well-designed strategy, with SSE as the delivery medium. The Sai education module celebrates universal spirituality, promoting love and respect for all faiths by focusing on their universal values. The five human values of Truth, Right Conduct, Peace, Love, and Nonviolence are elicited through lessons based on the interactive teaching techniques such as stories, songs, prayers, or quotations, silent sitting, and games or group activities. Conducted for children 5-13 years, the 9-year program is divided into three groups, each with 3 sub-levels. Upon graduation, young adults enter the society as mature and balanced agents of positive change.

Pointing to the program's lasting success, its National Joint Coordinator Mrs. Vidya Srinivasan, says "Even years after graduating, wherever our students go, they stand out in a crowd due to their radiant personality and the way they conduct themselves. In many places, a SSE diploma is seen as an edge by employers, for it tells them something positive about the person's moral fibre."

While academic lessons learnt in school help in honing one's IQ, SSE complements it rightfully by helping develop the learner's EQ or ethics quotient. The "strong grounding in ethics, good manners and human values as a Bal Vikas student have left a deep and positive impact on my personality" shares Mr. N. Sethuramon, Managing Director of W.S. Industries.

When delivered within a regulated institutional environment, its benefits are hard to miss. Rekha Agrawal, Principal of the Sri Sathya Sai Vidya Vihar New Delhi says, "SSE has helped our students excel in all areas of learning. The school's ambience, discipline, and values-based education focus on the holistic development of each child, and not academics alone."

Global educational reforms are still searching for a "new educational order" to eliminate religious fanaticism, violence, and fatalism that characterize today's society. For decades now, through SSE, Baba has been lighting the way to truth, triumph and transformation.

Healthcare of the Doorstep
SSS Mobile Hospital

The Sai Mobile Hospital is a unique and free rural outreach holistic health service launched on March 30th 2006 by Bhagavan Baba. A unit of the SSS Medical Trust, it operates from the 1st to 12th of every month at 12 base villages to each of which are attached another 6 villages. In practice however, patients are drawn from nearly 400 villages.

The hospital-on-wheels is managed almost entirely on voluntary basis. Five hundred doctors from the state of Andhra Pradesh belonging to 12 specialties serve in rotation. This diagnostic bus comes equipped with an ultra sonogram, x-ray plant with automatic processor and a laboratory which can perform most of the pathological and bio-chemical investigations.

Given the program's outreach, its larger agenda is based on a triangular approach of Curative thrust, Preventive focus and Spiritual base.

The curative thrust owes its strength to the presence of specialists belonging to Radiology Medicine, Surgery, Orthopedics, ENT, Dentistry, Ophthalmology, Gynecology & Pediatrics on any given day. They work under a common roof integrating their efforts to solve many an intricate problem. Six hundred to seven hundred patients are seen every day at each of the nodal points.

The curative work is further strengthened by pharmacy which ensures that parents with chronic ailments like epilepsy, diabetes, hypertension, heart disease and asthma are provided with continuous and uninterrupted supply of medicines (one month's worth till the next visit).

Patients requiring follow-up treatment like surgical intervention are referred to Baba's Super Specialty hospitals and their problems are monitored till the logical solutions are arrived.

On the diagnostic front, for the few tests that cannot be undertaken on the bus, the team has an innovative system in place. Samples are collected and delivered to the SSS Super Specialty Hospital for testing and reporting.

The preventive work consists of health education based on five major themes: cleanliness, nutrition, healthy air and water, harmful effects of smoking and alcoholism, proper physical exercise and mind relaxation.

Education on these subject is offered through audio-visual presentations, demonstrative sessions, interactive meets and photo exhibition. It is further reinforced by regular screening through the local cable television.

The spiritual base of the service involves educating and motivating the villagers on the importance of positive thinking, human values and age-old practices like prayer and meditation all of which foster positive health.

With this holistic strategy, ninety percent of community's health problems are solved because the approach is professional, proactive and integrated and takes care of common ailments, chronic ailments, preventive ailments, asymptomatic diseases and endemic diseases. Only problems requiring major surgical intervention are referred to the base hospitals.

The impact of the service is tremendous. On the curative front it has given a sense of great security to people living in hundreds of villages around Puttaparthi. It is a boon for patients with chronic ailments who can never dream of buying medicines on a continuous basis. The preventive services have created a huge wave of awareness on major health issues, thereby translating into positive lifestyle changes. The spiritual component of the service has strengthened the community bonds, reviving the practice of human values as a way of life for achieving health and happiness.

Inspired by Bhagavan Baba's call to fulfill their social responsibility through selfless service, medical professionals including doctors, paramedics, lab technicians and pharmacists are seizing this opportunity to express their gratitude to society, which nourishes and nurtures them. The success of this project has triggered a domino's effect in other states such as Maharashtra where a fleet of 29 such hospitals on wheels are being deployed by the Sai Organization to serve six hundred thousand villagers in the interiors of Maharashtra. The Sai Mobile Hospitals bring to rural India not only a state-of-the-art healthcare but also a state-of-the-heart caring and loving services.

ICONIC SPEAK:

- Mr. Ashok Chavan, Former Chief Minister, Maharashtra

Baba is silently promoting values education and spiritual transformation through social service projects on a massive scale globally. His message of unity of faith and the fatherhood of God and brotherhood of man has reached the farthest corners of the globe. My family has been enriched by Baba's blessings.

- Ms. Mallika Srinivasan, Vice-Chairperson, TAFE & Mr. Venu Srinivasan, Chairman & MD, TVS Motors, Past President, Confederation of Indian Industry

We are indeed blessed to have been brought into Bhagavan's fold by his divine grace. He has moulded our lives and those of our children as well, installing in all of us the principles of hard work, good values and, above all, devotion to God.

At times of adversity and personal loss he has been the sole source of courage, assuring us that he is taking care. He has opened our eyes and made us understand that true devotion to him can only be demonstrated by serving and caring for others around us. The only power he uses to transform us is the power of his love.

Acceptance of his will and living by his teachings has filled us both with a sense of inner peace and to him we are both most grateful.

- Ustad Amjad Ali KhanSarod Maestro

In the early 1970s, I first saw Baba with the then Police Commissioner of Bangalore Mr. Nizamuddin. After my marriage to Subhalakshmi, we performed during the 70th birthdsay celebrations. Both my sons Amaan and Ayaan have received Baba love and blessings. Baba has always had special bond with all musicians of India. We are amazed by Baba's vision to create free hospitals, schools, colleges and of course the water projects, which are a testimony of his love for humanity. Once three days prior to my departure for India, I broke my nose. The pain was unbearable. On the flight I even caught a cold. Upon reaching the ashram, Baba granted me an interview. I had not told anyone of my accident. In the middle of the conversation, Baba suddenly stretched his hand and caught hold of my nose, shaking if from side to side for about 20 seconds. I felt no pain. When he released his grip, my nose was completely healed, bone fused and the cold gone. Baba is not only healing broken noses but more importantly the hearts and minds of millions in Latin America and the world.

- Mr. Leonardo Gutter, Argentina-Member-Prashanti Council

I was raised to believe that happiness comes from acquiring wealth, high positions and power. However, experience taught me otherwise. In my first interview with Sai in 19* he said "Material things always change, change, change. Only love lasts." I subsequently learned through practicing Baba's teachings that true love is Love-in-Action, and it manifests and grows through self-denial and selfless service to others in need, filling one with true joy eternal.

- Mike Congleton, M.D., PhD., Presidenet, Pacific RegionSouth-SatHya Sai Baba OrganIzation of USA

This mystical ancient land has gifted the world with endless enlightened beings. If the world is a spiritual train, *Bharath* (India) is its engine and Sri Sathya Sai Baba its current enginner. Sai's boundless love is evident in his historic and unequalled philanthropic achievements in aiding the poor and the suffering. He is your national treasure.

- Mr. Issac Tigrett, Enterpreneur, Founder—Hard Rock Café, House of Blues

At the age of 17, I had a mystical experience a voice said to me, "What would you want to do with this life?" After nine years of searching in vain for thisi inner 'Voice', Sai came to me in a vivid vision. I simply dissolved in the ocean of his Love! Without speaking, he communicated, "I am the one you have been looking for". In that stillness of his presence, I knew him to be that voice! From then he has been teaching me how to be like Jesus.

- Reverend Father Charles Ogada, Catholic Priest, Nigeria

Baba is always there for our family. There are so many instances of difficult times, when he has thrown light on our paths and guided us. With Sai by our side, we feel no fear.

- Dr. L. Subramaniam & Kavita Krishnamurthy Subramaniam, Musicians

Sai personifies *atmic* reality, inspiring me to write three books about him and our family to host a Sai Baba Centre in our home for the past 37 years. His path of loving all, serving all is essential at this perilous time when there is a global disregard for truth and *Dharma*. In my view, he embodies the sacred soul of Mothr India.

- Samuel H. Sandweiss M.D., Psychiatrist—San Diego, USA

Only Sai can lead one to peace, prosperity and potential power in life. By his example, he shows us what constitutes pure love, kindness, charity and real devotion in life. Those who been blessed by him can realize the true presence of God in every atom of the universe, and experience the bliss of eternity.

- Ustad Dilshad Khan & Begum Parveen Sultana, Hindustani Classical Singers

Who among men knows everything that we have thought, felt, said, done and even dreamed? Who among men, cannot be constrained by the laws of time and space or matter and energy as far as our meager knowledge permits us to understand God's creation? Who among men has given his life for the welfare of mankind so magnanimously and selflessly, always giving and forgiveing and never getting and forgetting? Who among men speaks the eternal truth spontaneously and with ultimate authority?

It has been my experience that Bhagavan Baba has these qualities. Four generations of my family and I have basked in Sai's incomparable love.

- Michael Goldstein, M.D., USA—Chairman, Sri Sathya Sai World Foundation

Visiting the Sai Medical Institute and coming face-to-tace with Sai Baba is an experience that awakens even the unprepared mind of a research oriented orthopaedic surgeon. Although completely naïve to religious experience, I could understand the power of love and kindness generated by Baba, and appreciate the peace felt by his devotees. I learned that Sai Baba's community includes all of us. We all can share this miracle, learn to devote ourselves to others, and do our part to serve and improve our world.

- Dr. Leo A. Whiteside, Orthopaedic Surgeon-Inventor, St. Louis, Missouri, USA

Who can ever gauge the relief that his water projects have brought to millions in Andhra Pradesh and Chennai, the free education from elementary to university and the medical care of the highest standards—all free of cost! I pray that Sai completes the century of life and continues to bless us.

- Mr. Sunil Gavaskar, Cricketer

When Sai looks into my eyes, I feel an amazing peace which fills me with a higher energy and understanding. I always return from Prasanthi Nilayam recharged with greater inner clarity, motivated to accomplish the Sai service projects in New Zealand with abundant love.

- Mr. Douglas Saunders, National Chairperson, Sri Sathya Sai Service Organziation, New Zealand

Human love is restrictive, and has causation conditioned by time and space. Sai's love manifests in his compassionate look, loving conversation, protective touch, fervent public speech, annihilation of ignorance through educare and self-less service to mankind and above all, non-dual cosmic love for all creation.

- Mr. Indulal Shah, International Advisor, Sri Sathya Sai Organzations

For over 40 years, Bhagavan Baba's teachings have guided my footsteps and inspired all my actions. He says, "God resides in every human being, therefore service to man is service to God." He does not ask us to renounce the world, but to live in the world, serve mankind selflessly without expectation of any reward and surrender ourselves wholly to the Lord. Baba exhorts us to look past the differences of race, religion, language or caste and seek their underlying oneness.

- Honorable P.N. Bhagwati, Former Chief Justice of India

Sri Sathya Sai Baba is a truly outstanding humanitarian. The Sai Trust's facilities, including the Sai University and the Institute of Higher Medical Sciences are most impressive and I am overwhelmed by the quality of facilities and the professionalism of the staff. These institutions are a standing tribute to Baba's vision and attention to detail. He has given so much. The world needs his kindness and service to humanity.

- Mr. Ratan N. Tata, Chairman, Tata Sons Limited

We are fortunate that Bhagavan Sri Sathya Sai Baba has chosen to share with us his divine wisdom. In a world full of conflict and difficult choices, Bhagavan is a beacon of light and hope in humanity's search for peace and understanding of the divine. The 85th anniversary of Bhagavan's advent is an occasion for rejoicing and praying that his message of universal love, tolerance and unity is imbibed by all.

- Mr. K.V. Kamath, Non-excecutive Chairman of ICICI Bank

I congratulate *Bhagavan* Baba for his enlightened vision, wise leadership, strong emphasis on character building, integrity, civility and compassion. I am particularly impressed with his focus on promoting the principles and values that are common to all regions and cultures of the world. The circumstances of the last several years have demonstrated the critical importance of his idea that only by thinking and working together, as one human family, can we reach the promise of a peaceful and prosperous global society.

- His Excellency Sheikh Nahayan, Mabarak Al Nahayan, Minister of Higher Education and ScientificResearch and Chancellor of the Higher Colleges ofTechnology (HCT), UAE

Love personified, Baba is the most divine being that ever walked this earth practicing and teaching universality and oneness. He guides from within, transforming us silently and subtly. This is the biggest miracle he performs, the miracle of inner transformation. He has stilled the waves of anger in me and taught me to forgive my enemies. He has guided me to serve the needy. In short he is the only reality of my life.

- Dr. J. Geeta Reddy, Minister for Information, Public Relations and Tourism, Govt. of Andhra Pradesh

219

Sri Sathya Sai Baba is an expression of truth in this age. He has moved millions by his spiritual teachings. His five human values have come to be accepted as ethical norms. His contribution to our nation and the world in all areas of human growth and development has been tremendous. The university of Sai Baba embraces the ethics of all faiths, transcending all boundaries. His teachings have an international appeal, breaking barriers of class, country and culture.

- Maulana Wahiduddin Khan, Founder—CPS International, President— Islamic Centre, New Delhi

Sri Sathya Sai Bsaba is an expression of truth in this age. He has moved millions by his spiritual teachings. His five human values have come to be accepted as ethical norms. His contribution to our nation and the world has ben tremondous. The unversality Sai Baba embraces the ethics of all faiths, transcending all boundaries. His teachings have an international appeal breaking barriers of class, country and culture.

(Courtesy: *The Times of India*, 2010)

28

Sai's Precious Teachings

—Dr. Samuel Sandweiss

Swami (devotees addressed Sri Sathya Sai Baba as *Swami*) awakens us to our divine nature. The mind struggles and doubts, but Swami's love tames it and gives confidence. Resting our minds in Swami's teachings and remembering his words bring us freedom.

"The end of wisdom is freedom."

Spiritual Pilgrimage

I would like to look into Swami's endless stream of wisdom that fosters, protects and leads us to God. his wonderful life-giving teachings are the essence of the Vedas.

"My main tasks are the fostering of devotees and the fostering of the Vedas."

Swami's teachings are practical guidelines for a worthwhile life and peaceful society. First he brings us close to him and becomes our omnipresent friend. Then he instructs us to see him in each other.

"See him in every being, every moment of existence."

With this vision firmly planted in eye and heart, he instructs us to practice his teachings in the community. So, the community becomes his very form— love, harmony and unity. This is a critical step in the spiritual pilgrimage—*the practice of spiritual principles for the uplifting and betterment of the community.* Swami has said that his "miracles" attract because of their inexplicability in order to "transform, reconstruct and reform" so that the person is made useful and serviceable for society. In the process, the ego is effaced and the person affirms the unity of all beings with God.

The person who has undergone this transformation becomes a humble, humane servant of those who need help. Service of this kind, done with reverence and selflessness, prepares man to realize the one that pervades the many. So, spirituality leads devotees to become befitting servants set upon building Dharmic communities as a crucial step on the path to union with God.

"The Lord incarnates in human form to re-establish righteousness on a firm footing, and to re-educate the human community on the paths of peace."

Swami has come to save the world community and to re-establish Dharma on a firm footing. He is calling each one of us to this high task. How glorious that an Avatar has come to rally us to this task! For me, meditating on Swami's teachings has helped me to serve the community better.

I have been meditating on Swami's marvelous teachings each morning since meeting him 28 years ago. One day, about a year ago, I felt something—the emergence of a clearer overview. I listed eight core elements which helped me deal more effectively with disturbing problems. as I rest my mind on each element, they speak to the problem and help me put it in proper perspective. My mind finds a place to settle, where confusion can clear.

Eight Elements

1. Remember—Man is God: What a gloriousrevelation! We can believe this incredible truth because Swami shows us his divinity—which awakens us to our own. We are infinitely blessed, because he does not show everyone, only a rare few. So, we must not lose this opportunity of achieving unity with God. this is a new insight for many people. It is an insight that transforms our lives. Remembering turns the mind from the outer world of sensory objects. And he helps us remember. Just being in his presence or hearing about him helps us remember him.

Dr. Hislop told me he saw Swami change into Lord Krishna, and Professor Kasturi told me he saw Swami transform himself into Lord Shiva. Many experiences have convinced me of Swami's loving omnipresence. What grace— God himself is our friend and teacher! Swami's closeness, closer than our breath, helps us remember that man is God! Loving Omnipresent Sai and feeling his love brings confidence in our own divinity and ability to overcome earthly problems.

"This confidence generates immense internal power."

2. The mind is the key: We are unaware of our divine nature because of the limitations of our mind. The mind however has the capacity to overcome its own limitations when aware of them.

"It is the thorn that removes the thorn."

Turn the mind to the left, through the senses to the outer world of objects, and we are trapped in delusion. The mind is attracted by external objects and becomes attached, addicted and deluded. We become locked in the dual world of pleasure and pain, birth and death, happiness and suffering. Turn the mind to the right, inward to God, and we open to our own omnipresent divinity. This is the way to transcend the "mad monkey mind".

3. Develop a relationship with Sai: The only way to tame the mind is to attach it to God, through love. Swami instructs us on the nine steps of devotion, which bring us closer to him. These steps turn the mind/key to the right, to Swami. They include listening to stories about him, singing his glories, contemplating on him, serving his feet, prostrating before him, worshipping him, offering service to him, taking him as friend and surrendering to him.

4. See Sai in the World: One of Krishna's great promises, which Sai Krishna also extends, is to "bear the burden of your welfare", when we offer all acts to him. This teaching instructs us to attach consciousness to God at all times and in every place. We can find him in others and in the outer world once we develop a strong inner contact with God. Thus, we begin the process of attaching to God and detaching from the outer world of sense objects.

5. Bring Sai into the Community: Swami has come to re-establish righteousness on a firm footing so that man can live in harmony and love. This involves practicing spiritual principles. Swami gives us guidance. Right action grows out of holding to virtue and acting according to our conscience, he says. This is accomplished when we constantly ask,

"Is this what Swami wants?"

Swami has given us the prototype fo a Dharmic community in his centres. Dharmic communities are built on the foundation of worshipping God through devotion, service and education programmes. To become good instruments of untiy and love in the community/centre, we must overcome differences. Finding oneness through love and helping to create unity through selfless service is the spiritual path in the outer world that leads us to inner oneness with him. Practicing Dharma requires using our intellect to understand the needs of the community and then to discipline and develop ourselves to serve these needs as an offering to Sai.

"Help ever, hurt never."

6. Commit to the Process of Purification: When we commit ourselves to any relationship such as building a Dharmic community as an offering to Sai in addition to experiencing love, we have to be ready to face problems. Today, commitment is difficult for most of us. (In the U.S. 60% of marriages end in divorce.) A marriage to Sai must overcome the tendency to run away from commitment. It requires the understanding that in order to "Follow the Master", we must be willing to sacrifice.

"Follow the Master, face the devil, fight to the end, finish the game."

We can expect to face trials, tribulations, troubles, fears, anxieties and sasdness along the path. When we stay steady and focused, offering all to Swami, we go through a process of purification and the giving up of our pain.

7. Control the Sense/Mind: Swami has given us tools for controlling the mind and releasing our pain. At the Ashram, he teaches us to remain calm and peaceful and turns us inward by making us sit silently and wait for him.

"Silence is the speech of the spiritual seeker."

And he teaches us to further quiet ourselves by putting a ceiling on desires.

8. Merge in Sai's peace: All the other elements are part of the process of merging in Sai and finding contentment by knowing that all is a gift from him. And Swami tells us there is a final state of oneness with him as well when he and I are one. Sai promises that if we follow the path, it will free us from fear—

"You will draw near to me, you will approach me, you will understand my mystery, you will enter into me, you will melt in me, you will merge in me, you will become me."

Keeping Swami's teachings in mind all the time will bring peace and love to ourselves and our communities. It will guide us to oneness with him. How fortunate we are to have the supreme authority, the embodiment of peace and boundless love to be our guide, guardian and God. Swami has come when we are so beaten and bewildered; he has come with a love that will make us whole and happy. I pray that we immerse ourselves in his love and with dedication, discipline and discrimination become bright instruments of his love and Dharma. We are beholden to you, Swami for being such a clear bright loving light that illumines our minds and dispels the darkness. Let us all *"Be good, do good, see good."* God ServesWhen you offer milk to a hungry child or a blanket to a shivering brother on the pavement, you are but placing a gift of God into the hands of another gift of God! You are reposing the gift of God in a repository of the Divine Principle! God serves; he allows you to claim that you have served! Without his will, no single blade of grass can quiver in the breeze. Fill every moment with gratitude to the giver and the recipient of all gifts.

29

Sri Sathya Sai Baba's Messege for the 21st Century

—S.P. Ruhela

Bhagavan Sri Sathya Sai Baba, the *Purnavatar* of the age, whom all his devotes lovingly address as 'Swami', has covered the entire gamut of morality religion and spirituality in his countless discourses, messages, teachings and pieces of advice to individual devotees all through the year since he launched his Avataric career at the age of 14 in 1940. In the numerous worldwide deliberations of his latest and the most favourite programme of 'Sai Educare' lots of things are being mentioned as his significant messages by speakers bubbling with enthusiasm and devotion.

Swami's messages or teachings have by now assumed the shape of a very vast ocean. So it is really difficult what to select and what to omit out of this vat ocean of his messages when one is asked to make their judicious assessment and clearly state as to what are his salient, radiant or distinctive messages. Based on my about three decades long involvement with the study, research and writing of the Sai movement, I have judiciously come to the conclusion that the following points can be identified as the salient or most distinctive and truly representative messages of our Swami for the new millennium, sand they deserve serious attention of and consideration by all Sai devotees and other enlightened inhabitants of the word.

1. The distinction between the worldly life and spiritual life should be done away with, and one should be believe that "All life is spiritual."

2. Love all and serve all. This is the only penancea for all sorts of hatred, conflicts, tensions, exploitation, wars, suspicion etc. throughout the World Man must become Supreme now in the 21st century. Sri Aurobindo had also greatly emphasized this point that man has for a very long period of his existence on his planet been merely 'Animal man'; for some recent centuries he has been claiming to have become 'Man', but this claim is dubious and unacceptable in view of the widespread anomie (normlessness) prevailing in the world. It is high time that man should now actually and seriously strive to become 'Supreme'—the sooner

he does so, the better it will be for the mankind and the world. Swami seems to be hammering this idea constantly that the functional sort of spirituality for the New Millennium and particularly for the 21st century per se must essentially consist of a genuine commitment to the five foremost universal values—Truth, Righteousness, Peace, Love and Non-violence.

The New Millennium can ill-afford to put up with dishonesty, hypocrisy, jealousies, conflicts, religious and cultural fundamentalism, tendencies of separatism and alienation, violation of norms, laws and rules, crimes exploitation and all kinds of disjunctive social processes which are detrimental to the unity, integration, progress and dignity and moral and spiritual elevation of man. It is necessary of all people in the world to thoroughly understand and intrinsically believe in this fact that sense of security, trust, understanding, unity, purity, commitment to virtues, ideals, and time tested good traditions and customs and noble precedent prerequisites for the future survival of mankind and its progress and advancement in the real sense of these terms. The world has already become a 'global village' and the people of all the nations have became one another's neighbours over riding the geographical distances and their political territories due to radio, T.V., computer, internet and tremendous and frequent explosions of knowledge and the global urge for peace emerging from the hearts of peace people of the world.

3. Swami has shown us the way, set ideal models of social services and social engineering. Like a teacher educator, he has given model lesson to us to emulate his strategies. His examples, strategies, models, concepts and behavioural attributes as innovator, leader, planner and executor of socio cultural and spiritual projects for the bettering the socio-economic, cultural, moral and spiritual lot of the 21st century mankind should be studied closely, understood, properly assessed and then duly followed by all those social planners, social engineers, cultural and spiritual leaders, innovators and political leaders who have the earnest urge in their hearts to improve the battered and burnished lot of the vast majority of the human beings who are living in conditions worse than those of animals.

The following five major thrusts of Swami must be recalled in this connection:

(i) Swami says that free medical care to all people who are ill should be available. He established an excellent Super-Specially Hospital at his Prasanthi Nilayam town in which totally free treatment is given to patients irrespective of their social-cultural backgrounds. Another

Super-Specialty has started functioning at Bangalore on a tract of land donated by the State Government of Karnataka and Swami is providing the same sort of free Medicare therein.

We know that there are countless rich people in many countries who are rolling in obnoxious luxury and debasing vices of all kinds. They are wasting millions of dollars on their immoral and meaningless pursuits, and many of them just do not know how and where to spend their money on good causes. If their conscience can somehow be raised by informing them about the unique models of social service presented by Sri Sathya Sai Baba in South India, surely some of them (if not many) will be most happy to give funds for establishing similar free hospitals for the poor country men in their own countries and also in other poor countries. Not only rich people have given and still giving large donations in the forms of funds, machines and costly medicines to Swami's hospitals, many Sai devotees regular render their voluntary services to Swami's hospitals, many Sai devotees regular render their voluntary services in these hospitals with great dedication. This exemplary model service can be emulated by those peoole who cannot afford to donate funds or equipments.

(ii) Swami holds that free education should be given to all students. In his schools and colleges, this ideal has been put into practice. Only some annual charges for boarding and some other items are taken there.

(iii) Swami wants that Education in Human Values must be given to all students—not only children in schools but even to adolescents and adult students in colleges and universities. A massive programme of education in human values, now renamed as "Sai Educare" programme, is being carried out by dedicated devotees in majority of the countries now.

(iv) Swami likes social service in villages, slums and poor localities. He says that service to man is service to God.

(v) Swami has provided drinking water to thousands of villages in Andhra Pradesh by mobilizing contribution from rich people in India and abroad.

4. Swami greatly emphasizes the sanctity and unity of the human family the basic social unit and the first and the foremost agency of socialization of children. The family must be a caring, shsaring, loving happy kind of family.

5. Swami teaches that one must pay the highest respect to other rand offer due courtesy towards all females.

6. Majority of the people inhabiting our planet are old, and so the future of the world is really in the hands of the youth, who ought to be given due guidance, encouragement and opportunities to develop themselves fully and contribute to the nation's unity, progress and advancement and work for global harmony and peace. They should be saved from the currents sadist fads, vices, fashions and all other variants of the sensate culture.

7. Swami does not like ritualism and exploitation of the people in the name of irrational rituals conducted by priestly class. He wants that all diehard, outdated and harmful religious and spiritual rituals, customs and practices should be discarded and people all over the world should be educated and sensitized to understand and appreciate the finer attributes and teachings of all religions and schools of spirituality and the emerging concept of Universal Religion for the New Age of the Humanity.

8. The concept of 'Global village' and its synonym 'Sai family' must be put into actual behaviour. All narrow, artificial and dysfunctional differences and conflicting tendencies must be quickly done away with. In the present age of sophisticated satellites, computers, super-industrialization, globalization and the widespread impatience or yearning for the early dawn of the New Age, there is no room for favouritism, discriminations, trade union tactics, corruption, bossism, dictatorship, exploitations and all those things which seek to create frustration, agony to the human mind and to degrade human dignity and deny them their legitimate rights.

9. All sorts of bad bahits or vices like drinking, gambling, sexual immorality, economic corruption, exploitation, hypocrisy, vantom destruction of precious natural resources, indecent public behaviour, polluting the environment etc. should become be curbed and human beings should be taught to lead healthy, moral and socially accountable lives.

10. Swami's foremost and constant emphasis during the last six decades has been that people must truly become godly, firm believers in the Karma theory, *Karma Yogis*, real servants of society and saviours of the ecological balance, and faithful adherents of the ideals of their religion and culture and have patriotism for their country of their birth.

11. Swami has been greatly emphasizing bhajan-singing, joining his Sai mission, attending Sai *bhajans*, becoming Seva dal, doing seva, etc to transform human beings into ideal moral and spiritual personalities. But Swami is a strict disciplinarian. In a number of his discourse he has severely criticized the permanent residents and functionaries or workers of his Prashanthi Nilayam Ashram, functionaries of other Sai organizations, seva dals and Sai devotees for their lack of courtesies, rudeness, artificial behaviours and non-observances of the high values taught by him. The message emerging out of such occasional critical comments of Swami is that liberation will not be automatically come to anyone merely by attending bhajans, becoming a functionary in the Sai organization or donning the seva dal's scarf. Liberation will have to be earned by genuine love, sincerity, transparency in character and behaviour and adherence to the high values of ethical and spiritual life. We see that so many corrupt politicians, discredited leaders, businessmen, industrialists and other professionals of doubtful have also been going to Swami for getting his blessing, grace, and gifts of materializations of *vibhuti* (holy ash), rings, statues and the like. Although outwardly *Swami* seems to be welcoming them in his *Ashram* and obliging them, yet one should not infer thereby that such violators of the basic laws of ethics, morality, culture, public decency and spirituality will be favoured by him and granted liberation preferentially. When he has declared himself to be God—God of Truth and Justice, how can he himself break his own established spiritual laws and show undue favouritism to them at the time of granting liberation?

12. Swami once said "We cry when we are born, we cry when die, in between we cry so many times, but do we cry when injustice is done to anyone in society?" This, I think, is the most important message of Swami, in the context of today's world which should be taken to heart by all right thinking men and women though out the world. Unfortunately we do not find this message ever mentioned and seriously discussed in the various deliberations of study circles in the Sai organization these days. The whole edifice fo peace int eh world and the very possibility of the dawn of the New Age or New Era in the near future rest on this very premise. Social reform and political cleansing is the crying need of every nation today, but unfortunately this point is not being badly stated by almost all devotees, organizational functionaries and spiritual seekers and even by most of the spiritual gurus of the present times. We hope and pray that Swami will stress on this vitally message of his more often in his future discourses, and Sai Study Circles will also follow the suit.

13. The last most significant point discovered by me in the countless messages of our *Swami* is the message of Optimism. Unlike most of the religious preachers and spiritual gurus who project themselves as the Prophets of Doom, mostly talking of sin, misery, despondency, hell, divine retribution guilt and the like, Sri Sathya Sai Baba hold before us the vision of optimism. All can and have to enter the Golden Age or the new, he exhorts us, by following his basic teachings and advices as highlighted above. He exhorts all his devotees and organizational functionaries to face the challenges of the new millennium with firm faith in God as well as in . . . own self, and to work for the early coming of the Golden Age for the humanity with determination, enlightenment, sense of commitment, purity and unity and belief in the inherent goodness in spirituality.

Thus not only Sai devotees but enlightened and objective followers of other spiritual gurus and all earnest inquisitive spiritual seekers who are really concerned about the moral and spiritual elevation of man in th New Millennium can clearly understand and appreciate the distinctive attributes of the Sai utopia of spiritual regeneration of mankind which is possible to attain by following he moral, social service and spiritual leads given your Swami.

Difficulties are bound to be there and they are already there. Intra organizational cleansing and inter faith collaborations are urgently called for. Mutual jealousies, bossim's, suspicion towards others and the tendency of considering oneself to be better or holier that others are found to be there in all religious and spiritual organization at the commencement of the New Millennium.

Let us not be oblivious of the fact that there are so many saint, God men and God women and other Gurus in the world who are also presently engaged in the crucially task of reforming and elevating the mankind. We all need to respect them as we do our Swami and know how to seek mutual collaboration with them and work for the same noble task.

(This article is the summary of a long lecture on this very theme delivered, on invitation, by the author at the Foreigner's Library—'The Joy Thomas Archives and Collections and Reading Room' at Shanti Garden, Shanti Lane, Prasanthi Nilayam, outside *Swami's ashram* on Janurary 3, 2000, with was attended by Sai evotees from a numberv of countries.)

30

Sathya Sai Education in Overseas Countries

—Dr. Pal Dhall

The formal Education system developed over the last two hundred years in the West and now universally adopted is flawed. It fails to meet the real needs of the children, the family, the community or the nation. It was developed in the industrial age and its main objective was to secure economic well-being of nations. It promotes inequality and competition and divides the world into rich and poor nations. Such an education with its emphasis on technical and academic achievements does not promote holistic development of the child. Crime, drug addiction, depression, anxiety, family tensions, violence, delinquency and suicides are on the increase in all the countries of the world. the natural resources are bing freely exploited and the planet is reaching non-sustainability. Educationists agree that most of these problems could be solved if we reform education to meet its two goals—development of character and academic excellence. But they have not been successful in reforming education to attain both these goals.

Philosophy of Sathya Sai Education

Sathya Sai educational institutions are based on the philosophy of education propounded by Bhagavan Sri Sathya Sai Baba. He gives equal importance to educational achievements and spirituality. He emphasizes that education must give technical knowledge as well as skills to lead a balanced life. The children must develop insight and understanding into their own life's purpose. They must develop a lively social conscience and serve society, and develop a strong identity with their family and culture, nation and humanity. Sathya Sai Schools are base don these central features fo Bhagavan's philosophy. They aim at human excellence through developing all personality domains—physical, intellectual, emotional, social and spiritual, and not just the intellectual. These schools do not charge any fees. They follow the mainstream government curriculum. In these schools, the culture is suffused with human values of peace, love, truth, right conduct and non-violence. There are now dozens fo Sathya Sai Schools in overseas countries. Many of these schools wer estarted in the 90's, and more and more are being established all the time. They are models of how human values can be integrated with the school curriculum to achieve the real aims of education—character development and academic excellence.

Institutes of Sathya Sai Education were established to manage and oversee standards in the Sathya Sai Schools, to train teachers in Education in Human Values (EHV) and to form professional links (or partnerships) with government or private schools for EHV (Education in Human Values). They have the task of developing EHV programmes appropriate to their local culture, to create awareness and guide government schools to establish such programmes. The question arises as to what extent the Sathya Sai Schools and Institutes have succeeded in their avowed aims and objectives. What is the impact of Sathya Sai Education?

Impact of EHV on Children

There is a global trend towards a materialistic culture based on technology and commerce. In this culture, television, rapid communication, mobile phones, internet, computers and CD players are important elements. Children's main entertainment is from watching TV, and a significant part of their time is spent with the computer, isolated from others. A lot of values, language and role models are based on what they watch on the TV. The programmes often glorify violence and are sensual. Children are, in general, more lonely now because the size of the family is smaller (with fewer children), and neighbourhood where the children can play with others is less safe. Moreover, both the parents work away from home and the time spent with the family has decreased. As a result of all these trends, children now have less well-developed social and emotional skills. Their language is not anchored in values and their morality is weak. Many children have problems with concentration because they have become passive from watching too much television. The violence that they see on the television makes them fearful and indifferent to pain and suffering. In fact, they see war and violence as a part of everyday life from watching world events.

Sathya Sai Schools counteract these by giving children capacity of focus through silent sitting. Their discrimination is nurtured as also their problem-solving skills. Many techniques used in Sathya Sai Education give children good social and emotional skills and enhance their understanding of morality. Transformation of children is the main purpose of these schools.

People observe that when children from many schools are gathered together, those from Sathya Sai Schools are identifiably different. They are more disciplined, gentle, kind, friendly, and in general have better social skills. Parents are the first to notice their chidlren's transformation. Their children become more respectual, assume greater responsibilities, go to bed and rise early, do not watch as much television, are more attentive and focused, more interested in their studies, and more diligent with the tasks assigned to them. Several parents have commented that their children have become aware of wastage and are conscious of the need to recycle toys, clothes, paper and water. They say their prayers before eating and show respect for food. In a number of Sathya Sai Schools—Australia, Thailand, Africa, Latin American countries, Taiwan, parents have expressed delight to notice how their children are fresh and content when they come home from the school and believe that silent sitting, daily prayers, and vegetarianism promoted by the schools contribute to this. Some parents remark on the peace and harmony in the classrooms and have observed that the school atmosphere is conducive to learning; the teachers are dedicated, caring and good role models. Many parents move from other areas specifically to be close to a Sathya Sai School in order to enroll their children.

Experienced teachers who come to Sathya Sai Schools from government schools have noted that the children are eager to learn. They are loving, more friendly, caring and helpful to others. In the Australian Sathya Sai School, children were friendly even to a violent child, regarding him with affection. They are keen to look after the school, attending to cleanliness and tidiness and their honesty is obvious. In the Australian School when a newly enrolled child could not find his pencil, he said, "Someone has stolen my pencil". The other children looked with amazement at him and one replied, "But no one steals in this school". They take care not to damage books and computers. They are respectful towards the teacher. They trust the teachers more and are open in their communication. Regarding the teacher as part of the family. Similar results have also been seen in the government schools which have had EHV programmes introduced by the Sathya Sai Institutes. The Australian experience is a good example. In Australia, indigenous (Aboriginal) education has beeen a challenge to the government. Pouring in more and more money and creating better educational facilities did not provide a solution to the poor achievement levels, high dropout rates, and high educational failure in this community. In one such school, a teacher noted that the attendance was poor, often only 5 or 6 chidlren in a class of 30, and the children in the afternoon were not the same as the ones in the morning. There was hardly any discipline—the playground was a place of fights. The school had litter all over and the windows were broken. The children had poor social skills, and educationally the school was a failure.A new principal appointed in the school invited the Australian Sathya Sai Institute to establish a partnership in EHV in this school. The teachers were enthusiastic about the programme and implemented it diligently. The results are nothing short of miraculous. Two years later, research by one of the teachers at the school for a thesis tracked the progress of the children and the school culture. He found that the school was a clean and tidy campus. The children were focused and interested in their studies. They had developed good social skills and were now able to resolve their own differences; schools fights were rare. To solve their differences they either negotiated with each other peacefully or took their problem to a teacher rather than resort to fights. Academic levels are now at par with other camparable schools.

Education Queensland (the Government Department of Education) has located a research unti in this school. The school principal was "The Queenslander of the Year" and the teacher who had acted as the human values education coordinator in this school, recognized for her work, was chosen as one of the seven teachers in the state to receive "Teacher of the Year" award. This school is now regarded as a model for Aboriginal education.

Another success story is the Sathya Sai U-Turn Training School in Australia. This school runs programmes for adolescents, boys and girls in grades 7, 8 and 9 who are identified as 'at risk' of educational failure by their own Government High School. The High School refers 'at risk' adolescents to the Sathya Sai U-Turn Training School. Here they are exposed to human values through a programme based on the teaching of Bhagavan through the world "WATCH": watch your words, actions, thoughts, character and heart. The programme gives these adolescents social, emotional and moral skills, while the adolescents are engaged in blacksmithing, woodwork, leatherwork, sewing, painting and knitting. They work closely with the teachers. This builds thei self-confidence and trust and they are transformed. To date almost all of the 43 'at risk' adolescents who have attended the Sathya Sai U-Turn Training School in Australia have improved their educational performance. The local High School, the local Museum and the Municipal Council are now partners in this programme. Both the parents and the teachers regognize the U-Turn Training School as an institution to reclaim 'at risk' adolescents. Schools in Zambia, Thailand, Kenya, Nigeria, Malaysia and several Latin Amercian countries have had similar experiences with EHV for adolescents 'at risk'. There seems little doubt that EHV is an excellent method for reclaiming adolescents who are heading towards educational failure.

Impact on Education System

Because of the benefits both to normal and educationally challenged children, it is not surprising that EHV is being introduced or being contemplated for introduction into mainstream education in a number of countries. For example, in Kazakhstan, an Islamic country, EHV is being introduced widely into the government schools. In fact, it seems wherever there are favourable circumstances—open and receptive societ, belief in God, general awareness of the need for values in education, generous donors (for Sai Schools) and good leadership in the Sai Organization and Institutes—EHV is taking root and is being accepted by the government schools. Latin America is a good example. 40% of all Sathya Sai Schools are within Latin American countries. Eleven Sathya Sai Institutes are active in training teachers from government schools. In Chihuahua, with a population 1,25,000, EHV programme is being run in 35 schools. The Ministry of Education has set up its own Human Values Committee and is running its own courses in ethics and values. However, surveys by the local Sathya Sai Institute show that the teachers prefer the courses of the institute as these are transformational.

In Thailand, the government regards the Sathya Sai School as a model of education for wide adoption. Following a seminar of Human Values in Education and Family in 2003 in Malaysia, almost 60 schools expressed interst in EHV programmes in their schools. In Chinda, the government acknowledges the need for education reform to include an emphasis of values. Apparently, the widespread single child family there is producing a generation of self-centred children with poor social skills. These effects are being compounded by the rapid economic progress, which is heightening materialistic trends in that society. A Professor of Education in Guanzao is working on a phased introduction of EHV programmes into the public school system—6 schools at a time. He has had good results and is enthusiastic about the future of EHV in China.

In Sri Lanka, the Sathya Sai Organization and the institute held a seminar with the educators from the local universities and officials from the Ministry of Education in 2004. The institute regards EHV as the programme that would spearhead education reform in the country.

Impact of Parents

Partents become aware of Human Values through the newsletters and the parent link material that requests them to support their child by practicing values at home. The community service that the children undertake through the school also influences the parents as also do the courses in human values for the parents that many Sathya Sai Schools run. In many Sathya Sai Schools, the children stage an annual event, a human values school play or a musical that the parents are invited to attend. In the Sathya Sai School in Australia, parents are actively involved in service to the school. Some take classes in art, yoga and music. The impact of all these activities is enormous. The parents become aware of their role in the values education of their child. Their relationships in the family improve and are spiritualized. In some cases, the children become values activists in the family, many times correcting even their parents.

Impact on the Community

Sathya Sai Schools are acting as the nuclei for creating better understanding in communities devided by ethinic, political and religious differences. In Fiji, the division between the Pacific Islanders and the Fijians of Indian descent has been deep for generations resulting in serious political turmoil including an attempted coup. The Sathya Sai School in Fiji is located near a local village; 40% of the children at the school are of Islander descent and the rest are of Indian origin. The children learn both Hindi and Fijian and the parents from both ethnic groups have reached levels of understanding never seen before. The Prime Minister observed in the Parliament that if politicians could follow the example of the children and parents in the Sathya Sai School, then all their problems would be solved!

In the Kesaju Sathya Sai School in Kenya, the local Imams, suspicious of the "free education" objected to their children praying with children from other religions. The Imams were invited to hold prayers in the school. Now the Muslims are accepting prayers of other religions. This has been deeply unifying for the community. Similar experiences are reported from some of the Latin American countries where Catholic nuns have run EHV in Catholic Schools. They have been able to convince Mother Superior and the Bishops that they do not see conflict between Bhagavan's and Christ's teachings.

31

Some Thrilling Miracles of Sri Sathya Sai Baba

Sri Sathya Sai Baba has been worldwide wellknown for his miracles of diverse kinds experienced by innumrrable persons of all races, religions and, countries an—devotees and even non devotees—throughout the world. His mirszcles asre still happening in many places even though he shed his shed his motal coil in 2011,

❖ **The Miraculous Vibhuti in Australia in mid 1970's**

How the faith of a little girl Mayan gave her a new life.

Howard Murphet and his wife Iris met the Harrison family in 1976 and through them could see the unfolding Australian miracle: For a detailed account of this incident, over to Howard Murphet's *Man of Miracles*:

Early in 1976 in Australia my wife and I became acquainted with Pearl Harrison, a retired secretary of the faculty of a university in Sydney. At first we thought this seemed to be just a chance meeting, but later we thought this seermsed to be just a chance meeting . . .

At that time the manuscript of my book 'Sai *Baba Avatar'*, after much rewriting, was ready for the final pblication. Pearl, although busy with volunteer welfare work, expressed a desire to type of the manuscript. Why she should desire she did not understand, but she does now. Anyway, arrangements were made for her to do the typing, and thus she was introduced to the miracles of Baba. One of her two grand daughters, eight-year-old Mayan Waynberg would, at times, help Pearl by reading the material to be typed. While the grandmother felt skeptical about the miracles, the granddaughter accepted it without question. To the child they seemed quite natural. The typing of the first few chapters had been completed when Mayan, who had lately been looking very pale andwas taken to a doctor for a blood test. The doctor was appalled at the results. He strongly advised that the child should be collected from her school and home to rest without delay. He also made immediate arrangements for her to be given a bone-marrow Prince of Wales Hospital in Sydney. At this stage the family became very worried indeed. Pearl told me about it when I called to find out how the progressing. I could see she was afraid, very afraid, that he rlittle granddaughter mighthavesome dreadful disease, like leukemia. It proved nto to be leukemia, but something equally lethal. Her blood picture at that time showed the haemoglobin count at less than half normality, the white components of blod about a third the normal level and the platelets way down to one-fifteenth of the normal count. A specialist told her mother that the only treatment was the use of certain drugs—, Prednisolone and Fluoxymesterone. From both of these, distressing side effects could be expected, such as stunting the child's growth, causing and obesity, hair growth on the face while causing baldness on the head. The patient would need to have blood and bone marrow tests to monitor her condition. As Mayan had a deep phobia about needles piercing and blood vessels, this was a frightful ordeal for her and everyone else concerned. But the most tragic part of the situation was that, after going through this treatment and suffering its side she would still not be cured. The best that could be expected was a few more years of life, with very limited* drug therapy was not a cure, the elders were told; all it could do was to delay the inevitable for a time. No one knew how long that period would be.

In this sad situation Pearl thought about the Sai miracles she had been typing. She writes:

"I must admit to complete lack of faith in religion, considering myself a Jewess by tradition but not uninfluenced by the typed about many miracls that Sai Baba had peformed, and had thought how interesting it all sounded had not this deadful disease not occcured to my own grand daughter, I might have let go at that. Then it was as if my mind suddenly opened with a jerk, and I began to think that perhaps there was something all I had typed. Howard and Iris Murphet were most concerned when I told, them about Mayan. They said * bring some *Vibhuti* over and Mayan could start taking it immediately."

It has often been said and written that Sai Baba is specially interested in anyone in whom his devotees are. So the link was there. Yet, I remembered him saying emphatically that two necessary ingredients of divine faith and surrender. Could we find such ingredients in this Sydney suburban home, where no one semed to ave religious or spiritual interests, and Sai Baba was a remote, almost fictional, figure in a far-off foreign country?

Well, we could but try. To Mayan I said earnestly, 'You must really and truly believe in the power of Sai Baba! 'Oh, but I do', she replied, and in the way she said it I sensed the simple, child-like faith she had in Christ. A little later, Grandfather Jack Harrison made me feel that he too may be fertile soil for faith. He said, stan garden of their home, 'I am going to India as soon as I can to thank Sai Baba for curing Mayan.' He did not cures her.' The Sai treatment had hardly begun, yet he seemed to have no doubts about its effectiveness. We may be born with faith, that inner certainty of the omnipotent Supreme, or we may acquire it, but we acquire it through reasoning and logic. In fact, the reasoning mind can be a handicap, blocking the birth of knowledge that men call faith.

Grandmother Pearl had her intellectual barriers but a very warm heart. Mother Helen was non-committal. she was atheistic but she was willing to try to *Vibhuti* treatment. We kept assuring the far importance of prayer—constant prayer. They agreed to pray to Swami for his help. My wife and I pray fervently and regularly.

By a stroke of good fortune, our friend Lynette Penrose was about to set off on a visit to Sai Baba. Indident had been in Lynette's home in Balmain that we first began Sai meetings in Sydney. Lynette agreed to take the photograph of Mayan, and letters asking the vital question about drug treatment. We hoped, moreover, that we might have the opportunity of asking him this question, herself, orally. She went off to India, and we all eagerly awaited to hear from her. It was not long before an airmail letter arrived.

Lynette told us that she had been granted an interview and had given the photograph and letters to Swami looked at the photograph, she wrote, 'His face had become very, soft and ompassionate'. About the drud, his reply was, 'No, no drugs, just *Vibhuti* in water twice a day'.

Pearl Harrison writes: 'When this message came back, we had to decide whether to take her off the drugs and take *Vibhuti* only'.

Mayan made up our minds for us. She said, 'If Sai Baba says I should not take drugs, then I won't take them'.

So after just three weeks on the drugs, she went off them and took nothing but *Vibhuti* . . . We felt some responsibility as we had been the channel through which they ahd heard of Sai Baba. We suggested that they start holding Sathya Sai meetings at the Harriso Greenacre. They readily agreed to this, and their house in Latvia Street became the second centre opened for Bhajans and study. The meetings were a success from the start, people coming from all parts of the metropolitan area, and various places in the Blue Mountains and the south coast. Soon Jack Harrison decided to convert his large garage intyo temple, buying a new carport to shelter his car. Within the Sai temple, lined and decorated and beautiful shrine was erected. The place acquired a sacred atmosphere and the size of the group was surprising to see, both at the Greenacre temple and at Balmain, how quickly and wholeheartedly they were singing *Bhajans*.

Many learned to lead the *Bhajans*, the child Mayan being one of them. Mayan's health was soon showing improvement. The family decided it might be better to let the doctors think, for the time being, that Mayan stoppd their drugs. Every two weeks she was given a blood test at the hospital, and the medical people were delighted with the results. No doubt they were surprised too.

There was a dramatic rise in her red blood cell count, a good improvement in the number of white cells, and their count was creeping upwards. After a few months of the Sai *Vibhuti* treatment, with no medical assistance red and white cell count was back to normal . . . . Even though Mayan's condition was showing satisfactory improvement, the platelets were still far from normal it was felt that such a graft would help in arresting the disease. Thus another question was posed to the family should the operation be performed?Fortunately another Australian devotee, just leaving for Puttattaparti, was able to ask Swami wheter operation should be done or not. Swami's reply was deinite: 'She is getting better and will soon be alright. There is no need for such an operation.'

The news came back to Greenacre quickly, and immediately it was decided, to the great relief of Mayan, and all concerned, that there would be no operation. The family felt confident now that nothing was needed. The doctor also agreed to accept a copy fo the book, 'Sai Baba: *Man of Miracles*'. When Pearl handed it to him, she said: 'now don't let it just lie on the shelf; read it, and then pass it on to else. If you feel you don't want to read it, please send it back to me.' It has never come back.(Reference: "*Sai Baba: Invitation to Glory*" by Howard Murphet. Page: 33-41. Published by Macmillan, 1982)

❖ **Mind Boggling Miracles of Sathya Sai Baba By Sri Ghandikota V. Subba Rao.** From '*Sri Sathya Sai Avatar of Love*' Prashanti Society, November 23, 1993

(Mr. Ghandikota V. Subba Rao has been a devotee of Swami for many years. He served with UNICEF and the United Nations, as head of the Energy Section, for 34 years and took early retirement in 1985 to return to India to be with his 92 year old father, Sri Ghandikota Subrahmanya Sastry, the Rishi of the Sathya Sai Gayatri and a renowned Vedic scholar. Mr. Subba Rao has been living in Prashanti Nilayam since 1985, on occasion translating Swami's speeches, giving lectures to overseas devotees, and editing publications of the Sri Sathya Sai Books and Publiications Trust.)

o **Shirdi Sai and Sathya Sai Connection**

That Baba knows our thoughts—indded our past as well as future, has been repeatedly attested to by a large numberof devotees. Just one such example from his writer's own experience is recounted here. For many years, I developed a deep yearning to visit Shirdi. I made several attempts to pay my respects at Shrdi Sai shrine at Shirdi itself but to no avail. The closest I could come to the point of realizing this dream was in 1983, when I planned on my home-leave trip from New York to India to visit Shirdi after our landing in Bombay. Unfortunately, the whole family developed a stomach virus after our first meal in India at a Santa Cruz airport five-star hotel—precluding any extensive surface travel all the way to Shirdi. It was once again a great disappointment.I was thinking of this escapade while intensely gazing at Shirdi Sai's shining silver idol and his giant size picture in the background of the Prashant Mandir Bhajan hall, and also wondering about the connection of Shirdi Baba with Parthi Baba, about which I found numerous references in the Sai Literature. I closed my eyes, with Shirdi Baba in my mind, when to my utter amazement Parthi Baba stood right in front of me while I continued in my reverie. Swami waited till I fully opened my eyes, when with a burst of bliss I clasped his soft lotus feet and hung on to them like a child. Swami beckoned me inside the interview room and materialized a rather large silver ring with an inlaid multi-colored enamel picture of Shirdi Sai—saying that 'I am he'. I was stunned and electrified and I blurted out that at long last my long-cherished desire was fulfilled now! The shining large Shirdi ring on my finger used to attract the attention of my diplomatic acquaintances during my frequent elevator rides in the forty-story UN headquarters building in New York, leading to many inquisitive queries on the strange-looking personality on the ring-face. One thing led to another and before long I found myself presenting Sathya Sai literature to the UN Secretary General in his office!

o **Sri Sathya Sai Study Circle at the UN**

Sensing the growing interst in the story of the glory of Baba, we had founded, with Baba's blessings, a Study Circle at the United Nations headquarters, with regular Thursday gatherings in delegates meeting rooms situated right underneath the UN General Assembly Hall, and sometimes under the Security Council Chamber. Before long, Sai Bhajans began to reverberate in the after-office hours in the United Nations! The annual celebrations of the Study Circle attracted a large number of UN staff members and country delegates. I remember the occasion when the president of the International Court of Justice came rushing along with a couple of delegates seeking Sai Vibhuti (sacred ash). He proudly showed me a picture of Baba in his wallet!

o   **Shirdi Ring Replaced by Sathya Sai Ring**

A few years after Baba gave me the Shirdi Baba ring, Swami called me again for a brief interview, and suddenly inquired of me whether I still wanted the old man or was now ready for the younger man! I then replied thathaving lived with the old man till then, I would welcome the change into company of the younger man! Swami graciously took out the somewhat worn-out big Shirdi ring which then disappeared right in front of my eyes and, then and there, materialized a well-fitting similar silver enameled ring with a picture of Swami showing his Abhaya Hastham—a raised palm assuring protection. This creative gesture and gift signified to me my spiritual (mental) journey from Shirdi to Parthi guided by Bhagavan Sathya Sai himself. As a result, I found myself and family settling at Baba's Lotus Feet in Prashanthi Nilayam—indeed the very abode of peace.

o   **Three Sided Oblong Stone**

This leads me to remember another miraculous manifestation of a triple-sided gray stone Baba materialized for me ten years earlier. Not knowing what to do with it, I kept it as a curio in my UN office desk drawer for two years. On my subsequent home-leave trip, in an interview with Baba, I held up the three sided stone and asked Baba about its meaning and significance. Baba then endearingly chided me for keeping it aside in a drawer and asked me seriously whether I was interested in knowing the meaning (Artha) of its shape or in reaping its beneficial effects (Phala). I replied categorically that my interest was in the benefit it would yield me!

Baba then explained that the triple-headed stone was given as a protective talisman in my numerous global air travels, and therefore I should wear it on my chest. A thought crossed my mind as to how I could wear an odd-shaped piece of stone on my chest. Baba sensed my inner doubt, took the stone from my own hand, held it up and blew, and lo and behold there appeared a twine-sized hole running through the point of the stone. Only a laser could drive a hole of that size through the sharp points on the opposite ends of the oblong stone. Swami then instructed me to insert or a thin wire and wear it like a chain around my neck with the stone resting on my lower chest.

o Materialization of Ganesha's Idol

Whatever article he materialized had a powerful purpose behind it. His materializations are not for exhibition but they are purposive evidence (*Nidharshana*) of their beneficial effects on the receiver. Around the early 1970s, Baba materialized for me a silver diol of Ganesha, saying that this would help me overcome obstacles in my spiritual and professional efforts. That was the time of our founding a Ganesha temple in New York, practically the first traditioanal Vedic style temple in the Western Hemisphere. A stone structure of the *Sarva Dharma* Symbol of all religions adorns the entrance of the Ganesha temple. This symbol was earlier strongly resisted by some of the tradition-bound Hindu devotees of the temple but after Swami appeared in the dreams of several trustees, the opposition melted away to the point that the temple management welcomed the holding of Sai Bhajans in the main hall of the temple facing the Sanctum Sanctorum itself! Today, the Sathya Sai Bhajan Mandali at the Ganesh temple in New York—dating back over twenty-five years—is perhaps the oldest, the most well-attended regularly organized *Bhajan* group in the western hemisphere. Hail to the Sai devotees in the New York Ganesha temple!

o *Vibhuthi* Storm in Connecticut

That the mind-boggling miracles of the Sathya Sai are not confined only to India but spread across the world has been attested to by many overseas devotees. Suffice it here to cite just one striking example repeatedly witnessed by this writer—a virtual *Vibhuthi* storm for a continuous period of nearly two weeks in the house of a Connecticut Sathya Sai devotee. I was overwhelmed by the unending flow of *Vibhuthi* in practically all rooms of that devotee's house and by the Amrith (nectarine fluid) on the Sathya Sai pictures taken and kept by this writer in that house. Inevitably such a miracle draws a large number of curiosity seekers disturbing the meditation of the devotees and Swami therefore advises against any undue publicity to such miracles.

o Revelation of Sathya Sai Gayatri

Some of my most unforgettable experiences of Baba's miracle relate to my father, the late Sri Ghandikota Subrahmanya Sastry, a great doyen of

Vedic learning and wisdom. A collection of the talks and articles on Baba by this great Vedic scholar was published in Telugu as *Sri Sathya Sai Avatara Vaibhavam* (Glory of Sr Sathya Sai Incarnation. My father had received in his long life, many honors but none of these compared with the joy and bliss conferred by Baba on his venerable Vedic scholar who was chosen by Baba as one of the founding members of the Prashanthi Vidhvan Maha Sabha, and who was often invited by Baba to preside over the Dassera Yagna Ceremonies and to deliver Vedic discourses in Baba's august presence. This revered Vedic Pandit was inspired to reveal, in the presence of Baba on the Christmas eve of 1977 in Brindavan, Bangalore—the *vision to Sri Sathya Sai Gayatri*, and electrified the gathering by his subsequent exposition of its meaning and significance. At the insistence of the late Kasturiji, I transcribed this event into an article in *Sanathana Sarathi* of April 1979. The Sathya Sai Gayatri conforms to the Vedic mould and characteristics similar to the other Gayatri Mantras and reads as follows:

"Om Sayeeshwaraaya Vidmahe Sathya Devaaya Dheemahi Thannassarvah Prachodhyaath"

(It means: 'We realize that Sai is the Supreme Lord. We meditate on this God of Truth. Let that All-in-All entity inspire and enlighten us.)

Baba called this Vedic scholar a *Maha Rishi*—a seer and revealer of *Vedic Mantra*—and showered on him compassion and grace in abundance.

o   Rescuing a Vedic Scholar from the Jaws of Death

When my revered aged father was completely bed-ridden with severe complications after a compound fracture of the hip, one morning he even passed into a long coma and the doctors warned us of the impending doom. When we gave up all hope, a telegraphic message reached us in our home town that all would be well soon and that I should bring my father to Puttaparthi for Baba's sixtieth birthday celebrations. My father woke up shortly thereafter with a smile on his lips and narrated, to the astonishment of the doctor, that all through that period Baba was sitting close to the bed, conversing with him, and even invited him for Baba's 60th birthday celebrations. When I inquired with my father whether it could have been a dream or hallucination, he emphatically declared the divine presence of Baba at his bedside and wondered why we did not notice it! The learned Vedic scholar also asserted that when Baba was speaking to him, Vedic passages flashed across his mind and that Baba was indeed the *Veda Purusha* (embodiment of Vedas) himself, exuding the fragrance of *Vibhuti* all around.

With all these happenings, there was no doubt in my mind that the devoted Vedic scholar was rescued by Baba from the very jaws of death. The Vedic scholar lived for a year and a half in *Prasanthi Nilayam* where he received Baba's *darshan, sparshan* and *sambhashan*, i.e., seeing touching and conversing with divinity practically every day.

o Baba—*Shiva Shakti Swarupa*

A few years earlier Baba lovingly performed the 90th birthday ceremony of my venerable father, when he materialized a most beautiful 42 diamond-studded automatic gold watch with gold wrist band. He also materialized a picture of his Shiva Shakti form, reiterating his Avataric source as *Sathyam* (Truth), *Shivam* (goodness) and *Sundaram* (divine beauty).

During my father's stay at the Lotus Feet of Bhagavan towards the end of his life, Baba used to materialize *Vibhuti* (sacred ash) frequently and would himself put it in the mouth of this renowned Vedic scholar and devotee. Once Swami manifested for my father a Shiva Linga of Neelakanteshwara—the blue throated form of Shiva, and instructed that he daily drink the water poured on it for his better health. Another time Baba pulled from the air a small silver medallion of Shiva on one side and the *Shiva Panchaakshari Mantra* (five syllable holy formula of Shiva) on the other side. He inserted, with great dexterity, this medallion onto the sacred thread worn by my father. Swami then stated that Shiva being my father's favourite deity, the silver medallion still wet with sandal paste was brought by celestial Sai messengers as Prasaadam immediately after Shiva Puja in Kailasha (abode of Shiva)! Hail to the glory of Shiva Shakti!

o The Ghandikota Secret Revealed

A day prior to the passing away of my revered father, Swami spoke to me in the verandah of the Prashanthi Mandir and somewhat cryptically told me that my father would go home the next day, being the first day of the Dassera festival, and that Swami would come to our apartment. Since my father's condition was improving, I interpreted Swami's remarks to imply that my father would return home from the hospital the next day. But something prompted me awake at 5 AM of that fateful day, and I sleep-walked my way from the ashram apartment to the hospital nearby. My father's eyes lit up as I lifted him up in my arms when, saying SAI RAM, he passed away in serenity and peace. That same evening after the cremation was over, Baba graciously visited our apartment in Prashanthi Nilayam and consoled us, explained the mystery of birth and death and declared that my father's life was fulfilled in Vedic and Vedantic terms and that he attained final liberation as he was a *Brahma Jnani*—steeped in Brahmic consciousness. On the tenth day of my father's passing away, Swami once again visited our apartment and later in the Poornachandra auditorium, Swami eulogized Subrahmanya Sastriji for his unsurpassed Vedic wisdom and his Vedantic living, called him an immortal soul, and declared that his Vedic scholar lived in the strong conviction of the Truth that Sri Sathya Sai is the embodiment of all divinites. When I heard the last statement from Swami's lips I recalled exactly the same words in Sanskrit imparted and thrice repeated in secret confidence a month earlier by my father. The secret Mantra was revealed by Baba himself to devotee sin Poornachandra auditorium.

o   See God in Rituals and not Rituals in God

Just a few minutes after my father passed away in my very arms, I received a telephonic message of condolence from Baba, and that if we wished the arrangements could be made for the body to be taken to our home town for cremation. On my stating that our sole refuge as well as that of my just departed father was Baba's lotus feet only, Baba promptly made arrangements in the minutest detail for the large funeral procession led by a number of Vedic chanting priests in front and *Bhajan* singing devotees at the back and for the cremation of the body on the river bed of the nearby dried Chitravathi river. Amazingly by the day of the bone-interring ceremony, unexpectedly the river swelled to such an extent as to wash away the bones and ashes—a sign of ritual fulfillment and a miracle in itself!

As promised, Baba visited our apartment the next day to console us personally. He directed me to perform post-funeral ceremonies for a period of ten days in strict Vedic style. When I expressed my ignorance and inability to perform them in the strict scriptural manner and wondered at the necessity of performing elaborate rituals, Baba stated that it was my bounden duty to perform them in memory of my learned father who, for a long period of his life, strictly followed *Vedic Karma Kaanda*—ritual actions. Swami arranged for a priest who was not only an expert in funeral rities but also learned in their significance. Swami instructed me to first understand the importance of each of the numerous ritual actions, before I performed the actual ritual on the ground. The daily rituals used to begin at 8 o'clock in the morning and ended in the late afternoon with a repeated number of baths and fire sacrifices. Swami advised one to read the *Garuda Purana* during this period. When Baba visited us again on the tenth day, he explained why he insisted on my performing these esoteric rituals strictly. Having been abroad all these years, I was like a cooking vessel kept far too long in the attic gathering grime and dust. The vessel had to be thoroughly cleansed and rubbed free of dirt. Baba made it clear that my departed father, being a *Brahma Jnani* steeped in Brahmic consciousness did not require these funeral ceremonies. But it was I that needed purification and understanding through the performance of rigorous disciplines or penance!

Initiated, I thought, by Baba himself into Vedic ritualism, I took to it like a duck to water, with the zeal of a "new convert"! Baba sensed this and promptly applied the brakes. He cautioned me about priestly ritualism and when I remonstrated that it was Swami who got me into it, he told me that the substance of spirituality should not be sacrificed for the shell of ritualism. He opened my eyes when he stressed that loving remembrance and expression of heart-felt gratitude to our forefathers is more important than mechanistical ritual action and that Ashru Tarpanam (offering of tears of gratitude) is more important than Thila Tarpanam (offering of sesame seeds with water).

Swami as a *Vedantic Guru* Par Excellence

Swami is primarily a Divine Aadhyaatmic Guru; he imparts profound spiritual lessons to the devotees on an individual, group and collective basis. His teachings are the quintessence of Advantic nondualistic Supremem Reality. A few experiences of this writer in this regard are given below.

o   Once this writer, just on the eve of his departure from Puttaparthi in a hurry to catch a plane that very morning in Bangalore, was called by Swami to his modest living-cum resting room in the upstairs of Prashanthi Bhajan Mandir. Without being told that I was studying *THAITTIREEYA UPANISHAD* during my week end spare time in Delhi (where I was then a resident representative of a UN agency) Baba, in his infinite grace expounded for nearly one full hour the essence of this famous *Upanishad*. When I began to write it all down, Baba remarked that there was no need to take notes; he assured me that whenever the need arose, I would automatically recall his teachings!

While Baba's teaching was proceeding, Kasturiji came up to request Baba for Swami's article for the monthly Sanathana Sarathi, the issue of which was just then going to the printer. Swami, with a wave of his hand, produced the article and gave it to Kasturiji in my direct presence! When Swami concluded his Upanishadic teaching, he materialized a king-sized hot *laddu* (a type of Indian sweet) as his prasadam to be distributed to members of my family. Furthermore,

Swami assured me that I would definitely catch the plane as it was flying late that day. I reached Bangalore airport with all anxiety but to my pleasant astonishment I was the last passenger on the long delayed flight!

I recall another individual teaching session with Baba also in the Prasanthi Mandir upstairs room. Baba explained to me for almost an hour the five most significant *Brahamasutras*—analytical aphorisms on the supremem Reality. As the saying goes, *Brahma Vidhyaa Vidhyaanaam*—the Brahmic knowledge is the came of all learning. The teaching by Swami was marked as usual by profundity and simplicity, using parables, and filled with good-hearted humor on the other side.

Apart from these exclusive individual teaching sessions, I had the greatest good fortune of listening in the interview room to Baba's teachings on the Bhagavad Gita. Thus I was initiate by Baba himself into the Vedantic lore of the holy scriptural Texts called *Prasthana Trayee*, viz. *Bhagavad Gita, Brahma Sutras* and *Upanishads!* Hail to Bhagavan Sathya Sai, *The Gyan Bodhka Guru.*

When he performed the *Upanayanam* of my eldest son in the early 1960s and also of my youngest son in the early 1980s, he not only materialized turmeric-anointed *Yagnopaveetham* (holy threads) but also patiently taught the *Vatus* (the young boys) the meaning and significance of Gaayatri Mantra recitation, the *Sandhyavandana* (daily prayers) ritual, and the importance of celibate living. Salutations to the world teacher Sri Sathya Sai Baba, *Sayinam Vande.*

Jagadgurum (World Teacher, Universal Master)

Sankalpa refers to the *powers of Siddha Purusha* with acquired—and therefore depletable Yogic powers, whereas *Sankalpa Siddha* signifies the state "mere Willing is Fulfilling"! Swami's undepletable miraculous powers are the most natural and spontaneous manifestations of his love and grace to the devotees.

See and Enjoy Swami's Miracles

That it is not possible to fully understand Swami is aptly expressed by Baba himself when he stated: "In order to understand me, you will have to understand me for so long that your legs are likely to collapse!" Then, what about experiencing him? To this Swami replied that experience is something like experimentation, with yesterday's experience being different from today's and one's experience being very different from other's. Experimentation is "mentation"—a mental act and the Lord cannot be reached, understood or experienced by the mind, *Apraapya Manasa Sah* as the *Thaittireeya Upanishad* states. If one cannot fully understand or experience, what then, Swami? He says, Enjoy—be in joy and end (your mind) in joy! Just as in the Upanishad saying *Aanandho Brahmano Vidhvaan*—The knower lives in Brahmianc Bliss alone.

❖ Apparitions

Over the years, many people have reported that Sai Baba has appeared before them in various places around the globe in a living form—yet he has 'physically' left India only once. One example is Connie Shaw, the American author and lecturer, who states in her book *Wake Up Laughing* that Baba has appeared in her home in Colorado over fifty times! At one point he appeared in the middle of the night, waking her from sleep with a tap on the shoulder, to request that she take over the presidency of a local Sai Center. Since the center was mainly comprised of Indians and she felt it would be inappropriate for a Westerner to lead them, she refused his request. The next night he came again, and again she refused. When he appeared for the third consecutive night she finally relented and agreed to lead the center. When she reluctantly told the president of the center about the apparitions, he confessed that on the same three nights Baba had appeared in his home as well, requesting that he resign so Connie could take his place!

Another example is James Sinclair, an American businessman who had never heard of Sai Baba, and who saw, on two occasions, an orange-robed man with an afro appearing and disappearing in his house in the USA. Inquiring at a spiritual book store if any living Master fit the description, he was shown a photo of Sai Baba, whom he instantly recognized as the man in his home. When Sinclair finally made it to Baba's ashram, the first thing Baba said to him was, "I came to you twice!"

❖ Miracles at Sri Ranga Patna orphanage in India

The Sri Rangpattanmam orphanage, founded by an humnle Sai dveotee Halgappa as advised and blessed by by Sathya Sai Baba in 1968. It is manahged by Halgappa in the spirit of selfless service. It has 50orphan boys, It is run on the support of donations and dedicated staff. It is located on the Bangalure-Mysore highwaymsome 5 kms. North of Mysore it has a small temples in which two great miracles are constantly happening which can be seen by all visitors freely. Vibhuti is constantly manifesting oin the photos of

250

Sathya Sai Baba and Shirdi Sai Baba, and jasmine scented *amrita* (honey) constantly ooze from two small porcelain amulets given by Sathya Sai Baba. Countless visitors from India and foreign countries have been coming here and have been wonderstruck by these miracles.

Testimonies:

A detailed decription of this miracle with its actual photographs and accounts of visitors is avaible on the internetin these files::

File:://1:Sathya Sai Miracles—Miracle at Sri Ranga Patne orphanage IN Mysore, I . . .

http://groups.yahoo.com/group/saibabanews/message/2258

❖ **Miracle I had witnessed at Sai Baba's ashram in 1996.** In the middle of his Christmas discourse, Baba waved his hand and materialized a small gold-covered book—bringing a gasp of amazement from the crowd of 50,000, me among them! (I was seated very close to Baba—and was certain it was a genuine miracle). That night at around 9 o'clock I heard that Baba had announced earlier that angels would be flying above the ashram that evening.

❖ **Baba Takes Lord Venkateshwara's Place**

I was recently a partial witness to an incident which provides another powerful due to Baba's identity. One of the most famous shrines in India is the hilltop temple to Lord Venkateshwara (a form of Vishnu), in Tirupathi, Tamil Nadu. Venkateshwara is considered by many Hindus to be the Supreme Lord, and the idol in this temple is known all over India for the powerful blessings it bestows. As with many of the subsects in Hinduism, there is an understandable quality of exclusivity in the devotees of that shrine, especially among the priests who perform the worship; for generations their families hav been single-mindedly devoted to Venkateshwara alone. One day in late November, 1998, the priests were performing a special *paad puja* (worship of Feet) ceremony to the Venkateshwara idol, when suddenly the idol's feet were transformed before their eyes into the feet of a living man. Looking up, they beheld, in place of the Venkateshwara idol, the living form of Sathya Sai Baba. "If you want full darshan", he told them, "come to whitefield next week!" Baba then disappeared, elaving Venkateshwara in his place.

I was in Sai Baba's Whitefield Ashra on December 6th, 1998, the day the priests from Tirupathi, dozens of them, arrivedt o receive the full *darshan* of the living God who had appeared before them in their shrine. (Courtesy:R.D.Awele)

❖ Baba and Ramana Maharshi

And speaking of *Jnanis*, at the moment of the death of Ramana Maharshi *anis* (*self* one of the greatest Self-Realized Masters of the last century), an extraordinary event occurred in Baba's ashram, giving us a clue both to Baba's identity and his relationship with Ramana. A Sai devotee named Vaadu reported what happened:

". . . the night when Ramana Maharshi passed away in Tiruvannamalai [14th April, 1950], I was with Swamiji [Sai Baba]. Krishna [another young devotee] and myelf were both there. That evening, around 9:00, we continued whatever it was we were doing (I think we were doing a puja) when suddenly Swamiji looked up at us. There was a peculiar way of looking he has which means that he wants to go to his room. The moment Krishna and I went through the door into the room and closed it, Swami fell down. I was ready for it. Krsihna and I both held hands, and Swami was lying across them. Then he rose up into the air, from our arms. He was a stiff as a board. He started murmuring—something about 'Maharshi has reached my lotus feet.' And then the sole of his right foot split open, and nearly two kilograms of beautiful, well-scented *vibhuti* poured out from the sole of his foot. I collected the *vibhuti* while he was still levitating in the air.

Then he came down and returned to his senses and asked what he said. I said, "Swami ji, this is what you said: 'Ramana Maharshi has passed away'. And this is what came out of your feet." He said: "Put it into packets and give it out as prasadam."

A day or two after this incident that we learned from the news papers that Raman Maharishi had died. It had been at that time that Swami said "Maharishi had reached His Feet."

So, at the time of his death, Ramana Maharshi merged in Baba's feet! Is it not therefore clear that Sai Baba is a full embodiment of the Divine Self, the supreme Atmic Reality that Ramana had realized at the age of 17.

❖ Sri Satha Sai Baba—*Namaskar* Miracle in UK

There has been huge mention across the world of Baba's "Namaskar" actions in Sai Kulwant Hall a few days before being admitted into hospital (in

March 2011). As many of you already know, Baba never ever has done this and it is thought it was his way of bidding farewell to all his beloved devotees and ensured it was caught on camera. Please see images below;

However, one devotee in London, UK has been extremely lucky to experience Baba in his own home. There are photos and statues of different Gods covered in vibhuti of different colours. I personally go to his home every week for bhajans and the house has a feeling of warmth and positive vibrations. The family is very kind in opening up their home every week for devotees to pray and join in the bhajans with them.

Yesterday, there was a birthday in the family and Baba was sure not to miss out on giving his blessing. The devotee I mention had printed an image of Baba's "farewell" namaskar, framed it and placed it in Swami's chair. Yesterday wonderful miracle occurred and the photo was bless with vibhuti—confirming to us ALL that Baba may have left us in physical form but will ALWAYS be around us and protect us."

File:"//1Sri sathya Sai baba Namakar Photograph Miracle in UK 2011, htm

Counltess Sai miracles are still happening in many counties and they have been and are still every day being reported on the internat and in many journals and books.

32

Sri Sathya Sai Baba's Miracles in My Life

—S,P.Ruhela

I had the first *darshan* of Sri Sathya Sai Baba in one forenoon in early April, 1973 standing outside the gate of the house No.16, Golf Link, New Delhi owned by Shri Sohan Lal Ji, President of the Sai Organization of Delhi, on hearing from one of my friends that a God man Sai Baba had come on a visit to Delhi to bless people.

1. I reached late. He had already given public *darshan* in early morning which I later came to know on reaching the place, but I decided to wait outside the gate in the hope that he might come out any time and I might have his *darshan*. After some time at about 10 AM, Sai Baba was seen coming out of the building moving towards a waiting car to go somewhere. It was bright sunlight and I was struck by the sight of a dazzling white halo or aura around Sai Baba's head just similar that we often see in the pictures of the prominent gods and goddesses venerated by all Hindus.

I was immensely impressed by this first *darshan* of Baba. I was then facing a very serious problem of life and death in my professional life. A conspiracy had been engineered by my three extremely jealous colleagues in nexus with their crooked friend—the then director of correspondence courses of Himachal Pradesh University under which I had enrolled for Master of Education by correspondence course in 1971 and I had appeared in the M.Ed. Examination 1972. Those antagonists of mine had maliciously conspired and succeeded in getting me declared as pass in just III division in the M.Ed. examination although I was already a Ph.D. in Sociology and was teaching Sociology of Education subject to M.Ed, class in my college in New Delhi. and had been requested and engaged by the Director of Correspondence Courses of the same university in that very year to act as their Guest Faculty to deliver a number of lectures to their M.Ed. Correspondence Course students some centers. I had done very well in my all the written papers of the M.Ed. Examination but. It was a murderous academic attempt Their mean and dirty goal was to get me disgracefully removed from the post of as Reader in Edu the newly created post of Reader in Education (Sociology) to which I had been appointed, while one of them had not been selected in open selection for that post as he was not at all qualified and competent to teach Sociology of Education to M.Ed. class in the Jamia Millia Islamia which was then a Deemed University. They were conspiring to get me removed by the University disgracefully and rendered jobless for no fault of mine but because of their malice and self interest. As ill-advised by his some of his very friendly colleagues, he had filed a case against the university n Delhi High Court against my appointment despite my having doctorate in Sociology and.B,Ed. degree and more than three years and a experience as Lecturer in Sociology of Education in the NCERT. And had publications to my credit. .The petitioner had not studied any such qualifications in Sociology, teaching research, experience and publications in the specialized field of Sociology of Education consequent to my selection in the open contest, which was then still going on since 1970. They were bent upon destroying my professional career. I had aleady resigned my services as a permanent employee of the Government after successfully completing one year of probation as Reader in the Jamia Miillia Islamia Deemed University in December 2000, and so I had no job to return to. This grave anxiety had seriously affected my health—even my hair on the head had fallen and I became very seek.

Immediately after knowing the unjust M.Ed. tesult in 1972 I applied for re-evaluation of all my examination scripts, the the Himachal Pradesh University first denied it saying that there was no provision for re-evaluation in that new university as the then Vice Chancellor was the Godfather and defender of the corrupt and mischievous director of correspondence courses. But when the Prime Minister Mrs. Indira Gandhi's office wrote to the Vice Chancellor to look into my compliant and report back soon and the leader of the Opposition Party in State Legislative Assembly Shanta Kumar of BJP intervened in this serious matter of academic mischief and bungling thus exposing extensively the widespread corruption done by the director of correspondence courses in 1971-72, the University Vice-Chancellor had to relent and ultimately get the re-evaluation of all my examination scripts done. The re-evaluation had been taking unusually very long time—over ten months and I had almost been totally shaken and shattered in body, mind and spirit,

Soon after my having Sai Baba's *darshan* (holy glimpse) in early April, 1973, about two weeks later in the fourth week of that very month, I received my revised mark sheet from the Himachal Pradesh University with no covering letter and posted to me by just ordinary post. The new mark sheet showed that I had passed the M.Ed. examination with 334 marks out of 600 marks) i.e. with good 55.62 % marks. I then heaved a sense of relief and I felt that was only due to Sathya Sai Baba's divine grace. Although I deserved to get First Division marks had there been a proper re-evaluation, but at least my protest, honour, professional security, and my life and family were saved by the reevaluation. and I was greatly relieved. Much later I heard from one of the professors in the National Council of Educational Rsearch&Training, New Delhi that the Vice Chancellor of the Himachal Pradesh had himself come to meet him in New Delhi with my one of my scripts and requested him personally to favour him by re-evaluating my script in one paper most rigorously then and there before him and award the least possible marks on scripts. It was later on heard by me that each of my six examination scripts were got re-examined by him in Delhi in the similar manner, and then the average of the total marks of the both the marks on the re-evaluations and the originally awarded unjust marks was most unusually taken. Even then my position was fourth among all the 904 M.Ed. candidates.

By Sri Sathya Sai Baba's divine grace, good days returned in my life, I was soon invited to come to Srinagar (Kashmir) to serve as an expert in Sociology by the Kashmir State Public Service Commission to act as expert member in the selection committee to select a Lecturer in Sociology. Thus I got the pleasant experience of visiting Srinagar which uplifted my spirit.

2. Before that, one night in April 2003 I had seen a dream in which Sri Sathya Sai Baba appeared before me and poured blue coloured *vibhuti* (holy ash) on my right palm and then he poured grey coloured *vibhuti* on my left palm and said to me, "You come to my *Ashram*, you come to that station but I did not mention the name of the station." I did not know where his *Ashram* was and which railway station I was directed by him to go. After some days I came to know from a book on the life Sai Baba—*Sathyam, Shivam, Sundaram'* (Part I) that one had to travel by train and drop at Penukonda railway station, and thence take a bus from outside the railway station to reach Sai Baba's Prasanthi Nilayam ashram and his adjoining Puttaparthi village.

I could fulfill my great desire to visit Sri Sathya Sai Baba's Prasanthi Nilayam ashram on the occasion of Shiva-Ratri festival in 1974. I stayed there for 4-5 days, saw the nearby Puttaparthi, the native village of Sri Sathya Sai Baba, met his elder brother Sesham Raju and elder sister in their homes and talked to some villagers and people in the market outside the Ashram. Thus I learnt many things about Baba. I most eagerly witnessed all the festive celebrations in the Ashram. Among them I still vividly remember three events. On the Shiva Ratri day in the forenoon Baba materialized a very huge amount of *vibhuti* by putting his hand in an empty small brass pitcher and rotating his fist therein vigorously. A big *paraat* (iron tray used by labourers) full of fragrant grayish *vibhuti* was thus miraculously created by Sai Baba in a few minutes, was showering on a small silver statue of Sri Shirdi Sai Baba kept in a big plate below the pitcher. Thus the *vibhtuti abhishek* (the sacred ceremony of bathing the statue of Shirdi Sai Baba with *Vibhuti* was ceremonially performed by him. There I learnt that Shirdi baba was his predecessor in the Sai Trinity and Sathya SaI had respected him by performing *Vibhati* Bath publicly,

The second thrilling event was in the night at about 9 PM. Sai Baba performed the miracle of materializing a huge most shining *Atma-Lingam* from his mouth, which was emitting light of changing colour. Baba again came to the dais of the Poorna Chandra Hall the next dawn and delivered a short discourse on the significance of the emergence of the miraculous *Atma-Lingam* which he had materialized in the previous night. He blessed the audience saying that all those who had witnessed the emergence of the *Atma-Lingam* were very privileged and fortunate people who would achieve *mukti* (liberation), that is they would have no more rebirth and be completely freed from the karmic cycle of birth, death, and rebirth, and that they should hence forth lead sacred life, This unique historical declaration in the discourse of Sai Baba and the photo of the *Atma-Lingam* miraculously created by him in the Shiva Ratri of 1994 were published in an important volume '*Vision of Divine*' by the eminent doctor, photographer and Sai devotee Dr. Fanibunda of Bombay in 1975 and its several reprints were brought out by Sri Sathya Sai Books & Publications Trust, Prasanthi Nilayam in later years in the 1970s.

The third event is still vividly remembered by me In the function in the Poorna Chandra Hall in the afternoon in which some devotee-speakers narrated their spiritual experiences and views, One school girl speaker narrated the very moving story of the ancient tribal old woman Shabari who had offered *ber* (berries) after tasting them to Lord Rama so that no sour *ber* fruit might go inside the mouth of divine guest Lord Rama. Baba listened to her narration of the thrilling story of the ancient tribal devotee Shabri with rapt attention closing his eyes and as soon as she finished and bowed down to offer *pranam* (salutation) at Baba's feet, he opened his eyes, stood up and instantly materialized a gold locket with gold chain and presented to her and thus blessed her before all.

Just before my visit to Prasanth Nilayam I happened to find and read the then recently published book "*A Value Orientation to Our System of Education t A Value Orientation to Our System of Education o Our System of to Our to Our System of Education*" (1973) edited by Professor V.K.Gokak, Vice-Chancellor of Sri Sathya Sai Institute of Higher Learning (then a Deemed University), in which were reported all the proceedings of the first Summer Course on Indian

Culture and Spirituality' organized by the Sai Trust in the premises of Sri Sathya Sai Baba's second ashram 'Vrindavanam' and Sri Sathya Sai college for men in Kadugodi, village near Whitefield railway station about 20 miles from Bangalore. I was greatly impressed by the fact that so many learned scholars from different parts of the country had been invited to the unique Summer Course on Indian Culture and Spirituality organized by and in the physical presence of Sri Sathya Sai *Avatar* and the summaries of the learned speeches of all had been given in that book.

As I was teaching theory of education in my institution and was keenly interested in value education, a wish sprang up in my heart that I should also contribute to the next Summer Course at Whitefield, if invited. After finishing my visit to Prasanthi Nilayam I travelled to Sai Baba's second ashram in Whitefield and met Professor V.K.Gokak, Vice Chancellor of Sri Sathya Sai Institute of Higher Learning, who then staying there. I met him and expressed my keen wish to be invited to deliver two lectures on Education in the 'Sai Sai Age India' in the ensuing Second Summer Course on Indian Culture and spirituality in May-June 1994. He replied that as the director of the Summer Course he would include my name in list of the guest speakers to be invited which he would submit before Swami for his final selection of the names of the speakers to be invited. This assurance gladdened my heart and I started praying to Baba for it.

My prayerful wish was granted by Swami and I was invited by Prof. Gokak to reach Swami's college in Whitefield and deliver two lectures on ':Education in the Sai Age India' in the first fortnight of June 1974. I was made to stay in the ground floor room just below Swami's room on the first floor, in the company of the famous Sai devotee Justice Bala Krishna Eradi of the Kerala High Court (who later on became the Chief Justice of Kerala High Court and then was elevated as Judge of the Supreme Court) and another ardent Sai devotee Sri Shastri, lecturer of English in a college in Nellore (Andhra Pradesh). We three slept on the floor of the small room. In the few nights stay there in that room, they narrated their own thrilling experiences of Sai Baba's miracles. My lectures on two days in June 1974 were well received. Then I was privileged to be called by Baba for a private interview in late night after his discourse. He assured me that he was and would always be with me in my life,. Thereafter Sunday came, all the students of the Summer Course did the (voluntary service) and cleaned the whole garden and space and assembled in the garden by 10 AM. Then Swami descended from his room and Professor Gokak, some other high ups of the Sai organization and we three speakers followed him and reached the garden where the students and others including the well-known Australian Sai devotee

Howard Murphet (author of *Sai Baba, Man of Miracles*) were sitting waiting for Baba. A mike was placed.

Reaching the mike, Baba asked the audience "Who will speak on Social Service?" After a prominent Sai devotee Chopra from Calcutta and the famous Australian Sai devotee Howard Murphet politely declined by tilting their head, in my youthful impatience an exuberance I raised my hand and Baba asked me to come before the mike. As soon as I wanted to speak on the mike, I saw a sea of utter darkness rolling in my mind, then I mustered courage and could hardly utter the two two words *"Hridayasi* Baba . . . (Indweller of heart Baba . . .), just then the electric current of the mike went away and it became mute Then from behind Swami quipped," *Baba hridaya mein nahi hai, peechoo khada hai.* (Baba is not in your heart, he is standing behind you). Alright you continue . . ." and instantly electric current returned and I gave a very short lecture on Social Service. After that Sai Baba gave a long and very interesting and informative discourse on the same topic in Telugu which was being translated sentence by sentence into English by Dr.S.Bhagvantham, retired director of the Indian Institute of Science Bangalore, who was Sai Baba's famous devotee. When the last sentence of Sai Baba's Telugu discourse was being translated into English, Baba stepped behind, came hear me and asked me *"Theek hai?"* (Is it (My discourse) O.K.?" I could not utter a single word then. How was I competent and how could I dare to comment on the appropriateness of the discourse of the *Purnavata*r (Full incarnation of God) of the age? It was his modesty and humanness to ask for my opinion on his divine discourse. I can never forget this poignant incident in my life.

3. In the personal interview at Whitefield in the later evening of 9th June, 1974 I requested Sai Baba to kindly come to bless my new house which was then under construction in Faridabad and he kindly agreed. I was short of funds but after returning from the Prasanthi Nilayam I was able to mobilize necessary funds to complete the house by November 1994. Then I sent an invitation to Sai Baba to kindly come on the inauguration day at my new house which I had named *"Sai Prabha".* Many Sai devotees from Delhi were invited by me to kindly come to my new house in six cars which were arranged by my uncle—by Swami's grace actually. They were told by me that Sai Baba had in the personal interview granted to me by Him in June 1994 had agreed to come on its day of inauguration of the house, and so all were very excited and expecting Swami's coming miraculously any moment.

Just as the *Sai Bhajans* were about to commence, the big garland of flowers placed on Sai Baba's framed photo suddenly broke which denoted the coming of Sai Baba; the *Bhajan* session enthusiastically started, a mysterious blue torch light was seen by all the people moving in all directions of the fall. After the *Bhajans*, lunch was served to all the guest Sai devotees. More than the invited and expected number of Sai devotees, friends, neighbours, car drivers and friends had come but by Swami's miraculous grace and blessing the food that was prepared by us for lunch to all multiplied, all people were sumptuously fed and still a lot of food t had remained in the kitchen.

While all the Sai devotees from Delhi left after taking their lunch with the full belief that Swami had indeed come in his subtle form in the *Bhajans* in my new house, my wife and I were intensely expecting Sai Baba to come to our house in his physical form and so we were waiting for Him even after all the Sai devotees and guests left. I as pained to think that Sai Baba had not kept his words given to me in the interview at Whitefield.

After some time a young girl of one of the rather distant neighbour came running into our house and excitedly told us that Sai Baba was coming. My wife, younger sister and I hastened towards the gate to receive Sai Baba, but not finding him, I asked that girl where was Sai Baba. She immediately pointed towards the vast open vacant space of plots from where a small black snake was seen hastily coming towards our house from the north direction. The snake stopped outside just close to the boundary of our house. It sat there sitting motionlessly at that very spot for over three hours from 2.30 PM till it became dark. Standing inside the boundary wall we just kept watching it constantly, A Keralite young man known to us who was present there told us that if we believed in the divinity and miracles of Sai Baba we ought believe the snake to be Sai Baba and worship him by placing *prashad* (consecrated food offering) near the snake and recite Sai Baba prayer. Readily accepting his suggestion my wife and I went outside the boundary wall placed the *prashad* near the snake, fearlessly stood very close to it and recited the Sai Baba *aarti* (worship tsong), and the snake just kept sitting there all the while without any movement of its hood or tail. After offering the *aarti* we came inside the drawing room to eat dinner, But within 2-3 minutes out of curiosity to see that snake we again came out near the boundary wall and found that the snake had already vanished in from there.

I had read in one of the books on Sai Baba that he sometimes appeared in the form of a snake and so I had to console my heart that Sai Baba might have come to my house also in the form of snake. But the doubt remained: even it be so, why did the snake not come inside the house. This became a puzzle to me. I really wanted confirmation from Sai Baba himself whether he had come near my house in the form of that snake on the day of the inauguration of the house, but since all my funds had finished by then there seemed to be absolutely no possibility of my being able to travel all the 2000 and odd kilometres to Whitefield or Prasanthi Nilayam to meet Sai Baba just to get the doubt lurking in my mind removed by Him by confirming that he had actually come near my house in the form of that snake.

4. By Sai Baba's miraculous grace, within a few days my former colleague in the National Council of Educational Training and Research, New Delhi Dr.B.S.Goel, Reader, invited me to go with him officially to act as a Resource Person in the NCERT workshop on text books that he was going to conduct as director in the Regional College of Education, Mysore. I agreed to do so believing it be the Sai–sent opportunity to clear the doubt lurking in my mind for several weeks.

Although Dr. B.S.Goel had been a hardcore Marxist and atheist for most of the years of his life, he had later on become a realized soul, a staunch believer in and devotee of Sri Sathya Sai Baba after some in early 1970s. Later he resigned his job in the NCERT, became Siddheswar Baba, established his own *ashram* at Bhagaan village in Haryana State and started teaching *Kundali Yoga* to spiritual seekers including many earnest foreigners drawn from France, Germany and a number of other countries

He had met Sai Baba some years back at Prasanthi Nilayam and received Sai Baba's blessings on his remarkable books, but he had never seen Sai Baba's Vrindavanam ashram at Whitefield near Bangalore. So we planned that as we would together reach Bangalore in early morning and from there we take another train for Mysore in night and in between, we would have the whole day-time at our disposal to visit Whitefield, see the Baba's *ashram* and have Sai Baba's *darshan* there as Sai Baba was generally living in Whitefield in winter season. Thus I got the Sai-sent (God-sent) opportunity to visit Sai Baba again at Whitefield. Both of us reached there in early morning and stayed there for some hours till Sai Baba came out to give public *darshan* in the compound at about 10 AM. Sai Baba while walking among the devotees came and stood just a few steps from where I was sitting in the crowd of the devotees. He gazed at me compassionately for some minutes. I saw the sublime sea waves of compassion rolling in his deep loving eyes and I could instantly realize that I thus got his positive answer to my query or puzzle in my heart which confirmed my belief that he had indeed come to my house in the form of that black snake on the inauguration day.

5. Some days after returning to Delhi my family witnessed another Sai miracle in our old house in Delhi where we were still living. One day we planned to go to our new house at Faridabad taking a neighboring Sai devotee's family for an hour's *bhajans* there. For that all lunch articles had to be prepared in the morning at our Delhi house itself to be carried with us to Faridabad for about 10 persons who would be going there. My wife was cooking *pooris* (puffed baked cakes) in the morning on the gas stove. Suddenly my youngest son Arvind stepped on the gas cylinder to fetch something from the loft of the kitchen and at once the gas cylinder as well as the frying pan full of a lot of boiling *ghee* turned upside down, the boiling *ghee* (clarified butter) sprinkled on my wife's feet and the floor, it spread all over the kitchen. My wife cried as she was feeling the burning sensation as both her feet were burnt by the boiling *ghee*. A serious accident was going to happen. Every one in the family and neigbourhood were at their wits end and cried. One of the daughters of the Sai devotee, whose whole family was to go with us to Faridabad for the *Bhajan,* ran to her house close by to bring Sai Baba's miraculous *haldi* (Turmeric) powder that had appeared on Sai Baba's photo in their house a few days back., That miraculous *haldi (turmericpowder)* was immediately applied all over her feet and that gave instantly soothing feeling of cold and complete relief to my wife. The gas cylinder did not burst and a major fire accident was prevented by Sri Sathya Sai Baba's divine grace on us. Normally even a drop of boiling water burns any one's skin, and a skin burnt by boiling *ghee* or oil requires hospitalization and very painful and costly treatment for a long time, but Sai Baba miraculously saved her from that calamity. instantly. After just a few minutes she recovered and was able to complete the coking of the *pooris* and other items of the lunch for all members of the party. We all could then indeed leave for my Faridabad house within two hours and have the *Sai Bhajans* and lunch together there as we had originally planned. We all then experienced Sai Baba's miraculous powers to save his earnest devotees from calamities, accidents and misfortune. "He is truly *aapad-bandhva'* (a true brother who comes instantly to save one at the time of calamity"—all of us then empirically realized and kept on saying so and thankimng Sai Baba for his miracle, compassion and timely divine help. My wife still after 36 years vividly recalls that thrilling incident and narrates it to us and others and gratefully acknowledges Sri Sathya Sai Baba's miraculous protection to her.

6. Sai Baba's *vibhuti* mark on his forehead in his photo inside the glass of the framed photo in our Delhi house us in mid-1970s suddenly appeared one day and remained there for some days,

7. My life was saved in 1975 from a serious car accident which was going to happen when I was driving my scooter, a speeding the car suddenly crossed me at the Income Tax Office Crossing in Indraprastha Estate, New Delhi. I was going to the printing press in which a booklet *"Education in the Sai Age India"* had been printed and I was driving my scooter to reach there and bring the printed copies. A speeding car suddenly came from the west direction. It could even have killed me then and there. My scooter and I were saved by the omnipotent, omniscient Sai Baba's miraculous grace and compassion.

8. I saw Sai Baba miraculously materializing a big gold chain and *mangal sutra* (most auspicious and essential bridal neckls of a Hindu woman *sutra* for the daughter of Prof.S.Sampat, the second Vice-Chancellor of Sri Sathya Sai Institute of Higher Learning at the time of her marriage which ceremony was performed in the big hall of Sathay Sai Baba's Vridavanam ashram at Whitefield in the day-time.

9. On the occasion of Sai Baba's 50th Birthday my book '*Sai Baba and His His Message—A Challenge to Behavioural Sciences*' with Prof. Duane Robinson, an American professor of Social Work and Sai devotee, whom I had met in the Second Summer Course on Indian Culture and Spirituality at Whitefield after my two lectures in June 1974 and planned the book, was printed by Vikas Publishing House, New Delhi and I went to present its copy to Sai Baba at the Prasanthi Nilayam. As soon as I entered the ashram I learnt from the Accommodation office that the famous American Sai devotee Mrs. Elsie Cowen had already arrived and she was staying in a certain room in the ashram. As I had included her earlier published the most thrilling story of the resurrection of her husband by Sai Baba at Madras some time back. I immediately went to her room and presented the first copy of the book to her, In the evening Dr. M.V. N. Murthi, zoologist son of Prof. N. Kasturi, Sai Baba's closest devotee, biographer and secretary, came searching for me among the thousands of Sai devotes who were then camping in the open ground space near the ashram office just to convey to me the most pleasant news that the first copy of my book which I had presented to Mrs. Elsie Cowen had already reached Sai Baba as after reading it immediately in the afternoon she had sent it through a close Sai devotee, with her brief personal note, to Sai Baba in his room requesting him to see the book and kindly let her know whether He would approve it and whether it was worthy of being taken by her to USA to be introduced to the Sai devotees in America. Sai Baba saw the book. Dr.Murthy came personally to convey the most thrilling news to me that his father Prof. Kasturi, 'who was

then Sai Baba's Secretary. was present there with Sai Baba, and then Sai Baba expressed his appreciation and approval of my book before him.; on coming to his room, Prof. Kasturi told his son Dr, Murthy about how my book had reached Sai Baba and how Baba appreciated it that afternoon. He told him to convey Baba's appreciation to me by searching for me out among the thousands of devotees and visitors camping in the open near the Ashram office Complex. Thus the book which I had carried to Prasanthi Nilayam for presentation to Sai Baba on his Birthday on 23rd November, 1975 by his miraculous grace reached him a day earlier.

I got the happy news of Sai Baba's appreciation and grace in the unique way. That book was published in as many as 13 editions/reprints between 1975-76 and 2000, and became one the best selling books on Sai Baba throughout the world. I returned to Delhi with my unfulfilled dream or fantasy that I would be presenting the book to Sai Baba on the stage before thousands of Sai devotees in the amidst a lot of publicity fanfare, but I think Baba did not want any ego to develop in me and so it was never done. After a few days, I was overjoyed to receive the following letter from Mrs. Robinson, wife of Prof. Duane Robinson and an eminent Yoga exponent and Sai devotee in USA and who had come to Baba's ashram unaccompanied by her husband to attend Baba's 50th Birthday and stayed there till the end of January 1996

Prasanthi Nilayam,
26th Jan.'76

Dear Prof. Ruhela,

After you left Prasanthi Nilayam a very interesting event took place which I want to share with you.

I was standing apart from other people, alone by the edge of the platform in the Poorn Chandra building. Suddenly Baba came out from behind the curtain, looked at me, walked away, turned around and came back and stood right in front of me. He called (mentioned with His hand to come closer and then said "Tell husband—GOOD BOOK, VERY GOOD BOOK."

He held out His hand for a copy of the book (Sai Baba and His Message) saying "GIVE IT TO ME" which was tucked under my arm and he thumped through looking at the page and saying "yes, very good book." He held out His hand again asking for the pen. Then He turned to the front of the book and inscribed message to Duane and signed His name. Giving the book back to me He said—"FOR HUSBAND"

Sai Ram.

—*Marjorie Robinson*

(Wife of Prof. Duane Robinson who had contributed two chapers to the book.)

10. One day I saw that while giving public *darshan* moving amidst thousands of people in Prasanthi Nilayam ashram Sai Baba suddenly made the gesture of throwing some thing with his empty palm looking at a boy, and the boy instantly caught it, it was found to be a lump of *mishri* (crystal *sugar)* that had miraculously materialized due to Sai Baba's love for the devotee. I also saw very beautiful pair of diamond studded gold earrings materialized and gifted by Sathya Sai Baba to an Italian adolescent girl in the ashram. She said that Sai Baba had earlier also materialized and gifted to a set of diamond studded gold earrings.

11. Once I had gone as a *Seva dal* (volunteer) with the Delhi State contingent of *Seva dals* to do social service in Prasanthi Nilayam. My duty was in the transport office of the Sai organization. Its Incharge was an ardent Sai devotee from Bihar state who was then permanently living in the Prasanthi Nilayam ashram. One day he told me about a beautiful silver container for keeping Sai Baba's sacred *vibhuti*, which had been miraculously created by Baba and gifted to him. On my request, the next day he brought it from his residence to show it to me.

12. I saw the collection of many small gold ornaments and other fancy items of gold that Sai Baba had reportedly miraculously created and gifted to a famous American lady devotee and writer of books on Sathya Sai Baba—Joy Thomas in several interviews given to her. She had donated all of them to the Foreigners' Library in Sai Baba's native Puttaparthi village adjacent to the Prasanthi Nilayam ashram. That small beautiful library having a very rich collection of rare spiritual books, was named after her—most probably she or her husband had donated a lot of funds and most or all her books, manuscripts etc to start that unique library. I visited it a number of times and in 2002 gave two talks in that library. Till then there no other public library of books on Sai Baba and other spiritual leaders and phenomena anywhere in the Prasanthi Nilayam ashram or Puttaparthi village of Sai Baba and perhaps still there is none for the intellectuals and inquisitive spiritual seekers from foreign countries as well as from India.

Not even 0.1 percent of the millions of Sai devotees and visitors to Prasanthi Nilayam/Puttaparthi complex might have ever heard of and visited this unique voluntary library which has been functioning so efficiently and peacefully for over two decades without any aid or support from the Sathya Sai organization or government or any other private organization or association as far as I know. This is very remarkable evidence of Sai Baba's miraculous grace that has been continuing for years and it is a tribute to the steadfast belief and unique devotion of the some of truly enlightened foreigner devotees of Sathya Sai Baba who established it and those who have been running it without any fanfare—in total silence—just as the fragrance of rose, *chameli* and other fragrant flowers spread in the neighbourhood. Sri Sathya Sai Baba always said that social service should be done by his devotees inspired by the ideal of fragrant rose.

13. In 1997 had applied for the post of Professor and Principal of the School of Social Work in my university as I had Ph.D. Degree in Sociology and the requisite Postgraduate teaching and research experience. Only two candidates were called for the interview—one myself and the other was a very mediocre one who was the principal of the same School of Social Work for many years—he had neither a decorate degree in Social Work or any Social Science, nor any writing and research experience, nor had he guided any doctoral research candidate in his life. He was known for having no taste for books, research, academic innovation or developmental activity but since he was a Muslim he was strongly supported by the then Vice Chancellor, Dean of Arts and Social Sciences Faculty and the two puppet experts who belonged to his community. In my interview, I showed all my books and research publications and replied to all the questions of the experts, but when I was asked what was my most recent work, I showed my book *"Sai Baba and His Message—A Challenge to Behavioural Sciences"* which I had edited in collaboration of the distinguished American Professor of Social Work Duane Robinson, the Dean of Arts and Social Sciences, an important member of the Selection Committee derisively laughed and commented: "If you believe in Sai Baba then how can you be a sociologist or social scientist?" And before I could say any thing, the Vice-Chancellor as the Chairman of the Selection Committee—Vice Chancellor firmly said to me. "Thank you. You may please go now." Thus I was rejected and the their other favourite inferior candidate was selected by the biased selection committee. All my intense preparation for the interview, my superior qualifications and Post Graduate teaching, research and publication experiences were ignored and naturally I felt very bad for some days, but I kept my faith in Sai Baba in tact.

After some months in September 1987 I was selected in the open interview for the post of Professor of Education in the Himachal Pradesh University, Simla i.e., in that very university which had done great injustice to me and caused great harassment and disturbance in my life five years back. I became the Professor and Head of the School of Education and also the Dean of Education faculty there, My earlier opponent and tormentor the Professor of Education and Director of Correspondence Courses was then in much disgrace as he had been facing corruption charges in the court and had been even kept in the jail for some days where he was very harshly treated by prison staff as was reported in a news item in a daily newspaper while I was the Professor, Head and Dean which positions he held some years back I believe that all this was Sai Baba's miraculous justice in my professional life.

After a year I resigned my post in the Himachal University as I was not getting the due cooperation of some of the subordinate teachers who were stooges of my earlier opponent and tormenter and they were constantly instigating students against me I was also facing many personal inconveniences and financial loss while staying in that university in Simla as my family was still living in Delhi and a property related dispute case of mine with a close relatives was going on in a Delhi court, and I was very much concerned for the safety and welfare of my children which necessitated my constant presence in Delhi. So in January 1979 I resigned my post of Professor in that university and rejoined my substantive post as Reader in Education (Sociology) in my parent institution Jamia Milllia Islamia. There too was a lot of politics and antagonism against me from the some members of staff. Although after about year I was appointed as the first Reader Head (founder head) of the newly created Department of Teacher Education & Non-Formal Education when the Jamia Millia Islamia was given the status of Central University and Facultization in the university and the bifurcation of the new Faculty of Education were implemented, yet again gross injustice was done to me. Another Reader of Education in the same faculty, despite his being junior to me, was selected as Professor of Education and Head of my Department in the open selection due to the communal bias. I had to bear this loss and injustice for one more year, Towards the end of 1992, the Merit Promotion Scheme of the University Grants Commission was implanted, in our university, and one post of Professor to promoted in our Faculty of Education. There were only two applicants—myself and the other one who was also Reader in Education junior and inferior to me in all respects but he had already been selected as Professor and appointed as the Head of my department about a year back. He was desperate to remain as the only professor in the department and spoil my chance to ever became a professor in the university. There was again intense lobbying in his favour in the university campus on non-secular l ground and the new Vice-Chancellor had come under the pressure of the lobbyists. The meeting of the selection committee started. My competitor was already sitting in the Vice-Chancellor's office when the interviews were to be held, as he had been invited to be a member of the selection committee being the head of the same department despite his being a candidate for the post. The Vice-Chancellor expressed his totally biased and illegal opinion before the two external experts—their favourite Muslim lady professor from another central university who already knew the Professor Head and was biased in his favour and the other expert who was a non-Muslim, a very reputed, logical, just and bold professor from Punjab University. While my competitor (Professor and Head of the Department) and the biased lady expert lady nodded in their instant and simultaneous gesture of accepting the Vice Chancellor advice, the other expert immediately sensed the whole foul game—the grand academic conspiracy and he retorted: "I totally disagree with you Mr. Vice Chancellor, both the applicants in their original status as Readers will have to appear before this Selection Committee for the Selection of Professor under the Merit Promotion Scheme and then we will see their performances and finally decide who has more merit and who should be selected by us now. He forcefully asserted that that since candidate Dr. A.B had already been selected as Professor by the earlier Open Selection by another interview committee about a year back, he could not be accepted as automatically selected by this Committee without interviewing him as he now was a candidate under the Merit Promotion Scheme of the UGC. He must either be asked by you to withdraw his candidature immediately if he to be eligible to sit as a member of this Selection Committee or he must immediately resign as Professor and HOD and you have to accept his resignation right nnow before us if he wants to be interviewed by us."

This upright and very bold retort by the external expert came as a thunder bolt from the blue and it at once foiled and crumbled down the whole the conspiracy. The Vice Chancellor took his favourite candidate to a corner of the room and advised him to withdraw his candidature and he at once did so, fearing the uncertainty of his selection as Professor again. After this high voltage drama in the VC office for about 20 minutes (about which I learned most reliably after many days), I was called in and interviewed for a long time and finally selected as Professor by that selection committee,

At the very start of the interview,. I was shocked to find that my full and correct curriculum vitae particulars/my original application and none of my several publications that I had sent to the University while applying for the post were not brought before the Selection Committee, all of them had been made to disappear as the crucial part of the conspiracy plan to reject me by all possible dirty tricks.

But Sai Baba's miraculous intervention in the form of that upright and bold expert in the selection committee foiled the conspiracy to ditch me and ruin my chance of ever becoming a professor in the university. I can never forget this great miracle of Sai Baba in my life.

I had to work for about 13 years as a Reader,(Associate Professor) whereas I have been seeing and hearing that even readers/ associate professors having not even 5 years standing and no significant academic and research contributions have become Professors in my university and in so many universities in India, and even those having no experience of teaching PG classes, guiding doctoral candidates and not producing any research wok and book have become professors of education.

Since I was the senior most Reader in the University and was now promoted as a Professor in 1983 under the Merit Promotion Scheme of the University Grants Commission very soon I became Dean of Education. And then being Senior-most Dean in the university I became a Member of the Executive Council and was privileged to be appointed as Officiating Vice-Chancellor of the University four times during 1983-1995 in which year I retired.

14. When I was reaching the age of superannuation (60 years) I applied for 5 years re-employment as professor in the university, as the teachers of central universities were then eligible for it provided they were of sound health and had outstanding academic record. The campus politics and the new Vice-Chancellor was also coloured by it and misled by my adversary, he was made biased against me because *was* a Member of the University Executive Council and also as Officiating Vice Chancellor in 1994, during the months before the time of my retirement I had boldly opposed his high-highhandedness and some crucial biased and unfair decisions. All my actions and protest were in based on the high values of truth, justice to all, righteousness, kindness, liberalism, secularism and espousing the causes of the suffering helpless employees who were victims of bureaucratic injustices. All my actions and protests as member of the Executive Council were based on five eternal values taught by Sai Baba. As a result of this, I was not given reemployment by the Vice Chancellor in the spirit of revenge, I was virtually denied this till the last day of my service without without any rhyme or reason. And so I had to move my case in the Delhi High Court. The university could not give any reply to the court as to why I was being denied reemployment when many other retired teachers had been given reemployment.

Ultimately after 11 months, the university gave me reemployment for 3 years which was later on extended to two more years. Thus I could work as Professor till February 2000 This was sole due to Sai Baba's miraculous grace.

As I go down the memory lane, I recall that I joined the teaching profession as an untrained matriculate assistant teacher in a govermnent high school in a town in Rajasthan on just Rs.70 as a poor pay pay of just Rs.50/—plus Rs.,20.—as Dearness allowance i.e., Rs.70/—per month only (which was much less than U.S $ 1.5 of today in 2013), how I privately passed my Intermediate, Graduation and Post Graduation and Doctoral examinationas as a modest teachrer candiate and woking very hard in severe financial stringency all throughout my youth, and progressed in my my professional career starting as school teacher in 1952 rising to the positions of *Professor of Education*, Heads and Dean oif Education and officiating Vice Chancellor of a Central University four times in Iindia's Capital.

On the basis of such long, difficult and thrilling experiences I am totally convinced in my conscience that Sai Baba's grace alone had helped me in steering through out the constant struggle in my professional life. I still gratefully remember that Sathya Sai Baba had given this assurance to me in my first private interview in June 1974 at Whitefield "I am with you, I shall ever be with you." I realized how truthful and valid his assurance full of genuine blessings proved in my life. I have tried to follow Sai Baba's teachings of five great human values—*Sathya* (Truth), *Dharma* (righteous), *Shanti* (Peace), *Prema* (love) and *Ahimsa* (Non–violence) and have been fearlessly fighting battles of my life as guided by my Spiritual Master Sri Sathya Bai Baba. I had no politician or influential bureaucrat as my God father to help me in my life.

15. I experienced miraculous Sai grace on me in the matter of the finalization of my pension. I had served as a government school teacher, teacher educator and senior teacher in school and then as a lecturer under the state government of Rajasthan, but the bureaucrats of that State government were denying and evading to pay the State Government's contribution to my university for this long service rendered by me before joining the Jamia Millia Islamia and this matter lingered for over 25 years. I had even retired from the university service but they were just not bothered to settle my claims. Ultimately I had to appeal to the Rajasthan High Court and after attending 25 court hearings and spending over Rs.75,000/—on litigation in three years, ultimately by Sai Baba's grace I succeeded in getting my due full pension.

16. Mr.Mohd Farah Aidid, Ambassador of Somalia (East Africa) to India became my friend in Delhi in May 1986. One day I told him about Sri Sathya Sai Baba but he showed no interest in Sai Baba. Soon he went to his country for some days. While returning to Delhi he visited Italy and met his friend Mr. Craxi, the Prime Minister there. When Mr.Craxi also told him about the God man Sai Baba and that his brother Antonia was a Sai devotee and Antonio's children were then studying in Sai Baba's school in Prasanthi Nilayam, Aided immediately made up his mind to meet Sai Baba. He came back to Delhi with one of his Somali close acquaintances Ali. He requested me to accompany him to arrange our visit to Sai Baba immediately. I sent a telegram to Prof,.S.N.Saraf, the Vice Chancellor of Sri Sathya Sai University, the Secretary of the Sai Baba Trust and Sai Baba that we three were coming to Prasanthi Nilayam to have the *darshan* of Sai Baba and two rooms may kindly be arranged for our stay in the ashram We three flew to Bangalore and from there drove to Prasanthi Nilayam by the evening. The ashram authorities very kindly allotted two rooms for our stay in the ashram and food was sent to our rooms. The next morning we sat just near Sai Baba's interview room, As soon Baba came out of his room he saw Aidid and his Somali friend Ali and gestured to then to go inside the interview room. I was not picked up by Sai Baba for interview with them. Inside the interview room. I did not know what talks Aidid had with Sri Sathya Sai Baba but when they came out I saw Aidid wearing a gold ring with a big white diamond and some lockets materialized and given by Sai Baba Later Aidid confided to me that Sai Baba himself had stated the conversation with him, saying "So you want to become the President of Somalia, Your wish will be fulfilled." Aidid had for many years been having this secret aspiration to topple the Somali tyrant President Said Barre and seize the President's post from him any how.

Since I had not been called with Aidid and his friend inside the interview room by Sai Baba that morning, I was deeply worried and frustrated throughout the day and passed the whole night sleeplessly worrying as to why Baba did not call me with Aidid and his friend in the interview room? "Baba, what was my fault for which you punished like this? "—I asked this question repeatedly in my mind throughout the mind. In the morning I got ready to go for Baba's *darshan,* and requested Adid and Ali to come with for *darshan, but* Aidid replied:" We have got his *darshan* yesterday and are fully satisfied with that. We are not going for it now. You may please go for His *darsha*n and after you come back we three shall leave for Bangalore in a taxi and return to Delhi by plane.".

So I alone went and sat at the same place near the entrance door of Baba's interview room. As soon as Sai Baba came out of the room for giving *darshan*, he saw me and asked me." You came with the Ambassador?" I said,"

Yes, Swami." He gestured to me to enter the interview room. After completing his *darshan* round among all the assembled people, he entered the interview with some others whom he had picked up by him for giving interview. In the interview room, he told me," I did not call you for interview yesterday with the ambassador as he had some personal problem to discuss with me, I know how much you were worrying and crying "Baba, why did you not call me for interview with the Ambassador? Baba. what was my fault for which you punished like this?'

After about one year Aidid and his wife Khadija did not get any favourable news and they did not foresee any possibility of his becoming the President of Somalia. So he told me one day, "Sai Baba had assured me that I would become the President. of Somalia. Already one year has passed but he did not tell me when I shall be able to fulfill my wish, five eternal values taught by Sai Baba.I and my wife Khadija both want to visit Sai Baba now. You kindly accompany us." We three reached Prasanthi Nilayam and were granted a common interview by Baba, In the packed interview room there were 18 persons including the famous old Gandhian Ram Chandran., former education minister of Madras state, Mrs. Ambika Soni, Congress leader from Delhi, Aidid, his wife Khadija, myself and other five Indian and some foreign devotees. First of all Baba miraculously materialized in his palm a bunch of fresh camera prints of his photograph with full postal address and gave to each one of the 18 people in the interview room, Then he materialized a small *Shivalinga* or *bazarbattu* type of object for the cure of the Mr. Ram Chandran's ailing eyes and materialized a crystal *jap-ma*la (garland of beads for name-chanting*)* for an Indian lady devotee. Then he asked Ambassador Aidid," How is your wife?" He replied "OK." Baba said, "Not OK. She has constant pain in her stomach, You take this (he immediately materialized a small *Shivering* and gave to him), put it in water and let her drink the water for some days for her cure. You can also drink that water," Later on Aidid disclosed to me that the two young daughters of Khadija were born in India by caesarean operations and so she had been feeling pain in her stomach since their births, "Sai Baba knows every secret of anybody he admitted. Then Baba took Aidid in the inner chamber for private conversation. Aidid never disclosed to me about that.

Again Aidid visited Sai Baba in Prasanthi Nilayam for the third time towards the end of 1989, and soon thereafter he relinquished the Ambassador's post, sent his wife and his two young daughters to one of the countries of the Middle East to live with her married younger sister Lull and he himself suddenly flew to USA and then to Ethiopia to mobilize army troops from there to throw out his adversary tyrant President of Somalia. After a lot of armed struggle he was ultimately able to topple President Said Barre and drag him out of the

Somali capital Mogadishu. But another Somali warlords declared himself as the new President of Somalia, Aided had to tight with him and defeat him and ultimately he did become the President of Somalia in 1994-95 but he was soon shot down by an enemy and so his Presidency was of very short duration.

17. I had the good fortune of coming under the divine grace of Sri Shirdi Sai Baba and Sri Sathya Sai Baba, visiting their holy places many times between 1974 and 2002 by their grace.

18. It was due to Sai Baba's miraculous grace only that I could hear about, meet and interview these three great spiritual lady saints of South India and to get their blessings:

- The 102 year old: Shivamma Thayee of Bangalore in 1994. It was due to Sai Baba's grace that I got the great fortune to meet this oldest surviving closest devotee of Sri Shirdi Sai Baba in 1994.
- The then 86 year old lady saintly lady Smt.P.Seethtamma, popularly known as 'Baba Patti' in 1995. She was the incarnation of Sri Shirdi Sai Baba's mother. She firmly believed in Sri Shirdi Sai Baba and in Sri Sathya Sai Baba as his second incarnation
- The then 61 year old Vasantha Sai (born in 1938) of Vadkampatti village in Madurai District of Tamil Nadu, who is now known all over the world to be the present reincarnation of Lord Krishna's beloved Radha, and great devotee of Sri Sathya Sai Baba who has been regularly appearing in his *sooskhma shareer* (spirit body) for the last over 25 years over three decades ago and revealed to her the future graphic history of Prema Sai Baba and of her as his onsort in her next birth in Gunaparhgti village in Karnataka. She is the founder and head of the Mukhti Nilayam ashram in Royapalyam Village, B.O., Tirumangalam S.O., Madurai-Virudh Nagar Road, Madurai District—625706t. She has already written over 50 books anda number of e books which have been published by Sri Vasantha Sai Publication Trust.

19. In 1997 I suffered heart attack and then in September 2007 I suffered a severe paralytic attack but my life was saved by the mercy and grace of both Sri Shirdi Sai Baba and Sri Sathya Sai Baba. After my paralytic attack I have considerably recovered in the last 3 years and have been able to resume my study and writing of some more books by Sai Baba's grace for which I am ever indebted to him.

20. By Sai Baba's blessings I was able to write and publish the following books on the birthday in the following years:

- 50th Birthday (23.11.1975) (Ed.) *Sai Baba and His Message—A Challenge to Bahavioural Sciences.*
- 60th Birthday (23.11.1985) (Ed.). *The Sai Baba Movement*
- 61st Birthday (23.11.1986) (Ed. *Human Values and Education*
- 65tth Birthday (23.11.1894) (Ed.). *Sri Sathya Sai Baba and the Future of Mankind*
- 68th Birthday (23.11.1986) (Ed.. *The Sai Trinity—Sri Shirdi Sai Baba, Sri Sathya Sai and Prema Sai Baba*
- 68tth Birthday (23.11.1894) (Ed.). *The Educational Theory of Sri Sathya Sai Baba*
- 70th Birthday (23.11.1996) (Ed.). *Sri Sathya Sai Baba as Kalki Avatar*
- 71st Birthday (23.11.1997) (Ed.) *In Search of Sai Duvine—A Comprehensive Review of Writings and Researches on Sri Sathya Sai Baba Avatar*
- 72nd Birthday (23.11.1998) (Ed.) *Sri Sathya Sai Baba and the Press*
- 72n Birthday (23.11.1998) *Sri Sathya Sai Baba—Understanding His Mystery and Experiencing His Love*
- 72nd Birthday (23.11.1998) (Ed.) *World Peace and Sri Sathya Sai Avatar*
- 73rd Birthday (23.11.1998) *How to Receive Sri Sathya Sai Baba's Grace*
- 76th Birthday (23.11.2000) (Ed.) *Lord Krishna and His Incarnation Sri Sathya Sai Baba*

21. In the last two decades, some mischievous, fraudulent deceitful persons posing as I devotees, friends and publishers came in my life and they caused me and my family great loss, pain and misery, but we could bear them and retain equilibrium and mental poise by the divine grace of Sai Baba, I and my family members are facing some difficulties and problems in our lives, but we firmly believe that Shri Shirdi Sai Baba and Sri Sathya Sai Baba shall continue to give us strength to withstand them and grant us due protection and ultimate victory over them. Sri Sathya Sai Baba sang the first *Bhajan* in 1940 *"Manass bhaj re Guru charnam, uster bhav-sagar tarnamuru maharaj jai jai, Guru maharaj jai jai."* (O man, meditate on the name of Guru (God), the oceran of life is difficult to cross.).

I have been following this advice of Sai Baba in my life since I heard him singing this *bhajan* in 1973 in New Delhi.

In the end, I wish to mention that countless Sathya Sai miracles have been experiened by people of over 170 countries in the last six decades, and many among them are still the recipients of Sri Sathya Sai Baba's divine grace, help and protection, and my experience of his miraculous grace may be not be more and profound than their's and especially of those thousands of the functionaries in his *ashrams*, organizations world wide who have been dedicately involved in the numerous on going projects and service activities and have been privileged to come in his inner circle of close devotees and so naturally they must be having far more greater and astounding experiences of his grace in their lives. I have never been privileged to be in their innner circles but observed all the going in the Sai kingdom *in the last 40 years* retaining my aloofness and objectivity as a sociologist and as an humble devotee and eanest spiritual seeker. My experrriences of Sri Sathya Sai Baba's miraculous grace, how-so-ever small, are geniune and important and unforgottable for me till I am alive.

Sri Shirdi Sai Baba and Sri Sathya Sai Baba both have again for the fourth time saved my life very recently on 27.2.2015 when I suddenly lost my breath in late evening. I had to be ambulanced to the Sarvodaya Hospital, Faridabad immediately, put on the ventilator throughout the night and then kept under treatment in the ICU for five days. I was discharged on 5.3.2015 on my great insistence. The doctors have told me that had divine grace would not have descended on me and had I not been rushed to the hospital within 5 minutes, I would have certainly died in such a critical condition..

Earlier also both my divine masters Sri Shirdi Sai Baba and Sri Sathya Sai Baba had mercifully saved my life from a likely car and scooter collusion in 1974, and when I had a serious heart attack in 1997, and when I had attack of coronary thrombosis and paralysis on the left side in 2007 and had then to be on complete bed rest and under medical treatment for three years.

Although I recovered partially I am still unable to speak, legibly, hear with the left ear, stand, walk, travel, write with hand and do any physical active yet by Sai Baba's grace I have been able to resume my spiritual writing work using my personal computer for some time daily and prepare my most cherished seven books for publication by good publishers during the three years despite my illness, very precarious financial condition being a small pensioner and without anybody's moral, financial and any other kind of support; my total faith in and complete surrender to both the Sai Babas and their continued miraculous help have been enabling me to cross all these grave hurdles anyhow.

I have been able to prepare these seven books and try to self- publish them under renowned publishers:

1. How I Found God- Role played by Fakir Shirdi Sai Baba and the Spiritual Masters in my Spiritual Training resulting in my God-realization (By; Yogi Minocher. K..Spencer, Ed. S.P. Ruhela). New Delhi; New Age Books, 2013.ISBN 978-081-722-352-00.

2. Maine Iswar Ko Kaise Paya (Hindi translation by Acharya Purshottamananda, Ed, S.P.Ruhela), Chennai; Notion Press (Under publication),

3. Shirdi Sai Speaks to Yogi Spencer inHis Vision..Bloomington, USA; Partridge India Publishing Co., Jan, 2015: ISBN: Soft Cover 978- 1-4828-2'. ISBN: e book; 978-1-4828-4395-5.

4. Essentials of Foundations of Education- New Useful Modern Concepts of Education for Teachers Under B.Ed. Training. Bloomington, USA; Partridge India Publishing Co. Jan., 2015. ISBN: Soft Cover 978- 1-4828-4162-6. ISBN: e book; 978-1-4828-4162-9. .

5. Select Spiritual Writings of Yogi Spencer- Harbinger of the New Age of Spirituality., Bloomington, USA,: Partridge India Publishing Co. (Under publication) ISBNS: Soft Cover 978-1-4828-4543-3 ISBN Book 978-1-4828-4542-6

6. In Search of Sai Divine – Exploring Sathya Sai Baba's Mystery and Unique Contributions to Humanity as the Harbinger of the New Age of Spirituality. Bloomington, USA,: Partridge India Publishing Co..(Under publication)

7. The Triple incarnations of Sai Baba-Sri Shirdi Sai Baba, Sri Sathya Sai Baba and Future Prema Sai Baba Soft Cover 978-1-4828-2293-9. e Book 978-1-4828-2292-2

Half the cost of publication of the first book and full cost of self publishing of the rest of the books have been borne by me. Although I have been having all these serious physical disabilities and problems in my old age, it is a fact that by the blessings of my spiritual masters. I still retain peace of mind and my morale is quite high.

Instead of bearing the grave exploitation and injustice by a publisher in India who has been publishing and selling worldwide as many as 38 books of mine, out of which 20 books are in English language and they bear ISBN and have been advertized and sold by many prominent web sites for over 15 years and even then the publisher has not been paying my due royalties. I have finally determined to fight out legally by deriving inspiration from Lord Krishna's great message in Bhagavat Gita; "Do not bear injustice, do not be impotent, and coward but do your legitimate Karma to fight for your rightful claim keeping God's name in your heart constantly and leave the would be fruit thereof to God." I unilaterally decided to move against the publisher in Delhi High Court in 2012 requesting appointment of arbitrator. The High Court has on 14.8.2014 appointed a sole Arbitrator to settle this Royalty dispute. I have changed my advocate and filed my claim petition in May 2014. The arbitration proceedings are presently going on and the judgment may be known in the next few months.

33

The Guru Who become a Living God

It is difficult to imagine that Puttaparthi was once a sleepy village called Gollapalli. But that was many decades ago, before a precocious teenager known for magically fishing out goodies from his bag like sweets, pens, watches and chains at 14 that he was a reincarnation of Shirdi Sai Baba.

The date of the proclamation was October 20, 1940. Now, 71 years later on a sweltering Sunday afternoon. Puttaparhi boasting of a super-specialty hospital, schools and colleges grieved much like the rest of the nation, the passing away of the person it owes its identity to: Sathyanarayana Raju, one of India's most popular godman, Sathya Sai Baba.

Sai Baba's 28-day battle with death had devotees praying for a miraculous recovery, their belief rooted in the many miracles he was credited with for performing during his lifetime. From creating ash (*vibhuti*) or even gold from thin air to miraculously pulling out cancer from a devotee's body (a much reported event in the case of a devotee named Rosy), Sai Baba's popularity soared. The miracles helped establish his divine identity among devotees.

Within four years of making his declaration that he was Shirdi Sai Baba's reincarnation, he embarked on a spiritual journey that would become bigger, greater and even controversial. By 1950, he had earned devotees committing their lives to serving the godman. Among them was Sakamma of Karnataka who funded the construction of Prashanti Nilayam (abode of highest peace) for her "Living God".

But then, Puttaparthi shaped up with Sai's increasing popularity, his spiritual enterprise turning the village into a town with metro-like facilities. Born on November 23, 1926, Sai Baba was the fourth child of Eswaramma and Ratnakaram Peddavenkama Raju. Sai fulfilled the wish of his mother Eswaramma when he decided to provide free medical care to the poor, particularly women and children, education and drinking water revealing his humane side. Sai Baba never really ventured out of Puttaparthi for long. He lived in Yajur mandir and gave *darshan* in Sai Kulwant Hall, which has a capacity of 4,000. During the summer months, he stayed in the massive

Brindavan ashram in Kadugodi, Whitefield, Bangalore. Occasionally, he visited Sai Shruit Ashram in Kodaikanal.

While he reached out to millions of devotees worldwide, Sai Baba never traveled to the West. The West came to him, as did other material comforts. He owned BMWs, Rolls Royces and Toyotas (all bearing No. 9999).

Nevertheless, the afro-haired Baba was either known for his divine powers to produce Shiva lingams, statues of deities sugar candy, gems, coloured string, herbs and amrita (a nectar-like honey) out of nowhere, or for his charitable work as he announced welfare schemes on his birthday every year. Of course, he was also known for his glorious list of devotees.

While his disciples revered him as *Swami* or Baba or *Bhagawan* (God), Baba's list of devotees read like a who's who from politics, business, entertainment, and judiciary and sports field. Almost all the presidents, prime ministers, Union ministers, governors, judges and chief ministers were his devotees who kept visiting Prasanthi Nilayam. One of his first VIP followers was former Andhra chief minister Marri Channa Reddy. When Sai Baba was 37, Channa Reddy, then minister for planning, inaugurated a primary school in Puttaparthi and remained a frequent guest at Sai Baba's abode.

Then there were devotees who aided significantly in boosting Sai Baba's popularity the world over or turned into interesting case studies themselves as they gave up their material life to serve him and work for his trust. Among them are Indulal Shah, trust member and chartered accountant from Mumbai who set up Sathya Sai international organizations, *bhajan* mandirs, health centres and schools. Today, the trust has 1,200 such centres world over with a combined membership of 10 million.

Then there is Hard Rock Café founder Issac Tigrett Burton. The American is said to have sold his stake in Hard Rock Café and donated his life's savings for the construction of the super-specialty hospital at Puttaparthi. When Sai Baba announced that he wanted to set up a super-specialty hospital in 1991, donations poured in from all quarters and the entire sum of Rs.300 crore could be raised. This facilitated the construction of the hospital in 80 acres in a record time of 11 months, says Sai Baba's nephew M. Shankar Raju, who admits that the hospital was the brainchild of Burton.

But Sai Baba had, over the years, only become too familiar with such generous donations. An American named Gold donated Rs.600 crore to the trust six years ago, sources say, adding that an NRI donated Rs.50 crore for the indoor stadium in 2009, while an Indonesian devotee gave Rs.50 crore for the music college. When the Sathya Sai Trust came out with *Vidya Vahini*, a street scholl project, Ratan Tata announced that TCS would provide software, laptops, food, clothing and teaching faculty for the project.

His devotees remind that Sai Baba always exhorted them to follow the five tenets of *Sathya, Dharma, Shanty, Prema* and *Ahimsa*. Hohn Hislop, author and former president of American Sathya Sai Organization, wrote in his book that Sai Baba did not have Osho's flamboyant lifestyle but remained rooted to Indian culture. Baba, a non-Brahmin of backward (Bhattraju) caste, had dropped out of school after Class IX, but devotees claim he could converse in Italian, German, Russian and French.

34

80 Ways to Serve Mankind

Sri Sathya Sai Baba has shown these 80 Ways of helping the less-privileged:

1. Organizing *Narayana Seva* by distributing food and clothes to needy people.
2. Organizing free food centres for needy people.
3. Providing *Amruta Kalasham* (bag of food items) to needy families.
4. Providing rugs and blankets during winter season to poor people.
5. Providing Sai Protein to meet the nutritional needs of poor people.
6. Organizing systematic poverty alleviation schemes for the most needy sections of society by adopting needy families.
7. Organizing *Grama Seva* in villages for conducting programmes of total village uplift.
8. Providing training and means of self-employment to needy people.
9. Providing training and efficient tool kits to plumbers, electricians, carpenters and other trained professional workers to make them self-reliant.
10. Organizing self-help groups in villages for maintaining sanitation and for constructing public utility conveniences like approach roads, water storage tanks, bus shelters, etc.
11. Constructing house/shelters for those who are without shelter.
12. Providing help in repairing of houses for those who live in dilapidated or unsafe houses.
13. Setting up orphanages to take care of destitute children.
14. Setting up old age homes for old people.
15. Organizing visits to old age homes to help aged people.
16. Providing drinking water to people in scarcity affected areas by digging wells and setting up water supply schemes in rural and remote areas.
17. Providing electric supply to remote areas which are still without electricity.
18. Organizing cleanliness drives in villages.
19. Adopting villages for village uplift programmes.
20. Providing the services of agricultural scientists to farmers at their doorstep to improve the agricultural yield.
21. Conducting mass marriages to save on wasteful expenditure on marriages.

22. Organizing rehabilitation programmes for homeless street children.
23. Providing tricycles to physically challenged persons to make them mobile.
24. Conducting *Seva* camps during religious fairs for providing sanitation, medical aid and guidance to pilgrims.
25. Conducting youth camps to guide the youth on the path of Seva and spirituality.
26. Conducting youth camps to provide training in disaster management.
27. Organizing disaster management during calamities like floods, earthquakes, etc., for saving lives of people.
28. Organizing relief measures for the rehabilitation of victims of disasters.
29. Setting up small-scale village industries for providing employment to villagers, especially the housewives to utilize their spare time and increase the income of the family.
30. Providing electronic devices like CARE developed by Sathya Sai Organization of Arizona (U.S.A.) to help the visually challenged persons to read books and to identify people.
31. Helping the villagers to make water safe for drinking by chlorination of wells and water tanks.
32. Setting up agricultural institutes for training the children of farmers in better techniques of farming.
33. Providing value-based education to students for proper use of water and other natural resources so as to avoid wastage.
34. Organizing tree plantation drives for planting more trees to combat deforestation.
35. Conducting surveys in villages for providing need-based services to the villagers.
36. Organizing *Bhajans*, meditation and lectures in jails for the reformation of the inmates.

Health care for all

37. Conducting health check-up camps and organizing health education meets to prevent the spread of diseases.
38. Putting up health education exhibitions to provide guidance to people on health education.
39. Organizing medical camps for providing free medicare to under-privileged sections of society in villages, urban slums and remote areas.
40. Setting up free homoeopathic, ayurvedic and allopathic dispensaries to dispense medicines to needy people.

41. Setting up hospitals for providing free medical treatment to less privileged sections of society.
42. Setting up hospices for terminally ill patients like the one set up by the Sathya Sai Seva Organization of Sri Lanka.
43. Organizing malaria eradication programmes like the Sainet Project started by the Sai Organization in Kenya.
44. Organizing visits to spastic homes to help spastic children.
45. Setting up leprosy home for rehabilitating lepers and providing treatment to them.
46. Setting up schools for deaf and dumb children for their rehabilitation.
47. Providing hearing aids and spectacles to needy people.
48. Providing artificial limbs to needy physically challenged people.
49. Organizing medical help and counseling to mentally challenged people.
50. Setting up schools for the visually challenged.
51. Monitoring and improving the health and nutritional needs of expecting mothers.
52. Providing health check-ups in schools and colleges for students.
53. Organizing special medical camps for drug de-addiction and freedom from bad habits like smoking.
54. Visiting hospitals and distributing gifts with humility and love to patients on various festive occasions.
55. Conducting free veterinary camps for treating domestic animals in rural areas.
56. Providing the services of livestock experts to villagers at their doorstep for improving the health of the livestock, and for the eradication of diseases of the livestock.

Education for all

57. Setting up schools, colleges and other educational institutions for providing free value-based education to students.
58. Conducting literacy classes to eradicate illiteracy in rural areas, urban slums and other backward areas.
59. Providing scholarships, books and other teaching and reading material to needy school children.
60. Conducting free coaching classes for helping needy students.
61. Constructing buildings for schools in villages with the help and cooperation of villagers.

Moral and Spiritual Regeneration of Mankind

62. Conducting Bal Vikas classes for providing education in human values to children.
63. Conducting seminars to provide value-orientation to school and college teachers.
64. Conducting interfaith meetings to foster love and harmony between followers of different religions.
65. Conducting summer courses on Indian Culture and Spirituality to spread awareness about Bharat's cultural and spiritual heritage.
66. Setting up forums of professionals like lawyers, professors, businessmen, doctors to provide value-orientation to professionals.
67. Setting up exhibitions to spread the teachings of Bhagavan on social service, village uplift and for spreading the values like *Sathya, Dharma, Santhi, Prema, Ahimsa* in society.
68. Conducting *Palaki Seva* (palanquin processions) and Nagar Sankirtan in villages, towns and cities for the spiritual regeneration of people.
69. Spreading awareness about the need of values in society through Ratha Yatra, seminars, conferences, etc.
70. Organizing cultural activities like drams, *Burra Katha* to spread values among people.
71. Holding exhibitions and seminars on Sathya Sai Parenting to educate the parents how to inculcate values in children.
72. Setting up Sathya Sai Human Values Institutes to train human values teachers.
73. Conducting *Bhajan classes* and *Bhajan centres*.
74. Conducting spiritual retreats and *Sadhana* camps for the spiritual advancement to people.
75. Conducting functions like Mass *Upanayanam* to initiate children on spiritual path.
76. Conducting *Yajnas* for the welfare of the world and promoting the teaching and learning of Vedas by setting up Vedic schools and honouring Vedic scholars.
77. Publishing books and magazines and producing films to make people aware of the humanitarian work of Bhagavan.
78. Producing serials on the Life and Message of Bhagavan for broadcasting to educate people about the ideals of Bhagavan like "Love All Serve All."

79. Producing CD's VCD's, DVD's on the teaching of Bhagavan to spread values in society.

80. Holding meetings at local, national and international levels to propagate the ideals of morality, ethics, spirituality taught by Bhagavan.

35

The Sai Empire

The worth of Sathya Sai Central Trust as per income tax estimates is said to be Rs.4,000 crore in Puttaparthi. The trust runs

- The university complex
- A specialty hospital
- World Religious Museum, Chaitanya Jyoti
- A planetarium
- A railway station
- Hill-view stadium
- A music college
- An administrative building
- An airport
- An indoor stadium
- A sports complex
- 1200 Sathya Sai Baba centers in the world
- Schools, cultural and health centres

Estimated total worth of the Sathya Sai Baba Empire is believed to be between Rs.40,000 crore and Rs.15 lakh crore

Dream Donation

Among one of Sathya Sai Baba's mega donors was Isaac Tigrett, who started Hard Rock Café. Sai Baba is said to have come in his dreams and saved him from a fatal disease. Tigrett apparently sold his care chain for $108 million and in 1991 gave the money to the Guru. This is how to famous Puttaparthi hospital was funded.

Vital Statistics

Rs.250 crore is the cost of Anantapur piped-water project. Benefits 750 villages in the district, 30 million is the estimated number of Sai Baba devotees.

The Sathya Sai Empire has over decades accumulated hundreds of acres of immovable property and cash assets in the form of donations that run into crores of rupees.

The Sathya Sai Central Trust manages medical and degree colleges, schools, Sadhana Trust of books and publications, the Eswaramma Women's Welfare Trust, *seva* organizations and super-specialty hospitals at Puttaparthi and Bangalore. In addition, there are general hospitals, eye hospitals and drinking water schemes in Anantapur, Medak, Mahabubnagar, East and West Godavari districts of Andhra Pradesh and Chennai (Tamil Nadu).

The Sai Empire has a presence in 186 nations and operates 1,200 organizations worldwide. Puttaparthi is the seat of the Sathya Sai University complex, the Chaitanya Jyoti Museum, a planetarium, an indoor stadium, an outdoor hill-view stadium, a general hospital, a music college, an airport, apart from the super-specialty hospital and Prasanthi Nilayam, ashram.

All these projects are managed by the central trust, exempted from taxes since it is a charitable body. Donations pour in from every corner of the world every year and there is no official figure available of this.

Sources said Isaac Tigrett Burton from Tennessee, USA, and founder of Hard Rock Café and House of Blues, donated Rs.300 crore for the Sathya Sai Super-specialty Hospital in 1991. Puttaparthi's super-specialty hospital was built at a cost of Rs.300 crore in a record 10 months. The Bangalore hospital cost around Rs.500 crore.

Daily Schedule of Prasanthi Nilayam

According to Internet:

Daily Schedule (at Sai Kulwant Hall)

Bhagawan has laid down the daily schedule to be followed in the *Ashram*. Every activity of the *Ashram* routine is suffused with deep spiritual significance. See the table below for the Ashram schedule:

Time	Activity
05.10 a.m.	Aumkar, Meditation and Suprabhatham
05.40 a.m.	Veda Chanting and Nagar Sankeertan (Circumambulating the Mandir)

06.30 a.m. - 07.30 a.m.	*Pooja* inside the Bhajan Hall (Entry for Devotees will start at 06.25 a.m.)
8.00 a.m. -9.00 a.m.	Veda Chanting
9.00 a.m. -9.30 a.m.	*Bhajans*
9.30 a.m. - 10.30 a.m.	*Darshan* of Bhagawan's *Mahasamadhi* and Prayer Hall
4.30 p.m. -5.15 p.m.	Veda Chanting
5.15 p.m. - 6.00 p.m.	*Bhajans*
6.00 p.m. - 7.00 p.m.	*Darshan* of Bhagawan's *Mahasamadhi*
6.30 p.m. - 6.40 p.m	Meditation for Overseas Devotees in Prayer Hall

Kindly Note:

- Ladies and gents are seated separately in the hall with separate entrances for ladies and gents.
- Devotees are generally allowed to be seated inside the Sai Kulwant Hall around 7.45 a.m. for the morning session and around 4.15 p.m. for the afternoon sesion.
- The prayer sessions and darshan are open to all. There is no restriction on any basis whatsoever, be it religion, region, status, caste etc.
- There is no amount collected from anybody for Darshan.
- Devotees are not permitted to carry along with them articles like books, bags, purses, mobile phones, cameras and other electronic etc. into the *Darshan* Hall during *Darshan* time. Devotees may however bring their Veda books to the hall.
- Small articles such as cell phones, can be kept in the cloak room located close to the entrance to the hall.

Aumkar: *Aumkar* is the chanting of 'Aum', the primordial sound, also called the 'Pranava'. The vibrations that emanate from chanting 'Aum' have the potency to purify the inner personality of an individual as well as the surrounding environment. That is why the day at Prasanthi Nilayam begins with the chanting of 21 *Aumkars*.

Suprabhatham: 'Su' signifies good, auspicious and 'Prabhath' means morning. 'Suprabhatham' refers to the morning prayers that are chanted in praise of the Lord to awaken the divinity present within each individual. It is the act of dedicating oneself to the Lord and praying for His blessings right at the start of a new day. For the text and MP3 audio of the prayer,

Veda Chanting: Vedas are ancient spiritual scriptures revealed to great sages and seers while in communion with God. Chanting or listening to these hymns confers spiritual as well as physical benefits. That is why *Bhagawan* gives a lot of importance to Vedas and encourages everybody to chant these hymns and understand their meaning. The students of Bhagawan chant these hymns in the early hours of the morning while circumambulating the mandir complex, and also during *Darshan* hours in the morning and afternoon sessions in the mandir.

Nagar Sankeertan: 'Nagar' means city or locality and 'Sankeertan' means devotional singing. After *Suprabhatam*, devotees circumambulate the mandir complex while singing devotional songs and clapping their hands keeping beat. It charges the atmosphere with holy vibrations and one begins the day with the name of the Lord on one's lips.

Bhajans: Bhajans means "Singing aloud the glory of God". *Bhajans* are unique as they are universal in their scope and appeal and emphasise the unity of faiths.

36

Sri Sathya Sai Organization Sites

"The main objective of the Sathya Sai Organizationis to help you recognize the divinity inherent in you. So, your duty is to emphasize the one, to experience the one in all you do or speak. Do not give importance to differences of religion, sect, status, or colour. Have the feeling of one-ness permeate all your acts. Only those who do so have a place in this Organization; the rest can withdraw."

Sathya Sai Baba
(Sathya Sai Speaks IX, 35, 187-188)

World Regions of the Sai Organization Zone Region

		India
		Dharmakshetra
		Delhi
1	11	United States, Isreel
1	12	West Indies
		Bahamas, Trinidad & Tobago, Surinam, Guyana, Barbados & other Caribbean Islands
1	13	Canada
2		Latin America and Puerto Rico
		Click this link to see much of www.sathyasai.org
		But in Spanish
2	21	Belize, Costa Rica, Cuba, Dominican Republic, El Salvador, Guatemala, French Guyana, Haiti, Honduras, Mexico, Nicaragua, Panama, Puerto Rico
2	22	Colombia, Equador, Peru, Venezuela
2	23	Argentina, Bolivia, Brazil, Chile, Paraguay, Uruguay
3		Australia & Papua New Guinea
3		New Zealand, Fiji, and Pacific Islands, Philippines, Nepal, Bhutan

3		Sri Lanka
4		Far East (South)
		Brunei, Indonesia, Malaysia, Singapore,
		Thailand, Vietnam
4		Far East (Middle)
		Afghanistan, Bangladesh, Laos, Myanmar
		(Burma), Pakistan
5		Far East (North)
		China PRC, Hong Kong, Japan, Japan (in
		English) Korea, Taiwan ROC
6	61	South Europe Croatia, France, Italy, Malta,
		Portugal, Slovenia, Spain, Switzerland
6	62	South Europe
		Albania, Bosnia & Herzegovenia, Bulgaria,
		Cyprus, Greece, Macedonia, Montenegro,
		Romania, Serbia
7		North Europe
7	71	Austria, Czech Republic, Germany, Hungary, Slovakia
7	72	Belgium, Denmark, Greenland, Iceland,
		Luxembourg, Netherlands, Norway, Sweden
7	73	Estonia, Finland, Latvia, Lithuania, Poland
8		East Europe Azerbaijan, Armenia, Byelorussia, Georgia,
		Kasakhstan, Kyrghyzstan, Moldova, Russia (Poccnr),
		Tagzhikistan, Turkmenistan, Uzbekistan, Ukraine (Ykpanha)
9		United Kingdom, Republic of Ireland, Africa,
		Middle East
9	91	United Kingdom, Republic of Ireland
9	92	South Africa, Botswana, Mauritius, Seychelles
9	93	Central & North Africa and Mauritius:
		Angola, Cameroon, Congo, Ethiopia, Kenya,
		Ghana, Ivory Coast, Libya, Malawi, Morocco,
		Nigeria, Rwanda, Senegal, Sierra Leone,
		Somalia, Swaziland, Tanzania, Uganda,
		Zambia, Zimbabwe
9	94	Middle East and Gulf (except Israel):
		Abu Dhabi, Bahrain, Dubai, Iran, Kuwait, Oman, Qatar, Saudi
		Arabia, Syria, Turkey

37

Sri Sathya Sai Baba Organization Centres Worldwide

Sai Baba of India—Sri Sathya Sai Baba Centres—Sai Baba Organization Worldwide 2 . . .

The Sathya Sai Seva Organization is a service organization with a spiritual core and base. The first Sai Centers were started in India as far back as 1965 under the name Sri Sathya Sai Seva * foreign countries. At present there are around 2500 centers spread over 137 countries.

Location and Addresses of Sai Centers worldwide—Sathya Sai Organizations: Zone/Region/Count Websites

Sathya Sai Centers and Sai Groups in various countries official and non-official) Location & addresses of Sai Centers

For official websites of the Zone/Region/Country click here Sathya Sai Organizations: Zone/Region/Country

Australia

- House of Dharma
  Devotional Centre, Located in Casterton, Victoria, Australia.
- Sai Centre of Homebush
- Sathya Sai Centre of Nunawading
- Sathya Sai Centre of Strathfield, Australia
- Sri Sathya SAi Casterton Devotional Group, Victoria
- Sri Sathya Sai Paddington Group
- Sai Events in Melbourne Australia region in simple Calendar like format

Bahrain

- Bahrain Sai Group (Yahoo Group)

Belgium

- Sathya Sai Baba Brotherhood. Sai Center in Belgium

Canada

- Sai Devotees in Burlington, Ontario, Canada (Yahoo Group)
- Sathya Sai Organization Montreal Young Adults (Yahoo Group)
- Bridletowne Sri Sathya Sai Baba Centre Information about Bhagawan Sri Sathya Sai Baba. Information, events and the happening at the centre, and more.
- Sai Centres in GTA (Greater Toronto Area)
- Sri Sathya Sai Baba Centre of Abbotsford
- Sri Sathya Sai Baba Centre of Calgary, Alberta
- Bienvenue sur le site officiel des Centres Sri Sathya Sai Baba du Quebec
- Sri Sathya Sai Baba Centre of Edmonton
- Sri Sathya Sai Baba Centre of Ottawa-Carleton
- Sri Sathya Sai Baba Centre of Toronto
- Sri Sathya Sai Baba Centre of Toronto East
- Sri Sathya Sai Baba Centre of Scarborough
- Sri Sathya Sai Baba Centre of Winnipeg
- Sri Sathya Sai Baba Centre of Vancouver
- Sri Sathya SAi Baba Centre, Victoria Park, Toronto, Ontario
- Sri Sathya Sai Devotional Group of West Island, Montreal
- Sri Sathya Sai Baba Spiritual Group—University of Waterloo

Colombia

- Sai Centers in Colombia

Denmark

- Sathya Sai Baba Landsforening
- Sai Baba—online forum

Hong Kong

- Sathya Sai Baba Centre of Hong Kong

Italy

- Centro Sathya Sai di Basilicata

India

- Addresses of the Convenors of the Sri Sathya Sai Seva Organization,

Mumbai

- Dharmaksherta, Sri Sathya Sai Seva Organization Mumbai, Maharashtra
- List of Convenors (sorted by Centre name)
- Sai Hyderabad Youth (Yahoo Group)
- Sai Youth Bangalore (Yahoo Group)
- Sai Youth Delhi (Yahoo Group)
- Sathya Sai Baba Centre of Mumbai
- Sathya Sai Youth Wing—Chennai (Madras Boys)
- Sri Sarva Dharma Smanvaya Trust, Karnataka
- Sri Sathya Sai Seva Organization—Fort Samithi (Mumbai)
- Sri Sathya Seva Organization Mysore
- Sri Sathya Sai Baba International Centre New Delhi
- Sri Sathya Sai Seva Organization Orissa
- Sri Sathya Sai Seva Organization Youth Wing, Bangalore
- Team of Young, Bangalore (Yahoo Groups)

Indonesia

- Sai Centers in Indonesia

Jamaica

- Sri Sathya Sai Baba Organization Kingston, Jamaica

Japan

- Sai Building Bhajan Group (Japanese)

Latin America

- Centros Sai

Malaysia

- Sathya Sai Centers of Malaysia
- Sai Sadhana Satsang Malaysia
- Sai Youths of Kuala Lumpur
- Sathya Sai Youth Wing Central Region
- Sri Sathya Sai Baba Bhajan Unit Kluang
- Sri Sathya Sai Baba Centre of Bandar Klang
- Sri Sathya Sai Baba Centre of Brickfields, Kuala Lampur
- Sri Sathya Sai Baba Centre of Johor Bahru
- Sri Sathya Sai Baba Centre of Melaka
- Sri Sathya Sai Baba Centre Taman University Bhajan Unit
- Sri Sathya Sai Baba Centres of Johor State
- Sri Sathya Sai Baba Puchong Nilayam
- Taman University Bhajan Unit
- The Abode of Peace—Sri Sathya Sai Baba Centre of Penang

Nether land

- Sathya Sai Baba Centrum Zaanstad

New Zealand

- Sathya Sai Service Organization

Oman

- Sai Centers in Oman

Portuguese

- Bhagavan Sri Sathya Sai Baba
  Pagina do Grupo Sathya Sai Boa Viagem.
  Republica Dominicana
- Centro Sai Santiago, Republica Dominicana

Scotland

- Sri Sathya Sai Service Organization of Scotland (Yahoo Group)
- Sai Youth Scotland Group, Glasgow (Yahoo Group)
- Sai Youth Scotland (Yahoo Group)

Singapore

- Sai Centres in Singapore
- Sai Baba Centres in Singapore
- Sai Baba Centre Katong
- Sai Singapore (Yahoo Group)
- Sai Youth Wing Singapore (Yahoo Group)
- Sathya Sai Baba Centre of Singapore
- Sathya Sai Baba Centre, Singapore
- Sri Sathya Sai Baba Centre of Singapore, Everton

Slovenia

- Sai Center Ljubljana 1

Spain

- Sathya Sai Baba Centre of Madrid
- Web del Centro Sathya Sai de Barcelona en castellano.

Sri Lanka

- Sai Baba Centre
- Sri Sathya Sai Seva Organization Sri Lanka

Switzerland

- Sathya Sai Centre Geneve
  Describes in French and English the activities of the Sathya Sai Geneva
  Centre

U.K.

* Birmingham Sai Kirtan Group
* Sai Baba Centre—Leicester Central
* Sai Baba Group, Cottingham
* Sathya Sai Baba Centre of Rosefields, UK
* Sri Sathya SAi Bbaa Centre of Hatfield
* Sri Sathya Sai Service Organization (Coventry)
* Sri Sathya Sai Service Organization UH—Sai Youth

U.S.A.

* Dallas Sai Center
  Schedule of Bhajans, Seva and Directions to the Sai center in Dallas,
* Deerhaven Hills, SW North Carolina USA
* East Brunswick Center, NJ
* East Brunswick SSSE
* Houston Sai Centers
* Las Vegas Sathya Sai Baba Center
  This is just a calendar of events for the Las Vegas Sai Center in Las Vegas.
* Nebraska Sai Bhajan Group (Yahoo Group)
* Ohio Sai (Yahoo Group)
* Om Sai Mandir
* Shri Sai Baba's magnificent temple in New York.
* Peninsula Sai Center, San Mateo, California
* Pittsburgh Sai Center
* Sai Baba Center of Greater Greenville, SC
* Sai Baba Temple, Houston (Yahoo Group)
* Sai Center Columbus, Ohio
* Sai Center of Canton, OH
* Sai Center of Cleveland
* Sai Center of South West Houston
* Sai Detroit
* Sai Spiritual Group in Beaverton, OR (Yahoo Group)
* Sai Young Adults Group of South Ozone Park, Queens New York (Yahoo Group)
* Sarva Dharma Service Centre, NJ
* Sathya Sai Activity: A journal of all the Sai activities & news going on and around New York.

* Sathya Sai Baba Atlanta Centre
* Sathya Sai Baba Centre of Central San Jose
* Sathya Sai Baba Center of Houston (Yahoo Group)
* Sathya Sai Baba Temple of Hollywood, Los Angeles, California Information about the location and schedule of the temple in Hollywood.
- Sathya Sai Baba's Home in Colusa, California
- Sathya Sai Baba San Francisco Centre
- Sathya Sai Center of Fremont (Yahoo Group)
- Sathya Sai Centre of Gordon (Yahoo Group)
- Sathya Sai Center San Francisco (Yahoo Group)
- Sathya Sai Memphis Group (Yahoo Group)
- Shri Sathya Sai Baba Center Activities in the West Boston area of Massachuss
- Sri Sai Baba Temple Society of Ohio
- Sri Sai's Shrine in South San Francisco
- Sri Sathya Sai Baba Center of Southfield, Michigan
- Sri Sathya Sai Baba center in Shelton, Connecticut
- Sri Sathya Sai Baba Center of Belle Mead
- Sri Sathya Sai Baba Center of East Brunswick, New Jersey
- Sri Sathya Sai Baba Center of Akron Ohio
- Sri Sathya Sai Baba Center of San Antonio, TX, USA
- Sri Sathya Sai Baba Center of San Bruno
- Sathya SAI BABA CENTER OF ATLANTA
- Sri Sathya Sai Baba Centers of Austin (Yahoo Group)
- Sri Sathya Sai Baba Centers of Austin
- Sri Sathya Sai Baba centers of Southern California
- Sri Sathya SAi Baba Organization Madison, Wisconsin
- Sri Sathya Sai Baba Devotees of Santa Rosa, CA and Vicinity (Yahoo Group)
- Sri Sathya Sai Bhajan Group Charleston, South Carolina
- Sri Sathya Sai Centre of Fort Wayne, Indiana
- Sri Sathya Sai Organization of Minnesota
- West County Sai Center (Yahoo Groups)

Others

- Centros Sai en el mundo
- Sai Divine Shrines and Temples in Various countries

Location & Addresses of Sai Centres Worldwide

State	Address
Argentina	Centros Sai Baba de Argentina
Belgium	Centers in Belgium
California	North and Nevada saicenters.org
California South	Sai Baba Centers of Southern California
Canada	Regions
Chile	Centros Sai en Chile
Colombia	Sai Centers in Colombia
Czech Republic	Sai Centrum
Denmark	Naermeste center eller grupee oplyses patelefon 35 38 23 43 eller Sai Info
Germany	Gruppen und Zentren
India	Sai Centres in India
	Sai Centres in India
Indonesia	Sai Centres in Indonesia
Italy	Centre Gruppi Sathya Sai in Italia
Latinoamerica	Organizacion Sri Sathya Sai Baba en Latinoamerica
Malaysia	Sathya Sai Baba Centres in Malaysia
Mid Atlantic Region	(USA) Sathya Sai Baba Centres Mid Atlantic Region
Netherland	Centra en Groepen in Nederland
New Zealand	Contacts-Sai House Centres
Singapore	Sai Baba Centres in Singapore
Spain	Direciones de los Centros * Grupos Sathya Sai
Sweden	Center och Grupper
Srilanka (Colombo)	webmaster@srisailanka.org
U.K. United Kingdom	Sri Sathya Sai Service Organization UK Regions
U.S.A.	Regions of U.S.A. Sai Organization

The Sai Organization

The inspiration of Sathya Sai Baba's example and message of unselfish love and service has resulted in the establishment of over 1,200 Sathya Sai Baba Centersin 114 countries throughout the world.

The Sathya Sai Baba Centres constitute a genuine spiritual movement. We are moving away from body consciousness and selfishness to God consciousness and selflessness. We are moving away from a world in which force maintains order, away from a world in which selfish goals are the foundation of human interactions and institutions. We are moving toward a world where acknowledgement of and love for God results in the harmonious and loving interaction of all members of the holy human family. Love is the fuel for our spiritual movement. The quality and constancy of our love determines the speed and duration of our journey.

The members of Sathya Sai Centers are united by a common bond—love of God—and a common goal—spiritual growth. Center activities include the study of the teachings of Sathya Sai Baba and the sacred literature of all religions, group devotional singing, spiritual meditation, and selfless service to the community, society, the world, and the environment. The membership includes people from all walks of life, and the center programs are compatible with all the major religions. There is never a fee membership in a Sathya Sai Baba Centre, and members are never required to purchase books or materials. Donations are never solicited.

38

108 Divine Names of Sri Sathya Sai Baba

(1)   Aum Shree Bhagwan Sathya Sai Naathay Namah

(2)   Aum Shree Sai Sathya Swaroopaya Namah

(3)   Aum Shree Sai Sathhya Dharma Parayanay Namah

(4)   Aum Shree Sai Sathya Vardaya Namah

(5)   Aum Shree Sai Sat Purushaya Namah

(6)   Aum Shree Sai Sathya Gunatmane Namah

(7)   Aum Shree Sai Saadhu Vardhanaya Namah

(8)   Aum Shree Sai Sadhujan Poshane Namah

(9)   Aum Shree Sai Sarvagyanaya Namah

(10)   Aum Shree Sai Sarvajan Priyaya Namah

(11)   Aum Shree Sai Sarva Shakti Murtaye Namah

(12)   Aum Shree Sai Sarveshaya Namah

(13)   Aum Shree Sai Sarva Sanga Parithyagine Namah

(14)   Aum Shree Sai Sarvantaryamine Namah

(15)   Aum Shree Sai Mahimatmane Namah

(16)   Aum Shree Sai Mahesh Swaroopaya Namah

(17)   Aum Shree Sai Parthi-gramod-bhavaya Namah

(18)   Aum Shree Sai Parti Kshetra Niwasine Namah

(19)   Aum Shree Sai Yash-kay Shirdi Wasine Namah

(20)   Aum Shree Sai Jodi Aadipalli Somappaya Namah

(21)   Aum Shree Sai Bhardwaj Rishi Gotraya Namah

(22)   Aum Shree Sai Bhakta Vatsalaya Namah

(23)   Aum Shree Sai Apantaratmaya Namah

(24)   Aum Shree Sai Sai Avatar Murtiya Namah

(25)   Aum Shree Sai Sarva Bhaya Nivarine Namah

(26)   Aum Shree Sai Aapastambha Sutray Namah

(27)   Aum Shree Sai Abhayapradaya Namah

(28)   Aum Shree Sai Ratnakar Vanshodbhavaya Namah

(29)   Aum Shree Sai Shirdi Abhed Shaktyavtaraya Namah

(30)   Aum Shree Sai Shankaraya Namah

(31)   Aum Shree Sai Shirdi Saimurtaye Namah

(32)   Aum Shree Sai Dwarkamai-wasine Namah

(33)   Aum Shree Sai Chitravatitat Puttaparti Viharine Namah

(34)   Aum Shree Sai Shakti-pradaya Namah

(35)   Aum Shree Sai Sharanagat-tranaya Namah

(36)   Aum Shree Sai Anand-daya Namah

(37)   Om Shree Sai Anandaya Nameh

(38)   Aum Shree Sai art-tranparnaya Namah

(39)   Aum Shree Sai Anaath-nathaya Namah

(40)   Aum Shree Sai Asahaya-Sahayaya Namah

(41)   Aum Shree Sai Lokbandhawaya Namah

(42)   Aum Shree Sai Lok-Raksha-Parayanaya Namah

(43)   Aum Shree Sai Sree Lok Nathaya Namah

(44)   Aum Shree Sai Deen-Jan-Poshanaya Namah

(45)   Aum Shree Sai Murtitray-swaroopaya Namah

(46)   Aum Shree Sai Mukti-pradaya Namah

(47)   Aum Shree Sai Kalush-Viduraya Namah

(48)   Aum Sri Sri Karuna Karaya Namah

(49)   Aum Shree Sai Sarvadharaya Namah

(50)   Aum Shree Sai Sarva—Hrudaya Wasine Namah

(51)   Shree, Aum Shree Sai Punya-fala-pradaya Namah

(52)   Aum Shree Sai Sarva-paap-Kshaya Karay Namah

(53)   Aum Shree Sai Sarva-Rog-Niwarine Namah

(54)   Aum Shree Sai Sarva-Badha-Haraya Namah

(55)   Aum Shree Sai Anant-nut Kartanaya Namah

(56)   Aum Shree Sai Aadhi-Purushaya Namah

(57)   Aum Sri Adi Shakhya Namah

(58)   Aum Shree Sai Apa-roopa-Shaktine Namah

(59)   Aum Shree Sai avyakt-roopaya Namah

(60)   Aum Shree Sai Kam-Krodh-Dhwansine Namah

(61)   Aum Shree Sai Kahkambar-Dharine Namah

(62)   Aum Shree Sai Adbhut-Charyay Namah

(63)   Aum Shree Sai Apadabandhavay Namah

(64)   Aum Shree Sai Prematmane Namah

(65)   Aum Shree Sai Prema-murtaye Namah

(66)   Aum Shree Sai Prem-pradaya Namah

(67)   Aum Shree Sai Priyaya Namah

(68)   Aum Shree Sai Bhakta-priyaya Namah

(69)   Aum Shree Sai Bhakta-mandaraya Namah

(70)   Aum Shree Sai Bhakta-jan-hrudaya Viharay Namah

(71)   Aum Shree Sai Bhakta-jan-hrudalayaya Namah

(72)   Aum Shree Sai Bhakta-paradhinaya Namah

(73)   Aum Shree Sai Bhakti-dana-pardipaya Namah

(74)   Aum Shree Sai Bhakti-dana-praday Namah

(75)   Aum Shree Sai Sugyana-marga-darshakaya Namah

(76)   Aum Shree Sai Gyana-swroopaya Namah

(77)   Aum Shree Sai Gitabodh kaya Namah

(78)   Aum Shree Sai gyansiddhidaya Namah

(79)   Aum Shree Sai Sundar-roopaya Namah

(80)   Aum Shree Sai Punya-purushaya Namah

(81)   Aum Shree Sai Punya-fal pradaya Namah

(82)   Aum Shree Sai Purshottamaya Namah

(83)   Aum Shree Sai Puran-Purushaya Namah

(84)   Aum Shree Sai Atitay Namah

(85)   Aum Shree Sai Kala-titaya Namah

(86)   Aum Shree Sai Sidhidh-roopaya Namah

(87)   Aum Shree Sai Sidhidh-Sankalpaya Namah

(88)   Aum Shree Sai Aarogya-pradaya Namah

(89)   Aum Shree Sai Anna-vastra-daya namah

(90)   Aum Shree Sai Sansar-Dukh-Kshaya Karay Namah

(91)   Aum Shree Sai Sarva-bhist-pradaya Namah

(92)   Aum Shree Sai Kalyan-gunaya Namah

(93)   Aum Shree Sai Karma dhwansine Namah

(94)   Aum Shree Sai Sadhu-manas—Shobhitaya Namah

(95)   Aum Shree Sai Sarvamersammataya Nameh

(96)   Aum Shree Sai Sarvasobhitaya Namah

(97)   Aum Shree Sai Sadhakanugraha-Vatavriksha Pratisthapakaya Namah

(98)   Aum Shree Sai Sakal Sanshay-haraya Namah

(99)   Aum Shree Sai Sakal-tatwa-bodhakaya Namah

(100)   Aum Shree Sai Yogishwaraya Namah

(101)   Aum Shree Sai Yogindra-vanditaya Namah

(102)   Aum Shree Sai Sarva-mangal-Karaya Namah

(103)   Aum Shree Sai Sarva-Sidhi-Pradaya Namah

(104)   Aum Shree Sai Apanniwarine Namah

(105)   Aum Shree Sai Aartiharaya Namah

(106)   Aum Shree Sai Shantmurtaye Namah

(107)   Aum Shree Sai Sulabh-Prasannaya Namah

(108)   Aum Shree Bhagwan Sathya Sai Babayaya Namah

SECTION III

The Future Sai Baba
The Third Sai Baba
SRI PREMA SAI BABA
Future Incarnation in the 21st Century

Vasantha Sai holding the picture of Sri
Sathya Sai Baba in her hands

Prema - the wife of the futrure Prema Sai
Baba-the incarnation of Vsasntha Sai;
miraculous creation of Sathya SaI Baba
given to Vasantha Sai

39

Earlier Indications by Sri Sathya Sai Baba till 1995

Although on 6 July, 1963, Sri Sathya Sai Baba made his first full-fledged public declaration about the advent of his next incarnation as Prema Sai Baba, who would be Goddess Shakti, born in that body, in the same Bhardwaj *Gotra* (lineage) of Rishi Bhardwaj to which the Shirdi Sai Baba and Sathya Sai Baba belonged, in Mysore (Karnataka) State in the 21st century, our research has led us to the discovery that Swami had predicted about the Prema Sai *Avatar* to some village women much earlier than that date, in the 1950's, when he used to live in Patta Mandir (Old Temple) in Puttaparthi village.

Mrs. G. Sujatha, an old Sai devotes from Andhra Pradesh, revealed as under:

"Once before the commencement of *Bhajan*, the women were gossiping and one of them said that some thought the Baba was playing games (joking), and there was another Baba at Shirdi who was endowed with supernatural powers. Suddenly, the voice of Swami was heard announcing that "another Baba will appear". Later, he presented a locket which contained the pictures of all the three Babas. This is still preserved in my mother's house."

Since then, the Baba had been disclosing to his close devotees very small bits of information about the future Prema Sai Baba from time to time. We have tried to gather all those bits of rare information and pieced them together. We present this profile of Prema Sai Baba as predicted by Sri Sathya Sai Baba. Baba had also miraculously produced some rings, lockets etc., of Prema Sai Baba, for his close devotees like Sujata Devi's mother, Hislop etc.

Sri Sathya Sai Baba had predicted that Sri Prema Sai Baba would be born in Gunaparthi village on the bank of Kaveri river in the Mandaya district of Karnataka, about eight years after the passing away of Sri Sathya Sai Baba.

The parents of Prema Sai will be very spiritual people. It was heard in Prasanthi Nilayam that the Baba had said that late Prof. N. Kasturi, who had been the Baba's ardent and long time devotee, official biographer and the first editor of *Sanathana Sarathi* and a very highly realized soul, would be reborn so as to be the mother of Prema Sai Baba. The person who would be the father of Prema Sai Baba has already taken birth. Baba had disclosed to his college students at Brindavan, Whitefield, that he was profoundly happy on that day because the father of Prema Sai had been born just on that day.

Prema Sai Baba will have long hair falling from his head to his shoulders. He will have a moustache (like the moustache of Lenin or Sam Pitroda). He will not have a crown of hair like Sri Sathya Sai Baba. He will be thin, tall and his face will be very peaceful and will radiate peace and divinity. Baba materialized a ring with the image of Prema Sai on it and gave it to Hislop. Hislop has recorded the following in this connection:

"The ring itself was silver in colour, that unique 5-metal alloy peculiar (*Panchdhatu*) to Indian. The stone was a cameo of Prema Sai, the loving Lord of Creation, destined to appear on Earth, and glazed; sculptured in profile, the bridge and length of nose visible with the suggestion of an arch over the left eye. It was a noble head with shoulder length hair, moustache and beard; the head resting on, or emerging from a lotus flower. His countenance was tranquil, peaceful and majestic."

The Baba said, "He is now in the process of birth so I cannot show any more of him. This is the first time I have shown it to the world."

This author had personally seen that ring on the finger of Mr. Hislop, at Whitefield, on 26 May 1992.

A staunch Sai devotee Mrs. Veena Verma (now resident of C-5/7557, Vasant Kunj, New Delhi) had informed me in 1992 that according to a miraculous Sai messages received by her, Prema Sai Baba would be a tall man, fair in colour and handsome; he will study in Sri Sathya Sai Institute of Higher Learning at Prasanthi Nilayam; he will marry a very pious lady and he will have only one issue, a very learned and virtuous son. According to her, several very devoted and spiritually advanced women had for years been praying so that one of them could be fortunate enough to be reborn to become the consort of the future incarnation of Prema Sai Baba. Such messages recorded in her diary were shown to the author in 1992.

The two pictures of Prema Sai, reportedly materialized by Sri Sathya Sai Baba and given to some devotees, ultimately found their way to the shops at Prasanthi Nilayam on the Baba's 60th birthday in 1986 in the form of printed copies. They reveal that Prema Sai will, in his later years, look like Christ, he will keep a stick in his hand and have the above mentioned facial features.

Mrs. Sarojini Palanivelu, in her book *Sri Sathya Sai's Miracles & Spirituality* (Vol. I) had revealed that the first portrait of the future Incarnation of Prema Sai Baba was drawn by an African female artist on the basis of a series of dreams in which Sri Sathya Sai Baba appeared as a "still life model" in the Prema Sai form, and when the portrait was completed, *Vibhuti* appeared on it. A Thai devotee showed a photo of that portrait to a Sai volunteer, Srinivasan, from Trichi at Puttaparthi in November 1986 and Srinivasan immediately took it to Hislop to compare it with the profile of Prema Sai on the ring given to Hislop by Sri Sathya Sai Baba. "The completely formed figure of Prema Sai on the ring and the copy of the portrait given by the Thai devotee are identical. Hence, it is confirmed that this portrait is that of Prema Sai."

Prema Sai will establish a separate *ashram*, in which there will be a big Shiva Temple with statues of other Gods and Goddesses also. Prema Sai will not inherit the Prasanthi Nilayam complex of Sri Sathya Sai Baba but will carry forward the great spiritual task of spiritual upliftment of Mankind, which Sri Sathya Sai Baba has been doing.

The purpose or role of Prema Sai Baba incarnation, as predicted by Sri Sathya Sai Baba, will be as under:

". . . Prema Sai, the third Avatar, shall promote the evangelic news that not only does God reside in every body, but every one himself is God. That will be the final WISDOM which will enable man and woman to rise to be God . . . He will work for the good and welfare of the world and with his efforts love, good will, brotherhood and peace will abound throughout the world. He will receive universal recognition from mankind."

This shows that Prema Sai will uplift mankind to a very high level of morality and spirituality, for which a lot of ground work has been done by Shirdi Sai Baba and Sathya Sai Baba. During his time, i.e. in the later half of the 21st century, the world will see the golden period of human civilization; there will be love, peace, happiness and spiritual awareness all over the world.

There are indications that a number of the present day close and blessed devotees of Sri Sathya Sai Baba will be born again so as to help or serve the mission of Prema Sai Baba. Swami has already disclosed this to some such fortunate ones. At least three concrete examples are available in print. One of them was of Dr. D.J. Gadhia, an eminent doctor and Sai devotee of Gujarati origin, domiciled in England. The second one is Mrs. Laxmi Deshmukh, a simple but staunch devotee of Atpadi village in Maharashtra. She will be born as a woman and live in close proximity to Prema Sai Baba. The third one is Mrs. Seethammal—88 year old lady of Chennai, known as 'Baba Paatti'. According to an ancient Tamil *Naadi*, she will be reborn as the elder brother of Prema Sai Baba. This information was made available to the preset author when he interviewed her at her house in Chennai on 27 November 1996. (See: Ruhela, S.P., *Shirdi Sai Baba's Mother and Her Re-incarnation*, 1998).

Dr. Gadhia had himself written about this prediction of Sri Sathya Sai Baba in his case in as under:

Passport for New Life

Kaya Kalpa (Transformation) of Soul

"In the interview room, beloved Swami (Sri Sathya Sai Baba) asked all the invited devotees (from U.K.) who were sitting around him: "Any Question?" Everyone started looking at each other. Sensing the situation which had developed, the Swami announced, "Let Gadhia ask a question". I was taken aback. Perhaps, he had known the turmoil inside me. I asked Swami:

"When you were in your previous body as Sri Shirdi Sai Baba, you had mentioned to one of your favourite devotees, Mr. Shyama that he was connected with you for the last 72 generations. At another occasion you had mentioned that all the members of the Dhurandhar family were also connected with you for 60 generations. May I know, my beloved Swami, since how many generations have I—a poor soul, been connected with you?

He appreciated my unusual question and replied with a smile on his lips replied. "You have been connected with the Swami for many generations and will continue to be connected for more generations. I asked "Are you not going to give me *Moskha* (liberation from further births and deaths) "*Moskha . . . ?*" The Swami asked in a loud voice "If that is what you wish, then you are a first class hypocrite." The Swami toned down . . . You are always singing in public *"Tumhi Mere Ram Ho, Tumhi Mere Pran Ho, Janam Janam Ke Sathi Ho"* (You are Rama to me, you are Krishna to me, you are my soul and companion for generations). That means what you sing loudly in public is quite contrary to your inner intentions! That surely means you are a hypocrite."

In an affectionate tone, the Swami disclosed that he is coming back, as *Prema Sai* in Mysore state and my next birth will also be there to serve the Swami, in the same way that I am serving him now. "Would you not like to come with Swami?" He asked looking straight into my eyes and issued a passport for my next birth."

Mrs. Laxmi Deshmukh's reference has been published in Sarla Joshi's Hindi book *'Kaliyug Ke Tirthsthal'* (Pilgrimages of Kaliyuga).

"After that, the Baba told Laxmi about Prema Sai's incarnation and said to her that in that period of incarnation, Laxmi also would be very close to him. Having said this, the Baba showed her a very big temple of Mahadev (Shiva); Laxmi had put on a very costly blue saree and was decorated with ornaments. Baba was holding her finger and lovingly showing her the statues of Nandi (Shiva's Bull), Parvati, Shirdi Sai and Prema Sai."

It was learned that (Late) Sri Brahmananda Reddy, State President of Sri Sathya Sai Organization of Orissa, who died in 1998, will be reborn as *Mausi* (mother's sister) of Prema Sai. Sri Sathya Sai Baba is reported to have predicted this to some Oriya Sai devotees.

In April 1999, a Sai devotee C. Krishnamoorthy, Deputy Executive Engineer, Anantapur (A.P.), has discovered that ancient Tamil *Suka Naadi* (Palm leaf records) also contain the prediction that Sri Sathya Sai Baba will have another *Avatar* namely, Prema Sai Baba. This Naadi is with Dr. A. Karunakaran Naadi Astrolger, Sri Sughar Agasthiyar Naadi Jyothide Nilayam, 14, Mannar (Reddy) Street, T. Nagar, Chennai-600017.

A number of Sai devotees from India and abroad in recent years, have revealed that the Sri Sathya Sai Baba had told them that they would be reborn during the time of Prema Sai Baba and serve him.

In his article on Shirdi and Parthi published in *Sanasthan Sarathi* (Speical issue, November 1999), Dr. D.J. Gadhia had recalled that when he went with Swami Shadhanand, a disciple of the late Swami Nityananda of Ganeshpuri near Mumbai, to Sri Sathya Sai Baba, after the interview, Sri Sathya Sai Baba maternized a beautiful medallion and handed over to him. Swami said "It is Prema Sai as a boy sitting behind a black flower. Gadhiva, have you seen black flowers in America?" "Yes, Baba". The Baba continued, "Prema Sai's right leg is on his left leg just like Shirdi Sai Baba. His hand style is like Swami and do you know why he is sitting behind black flower?" The Swami inverted the medallion upside down and said, Black flower becomes the hair of Swami, and the body of Prema SAi Becomes his face . . ." (*Sanathana Sarathi*, November 1999)

40

Information on Future Sri Prema Sai Baba gathered by me after 1995

I had the great fortune of coming under the divine grace of Bhagavan Sri Sathya Sai Baba when I was just 38 years of age in April 1973.

It was on my first visit to Puttaparthi/Prasanthi Nilayam ashram in February, 1974 that I had first of all heard that there would be third Sai Baba incarnation bearing the name of Prema Sai Baba, probably eight years after the *Samadhi* or *Nirvan* of Sri Sathya Sai Baba.

Since then I had been very much interested in Prem Sai Baba and very eager to collect information about the third Sai Baba—the future Prem Sai Baba as well. Thus whatever information I could any how gather from different sources till 1993 was presented by me in my book *The Sai Trinity* which was originally published by me through Sai Age Publications, Faridabad in 1994 and its next two editions in 1994 and revised enlarged edition in 2000 and several reprints were published by India's Vikas Publishing House.

I had gathered further very interesting new information about Sri Prema Sai Baba by coming in contact with Mrs. Vasantha Sai in the years 1999, 2000 and thereafter. I had the good fortune of meeting her and learning a lot from her, and from her close devotees and books. In 1999, I with my wife had gone to Anantapur (Andhra Pradesh) on 19th June *en route* to Prasanthi Nitayan. She had very kindly come there with her husband, her foremost devotee S.V. Venkataraman and a her family friend from Madurai. I interviewed her for 8 hours from 10 AM to 4 P.M. in order to grill her and discover the truth of her claim that she was the reincarnation of Lord Krishna's closest beloved Radha about 5000 years age and was ardent devotee of Sri Sathya Sai Baba. She and her party showed the copies of the most precious ancient records of *Agastya Mahashiva Nadi* and *Suka Nadi Agastya Muni* predicted about her that she was a unique spiritual being who was indeed Lord Krishna's beloved gopi (close female devotee) Radha. I had recorded her interview with the help of tape recorder and took very copicious notes and then that interview booklet entitled *'Radha's Reincarnation as Vasantha Sai'* (1999) was prepared. It was published by Sri Vasantha Sai Books and Publications Trust in 2000 and soon got into the internet and was known all over the world.

Thereafter, Vasantha Sai very graciously came to my Faridabad house and stayed with my family on three occasions. On 30th April, 2000 she along with her husband Sri M. Manoharan and her Tamil acquaintance a young man Arul Anant came to Faridabad and stayed with us for 21 days, trying to obtain Visa for their visit to Canada as they had been invited by one of her Indian devotees living there, but the Canadian Embassy did not give them Visa. In her book *Prema Nivarana Sayee* (2000) she poignantly recorded the highlights of her memories of interactions and impressions with Sai devotees in Faridabad in her daily diary.

Her second visit to our house at Faridabad was with two of her close Indian female devotees Geeta and Yamini in the next year. Her third visit to and stay with us in our house was with her four devotees—Fred, Eddy, Serena and one more foreign lady. Her last visit to our place with her close devotees Ventatraman, Fred, Geeta and Yamini was in the month of April 2002.

Thereafter, I also visited her native home at Vadkumpatti village in Tamil Nadu with an American devotee Martin Evind in early 2005, and then my wife and I visited her at the auspicious occasion of the inauguration of her Mukhti Nilayam ashram near Royapalyam village in Madurai District in February 2006 and witnessed the grand function there the readers of this book should know about this most unique event of the inauguration, construction, erection and divine importance of this Mukhti Stupi (Liberation Pillar). It is a unique temple of *Kundalini shakti*. 'It is the centre for all paths of yoga, worship, devotion and worship, and has has power to liberate the entire world. It is a symbol of universal love and sacrifice. Nowhere in the world such a temple of the deity of Kundalini exits. It was suggested by merciful Sri Sathya Sai Baba to Vasantha Sai in her meditation sessions to build it for bestowing the divine grace of achieving liberation on all those who wuld visit it. It was constructed as per the most elaborate spiritual directions of the *nadi* revelations by the most celebrated ancient saint Kakbhujander and by the world renowned architect and Vastu expert Sri Ganapathi Sthapati.

In course of all the above mentioned my contacts with Vasantha Sai and the mutual visits during 1999-2006 I have been hearing and learning a lot of most astounding spiritual secrets from her, her close devotees and ashramites and from all her above 50 spiritual books.

While publicizing the book *Beyond the Vedas Prema Sai Avatar* (Part II) the following information about the author Vasantha Sai has been posted by Vedic Books Com worldwide on the Internet since 2006:

About the Author: Vasatha Sai: VedicBooks advertisemement on Internet

Thirumathi (Mrs.) Vasantha Manoharan comes from a village called Vadakkampatti which is situated three kilometres west of Kallkudi near Thrumangalam in Madurai District of Tamil Nadu (India). Her father Madurakavi Azhwar was a great patriot and freedom fighter of the congress party. He cultivated cotton plant in his own house, obtained cotton, coverted it into yarn and then wove a cloth and offered it to Mahatma Gandhiji. Her mother was Vedavalli. She belongs to a family of orthodox Vaishnavite tradition.

Vasantha is a great and ardent devotee of Sri Krishna. The small sparks of love developed in due course and started raging as a fire, and later as a forest fire and it started burning her. When she was thirty five years old, one day during meditation Lord Sri Krishna appeared to her and said that he had incarnated as Sri Sathya Sai Baba at Puttaparthi. From that day, she has taken Sri Sathya Sai Baba as Sri Krishna and became his ardent devotee. She composed a garland of hymns "Sri Sai Ganajali" and offered it at the holy lotus feet of Sri Sathya Sai Baba.

Baba started appearing in her vision everyday. Later he started to enrich her with incredible divine experiences. Thrilling accounts of her experiences are condensed into some of her books which Sri Sathya Sai Baba has prompted her to write and dictated to her. Vasantha Sai, unique God woman of the contemporary world, the most unassuming, simple, shy, unostentatious, softly-spoken and genuinely lovin sanyasin possessing a very high level of spiritual attainments, is profusely admired and deeply loved by her countless devotees, friends and other spiritual seekers not only from India but from many foreign countries.

With all this knowledge, I have conclusively come to believe:

- That Vasantha Sai is really the reincarnation of Radha—Lord Krishna's close beloved devotee Radha about 5000 years back, as repeatedly told and confirmed to her by Sri Sathya Sai Baba in her thrice daily *dhyan* (meditation) sessions for many years and through innumerable miracles done by him to authentically prove it in spiritual contact and constant conversations all these year.

- That Sri Sathya Sai Baba had been always telling and repeatedly confirming to her in her meditation sessions that her ardent wish to be the consort/wife of God would certainly be fulfilled, she would certainly be united with him as His Divine Consort (Wife) bearing the name of 'Prema' in his next incarnation as Prema Sai Baba.

- That Sri Sathya Sai Baba had miraculously materialized for, in her devotee's house in Coimbatore and sent to her in her Mukhti Nilayam ashram, a very beautiful picture of 'Prema' in whose form the present Vasantha Sai would be incarnating. Her Mukhti Nilayam Ashram Trust has already published that unique coloured photo of Prema on the inner page of the back title of her book *'Prema Sai'* (Part I, April 2006) which all those who had purchased or seen that book must have surely seen.

In these two books on Prema Sai Baba, Vasantha Sai has narrated very fascinating, detailed, graphic details of the future life history of Prema Sai Baba (whose name would be Raja till he becomes 'Prema Sai Baba' at the age of 40, and of his beloved wife/divine Consort Prema—especially their childhood, marriage, their pilgrimage after marriage to certain holy places in North Indian like Badrinath, Ayodhya etc., and the certain intimate and special features of their only son 'Rema'. Not only these, she has even published the names of the future parents and close relatives—brothers, sisters, nephews, nieces and friends of both Raja (Prema Sai Baba) and Prema. She has even clearly given names of those among her ashramites at Mukhti Nilayam and her close devotees in South India who would be reborn as the relatives, friends and helpers of Prema Sai Baba and his would be wife/consort Prema. She has repeatedly mentioned fearlessly that Swami (Sri Sathya Sai Baba) only had foretold all these crucial pieces of information. She has published the genealogical tables of both Raja (who would become Prema Sai Baba) and his wife Prema.

All the above mentioned information and the following finer details about the life of the future Incarnations of Prema Sai Baba and his divine consort Prema mentioned by Vasantha Sai in her books boldly about 15-20 years or so ago in advance are really very pertinent, compelling, significant and very thrilling. Most of the people in this present day materialistic world who are not aware of and believers in spirituality, miracles of Sri Sathya Sai Baba or very orthodox and narrow minded will like to outright dismiss them as mere conjectures and improbabilities.

But since I have known so much about the genuineness of Vasantha Sai's claims as a great spiritualist and her being a very ardent devote and lover of Lord Krishna and Sri Sathya Sai Baba, I have total faith in her words—spoken as well as written. I am an ordinary human being and like most of the people I cannot know and predict any future event. I am a spiritual seeker. Every spiritual seeker is supposed to have faith and firm conviction in his/her belief emerging out of his own experience, and I have total belief and faith the divine personages of Sri Sathya Sai Baba and Vasantha Sai who is popularly known as Vasantha Amma. That is why I am mentioning all this which I have gethered as the most precious information about the future Prema Sai incarnation.

Having herself fully convinced of her beloved Bhagavan Sri Sathya Sai Baba's repeatedly given loving firm assurances to her in her thrice a day regular meditations in 2005-2006, Vasantha Sai has already six years back very boldly and publicly disclosed the following thrilling revelations about the future coming of Sri Sathya Sai Baba in the form of the third Sai Baba i.e., Prema Sai Baba at Gunparthi village in Mandya Distirct of the Karnataka State and also about her own rebirth there. In the beginning itself of her book *'Prema Sai'* (Part I, April 2006) she quotes Sri Sathya Sai Baba, Vasantha Sai Baba is making (my) dreams true." He says that he will come as Prema Sai in Sathya Yuga and (our) marriage will happen then. In Prema Sai Avatar, I wanted Swami to be with me at the time of childbirth.

On page 10 of that unique and most thrilling book she exhorts and invites all her readers: "Dear Readers, now you are ready to watch the Prema cinema unfold on the screen. Allow this prestine epic to shine the light of wisdom. Let the curtain of ego go up!

The most interesting and thrilling highlights of her divine futuristic cinema story scripted by Swami and Vasantha Sai may be presented as under:

- Both Raja (name of the next Sai incarnation till he publicly announces his avatarhood as Prema Sai at the age of 40 and his would be wife Prema will also be born in Gunaparthi Village in his neighbourhood. Their fathers would be friends and they will make a friendly promise or pact that that if their next issues would be a son and daughter they would be married to each other. Thus Raja and Prema would be married. Their marriage would be love marriage but arranged by their parents. Swami told her in mediation that ". . . we will be betrothed before birth."

- Raja (Prema Sai Baba) will the fourth child of his parents.

- Raja and Prema would know and love each other from their childhood and play together. Their play mates will include Vasantha Sai' present foreign devotees/ashramites (Fred and Eddy) who will be reborn to be their relatives.

- Raja's father would be Shirdi Sai Baba's contemporary devotee and also Sri Sathya Sai Baba's contemporary most eminent devotee and his ashramite in Prasanthi Nilayam Pedda Bottu reborn as a male, and his mother would be Prof. Kasturi who was the closest devotee, biographer and secretary of Sathya Sai Baba's eminent devotee, biographer and closest and most trusted ashram functionary, reborn as a female. It was heard by me also in 1974 that Sri Sathya Sai Baba had disclosed this rare piece of information to some of his devotees many years back and it was in the known to many people—much before Vasantha confirmed it in her prophetic spiritual book in April 2006. It had already been known to most Sai devotees as well. All those who have been privileged to read Vasantha Amma Sai's books or meet her and her chosen group of ashramities since 2006 have been knowing it as very confirmed truth about Prema Sai's future life history.

- Prema's parents' names will be Mathurakavi and Vedavalli—the same which were the names of the parents of Vasantha born in Vadkampatti in 1938.

- The parents of Vasantha Amma's devotees (who were Lord Rama's wife Sita's uncle and aunt) will come as Prema Sai Baba's father' elder brother and his wife. Vasantha Amma's devotee one Varmaji will be reborn and be Prema Sai Baba's uncle.

- Prema Sai Baba's uncle will come with his four sons, daughters-in-law, grand sons, grand daughters, sister and sister's husband. 'The sorrows of many births will (thus) be removed and they will enjoy the bliss of living with God.'

- Vasantha Amma's devotees Mandvi and Shrutkeerti will come as Prema's father's elder brother and his wife.

- Vasanta Amma's following present ardent devotees and ashramities will be reborn to play their future roles in relation to Sri Prema Sai and Prema

- Vasantha Sai's principal devotee SV. (K.S. Venkatraman) of Madurai will be born as Prema's brother Vijay. He will be one of the playmates of Raja and Prema in childhood, he will not marry, and after their marriage he will come as *Sri Dhan (Stree Dhan?)* with his sister Prema to her matrimonial home and live there for the rest of his life in order to serve her and her divine husband. He will not marry in that birth.

Swami had solemnly assured Vasantha Sai that her present Ashramities will be reborn as under:

- Her American devotee Fred will be reborn as the son of Prema's father's elder brother. His name will be Madhu.

- Her British devotee Eddy will be reborn as the son of Prema's father's elder brother. His name will be Kanha. He will not have married life.

- Vasantha Amma's foreign female devotees Sandy and Nicola will be reborn as Prema's friends.

- Vasantha's present devotees Dr. Bagchi, Vimala, Galatia will come as her relatives. Vimala will come as Prema's aunt—her mother's sister, i.e., *mausi*; her name will be Amrita. Dr. Bagchi's name will be Krishna.

- Vasantha's ardent devotees Bose, Rao, Govindrajan (who had been Lord Rama's friends in Gurukula) will come as relatives of Prema Sai Baba. In Prema Sai Avatar, Bose (who does not have any child in his present birth) will have two sons like Lord Rama's twin sons Lava and Kusa.

- Vasantha Amma's son Manovannan and Yamini will be brother and sister, and be cousins of Raja (Prema Sai Baba).

- Yamini, Meenakshi and Galgotia will be reborn and be Prema's friends.

- Vasantha Amma's daughter Kaveri will be the adopted daughter of Raja (Prem Sai Baba) and Prema; she will remain unmarried.

- Yamini (who was Lord Rama's wife Sita's sympathizer Trijada, when she was in the captivity of Ravana in Ashok van, and was thereafter reborn as Lord Krishna's sister Subhadra who was married to Arjun and was the mother of Abhimanyu) will be born as Prema Sai's sister 'Vasantha' in 1927 or 1928.

- Vasantha Amma's ardent devotees Mr. and Mrs. Anyaswamy will come as Prema's uncle and aunt. Fred and Eddy will be their sons Kanha and Madhu.

- Raja and Prema shall go to college.

- Raja will give to his bride Prema immediately after marriage that very ring which Lord Rama ring had gifted to his bride Site, saying "We came in *Treta* (Yuga) as Sita and Rama. I gave this ring to Hanuman, In *Dwapara* (Yuga) we came as Krishna and Radha. We are born for each other. No one can understands our love. In *Kali* (*Yuga*) we came to establish *Prema* (love), as Sathya Sai and Vasantha. You made me mad. Your boundless love has made me take another Avatar."

- Her devotee Kodai's parents will be reborn and will be Prema's relatives.

- Her devotees Mr. and Mrs. Anyaswamy will come as Prema's uncle and aunt. Fred and Eddy will be their sons.

- Raja and Prema's wedding will take place in morning. It will be attended and blessed by *Devas* (Gods). Both Raja and Prema will go on a motorbike to the local temple in Gunaparthi to hand over the first copy of their weddinginvitation card to God (Narayana) in the temple and the priest there will happily receive it and bless them profusely.

- Vasantha has written that she had put three conditions before Swami that as his future wife—she will not go to a hospital, only Swami should assist her in child birth, her blouse should not be stitched by a tailor', and she must never be forsaken by her husband. Swami fully agreed to abide by them.

- "In Prema Sai Avatar, nobody will be able to tell the difference between paternal and maternal cousins. All nephews and nieces will be united in love. No one will be able to tell the families apart, it will be one large family of brothers, sisters, friends, and their children. It will be an extended family of many families, an ideal example in the world."

- Three years after marriage, their only son will be born in the same month, at the same time and at the same time of Lord Rama's birth on Rama Navami day (Lord Rama's Birthday). His too will be named "Rama". He will be conceived at Ayodhya when Raja and Prema would be staying in course to their camping at that holy place of Lord Rama while returning from their pilgrimage with a party of their close relatives to north India's holy places—Badrinath, Naranarayan Gufa, Rishikesh, Haridwar, Kashi etc.

- In his features, their child Rama will resemble his father Raja. The future Prema Sai i.e., Raja will assist in his son Ram's birth. He will take the child from Prema's stomach. The child would not cry after birth. He will be a child of wisdom. He will always be blissful. He will be very attached to his father. He will live with his parents. He will be unique. *Devas* (Gods) will give him boons whenever he wants.

- Vasantha Amma's son Arvindan will be born as Prema Sai and Prema's son Rama. He will be Kamdeva's reincarnation—Vasantha Amma has written this as having been told by Sri Sathya Sai Baba in his spirit form in her meditation. His present wife also will come as his future life.

The following rare information is already available also on the internet as under:

13 September 2010 Meditation

Vasantha: Swami, My *Prabhu* (. . . God). How to write about my family?

Swami: Arvindan is the aspect of Kamdeva. He did not see the girl before marriage, he said: "Whatever my parents have decided, it is okey. Rama never saw Sita before their marriage. He said that only after his father came and fixed the marriage, he would see her. Arividan had told the same. Is he Kamadeva or Rama? That is why he will be born as our son. His two sons are aspects of Gandharvas, (celestial musicians). Manivannan also did not seek his bride. He only saw he face when he tied her Mangala Sutra, He and his wife are the aspects of Uddava (Lord Krishna's devtoee and most trusted friend). Their daughter Vaisnavi Yoga Maya, Kaveri was born through the feelings (of) Radha (and) Krishna. Her husband is a *Gandarva* (celestialsinger) also. Sathyan (their son) is an aspect of me, and his wife Sree is an aspect of you. All have been brought for our task, they demonstrate how to live a moral life ever in thought of God."

- Vasantha Sai's book *Avatar's Secret*, pp. 11-13

Internet (*file://Swami's Children and Vasantha Sai's Vaikuntha—Heaven on Earth.html*)

- Raja will reveal his identity much later as Prema Sai Baba (after the age of 40) to the world, till 40 "He will hide his divinity in order to fulfill his debt to his wife." He will not desert his wife Prema, as Lord Rama did with his wife Sita. He will tell her, "I am not like Rama. I will not leave you alone. We have come to show an ideal life without the fault of Rama and Krishna Avatars. I will not separate from you, our child and the family. This a promise."

All these things have been revealed by Vasantha Sai on the basis of her Lord Sri Sathya Sai Baba's solemn divine assurances to her and published by her some years back in 2006 with his divine consent. He had even materialized and sent her a wonderful coloured beautiful picture of Prema Sai Baba's beloved wife/consort Prema in a house of Vasantha Amma's devotee of Coimbatore and she published the same as was authorized and prompted by Swami, miraculous pictures of future Prema appear in the above—mentioned book first published in 2006 and known to her devotees.

41

Recent News & Rumours

Despite this treasure of spiritual and mundane information about Prema Sai Baba having been unearthed and world-wide informed to her devotees by Vasantha Sai during the last 6-7 years, it is indeed very astonishing to me as to why these thrilling revelations have not yet found their entry into the repertoire of the belief system of the leaders and bosses of Sai Organization and countless Sai devotees in the world. May be it has been due to their ignorance of these revelations, or their reluctance to recognize and accept them out of prejudice or envy or their lack of full belief in the miraculous and mysterious powers of Sri Sathya Sai Baba and Vasantha Sai. It is indeed surprising that while Sri Sathya Sai Baba and the countless miraculous messages sent most mysteriously to many throughout the world by him, why they have been just ignoring his messages in regular intimate spiritual conversations with her for so many years. It is high time when their ignorance or prejudice as such should end—the earlier the better.

- Recent News, Speculations/Wild Rumours About Sai Baba Circulating Since Sri Sathya Sai Baba's Passing Away: A Review:

Since the very time when Sri Sathya Sai Baba left his mortal body on Sunday, the 24th April, 2011 in the Sri Sathya Sai Super Specialty Hospital at Prasanthi Nilayam at 7.40 A.M., a lot of news about his next incarnation as Prema Sai Baba has come on TV and Internet and in newspapers. A brief review of them is essential and is therefore presented here as under:

1. India's most prestigious and widely selling news paper *The Times of India* (New Delhi edition) of 25th April, 2011 published the following news item:

Abandoned baby next Sai Baba?

Mandya: If the words of Halgappa, an ardent devotee of Sathya Sai Baba are to be believed, it was in the early 1960s that Baba had broached the issue of his reincarnation as 'Prema Sai', in a village on the banks of river Cavery near Srirangapattana in Karnataka.

"Although Baba did not reveal the name of the village, he said it would be called Gunaparthi", he claimed. He added that he would not insist on knowing the name of the village as he had the impression that the village may be called Gunaparthi after Baba's incarnation. According to Halgappa, Sai Baba's reincarnation will be found deserted on the banks of Cavery in Mandya. There isn't much clarity on who the child's parents will be. A fisherman will take the baby and groom him, and he will be named Prema SAi Baba, the third avatar of Sai Baba." TNN

This news item stunned me being very conjectural one. I personally do not believe in it at all. It is in total disregard to Sri Sathya Sai's earlier clear hint that Patta Boddu and Kasturi will be reborn to be the parents of Prema Sai Baba. This strange story is in total disregard to my information collected in several years, especially since I strongly believe in the spiritual personalities of Sri Sathya Sai Baba and Vasantha Sai. I know that Vasantha Sai's first book 'Now *Liberation! Itself! Right!'* had actually been blessed by Sri Sathya Sai Baba in the house of P.S.A. Subramaniam Chettiar, President of Sri Sai Paduka Trust, Madurai on 5th May, 1997 and the photo of Baba blessing it by writing *'With Love Baba'* in the presence of Chettiar was taken and published in the book, all the manuscripts and books of Vasantha Sai were blessed by Baba in innumerable ways like Baba's written messages, signatures, materialization of *vibhuti, kumkum,* fantastic drawings etc., and her conversations with him in all her meditation sessions for many years were authentic and known to her thousands of devotees spread in many countries of the world. Swami had sent his messengers and devotees of many countries a number of times to her in her Vadkampatti village and Mukhti Nilayam to convey his love and blessings and enable them to receive her grace as she has been functioning as his alter—ego or complementary avatar.

I have been a firm believer in the genuineness of her revelations about herself and her divinity as a living goddess who has been playing the supplementary Avataric role of blessing and guiding many earnest spiritual seekers. I have not even a trace of untruth in her behaviour, role functioning as Avatar, her confirmed and cent per cent confident declarations that she is Radha's reincarnation, she is genuinely in highest love with Swami and that she has indeed been promised by Swami that in Prema Sai Avatar he would certainly marry her, and that Sathya Yug has already been commenced by both Baba and her on 23rd October, 2010 with celebration of *'Sathya Yuga Pravesham'* done by her in her Mukhti Nilayam Ashram, which was attended by many Indian and foreign devotees. How can I the least doubt or disbelieve in her spirituality and her spiritual romantic future history of Prema Sai Avatar?

I had long back heard and read about and actually observed the unique miracles happening with Sri Halgappa for many years—*vibhuti* and *chameli* (jasmine) flavoured honey constantly appearing in the Sri Sathya Sai temple in his ashram on the bank of Cauvery river on Bangalore-Mysore highway. I still possess the miraculous honey, which has constantly been oozing out of the two amulets given to him by Sri Sathya Sai Baba more than two decades back (readers can read about this unique miracle on the internet (file://1/ POTENT EVIDENCE—htm: by R.D. Awle, 2001) very lovingly given to me by him when I visited his temple and orphanage in Mandya about 15 years back. Despite all this, I have to outright dismiss his imaginary, baseless, wild story about Prema Sai Baba. I cannot ever believe that Prema Sai Baba will be an abandoned boy discovered and brought up a fisherman. I can not be unture to my conscience and waver in my belief in the divine announcement of Vasantha Sai.

2. I have come to know about a news on the internet (file://1: Sathya Sai Maddur Baba reborn as Prema Sai Baba on 24 April, 2011 usearched_info. htm) that Prema Sai Baba will be born in Doddmallur village that lies between Channapatam and Maddur around 90 kilometers away from Bangalore.

'With the funeral (burial) of the Sathya Sai Baba over, the focus has now shifted out of Puttaparthi to a small village named Doddamallur, which lies between Channapatna and Maddur around 90 kilometres away from Bengaluru.

Doddamallur will play a significant part in the days to come, as this has been the village that has been identified by Sathya Sai Baba to be the place where his next incarnation Prema Sai Baba will be bron.

With the reincarnation stories doing the rounds, a great deal of interest has already been generated in his small village. The sleepy hamlet has had just one great story to tell in all these years—that Lord Rama had prayed at the Shri Ambegalu Shri Krishna temple before he set out to Lanka to battle Ravana.

There was a great deal of confusion regarding this place as far as stories of Prema Sai Baba were concerned.

Earlier, it was being said that he would be born in a village called Gunaparthi near Mandya, but now it is official that the reincarnation would happen at Doddamallur.

The villagers are in frenzy. They are aware that if this happens then their village will become hugely important and what is more they all believe that Sathya Sai Baba's reincarnation will be born in their village.

Prema Sai Baba, according to the discourses given by Sathya Sai Baba, would be the third and the last incarnation of Sai Baba, the first being Shirdi Sai Baba.

This has also been documented in a book written by a lady by the name Kannamma who herself is a great devotee of Sathya Sai Baba.

The people from Puttaparthi have been showing a great deal of interst in Doddamallur. What is more ironical is that two months back, Baba himself had dispatched a team of around 700 members to Doddamallur. The villagers were a bit taken aback to see such a large contingent.

The group headed straight to the temple at Doddamallur and offered 'Laksharchana' and 'Kumkumarchana' pujas, which were conducted for nearly 10 hours. Temple trust Chairman Venu confirmed this.

Venu goes on to add that this was the moment that they are all waiting for. They have no reason to believe that this will not happen and the whole village thinks that the prophecy by Baba will come true.

What we were given to understand is that there is no date specified for the birth of Prema Sai and so it could happen any time in the near future, he said, adding, the age factor which is being debated was also clarified to us.

We expect the people from Puttaparthi to come down and identify Prema Sai for us. Although we are on the look out for the possible parents of Prema Sai, we would still wait for the people from Puttaparthi to do the needful. All they have told us is to inform them if they find something strange or a miracle, which is bound to happen around the Shri Ambegala Krishna temple, Venu said.

Regarding the birth of Baba's next incarnation, the trustees said the spiritual leader had not given any specific date for the brith of Prema Sai Baba.

. . . In incarnation, as Prema Sai, had been born in the southern Indian state of Karnataka in the early 1990s, during a talk with students, Sathya Sai told them "that the father of his next. He also said that the body of Prema Sai was in the process of being formed." It is also said that Prof. Kasturi will be the mother of Prema Sai", who is now already reborn.

The future incarnation of Sathya Sai is to include the roles of being a husband and father. It is said, at a certain time, Prema Sai will be married, and be the father to one boy.

Prema Sai Baba is said to complete the mission of the Sai Avatar to end this age of darkness and to usher in the golden age of mankiind. Around 2105, the incarnation will finish as Prema Sai Baba (then 86) will enter into *mahasamadhi*.

The following extract of Internet fi://1: le*NEWS ABOUT PREMA SAI BABA* <<*saiprema's Blog.htm i*s worth serious consideration at this juncture:

About Doodamallur: ". . . Someone like Sri G. Vekataran or Sri Prof. Anil Kumar would not stop laughing it this news as it is completely an imaginary. Of course our monkey minds are very keen to know more about his place. As far as I know, Swami never sent atlest 7 people to anywhere for such meaningless reason and 700 people is completely unimaginable. Knowing Swami. He would never do so.

". . . When it was announced that Swami left his body on the 24th April, 2011 at 7.40 a.m. two days later there was one news channel which showed one young couple. Apparently they had a baby on the 24th April, 2011 at 7.42 a.m. (two minutes after Swami left his body. This young couple happens to be from Mandya District where Prema Sai is predicted to be born . . . Now the couple who seemed to bedaily wag labourers claim that their child is Swami's reincarnation."

3. In the *Asian Age* of 25th April, 2011 this news was published:

When will Sai Baba be reborn?

(C.R. Gowri Shanker and S.V. Krishna Chaintanya)

No sooner has news of the demise of Sathya Sai Baba spread then there are predictions of his rebirth. A family in Mysore claims that Baba will be reborn as Prema Sai in 2012 near the Ambegala Krishna temple in Doddamallur in Maddur *taluk* of Mandya district. "This is not our prediction. Sai Baba himself revealed it to my mother Kannamma and grandmother Nammagiriamma during one of his visits to our residence in Mysore", a Sathya Sai devotee, Mr. Shankar, retired deputy director of the Central Food Technological Research Institute, told this newspaper. Mr. Shankar also claimed, quoting his mother Kannamma, that the Baba will be born to Narayana Kasturi, who authored the first four volumes of Baba's biography *Sathyam Sivam Sundaram* (Life of Sathya Sai Baba). It is in this book that Baba first claimed, in 1963, that he would be reborn. Several generations of Mr. Shankar's family are diehard devotees of Baba and the 90-year-old Kannamma is one of the closest devotees of the seer, who has visited her residence in Mysore six times. Kannamma's diaries describing her experiences with the Baba were published in the form of a book titled "Sri Sathya Sai Anandadayi", which also talks about Baba's third incarnation . . .

. . . This has also been documented in a book written by a lady by the name Kannamma who herself is a great devotee of Sathya Sai Baba.

The history of Prema Sai Baba began in 1963. During a Guru Poornima discourse, Sathya Sai Baba stated, "Shiva said that they (Shiva and Shakti) would take human form and be born in the Bharadwaja lineage, thrice: Shiva alone as Shirdi Sai, Shiva and Shakhi together at Puttaparthi as Sathya Sai, and Shakthi aone as Prema Sai, later." This is the first time Prema Sai was mentioned.

Some years later, Sathya Sai elaborated on the message and mission of Prema Sai. "Prema Sai, the third avatar will promote the evangel news that not only does God reside in everybody, but everybody is God. That will be the final wisdom which will enable every man and woman to go to God. The three avatars (Shirdi Sai, Sathya Sai, Prema Sai Baba) carry the triple message of work, worship and wisdom."

Clearing further confusion, Sathya Sai continued, "they (the three Sai avatars) are not separate. I have already mentioned the complete oneness of the three in the final objective of the mission. I will give you an example. Take a kilo of *gud* (solidified sugarcane juice). The whole of it tastes sweet. Next break it into small pieces. Each of them is sweet. Finally break them into small grains. You find the same sweetness in them. So the difference is one of quantity and not quality. It is the same with the Avatars. Their tasks and powers requisite to them differ according to the time, the situation and the environment. But they belong to, and derive from, one and the same dharma swarup or divine body."

On March 6, 2008, (during Shivaratri celebrations) Sathya Sai Baba gave further insight to the nature of the triple incarnation. "The Avatar came as a Trinity. The first was Shirdi Sai, the second is Parthi Sai, and the third will be Prema Sai. The complete unity among all will be achieved when Prema Sai comes."

In the early 1990s, during a talk with students, Sathya Sai told them that the father of his next incarnation, as Prema Sai, had been born in the southern Indian state of Karnataka. He also said that the body of Prema Sai was in the process of being formed." "It is also said that Prof. Kasthuri will be the mother of Prema Sai", who is now already reborn.

The future incarnation of Sathya Sai is to include the roles of being a husband and father. It is said, at a certain time, Prema Sai will be married, and be the father to one boy.

Prema Sai Baba is said to complete the mission of the Sai avatar to end this age of darkness and to usher in the golden age of Mankind. Around 2105, the incarnation will finish as Prema Sai Baba (then 86) will enter into *mahasamadhi*.

Professor G. Venkataraman relates a personal experience with Sathya Sai in which Prema SAi became the topic." A warden offered a peanut to Swami who first refused but later popped one but into his mouth. He then started giving us one nut at a time. Everyone put out his hand to receive the Prasadam from Swami and when my turn came I did the same. But what fell into my hand was not a piece of ground nut but an enamel billet with some art work on it. I gave Swami a puzzled look and he said, "See what it is." I tried to see what was on the billet but could not see clearly since I did not have my glasses on. Swami then made some teasing remarks and said, "This billet shows the Cosmic Form of the Lord. Embedded in it are the forms of Shirdi Sai and Swami. I have left some space for Prema Sai also. Shall I include Prema Sai also?" We remained silent, stunned by the experience. He then smiled and said, "No I shall not include Prema Sai because you faithless fellows would desert me and go after him!" We all laughed."

In 2004, Professor Anantharaman talked about an experience with Howard Murphet and Sai Baba. "Howard then asked what work would Prema Sai do? Sai said "He will have plenty of work. Prema Sai will elevate human consciousness to divine heights. Not only will there be a lot of work but he will also need a lot of help."

James Sinclair, an American, in 2005, described a series of dreams that "went on for years. I saw myself walking up a hill, led by three men in the darkness of night. One was an old man in white. One looked somewhat like Jesus Christ. The one in the middle had an orange robe." Fifteen years later, he describes finding a book about Sai Baba, and seeing his appearance, "recognized that the recurring dream had been of Shirdi Sai, Sathya Sai and Prema Sai walking up the hill night after night for many years."

42

Epilogue

Having gone through all the above various pieces of information, I am now finally of the view:

- That the information given by Vasantha Sai seems to be most authentic and it should be and ultimately, sooner or later, would certainly accepted by all Sai devotees and the organizers, bosses and functionaries of Sri Sathya Sai organizations in all countries of the world when they would study all the spiritual truths contained in the wonderful books written by her virtually inspired, guided and dictated by Sri Sathya Sai Baba who is going to reincarnate as Sri Prema Sai Baba in very near future! This timing seems to correct as Vasantha Sai has already written that Prema Sai's sister Vasantha (the future incarnation of her devotee Yamini) would be born in 1927-28.

- That the future incarnation of Sri Prema Sai Baba might in all probability will be in Dodamallur village, which will be renamed as Gunaparthi. I believe that Raja (future Prema Sai) and Prema (reincarnation of Vasantha Sai) would go to give the first copy of their wedding invitation to the Narayana (God) in the ancient Ambegalu Sri Krishna temple of this village only. Most of the people of my age would not be alive till then; those who live till then would be able to verify this prediction.

- Prema Sai may be in a low case as it would be will be born and brought up in Hindu family. It has already been prophesied by Sri foretold by Sathya Sai Baba a number of indications.

- That the families of both Raja and Prema would be religious, spiritual and cultured families and they would realize the importance of higher education for their wards; Vasantha Sai has already predicted that both Raja and Prema could receive college education.

- Most likely Raja would receive his college education in one of the Sai Colleges in or near Bangalore.

- It is likely that Prema Sai would not settle down in Prasanthi Nilayam to complete his Avataric mission, but he will most probably settled down at on a large tract of land near the Bangalore-Mysore highway,

Halgappa's Sai Temple and orphanage. That place would be very well developed and well connected to Bangalore and Mysore and will be accessible to the spiritual seekers and devotees throughout the world just as Prasanthi Nilayam has been so far.

Let us pray and hope that in Prema Sai era (probably starting from the sixth dacade of the 21st century will be free of crime, corrupton and political mischief and all mistrust and uncertainties and the Indians will have peaceful, contented, happy and ideal life and the glory of India as the Spiritual Centre of the world and the humanity will experience the glory and benefits of the Golden Age.

It has been predicted that Sri Prema Sai Baba will live up to a very long age—86 like Sri Sathya Sai Baba and he will have much work to do with the help of countless devotees. We already know that certain esteemed devotees of Sri Sathya Sai Baba like Sinclair of USA, Dr. Gadhia of U.K., Prof. Adhya Prasad Tripathi, Head of the Hindi Department of Sri Sathya Sai University, and countless others including the devotees and ashrimites of Sri Sathya Sai Baba and Vasantha Sai had already been given passport to get into the Prema Sai era by Sri Sathya Sai Baba. All those who have really belived in Sri Sathya Sai Baba and earnestly loved, followed and served Sri Sathya Sai Baba as *seva dal* and functionaries in his charitable institutions and organizations will certainly get the rare opportunity to serve Prema Sai. As the great British poet Milton had written: "They also serve who only stand and wait', all those who had been standing and only waiting at the doors of Sri Sathya Sai Baba will also be reborn to be in the army of Sri Prema Sai Baba in the second half of the present 21st century.

The Sai devotees have been eager to see the authentic image of future Prema Sai Baba. I have discovered that SaiDham, Nottingham has it. They have circulated it along with a page of write up on Prema Sai Baba on their web site saidham.UK mentioning that this image of Prema Sai Baba wasmaterialized by Sri Sathya Sai Baba.

A colored photograph of exquisitely beautiful girl 'Prema, who would be married to her neighbor, playmate and college mate 'Raja' (who will be later known as 'Prema Sai Baba' and venerated by billions of devotes throughout the world) was miraculously materialized by Sri Sathya Sai Baba and given to Vasantha Sai (Vasantha Amma). That rare colored image was published in her book 'Prema Sai Avatar' (Part 2, 2006). Sri Sathya Sai Baba had prophesied and assured her many times in her mediation that she would be reborn to become Prema, the wife of Prema Sai Baba incarnation.

BIBLIOGRAPHY ON
SRI SHIRDI SAI BABA

1. Agaskar, P.S., *Sri Sai Leelamrita*. Shirdi: Shri Sai Baba Sansthan, 1989. (In Hindi).
2. Aiyer, P.S.V., *Perfect Masters*. Calcutta: Author, 1973.
3. Ajgaonkar, Chakor, *The Divine Glory Sri Shirdi Sai Baba*. New Delhi: Diamond Pocket Books, 1998, pp. 126. (Ed. S.P. Ruhela).
4. _____, *Tales From Sai Baba's Life*. New Delhi: Diamond Pocket Books, 1998, pp. 183 (Ed. S.P. Ruhela)
5. _____, *What Saints & Maters Say on the Realm of Sadhna*. New Delhi: Diamond Pocket Books, 1998, pp. 88 (Ed. S.P. Ruhela)
6. _____, *Foot Prints of Shirdi Sai*. New Delhi: Diamond Pocket Books, 1998. (Ed. S.P. Ruhela)
7. _____, *Sri Shirdi Sai Baba Ki Divya Jeevan Kahani*. New Delhi: Diamond Pocket Books, 1998, pp. 164. (Trans. J.P. Srivastava; Ed. S.P. Ruhela). (In Hindi)
8. _____, *Sri Sai Geetayan*. New Delhi: Diamond Pocket Books, 1998, pp. 93, (Trans. J.P. Srivastava, (Ed. S.P. Ruhela): (In Hindi).
9. Anand, Sai Sharan, *Sri Sai Baba*. Bombay: Dinpushpa Prakashan, 1989. (In Marathi/Gujarati).
10. _____, *Sri Sai Baba*. New Delhi: Sterling Publishers, 1997. (Trans. V.B. Kher) (In English)
11. _____, *Sai; The Supeman*. Shirdi: Shri Sai Baba Sansthan, 1991.
12. _____, Awasthi, Dinesh & Blitz Team of Investigators, "Sai Baba The Saint of Shirdi", *Blitz* (Bombay Weekly), Nov. 6 & 13, 1976. (Article)
13. Balakrishna, V.V., Sri *Sayee Smaromstroram*.
14. Balse, Mayah, *Mystics and Men of Miracles in India*. New Delhi: Orient Paper backs, 1978.
15. Bharadawaja, Acharya, E., *Sai Baba The Master*. Ongole: Sri Guru Paduka Publications, 1991. (III Ed.)
16. Bharati, Sushil, *Sai Darshan Sagar*. Sai Prakashan, 1995, p. 62, (In Hindi).
17. _____, *Sai Upasana*. Sagar, Sai Prakashan, 1995, pp. 36, (In Hindi).
18. _____, *Sai Kripa Ke Pawan Kshan*. Sagar: Sai Prakashan, 1995. (in Hindi).

19. _____, *Sai Dham*. Sagar: Sai Prakashan, 1996. (In Hindi).

20. _____, *Sai Sukh Chalisa*, Sagar, Sai Prakasthan.

21. _____, *Sai Sandesh*. Sagar: Sai Prakashan.

22. _____, *Sai Mahima*. Sagar: Sai Prakashan.

23. _____, *Bachchon Ke Sai.* Sagar: Sai Prakashan.

24. _____, *Sai Geetmala*. Sagar: Sai Prakashan.

25. _____, *Sai Chintan*. New Delhi: Diamond Pocket Books, 1998, pp. 110.

26. _____, *Sai Sri Ke Adbhut Devdoota*. New Delhi: Diamond Pocket Books, 1998, pp. 216.

27. _____, *Sai Kripa Ke Pavan Kshan*. New Delhi: Diamond Pocket Books, 1998, pp. 126.

28. _____, *Sai Sarita*. New Delhi: Diamond Pocket Books, 1998, 1998, pp. 227.

29. Bharucha, Perin S., *Sai Baba of Shirdi*. Shirdi: Shri Sai Baba Sansthan, 1980.

30. Bharvani, A.D. & Malhotra, V., *Shirdi Sri Baba and Sathya Sai Baba are One and Same*. Bombay: Sai Sahitya Samiti, 1983.

31. Bhisma, K.J., *Sadguru Sai Nath Sagunopasama*. Shirdi: Shri Sai Baba Sansthan, 1986. (Marathi).

32. Chatturvedi, B.K. Sai Baba of Shirdi. New Delhi: Diamond Pocket Books, 1998. (Revised Ed. S.P. Ruhela).

33. Chopra, Parveen, 'Shirdi Sai Baba: Beacon of Hope', *Life Positive* (Monthly), New Delhi; Magus Pvt. Ltd. S-487, Greater Kailash, Part I, Jan. 1998, pp. 16-21 (Article).

34. Das, M. Machinder, *Sai-The God on Earth.*

35. Ganu, Das, *Shri SaiNath Stavan Manjari*. Shirdi: Shri Sai Baba Sansthan, (English Trans. Zarine Taraporewala, Bombay: Sai Dhun Enterprises, 1987).

36. _____, *Sai Harkathas*. Madras: All India Sai Samaj, Mylapore.

37. *Gems of Wisdom*, Nagpur: Sri Publicatins.

38. *Guide to Holy Shirdi*. Shirdi: Shri Sai Baba Sansthan.

39. Gunaji, N., Shri Sai Satcharita, Shirdi: Sai Baba Sansthan, 1944.

40. Harper, Marvin Henry, 'The Fakir: Sri Sai Baba of Shirdi' in *Gurus, Swamis, and Avataras: Spiritual Masters and Their American Disciplines*. Philadelphia: Westminister Press, 1972. (Article).

41. Hattingatti, Shaila, *Sai's Story*. Bombay: India Book House, 1991.

42. Hemadpant, *Shri Sai Satcharita*, Shirdi: Shri Sai Baba Sansthan, (In Marathi, Hindi, Gujarati, Telugu, etc.)

43. *Is Sai Baba Living and Helping Now?* Madras: All India Sai Samaj. Mylapore.

44. Jha, Radhanandan *Sai Baba: Sab Ka Malik Ek Hai*. Patna, Sri Sai Baba Trust, I-A, Aney Marg, 1997, pp. 65. (In Hindi).

45. Joshi, H.S., *Origin and Development of Dattatreya Worship in India*. Baroda: M.S. University of Baroda, 1965. (Chapter 12).

46. Kakade, R.C. & Veerbhadra. A., *Shirdi to Puttaparthi*. Hyderabad: Ira Prakastha, 1989. (In English & Hindi).

47. Kamath, M.V. & Kher, V.B., *Sai Baba of Shirdi: A Unique Saint*. Bombay: Jaico Publishing House, 1991.

48. Karunanada, Swami, *The Uniqueness of the Significance of Sri Sai Baba*. Panvel: Sri Bhagwati Sai Sansthan.

49. Kevin, Shephered, R, D., *Gurus Discovered* (Biographies of Sai Baba & Upasani Maharaj) Cambridge: Anthropoprahia Publicatiuon 1984.

50. Khaparde, G., *Sources of Sai History*. Bangalore: Jupiter Press, 1956.

51. _____, *Shirdi Diary*. Shirdi: Shri Sai Baba Sansthan.

52. Krishna, Indira Anantha, Sai Baba of Shirdi. (Adarsh Chitra Katha-Pictorial).

53. Krishna, S. Gopala K., *Understanding Shirdi Sai*. Hyderabad: Shirdi Sai Mandiram, Chikkadpalli, 1997, pp. 227.

54. Kumar, Anil, *Doctor of Doctors Sri Sai Baba*. Nagpur: Sri Sai Clinic.

55. Kumar: Sudhir, *Shirdi Ke Sai Baba: Chalisa aur Bhajan*. New Delhi: Author, (In Hindi).

56. Maneey, S., *The Eternal Sai*. New Delhi: Diamond Pocket Books, 1997.

57. Mani, Amma B., *Sai Leela Taranagini*. (Parts 1 & 2). Guntur: Authoress.

58. Mehta, Rao Bahadur Harshad B., *The Spiritual Symphony of Shree Sainath of Shirdi*. Baroda: Rana & Patel Press. 1952.

59. Mehta, Vikas, *Hridaya Ke Swami Shri Sai Baba*. New Delhi: Siddartha Publicatins, 10 DSIDC, Scheme 11. Okhla Industrial Area Part 11, 1995. (In Hindi).

60. _____, *Karunamaya Shri Sai Baba*. New Delhi: Siddartha Publications, 1996. (In Hindi).

61. Mittal, N., *World Famous Modern Gurus and Guru Cults*. New Delhi: Family Books, F 2/16, Darya Ganj.

62. Monayan, S.V.G.S., *Sai the Mother and Ansuya, the Amma*. Masulipattanm, Sai Ma Gurudatta Publications, 18/286, Ambani Agraham.

63. Munsiff, Abdul Ghani, "Hazrat Sai Baba", *The Mehar Baba Journal* (Ahmednagar): Vol. 1 1938-39 (Article.)

64. Murthy, G.S., *Understanding Shirdi Sai Baba*. Hyderabad: Sri Shirdi Sai Prema Mandiram, 1977.

65. Narasimhaswamy ji, *Who is Sai Baba of Shirdi?* Madras: All India Sai Samaj, 1980.

66. _____, *Sri Sai Vachnamrita*. Madras: All India Sai Samaj.

67. _____, *Sai Baba's Charters, and Sayings*. Madras: All India Sai Samaj, 1980.

68. _____, *Devotees' Experiences of Sai Baba*. Madras: All India Sai Samaj, 1965. Hyderabad: 1989.

69. _____, *Glimpses of Sai Baba*. Madras: All India Sai Samaj.

70. _____, *Life of Sai Baba*. Madras: All India Sai Samaj.

71. Narayan, B.K., *Saint Shah Waris Ali and Sai Baba*. New Delhi Vikas Publishing House, 1995, pp. 112.

72. Narayanan, C.R., *A Century of Poems on Sri Sai Baba of Shirdi*. Madras: Author, 1994 (11 Ed.)

73. Nimbalkar, M.B., *Sri Sai Satya Charitra*. Poona: Author, 1993 (In Marathi).

74. 108 Names of Sri Shirdi Sai Baba. New Delhi: Sterling Publishers, 1997. Pp. 108. (Pocket Book).

75. Osburne, Arthur. *The Incredible Sai Baba*. Delhi: Orient Longmans, 1970.

76. Paranjape, Makarand, 'Journey to Sai Baba', *Life Positive*, New Delhi: Magus Media Pvt. Ltd. Jan. 1998, pp. 22-23 (Article).

77. Parchure, D.D., *Children's Sai Baba*, Shirdi: Shri Sai Baba Sansthan, 1983. (In English, Hindi)

78. Parchure, S.D., *Shree Sai Mahimashstra*. Bombay: Tardeo Book Depot, 1990.

79. Parthsarthi, R., *Gold Who Walked on Earth*. New Delhi: Sterling Publishers, 1996.

80. _____, *Apostle of Love: Saint Saipadananda*, New Delhi: Sterling Publishers, 1997.

81. *Pictorial Sai Baba*. Shirdi: Sai Baba Sansthan, 1968.

82. Pradhan, M.V., Sri *Sai Baba of Shirdi*: Shirdi Sri Sai Baba Sansthan, 1973.

83. Ramalingaswami, *The Golden Words of Shri Sai Baba*. Shirdi, 1983.

84. _____, *Ambrosia in Shirdi*. Shirdi: Shri Sai Baba Sansthan, 1984.

85. Ramakrishna, K.K., *Sai Baba The Perfect Master*. Pune: Meher Era Publications, Avatar Meher Baba Poona Centre, 441/1, Somwarpeth, 1991.

86. Rao. A.S., *Life History of Shirdi Sai Baba*. New Delhi: Sterling Publishers, 1997, pp. 228 (Eng. Trans. Thota Bhaskar Rao).

87. Rao, A.S., *In Search of the Truth*, New Delhi: Sterling Publishing, 1998.

88. Rao, B. Umamaheswara, Thus Spoke Sri Shirdi Sai Baba. New Delhi: Diamond Pocket Books, 1997. (Ed. S.P. Ruhela)

89. Rao, B. Umamaheswara, *Communications From the Spirit of Shri Shirdi Sai Baba.* New Delhi: Diamond Pocket Books, 1998, pp. 160 (Ed. S.P. Ruhela).

90. _____, *The Spiritual Philosophy of Sri Shirdi Sai Baba.* New Delhi: Diamond Pocket Books, 1998. (Revised edition of *Bhava Lahari: Voice of Sri Sai Baba,* 1993) Ed. S.P. Ruhela.

91. _____, *Sai Leela Tarangini.* Guntur: Author, Flat 12, 'Sai Towers', 4th Line, Brindavan Gardens, Guntur-522006). (In Telugu).

92. _____, *Sai Tatwa Sandesham* (Part I & II). Guntur: Author, (In Telugu).

93. _____, *Sai Tatwa Sandesham.* Guntur: Author. (In English)

94. Rao, evata Sabhe, *Baba Sai.* Hyderabad: 76, N.H.I., Type Ramchandrapuram.

95. Rao, M.S., *Divine Life Story of Sri Sudguru KrishnaprIyaji.* Burla: Author, 1995.

96. Rao, Devata Sabha, *Baba Sai* Hyderabad: 76 N.H.I., Type 5, Ramchandrapuram (BHEL).

97. Rao, K.V. Raghva, *Message of Sri Sai Baba.* Madras: All India Sai Samaj, 1984. (Ed. By Dwarkamai Trust, Hyderabad, 1995).

98. _____, *Message of Shri Sai Baba.* Hyderabad: Shri Shirdi Publications Trust, 1992

99. _____. *Enlightenment From Sri Baba on Salvation of Soul.* Hyderabad: Dwarkamai Publications, 1994.

100. _____. *Golden Voice and Divine Touch of Sri Sai Baba.* Hyderabad: Dwarkamai Publications, 1997.

101. Rao, M. Rajeswara, *Shri Shirdi Sai Baba and His Teaching.* New Delhi: Diamond Pocket Books, 1998, pp. 76 (Ed. S.P. Ruhela) (Mini Book).

102. Rigopoulos, Antonio, *The Life and Teachings of Sri Sai Baba of Shirdi* (Ph. D. Thesis) New York: State University, 1992. (Delhi—110007): Sri Sadguru Publications, Indian Book Centre 40/5, Shakti Nagar 1995).

103. Ruhela, Sushila Devi, *Sri Shirdi Sai Bhajan Sangraha (Samprna).* New Delhi: Diamond Pocket Books, 1998, pp. 287. (In Hindi)

104. —, *Sri Shirdi Sai Bhajan Sangraha.* New Delhi: Diamond Pocket Books, 1998. Pp. 96.

105. —, *Sri Shirdi Sai Bhajanmala.* New Delhi Diamond Pocket Books, 1998, pp. 135. (Mini Book)

106. Ruhela, S.P., *My Life with Shirdi Sai Baba*—Thrilling Memories of Shivamma Thayee. Faridabad: Sai Age Publications, 1992. (New Delhi-110002: M.D. Publications, 11, Darya Ganj, 1995).

107. ——, *Sri Shirdi Sai Baba Avatar.* Faridabad: Sai Age Publications, 1992.

108. ——, *What Researchers say on Sri Shirdi Sai Baba.* Faridabad: Sai Age Publications, 1994. (II Ed. New Delhi-110002: M.D. Publications, 1995).

109. ——, *Sri Shirdi Sai Baba: The Universal* Master. New Delhi; Sterling Publishers, L-10, Green Park Extension, 1994. (Reprint 1995, 1996).

110. ——, *The Sai Trinity*—Sri Shirdi Sai, Sri Sathya Sai, Sri Prema Sai Incarnations, New Delhi-110014; Vikas Publishing House, 1994.

111. ——, *Sai Puran*, Delhi: Sadhna Pocket Books, 1996.

112. ——, *Shirdi Sai Baba Speaks to Yogi Spencer in Vision,* New Delhi: Vikas Publishing House, 1998.

113. ——, *Sant Shiromani Sri Shirdi* Sai Baba, New Delhi: Sterling Publishers, 1997.

114. ——, (Ed) *Divine Revelations of a Sai Devotee.* New Delhi: B.R. Publishing Corporation, 1997, pp. 270.

115. ——, (Ed.) *Sri Shirdi Sai Bhajan-mala,* (In Roman) New Delhi: B.R. Publishing Corporation, 1998, pp. 111.

116. ——, *Shirdi Sai Baba's Mother and Her Re-incarnation.* New Delhi: Aravali Books International (W-30, Okhla Industrial Area, Phase-II, New Delhi-110020). 1998, pp. 45. (Pocket Books).

117. ——, (Ed.) *New Light on Sri Shirdi Sai Baba.* Delhi: Indian Publishers and Distrributors, 1998, pp. 111.

118. ——, (Ed.) *Shirdi Sai Ideal and The Sai World.* New Delhi: Diamond Pocket Books. 1998.

119. (Ed.), *The Immortal Fakir of Shirdi*, New Delhi: Diamond Pocket Books, 1998.

120. ——, My *Life with Sri Shirdi Sai Baba.* (In Japanese).

121. *Sai Amritvani* (By:B.K. Bassi, 1/42, Panchsheel Park, New Delhi An excellent melodious prayer to Sri Shirdi Sai Baba. This very impressive impressive and highly elevating prayer is most attentively listened by countless Sai devotee throughout the world on Thursday—Sai Baba's favorite day. It may be downloaded from: http://groups.yahoo.com/group/ mysaiu baba20

122. *Sadguru Nityananada Bhagavan The Eternal Entity.* Kanhangad Pin Code 671315. Kerala: Swami Nityananda Ashram, 1996 (IIEd.)

123. *Sai Ma Ki Kripavrasti*—Souvenir, Mussorie, Sai Darbar, 2, Garden Reach. Kulri, 1997. (In Hindi)

124. *Sai Sandesh* (Sri Shirdi Sai Messages give to Devotee). (Parts I & II Hyderabad: Sai Prabha Publications (3050697/87. Telugu Academy Lane, Vithalwadi)

125. Seshadri, H., *Glimpses of Divinity—A Profile of Shri Saidas Babaji*, Bombay: Shri Bhopal Singh Hingharh. (It shows that Sri Shirdi Sai Baba and Sri Sathya Sai Baba are one and the same.)

126. *Sai Sudha.* Magazine—Golden Jubilee Issue, Special Number, Madras: All India Sai Samaj.

127. Savitri, Raghunathan, *Sai Bhajanmlal.* Mumbai: Balaji Bagya, Sudarshan Art Printing Press, 5 Vadla Udhyog Bhavan, Mumbai-400031, 1995 (24th Ed. 1986) (In Marathi). (It contains folk songs and Bhajans on Sri Shirdi Sai since his lifetime.)

128. Shepherd, R.D. *Gurus Rediscovered.* Cambridge: Anthropological Publications, 1985. Biographies of Sri Shirdi Sai Baba and Sri Upasani Maharaj).

129. *Shirdi Darshan*, Shirdi, Shri Sai Baba Sansthan, 1966, 1972. (Pictorial).

130. Shirdi Ke Sai Baba. Delhi: Ratna Book Co. (In Hindi)

131. Shivnesh Swamiji, *Sri Sai Bavani*, Shirdi.

132. *Shree Sai Leela: Sachitra Jeevandarshan.* 1939.

133. *Shree Sai Leela*, March—April 1992. (First Convention of Sai Devotees).

134. *Silver Jubilee Souvenir.* Madras: All India Sai Samaj, 1996.

135. *Spiritual Recipes*, Bangalore: Sri Sai Baba Spiritual Centre, Sri Sai Baba Mandir Marg, T. Nagar.

136. Singh. I.D, *Gagar Main Sai Kshir Sagar.* Faridabad; Sai Age Publications, 1996. (In Hindi). (New Delhi: Diamond Pocket Books, 1997)

137. Somsundaram, A., The *Dawn of a New Era: The Message of Master Ram Ram And the Need for Universal Religion.* Markapur (A.P.): Divine Centre, 1970.

138. Somsundaran, A., *The Dawn of New Era: The Vision of Master Rishi Ram Ram.* Markapur: Divine Centre, 1969.

139. *Souvenir: Maha Samadhi Souvenir.* Madras: All India Sai Samaj, 1966.

140. *Souvenir*, Delhi: Shri Sai Bhakta Samaj, 1972.

141. *Souvenir.* Secunderabad: Sri Sai Baba Samaj, 1975.

142. *Souvenir*: Secunderabad: Sri Sai Baba Samaj, 1990.

143. *Souvenir*: 26th All India Sai Devotees Convention: Golden Jubilee Year, 1991.

144. *Sri Harikatha—Special Number on Shirdi ke Sai Baba.* New Delhi: Srikath, B-5/73, Azad Apartments, Sri Aurobindo Marg (Bilingual).

145. Sri *Sainath Mananan.* (Sanskrit with English). A Symposium: All India Sai Samaj, Mylapore.

146. *Sri Sai Spiritual Centre and The Trinity* (Sai Baba, Sri Narasimha Swamiji, Sri Radhakrishna Swamiji). Bangalore: Sri Sai Spiritual Centre, Sai Baba Mandir Road, Ist Block, Thyagraja Nagar, Bangalore-560028), pp. 36.

147. Steel, Brian, *Sathya Sai Baba Compendium.* York Beach (USA): Samuel Weisner, 1997. Pp. 244-248.

148. Subramaniam, C.S., *The Life and Teachings of Great Sai Baba.*

149. *Tales of Sai Baba.* Bombay: India Book House, 1995. (Pictorial)

150. *Taravade*, S.V. May Sai Baba Bless Us All. Bombay: Taradeo Book Depot.

151. Taraporewala, Zarine, *Worship of Manifested Sri Sadguru Sainath.* (English translation of K. J. *Bhisma, Sri Sadguru Sainath Sahunopasan*). Bombay: Saidhun Enterprses 1990.

152. Towards *Godhood—Messages reveived by Autowriting at the Centre* (Third Annual Number). Coimbatore: The Spiritual Healing Centre, 1945. Pp. 6-8 (It contains some Spirit Message on and from Sai Baba received in 1940).

153. Uban, Sujan Singh, 'Sai Baba of Shirdi', *The Gurus of India.* London: 1977.

154. Verma, Subha, *"Shirdi, Sab Boom Sai Ki . . ."* *Saptahik Hindustan*, Nov. 12, 1992, pp. 17-25. (In Hindi). (Article).

155. Verma, Subha, *Sri Das Ganukrita Char Adhyaya.* New Delhi: Ansh Media Expression. Subha Verma, A-35, Chittaranjan Park, New Delhi-110019), 1997, pp. 46.

156. White, Charles, S. J., 'The Sai Baba Movement: Approaches to the Study of India, Saints', *The Journal of Asian Studies*, Vol. XXXI, (Article) No. 4, August 1972.

BIBLIOGRAPHY ON
SRI SATHYA SAI BABA

The *Sathya Sai Speaks* series of discourses are available from Sathya Sai Baba's principal ashram of *Prasanthi Nilayam* and, in many languages, from the national Sathya Sai Organizations in many countries.

1. *A Festival of Divine Love* (15 Nov.—23 Nov. 2010). Prasanthi Nilayam: Sri Sathya Sai Sadhana Trust, Dec. 2010, enquiry@sssbpt.org URL: www.sssbpt.org

2. Aditya, Sudha: 1996a *Sathya Sai's Amrita Varshini*, (2nd ed.), Prasanthi Nilayam: Sai Towers. [1st ed. 1992]

3. —1996 *Sathya Sai's Anugraha Varshini*, Prasanthi Nilayam, Sai Towers.

4. —1986a: *Redemptive Encounters. Three Modern Styles in the Hindu Tradition*, Berkeley, University of California.

5. —1986b: 'The Puzzle of Religious Modernity', in *India: 2000. The Next Fifteen Years*, ed. James R. Roach, Riverdale, Maryland, [n.p.] and New Delhi, Allied Publishers, pp. 59-79.

6. —1987: 'Sathya Sai Baba's Saintly Play', in Hawley, John S. (ed.) *Saints and Virtues*, Berkeley, Univ. of California Press, 1987, 168-186.

7. —1994: 'Sathya Sai Baba's Miracles', in *Religion In India*, (ed.) T.N. Madan, New Delhi, Oxford University Press, pp. 277-292.

8. Badaev, Serguei, Various articles and notes at www.exbaba.com and www.saiguru.net, 2002.

9. Bailey, D.: 1996 *Journey to love*, Prasanthi Nilayam, Sai Towers, 1998.

10. Bailey, Faye, *Another Journey to Love. Experiences with Sai Baba*, Prasanthi Nilayam, Sai Towers, 1998.

11. Bailey, David & Faye *The Findings*, Conwy, North Wales: Private publication, 2000. [See also www.snowcrest.net/sunrise/links.htm]

12. Balse, Maya, *Mystics and Men of Miracles in India*, New Delhi, Heritage Publishers, 1976.

13. Balu, Shakuntala, *Living Divinity*, London, Sawbridge, 1984.

14. Balu, V.: 1990: *The Glory of Puttaparthi . . .*, Rev ed., Delhi, Motilal Banarsidas. [1st ed., 1990]

15. —1992: *Shanti. Peace Collages*, Bangalore, S.B. Publications.

16. Balu, V. and Balu, Shakuntala, *Divine Glory*, Bangalore, S.B. Publications, 1985.

17. Barker, Joyce Darlene, *The Touch of Baba*, India, 1997.

18. Bashiruddin, Zeba: 1990: 'Truth of a Prophecy', in *Sanathana Sarathi* November, 1990, 298-300.

19. —1998: *Sai Baba and the Muslim Mind*, Sri Sathya Sai Institute of HigherLearning.(Alsoat:file://C:Windows/Temp/www.vinnica.ua/~sss/sb mm.htm—listed on http://groups.yahoo.com/group/saibabaleelas/links]

20. Baskin, Diana, *Divine Memories of Sathya Sai Baba*, San Diego, Birth Day, 1990.

21. Beyerstein, Dale, *Sai Baba's Miracles. An Overview*, Vancouver, [n.p.], 1992. http://seercom.com/bcs [forthcoming] and www.exbaba.de/db.shtml. See also: http://www.indian-skeptic.org/html

22. Bhagavantam, S., 'Lord of Miracles', in S.P. Ruhela (ed.),—*Sai Baba and His Message*, Rev. ed., New Delhi, Vikas, 1995, pp. 189-196.

23. Bhatia, Dr. Naresh, *The Dreams and Realities Face to Face with God*, Prasanthi Nilayam, [n.p.], 1994.

24. Bock, Janet, *The Jesus Mystery. Of Lost Years and Unknown Travels*, Los Angeles, Aura Books, 1980.

25. Brown, Mick: 1999: *The Spiritual Tourist. A Personal Odyssey through the Outer Reaches of Belief*, London, Bloomsbury, 1998.

26. —2000: 'Divine Downfall', in *The Telegraph Magazine and The Electronic Telegraph*, 28 October 2000. [Also in The Sunday Age, Melbourne, 12 November 2000]

27. Bruce, Rita, *Vision of Sai*, 2 vols, Prasanthi Nilayam, 1991 and 1994. Busto, Graciela, *Baba is Here. Conversations with God on His Omnipresence*, Faber, Leela, 1998.

28. Chopra, Parveen, '*Shirdi Sai Baba. A Beacon of Hope*', *Life Positive*, (Delhi), October 1997, pp. 30-40.

29. Dadlani, Sanjay K., 'Sai Baba. Shiva or Sadhaka?' www.exbaba.com, July 2002.

30. Devamma, N. Lakshmi, *Bhakthodhaaraka Sri Sathya Sai*, Prasanthi Nilayam, Sri Sathya Sai Books and publications Trust, [n.d.]

31. Divine Grace: Sathya Sai Baba: The India Today Group, Living Media India Ltd. Special Volume 2012.

32. Esposito, John L. et al (eds), *The OXFORD Encyclopedia of the Modern Islamic World*, Oxford and New York, 4 vols., 1995)

33. Fanibunda, Eruch B., *Vision of the Divine*, Bombay, Sri Sathya Sai Books and Publications, 1976.

34. Fuefuki, Panta, *The Naked Sai Baba*, Tokyo: Voice Inc., 2000.

35. Ganapati, Ra.:—1985: *Baba: Sathya Sai*, Part I, 2nd ed., Madras, Sai Raj.

36. —1984: *Baba: Satya Sai*, Part II, Madras, Sathya Jyoti. {adapted from Tamil original, Svami, 1981] [2nd rev. ed., 1990]

37. —1990: *Avatar, Verily!*, Madras, Divya Vidya Trust.

38. *Garland of Golden Roses*, Prasanthi Nilayam, Sri Sathya Sai Central Trust, 1975.

39. Gibson, Doris May, *Let Me Sow Love*, 2nd ed., Prasanthi Nilayam, Sai Towers, 1997. [Canadian 1st ed., c 1995]

40. Goel, B.S.: 1985: *Third Eye and Kundalini. An Experiential Account of Journey from Dust to Divinity*, Kurukshetra, Third Eye Foundation of India.

41. —1986: *Psychoanalysis and Meditation. The Theories and Practice of Psychoanalytical.*

42. —*Meditation*, Bhagaan, Third Eye Foundation of India.

43. Gokak, V.K.: 1973 (ed.): *A Value Orientation to Our System of Education*, New Delhi, M. Gulab Singh & Sons.

44. —1975: *Bhagavan Sri Sathya Sai Baba. The Man and the Avatar. An Interpretation*, New Delhi, Abhinav Publications. [2nd ed., 1983]

45. —1979: *In Defence of Jesus Christ and Other Avatars*, New Delhi, Abhinav Publications. [1996: Delhi, B.R. Publishing Corporation]

46. —1979: 'An Historic Letter of Baba', *Golden Age, 1979*, pp.1-9. Gokak V.K. and S.R. Rohidekar (eds), *Teachers Handbook for the Course in Human Values*, Prasanthi Nilayam, Sri Sathya Sai Books and Publications, 1983.

47. *Golden Age, 1979*, Brindavan, Kadugodi, Kingdom of Sathya Sai, 1979.

48. *Golden Age, 1980*, Prasanthi Nilayam, Sri Sathya Sai Books and Publications Trust, 1980.

49. Gries, David and Elaine, *An Index of Sathya Sai Speaks, Vols. I-XI*, Tustin, Sathya Sai Book Center of America, 1993.

50. Haraldsson, Erlendur: (1987) *'Miracles Are My Visiting Cards'. An Investigative Report on the Psychic Phenomena Associated with Sathya Sai Baba*, London, Century Paperbacks. (Also marketed for sale in India only by Prasanthi Publications of New Delhi.)

51. —(1996) *Modern Miracles*, Norwalk, CT, Hastings House. [The latter has the same content as the new Indian edition: personal communication.]

52. Haraldsson, E., and Osis, K., 'The Appearance and Disappearance of Objects in the Presence of Sri Sathya Sai Baba', *Journal of the American Society for Psychical Research*, 71 (1977), 33-43.

53. Haraldsson, E. and Wiseman, R., 'Reactions to and an Assessment of a Videotape on Sathya Sai Baba', *Journal of the Society for Psychical Research*, April 1995, 60, pp. 203-213.

54. Harvey, Andrew, *The Return of the Mother*, New York, Jeremy P. Tarcher/ Putnam, 2001. (1st ed., Berkeley, Frog Ltd., 1995)

55. Hislop, John S.: 1978: *Conversations with Sathya Sai Baba*, San Diego, Birth Day. (n.d.) *Conversations with Bhagavan Sri Sathya Sai Baba*, enlarged Indian edition, Prasanthi Nilayam, Sri Sathya Sai Books and Publications Trust.

56. —1979: 'Things are not as They Seem to Be', *Golden Age*, 1979, pp. 32-40.

57. —1985: *My Baba and I*, San Diego, Birth Day.

58. —1997: *Seeking Divinity* - Talks by Dr. John S. Hislop, Tustin, Sathya Sai Society of America.

59. Holbach, Paul, http://www.geocities.com/p_holbach/eng/main_e.htm or: http://p_holbach/index.htm. *The Indian Skeptic*, See www.indian-skeptic. org/html

60. Jagadeesan J. (also J. Jegathesan}: 1978: *Journey to God. The Malaysian Experience*, Kuala Lumpur, [n.p.]

61. —1980: *Bhagavan Sri Sathya Sai Baba. The Mission and the Message. (Some Often Asked Questions)*, Kuala Lumpur, [n.p.]

62. —[1981]: *Sai Baba and the World. (Journey to God, Part 2)*, Prasanthi

63. Nilayam, Sri Sathya Sai Books and Publications. [1st ed. Kaula Lumpur, 1981]

    K1A See Kasturi, 1961-1980, Vol. 1
    K1B See Kasturi, 1961-1980, Vol. 2
    K1C See Kasturi, 1961-1980, Vol. 3
    K1D See Kasturi, 1961-1980, Vol. 4

63. Kakade, R.T. and Rao, A. Veerabhadra, *Shirdi to Puttaparthi*, 6th ed. Hyderabad, IRA Publications, 1993.

64. Kant, Sanjay, *God Descends on Earth. As Prophesied by Nostradamus and Edgar Cayce*, Panjim, Goa, New Flash, 1990.(2nd ed., Puttaparthi, Sai Towers, 1998.)

65. Karanjia, R.K.,: [1994]: *God Lives in India,* Puttaparthi, Saindra. (Later editions by Sai Towers)

66. 1976 article in *Blitze* and other shorter ones from the same year.

67. 1976: Interview given by Sri Sathya Sai Baba to R.K. Karanjia, *Blitz*, Bombay, September.

68. —1976. ([Reprinted in Samuel H. Sandweiss, *Spirit and the Mind*, pp. 235-258.]

69. 1979: 'God is an Indian', *Golden Age*, 1979, pp. 128-135.

70. Kasturi, Narayan: 1961-1980: *Sathyam Shivam Sundaram. The Life of Bhagavan Sri Sathya Sai Baba*, 4 vols., Prasanthi Nilayam, Sri Sathya Sai Books and Publications.

71. —1968: *Sathya Sai Baba: The Light of Love in Africa*, London, Sai Publications.

72. —1979: *Garland of 108 Precious Gems. Ashtothara Sathanama Rathnamala*, (4th ed.), Sri Sathya Sai Education and Publication Foundation.

73. —1982: *Loving God. Eighty Five Years under the Watchful Eye of THE LORD*, Prasanthi Nilayam, Sri Sathya Sai Books and Publications, 1982.

74. —1984: *Easwaramma. The Chosen Mother*, Prasanthi Nilayam, Sri Sathya Sai Books and Publications.

75. Klass, Morton, *Singing with Sai Baba. The Politics of Revitalization in Trinidad*, Boulder: West View Press, 1991: 112-113.

76. Kaishnamani, Mani, *Divine Incarnation—A Mystresy*. New Delh, Rajan Publication, 2000

77. —, Sai or Himself, New Delhi: Rajan Publication, 2001.

78. Krystal, Phyllis: 1985: *Sai Baba—The Ultimate Experience*, Los Angeles, Aura Books. (Reprinted by Samuel Weiser, 1994)

79. —1993: *Cutting the Ties that Bind*, York Beach, Samuel Weiser.

80. —1993b: *Cutting More Ties that Bind*, York Beach, Samuel Weiser.

81. —1994: *Taming Our Monkey Mind. Insight, Detachment, Identity*, York Beach, Samuel Weiser.

82. —1995 *Cutting the Ties that Bind Workbook*, York Beach, Samuel Weiser.

83. —1995b: *Reconnecting the Love Energy, Don't By-Pass Your Heart,* York Beach, Samuel Weiser.

84. Kumar Malhotra, Anil, *The Wonderful Leelas of Bhagavan*, Prasanthi Nilayam, 1998.

85. Lee, Raymond L.M., 'Sai Baba, Salvation and Syncretism: Religious Change in a Hindu.

86. —Movement in Urban Malaysia, in *Contributions to Indian Sociology (NS)*, 16(1), 1982, 125-140.

87. Leslie-Chaden, Charlene, *A Compendium of the Teachings of Sathya Sai Baba*, Prasanthi Nilayam, Sai Towers, 1997.

88. Levi, S., *Faces of Love*, London, Sri Sathya Sai Book Centre, 1996.

89. Levin, Howard: 1996a *Good Chances*, 2nd ed., PN, ST [republished] 1996 [1st ed. Tustin, 1985]

90. —1996b *Heart to Heart*, Prasanthi Nilayam Sai Towers, 1996.

91. *LIMF* See Under Padmanaban, R. *(Love is My Form. Vol. 1)*. Lipton, Sheree, 'Sai Baba's Big Heart Hospital', in *Hinduism Today*, No. 94-01.

92. *Love is My Form*. See under Padmanaban, R.

93. Lowenberg, R.: 1983: *The Heart of Sai*, Bombay, India Book House.

94. —1985: *The Grace of Sai*, Bombay, India Book House.

95. —1985: *At the Feet of Sai*, Bombay, India Book House.

96. —1997: *The Omnipresence of Sai*, Prasanthi Nilayam, Sai Towers.

97. Lunshof, Geesje, *Inner Dialogue with Sai Baba*, Delhi, B.R. Publishing Corporation, 1999.

98. Manu Rao, B.S., 'Sai Baba lashes out at detractors', *The Times of India*, 26 December, 2000.

99. Marwaha, AnneMarie, . . . *and the Greatest is LOVE. My Experiences with Bhagwan Sri Sathya Sai Baba*, New Delhi, 1985.

100. Mason, Peggy and Laing, Ron, *Sathya Sai Baba. Embodiment of Love*, London.

101. Sawbridge, 1982. (3rd ed., Bath, Gateway Books)

102. Mason, Peggy, Levy, S. and Veeravahu, M., Eds.), *Sai Humour*, London, U.K. Sai Organization, and Sai Towers, 1995.

103. Mazzoleni, Don Mario, *A Catholic Priest Meets Sai Baba*, Faber, Virginia.

104. Leela, 1994. [Translated from the Italian: *Un sacerdote incontra Sai Baba*, Milano, Armenia Editore, 1991]

105. Menon, Amarnath K. & Ashok Malik, 'Test of Faith', *India Today*, 4 December, 2000, 38-43.

106. Murphet, Howard:—1971: *Sai Baba: Man of Miracles*, London. (Reprinted by Samuel Weiser, York Beach, 1973.

107. —1977: *Sai Baba Avatar. A New Journey into Power and Glory*, San Diego, Birth Day, 1977.

108. —1980: 'The Finger of God', *Golden Age, 1980*, pp. 35-40.

109. —1982: *Sai Baba. Invitation to Glory*, Delhi, Macmillan.

110. —1983. [Republished in USA in 1993 as *Walking the Path with Sai Baba*, York Beach, Samuel Weiser]

111. 1993a: *Walking the Path with Sai Baba*, York Beach, Samuel Weiser.

112. —1993b: *Where the Road Ends*, [N.S.W. Australia], Butterfly Books. (Later editions: Faber, VA, Leela Press.)

113. —1996: *Sai Inner Views and Insights*, Faber, VA, Leela Press.

114. Narasimhan, V.K., *Bapu to Baba*, 2nd ed., Prasanthi Nilayam, Sai Towers, 1997. [1st ed. 1985; 3rd ed 1998]

115. Orefjaerd, Curth, *Bhagavan Sathya Sai Baba. My Divine Teacher*, Delhi, Motilal Banarsidas. 1994.

116. Osis, K. and Haraldsson, E.: 1976: 'OBE's in Indian Swamis: Sathya Sai Baba and Dadaji', in J.D. Morris *et al* (eds.), *Research in Parapsychology 1975*, Metuchen, NJ, Scarecrow Press, 1976.

117. —1979: 'Parapsychological Phenomena Associated with Sathya Sai Baba', *The Christian Parapsychologist*, 3 (1979), 159-163.

118. Padmanaban, R. *et al., Love is My Form. Vol. 1 The Advent* (1926-1950). Prasanthi Nilayam, Sai Towers, 2000.

119. Penn, Charles: 1981: *My Beloved. The Love and Teaching of Bhagavan Sri Sathya Sai Baba*, Prasanthi Nilayam, Sri Sathya Sai Baba Books and Publications Trust.

120. —1985: *Finding God. My Journey to Bhagavan Sri Sathya Sai Baba*, Prasanthi Nilayam, Sri Sathya Sai Books and Publications Trust.

121. Penn, Faith and Charles, *Sai Ram. Experiencing the Love and Teachings of Bhagavan Sri Sathya Sai Baba*, Prasanthi Nilayam, Sri Sai Books and Publications, 1985.

122. Phipps, Peter: 1994 *Sathya Sai Baba and Jesus Christ. A Gospel for Golden Age*, Sathya Sai Publications of New Zealand, Auckland.

123. —1997 *Greater than You Know*, Sathya Sai Publications of New Zealand, Auckland.

124. Purnaiya, Nagamani, *The Divine Leelas of Sri Sathya Sai Baba*, Bangalore, House of Seva, 1976.(4th ed., Prasanthi Nilayam, Sai Towers, 1995)

125. Ralli, Lucas: 1985: *Sai Messages for You and Me*, London, Vrindavanum Books. 1987: *Sai Messages for You and Me, Vol II*, London, Vrindavanum Books.

126. —1990: *Sai Messages for you and Me, Vol. III*, London, (n.p.).

127. —1993 *Sai Messages for You and Me, Vol. IV*, Madras, (n.p.).

128. Ramnath, V., *Waiting for Baba*, Prasanthi Nilayam, Sai Towers, 1996.

129. Rao, M.N.: 1985: *Sri Sathya Sai Baba. A Story of God as Man*, Prasanthi Nilayam.

130. —1992: *Our God and Your Mind*, Prasanthi Nilayam.

131. —1995 *God and His Gospel*, Prasanthi Nilayam, Sai Towers.

132. —1998: *You are God*, Prasanthi Nilayam, Sai Towers.

133. Reddy, A. Adivi, *Uniqueness of Swami and His Teachings*, Prasanthi Nilayam, Sri Sathya Sai Books and Publications, 1995.

134. Roberts, Paul William *Empire of the Soul. Some Journeys in India*, New York: Riverhead Books, 1996. (1st ed. Canada, Stoddart Publishing, 1994)

135. Rodriguez, Birgitte, *Glimpses of the Divine. Working with the Teachings of Sai Baba*, York Beach, Samuel Weiser, 1993.

136. Ruhela, Satya Pal: 1985a (ed.): *The Sai Baba Movement*, New Delhi, Arnold Heinemann.

137. —1991: *Sri Sathya Sai Baba and the Future of Mankind*, New Delhi, Sai Age Publications.

138. —1993: *Sri Sathya Sai Baba. His Life and Divine Role*, New Delhi, Vikas.

139. —1994a: *The Sai Trinity. Shirdi Sai, Sathya Sai, Prema Sai Incarnations*, New Delhi, Vikas.

140. —1994b: *The Educational Theory of Sri Sathya Sai Baba*, Faridabad, Sai Age Publication.

141. —1995 (ed.): *Sai Baba and His Message*, Rev. ed., New Delhi, Vikas.

142. —1996: *In Search of Sai Divine. A Comprehensive Research Review of Writings and Researches on Sri Sathya Sai Baba Avatar*, New Delhi, MD Publications.

143. —1998, Sri Sathya Sai A Kalki Avatar. Delhi, B.R. Publishing Corporation, 1995.

144. —2000b *The Sai Trinity, 2nd Rev. Ed.*, New Delhi, Vikas.

145. —*How to Receive Sri Sathya sai Baba's Grace.* *, New Delhi: Diamond Pocket Books.

146. Sri Vasistha, *Sathya Sai Baba's 10 Avataras* in 1. Mukth Nilayam, 2002.

147. St. John, Gloria, *Ashes, Ashes, We All Fall Down. Becoming a Devotee of Sathya Sai Baba.* Prasanthi Nilayam, Sai Towers, 1997.

148. *Sanathana Sarathi*, Prasanthi Nilayam, Sri Sathya Sai Baba Books and Publications Trust. (A monthly magazine for devotees from Prasanthi Nilayam}149. Sandweiss, Samuel H.: 1975: *SAI BABA. The Holy Man . . . and the Psychiatrist*, San Diego, Birth day.

150. —1979: 'Sai Love', *Golden Age*, 1979, pp. 123-127.

151. —1985: *Spirit and the Mind*, San Diego, Birth Day. Sansthan Sai Sanjeevini, *Sanjeevini Healing Fragrances*, Gurgaon, 1996.

152. Sarin, V.I.K., *Face to Face with God*, Puttaparthi, Saindra Publications, 1990.(2nd ed. 1995)

153. *Discourses in Kodaikanal, April 1996*, ed. Pooja Kapahi, Prasanthi Nilayam, Sai Towers, 1997.

154. *Discourses on the Bhagavad-Gita*, Compiled and edited by Al Drucker, Prasanthi Nilayam, Sri Sathya Sai Books and Publications Trust, 1988.

155. *An Eastern View of Jesus Christ. Divine Discourses of Sathya Sai Baba*, translated by Lee Hewlett and K. Nataraj, London, Sai Publications.

156. *Benedictory Addresses*, Prasanthi Nilayam, Sri Sathya Sai Books and Publications Trust, [n.d.] [A compilation of Baba's annual Convocation addresses to the Sri Sathya Sai Institute of Higher Learning]

157. *Education in Human Values*, Compiled by Loraine Burrows, Prasanthi Nilayam, Sri Sathya Sai Books and Publications Trust, [n.d.]

158. *Sathya Sai Speaks* Series. (Compiled from the speeches of Sathya Sai Baba from 1953 to 1982 by N. Kasturi, and since then by other devotees. Thirty volumes have been issued. There are several different editions in India and U.S.A. See under Gries for *Index* to Vols. I-XI of the American Editions. See Steel (1997), pp. 228-239 for a Concordance by volume and chapter between the Revised Enlarged Indian edition, Vols. I-XI and corresponding volumes of the American Edition.])

159. Vijaya Kumar, *Other than You Refuge is None*. Bangalore, 1994.

160. Joshi, Sarla, Kaliyoug Ke Tirthretra, Pune, Saryesh Publication, 1999.

161. Ramamurthy, K., Sri Sathya Sai Anandadaus: Journey with Sai, Bangalore, Sai Prakashan Society, 2001.

Below are listed the volumes of the Revised Enlarged Indian Editions. Note that the similarly numbered American editions are often very different in content.

Summer showers Series Complied from discourses given by Sri Sathya Sai Baba during the Summer Courses on Indian Culture and Spirituality at Brindavan (Whitefield), 1972-1979, 1990, 1993.
The 1977 volume is titled *Summer Roses on the Blue Mountain* because it refers to the 1976 course held in the hill station of Ootacamund.
—*Summer showers in Brindavan, 1972*, Prasanthi Nilayam, Sri Sathya Sai Books and Publications Trust.
—*Summer Showers in Brindavan, 1973*, Bombay, Sri Sathya Sai Education Foundation.
—*Summer Showers in Brindavan, 1974*, New Delhi, Bhagavan Sri Sathya Sai Seva Samithi.
—*Summer Roses on the Blue Mountain, 1976*, Prasanthi Nilayam, Sri Sathya Sai Books and Publications Trust.
—*Summer Showers in Brindavan, 1977*, Prasanthi Nilayam. Sri Sathya Sai Books and Publications Trust.
—*Summer Showers in Brindavan, 1978*, Prasanthi Nilayam, Sri Sathya Sai Books and Publications Trust.
—*Summer Showers in Brindavan 1979*, Brindavan, Kadugodi, Sri Sathya Sai Hostel.

—*Summer Showers in Brindavan, 1990*, Prasanthi Nilayam, Sri Sathya Sai Books and Publications Trust.

—*Summer Showers in Brindavan, 1993*, Prasanthi Nilayam, Sri Sathya Sai Books and Publications Trust.

—*Sathya Sai Speaks, I* (Discourses, 1953-1960) American: 1953-1960

—*Sathya Sai Speaks, II* (Discourses, 1961-1962) American: 1960-1962

—*Sathya Sai Speaks, III* (Discourses, 1963) American: 1960-1964

—*Sathya Sai Speaks, IV* (Discourses, 1964) American: 1964-1965

—*Sathya Sai Speaks, V* [Discourses, 1965) American: 1965-1967

—*Sathya Sai Speaks, VI* (Discourses, 1966) American: 1967-1968

—*Sathya Sai Speaks, VII* (Discourses, 1967) American: 1968-1971

—*Sathya Sai Speaks, VIII* (Discourses, 1968) American: 1972-1973

—*Sathya Sai Speaks, IX* (Discourses, 1969) American: 1974-1975

—*Sathya Sai Speaks, X* (Discourses, 1970) American: 1975-1979

—*Sathya Sai Speaks, XII* (Discourses, 1973-1974)

—*Sathya Sai Speaks, XIII* (Discourses, 1975-1977)

—*Sathya Sai Speaks, XIV* [Discourses, 1978-1980]

—*Sathya Sai Speaks, XV* (Discourses, 1981-1982)

—*Sathya Sai Speaks, XVI (New Series)* (Discourses, 1983)

—*Sathya Sai Speaks, XVII* [Discourses, 1984]

—*Sathya Sai Speaks, XVIII* [Discourses, 1985]

—*Sathya Sai Speaks, XIX* [Discourses, 1986]

—*Sathya Sai Speaks, XX* [Discourses, 1987]

—*Sathya Sai Speaks, XXI* (Discourses, 1988)

—*Sathya Sai Speaks, XXII* (Discourses, 1989)

—*Sathya Sai Speaks, XXIII* ([Discourses, 1990)

—*Sathya Sai Speaks, XXIV* (Discourses, 1991)

—*Sathya Sai Speaks, XXV* (Discourses, 1992)

—*Sathya Sai Speaks, XXVI* (Discourses, 1993)

—*Sathya Sai Speaks, XXVII* (Discourses, 1994)

—*Sathya Sai Speaks, XXVIII* (Discourses, 1995)

—*Sathya Sai Speaks, XXIX* (Discourses, 1996)

—*Sathya Sai Speaks, XXX* (Discourses, 1997)

Vahini Series, or Teachings of Sai Baba on specific topics. (Translated from Telugu.) Published by Sri Sathya Sai Baba Books and Publications Trust of Prasanthi Nilayam and (by arrangement) by the Sathya Sai Baba Book Center of America.

—*Bhagavatha Vahini*.(Sai Baba's version of the *Bhagavata*-The Story of the Glory of the Lord]

—*Dharma Vahini*, 4th ed., 1975.(The Path of Virtue. Teachings on Righteousness)

—*Dhyana Vahini*. (Teachings on Meditation)

—*Gita Vahini*, 4th ed., 1978. (Teachings on the *Bhagavad Gita*, The Divine Gospel)

—*Jnana Vahini* (Teachings on Eternal Wisdom)

—*Leela Kaivalya Vahini* (The Cosmic Play of God]

—*Prasanthi Vahini* [The Bliss of Supreme Peace)

—*Prasnothara Vahini* (Answers to Spiritual Questions)

—*Prema Vahini*.(The Stream of Divine Love)

—*Sandeha Nivarini. Dialogues with Sri Sathya Sai Baba*, New Delhi.

Swami Maheshwaranand, *Sai Baba and Nara Narayan Gufa Ashram*, 3 Parts, translated by B.P. Misra, Madras, Prasanthi Printers, 1990-1992. (Parts I and II separately published as *Sai Baba and Nara Narayana Gufa Ashram*, Ahmedabad, Satsahitya Prakashan)

Bhagawan Sri Sathya Seva Samiti. (Clearance of Spiritual Doubts)

—*Sathya Sai Vahini* ([Spiritual Messages of Sathya Sai Baba)

—*Sutra Vahini* (Analytical Aphorisms on Supreme Reality. Spiritual Message of Sathya Sai)

—*Upanishad Vahini*. (Essence of Vedic Knowledge. Teachings Spiritual Discipline] *Vidya Vahini*. (Flow of Spiritual Education)

Schulman, Arnold, *Baba*, New York, Viking Press, 1971.

Selby. Richard: 1999 *Path of the Pilgrim*, Prasanthi Nilayam, Sai Towers.

—[n.d.] *My Trip to Sai Baba*, (n.p.).

Shah, Indulal: 1980: *Sixteen Spiritual Summers*, Prasanthi Nilayam,
Sathya Sai Books and Publications Trust.

—1983: *We Devotees*, Bombay, World Council of Sri Sathya Sai Organizations.

—1993: *Spiritual Blueprints of My Journey*, Bombay, Sarla Charity Trust.

—1997: *i, we and HE*, Prasanthi Nilayam, [n.p.], 1997.

Sharma, Arvind, 'New Hindu Movements in India', in James A. Beckford (ed.), *New Religious Movements and Rapid Social Change*, Sage Publications/ UNESCO, 1991, 220-239. (The pages on Sai Baba are 228-231)

Shaw, Connie: 1995: *Mary's Miracles and Prophecies. Intimate Revelations of a Visionary*, Colorado, Om Productions.

—1996: *Sai Baba in Brief*, 4th ed., Colorado, Om Productions.

—1998: 'Tapping Swami's Grace Anywhere', *Spiritual Impressions*, Nov.-Dec. 1998, 25-29.

Shepherd, Kevin R.D., *Gurus Rediscovered: Biographies of Sai Baba of Shirdi and Upasni Maharaj of Sakori*, Cambridge, Anthropographia Publications, 1986.

Aura of Divinity, Hollywood, Aura Productions, 1990.

David Bailey, Toronto, December 1996, The Video Education Co.

Dr. N.K. Bhatia of the Sathya Sai Institute of Higher Medical Sciences. How he came to Swami. The Video Education Co., 1993.

Christ in Kashmir. The Hidden Years, Richard Bock.

Christmas Days at Prasanthi Nilayam, Peter Rae, 1992.

Dr. Fanbunda: Blueprint, Practical Spirituality, The Video Education Co.

Lives in India, Holland.

Golden Chariot and Paduka Festival, The Video Education Co.

Dr. Jack Hislop at the 17th North and South Central Region Sai Conference, Missouri, May 1994, The Video Education Co.

The Hospital Video. The Beginning of the Sri Sathya Sai Institute of Higher Medical Sciences. Produced by James Redmond. The Video Education Co.

Interview with Dr. B.S. Goel, The Video Education Co.

Phyllis Krystal, at the San Diego Retreat, The Video Education Co.

The Miracle of Puttaparthi (On the building of the Super Speciality Hospital in Puttaparthi. (Includes an interview with the architect Professor Keith Critchlow.)

My Sweet Lord (A music and Darshan video), The Video Education Co., 1997.

On Personal Experiences with Swami, The Video Education Co., 1994.

Charles and Faith Penn, at the N. California Retreat, 1991.

Personal Experiences, Vol. 1, Tigrett, Shaw, Rahm, The Video Education Co.

Personal Experiences. Vol. 2, Ralli, Mason, Critchlow, The Video Education Co.

Prasanthi Nilayam, Christmas 1992, Torrensville, South Australia, P.G. Video, 1993.

Pure Love (Peter Rae, 1994), The Video Education Co.

Rahm, Seral, at the Texas Retreat, 1994.

Rahm, Seral, at the N. Carolina Retreat, November 1996.

Jonathan Roof, at the Texas Retreat.

The Rowdies, The Video Education Co.

Sai Baba and His Children, U.K.

Sai Baba. God on Earth, London, Golden Age Production. (BBC)

Sai Gayatri

Samuel and Sharon Sandweiss at the Western Canada Sai Conference, Calgary, July 1994, The Video Education Co.

Sathya Sai Baba. His Message and His Works.

Sathya Sai Baba—The Inner Voice, Denmark.

Secret Cave of India—Patal Bhuvaneshwar, The Video Education Co

Sixtieth Birthday.

G.V. Subba Rao, Avatar and Sri Gayatri. Dallas The Video Education Co.

Swami's Mission, Prof. N. Kasturi, Christmas 1984.

Tigrett, Isaac, at the 1993 USA North and South Region Sai Conference.

Travelling to India for the First Time, James Redmond, The Video Education Company, 1994.

Two in One: Aura of Divinity and The Lost Years of Jesus.

Two in One: Glimpses of Divine Mission and Shirdi Darshan (Hindi Commentary)

The Way to Baba Hartley Film Institute, U.S.A.

Who's Sai Baba? (Victor Tognola, Switzerland)

2. Discourses by Sri Sathya Sai Baba (The Video Education Company.

3. Internet: www.saivideos.com)

November 19, 1990: Service

November 20, 1990: Gaining God's Love

November 22, 1990: Education

November 23, 1990: The Motherland

November 24, 1990: The Biggest Miracle

April, 1991: Talk to Westerners (Kodaikanal)

November 22, 1991: Ideal Lives

November 23, 1991: Winning the Lord's Grace

1992 Discourse: Importance of a Name

March 3, 1992: Discourse on *Bhajans*

November 22, 1992: Discourse

November 23, 1992: Discourse

February 19, 1993: Shivaratri

Febraury 20, 1993: Shivaratri (with English sub-titles)

November 20, 1993: Discourse

November 23, 1993: Discourse

December 25, 1993: Christmas Discourse

January 21, 1994: Discourse

November 22, 1994: Discourse

November 23, 1994: Discourse

July 8, 1995: Discourse

July 11, 1995: Discourse

July 12, 1995: Discourse

November 18, 1995: Water Project Discourse

November 18, 1995: World Conference Inaugural Discourse

November 19, 1995: Women's Day

November 20, 1995: Discourse on E.H.V.

November 21, 1995: Discourse

November 22, 1995: Discourse
November 23, 1995: 70th Birthday Discourse
February 17, 1996: Shivaratri
February 18, 1996: Shivaratri
July 29, 1996: Hanuman
July 30, 1996: Guru Poornima
November 19, 1996: Ladies Day Discourse
November 21, 1996: Discourse
November 22, 1996: Discourse
November 23, 1996: Birthday Discourse
December 25, 1996: Christmas Discourse
March 7, 1997: Shivaratri
March 8, 1997: Discourse
July 16, 1997: Discourse
July 17, 1997: Discourse
July 18, 1997: Discourse
July 19, 1997: Discourse
July 20, 1997: Discourse
September 22, 1997: Sacrifice
September 23, 1997: Human Values
December 25, 1997: Faith
December 25, 1998: Sacrifice and Surrender
November 18, 1999: Discourse
November 19, 1999: Discourse
November 21, 1999: Discourse
November 22, 1999: Discourse
November 23, 1999: 74th Birthday Discourse
December 25, 1999: Christmas Discourse
July 16, 2000: Guru Purnima Discourse
Sri Sathya Sai Sadhna Trust Pranthi Nilayam-515134 (.A,P) http6/4/2014//
smashwords. com/profile/view sssstpd% E2%80%BE
On 1st January, 2009, Sri Sathya Sai Sadhna Trust (SSSST) commenced
commensed, and publishing an e newsletter 'Sai Spiritual Showers' for free
Distribution for those who are unaware of Sri Sathya Sai Baba's Spiritual treasure
may like to be enriched by it.

BIBLIOGRAPHY ON
SRI PREMA SAI BABA

1. Sujatha Devi, G., "Good Golden Days" in *Sathya Sai—The Eternal Charioteer*. Hyderabad: Sri Prasanthi Society, 1990, pp. 79.
2. Hislop, John, S., *My Baba and I*. Prasanthi Nilayam: Sri Sathya Sai Books & Publications Trust, p.56.
3. Palanivelu, *Sri Sathya Sai's Miracles & Spirituality* (Vol. II), Chennai: Saroj Moor Publishers, 1990, pp.155-162.
4. Karanjia, R.K., "God is an Indian", in *Golden Age*, Brindavan: Kingdom of Sathya Sai, 1979, pp.130-131.
5. *The Divine Grace of Lord Sri Sathya Sai Baba*. Wolverhampton, West Midlands, U.K.: Sri Sathya Sai Baba Centre, (30, Lonsdale Road), p.19.
6. Joshi, Sarla, *Kaliyug Ke Thirthsthal*, Pune: Amrendra Joshi, 1979, p.155 (In Hindi).
7. *Sanathana Sarathi*, November 1999.
8. Tripathy, A.P., Punarjama ki yachanan' (Hindi Poem), in Ruhela S.P., *Sai Puran*, Delhi: Sadhna Pocket Books, 1996, p.115.
9. Sai Vasantha, *Prema Sai Avatar* (Part I) Mukthi Nilayam, 2006.
10. Sai Vasantha, *Beyond the Vedas: Prema Sai Avatar* (Part II), Mukthi Nilayam, 2006.
11. Sai Vasantha, *Prema Sai Digest*, Mukthi Nilayam, 2006.
12. Sai Vasantha, *Avatar's secrets*, Mukthi Nilayam.

Vasantha Sai's books may be had from:

• Sri Vasantha Sai Books & Publications Trust
  'Mukthi Nilayam'
  Royapalayam Village
  Thirumangalam
  Madurai-Virudhunagar Road, Madurai District 625-706
  Tamil Nadu, India
  E-mail: mukthinilayam@gmail.com

• Vedic Book.com